CLARENDON LAW SERIES

Edited by

TONY HONORÉ AND JOSEPH RAZ

CLARENDON LAW SERIES

CONFLICTS OF
LAW AND MORALITY

R. Kent Greenawalt

Oxford University Press · New York
Clarendon Press · Oxford
1987

Oxford University Press

Oxford   New York   Toronto
Delhi   Bombay   Calcutta   Madras   Karachi
Petaling Jaya   Singapore   Hong Kong   Tokyo
Nairobi   Dar es Salaam   Cape Town
Melbourne   Auckland

and associated companies in
Beirut   Berlin   Ibadan   Nicosia

Published by Oxford University Press, Inc.
200 Madison Avenue, New York, New York 10016

Oxford is a registered trademark of Oxford University Press

Library of Congress Cataloging-in-Publication Data
Greenawalt, R. Kent, 1936–
Conflicts of law and morality.
Includes index.
1. Law—Philosophy.   2. Law and ethics.   I. Title.
K230.G74C66   1987   340′.112   86-8335
ISBN 0-19-504110-0

1 3 5 7 9 8 6 4 2

Printed in the United States of America
on acid-free paper

310263

To Sanja
Whose love sustains

Preface

This book aims to bring an understanding of modern legal systems to bear on classic problems of political and moral philosophy, in a way that illuminates choices about obedience to law made by ordinary citizens and officials. Because it combines much of the fruit of my life "in the law" as well as my education and study outside the law, the intellectual debts the book reflects are extensive indeed.

I had the good fortune to be the student of four great teachers of political and legal philosophy: J. Roland Pennock at Swarthmore and Sir Isaiah Berlin, H. L. A. Hart, and John Plamenatz at Oxford. They generated an interest in the question of why citizens should obey the law that has lain dormant for stages of my professional life but has never disappeared. What I have learned about the law from members of the Columbia faculty, initially as student and subsequently as colleague, has added a different dimension to my thought about this subject, one that has been further enriched over the years by exchanges with students in classes and seminars in Jurisprudence and Legal Philosophy, and particularly in a 1984 seminar on Conflicts of Law and Morality.

My progress toward a book has been greatly aided by opportunities to develop aspects of the general topic. An invitation to comment on a paper by Luther Adams at a 1968 meeting of the American Society for Political and Legal Philosophy led me to a strongly consequentialist position about obedience to law, one that I have progressively qualified as time has passed. My first serious thinking about conscientious objection was in response to an invitation to contribute to the 1971 Supreme Court Review. A 1980 conference at the University of Virginia honoring A. D. Woozley provided the occasion to develop broader ideas about official responses to moral claims to disobey the law; and I first addressed the troubling topic of violent disobedience for a conference on that subject at Emory University in 1982. For a 1984 Sibley Lecture at the University of Georgia, I had to focus my thoughts about underlying reasons to obey the law. This book builds on and integrates those separate treatments and has benefited greatly from the discussions of my presentations at Virginia, Emory, and Georgia.

My ability to put aside time for this effort was very generously supported for three years by the Richard Lounsbery Foundation. A summer research grant in 1980 from the Kayden Research Fund was critical at an early stage, and a similar grant in 1985 from the Samuel Rubin Program for the Advancement of Liberty and Equality Through Law enabled me to complete a near final draft. I finished a final draft during a sabbatical leave which I spent as Visiting Lee Distinguished Professor at the Institute of Bill of Rights Law, Marshall-Wythe School of Law, College of William and Mary, where I was afforded the chance to work largely free of the ordinary distractions of academic life. My father's encouragement contributed to my persistence at various points, and it saddens me that he is not alive for the book's completion and publication.

My debts to those who have written in this area and to colleagues with whom I have exchanged ideas are immense. My notes largely reflect the authors from whom I have learned the most, although others are not cited who have deeply influenced my thinking in ways that leave me no longer aware of precise contributions. Among the writers from whom I have most profited are many whose views are criticized in the succeeding pages; the points of disagreement, perhaps inevitably, are more sharply etched than the points of common view, and many positions I reject have themselves increased my understanding.

Bruce Ackerman, Milner Ball, John G. Bennett, Vince Blasi, William Heffernan, Paul LeBel, Henry Monaghan, Stephen Presser, and

Andrzej Rapaczynski are among the colleagues who made valuable comments on parts of the book. I am grateful to them and especially to Stephen Munzer, who gave me highly detailed and careful criticisms of the entire manuscript, and to John Simmons, who helpfully reviewed much of the near final draft under tight time constraints. I know the book would be better if I had had the insight and energy to put all their comments to good use; but it is now much better than it would have been without them.

During the years of work on the book I have been cheerfully and competently helped by members of the Columbia Law School Faculty Secretariat, supervised by Virginia Woods. Drafts of the entire manuscript were typed with marvelous speed and accuracy by Krista Page. Millie Arthur at the Institute of Bill of Rights Law managed the complex task of shepherding the final draft to completion. Rhonda Callison has provided secretarial assistance during the editing process. Steven Walt prepared the index and gave me valuable research help and criticism at the final stages. Had I not had such able, prompt, and gracious assistance, which allowed me to invest my energies in the substance of my topic, the task would have taken much longer.

Finally, I want to thank the members of my immediate family— Sanja, Robert, Sasha, and Andrei. On occasion, the needs of family life have reduced the time available for thinking and writing; but absent the emotional support and sense of meaning that that life has involved, I strongly doubt I would have maintained the commitment and patience required to complete the book.

Contents

I

THE CONFLICTING CLAIMS
OF LAW AND MORALITY

1

Introduction

When powerful emotion or pursuit of self-interest leads people to serious lawbreaking, they often do not believe what they do is morally justified and lack any plausible argument that it is. Sometimes, however, people do think they have good moral reasons for disobeying legal norms. This book involves philosophical and legal analysis of those occasions.

The study considers two different perspectives. One is that of the person facing a possible conflict between the claims of morality and law, who must choose whether or not to obey the law. The second is the perspective of those who make and apply laws; they must decide whether or not to treat someone with a moral claim to disobey differently from ordinary lawbreakers.

This brief introductory chapter outlines the scope of the topic. It is followed by discussion of what may loosely be called the law's claim to obedience. The third and final chapter of this preliminary part canvasses the variety of moral claims to disobey; it then addresses the nature of the moral evaluation done in this study, sketching the dimensions and limits of my aspirations. These chapters lay the groundwork for the main work, contained in Parts II, III, and IV.

Parts II and III adopt the viewpoint of the prospective lawbreaker. Part II inquires to what extent legal norms carry moral weight by virtue of their status as law. This examination of the moral reasons for complying with laws is closely related to one of the central themes of political philosophy: the obligations citizens owe to their governments. My enterprise differs in one very important respect from traditional treatments of political obligation, which concentrate on the possible existence of a single source of obligation that applies to all citizens, or residents, and all laws. I do offer some comments on that subject; but the person who is deciding whether or not to obey is primarily concerned with the obligations that constrain him in that situation, and with their strength, not with the breadth of their application to others or to himself in other situations. For this reason, I pay close attention to a moral ground for obeying the law even after concluding it does not have general application. I discuss the reasons officials as well as ordinary persons should obey the law of the state and also touch on reasons for obeying rules of organizations other than the state.

The first chapter of Part II deals with the assertion that to recognize a government as legitimate is itself to acknowledge an obligation to obey its rules. Longer chapters on promissory theories of obligation, utilitarian grounds of obedience, and the duty of fair play follow. I then consider a number of theories of natural duty that link the benefits government provides with a duty to obey its norms. Part II finally concludes that people often have powerful moral reasons for obeying the law, although the claim that all citizens, even in good societies, are obligated to obey the law in every instance is rejected.

To say that someone has an obligation, a duty, or moral reasons to obey the law does not settle the question whether or not, *overall*, he should obey on a particular occasion, for there may be conflicting factors favoring disobedience. Assessing reasons for obeying the law, the task of Part II, is an important first step in evaluating whether or not disobedience is morally appropriate; but it is only a first step.

Part III addresses some of the sorts of reasons advanced for violating the law and comments on their relation to the reasons for obeying. The focus of the discussion is not only on whether or not disobedience of some kind may be justified but also on possible limits on justifiable disobedience—must it be preceded by legal efforts to change a law or policy; must it be directed against a law that is itself unjust; must it be peaceful; must it be accompanied by a willingness to submit to punishment? These matters, often taken up in treatments of civil disobedience, are of the utmost importance for someone considering whether or not and how to break the law.

Confident conclusions about the occasions for justifiable violation of the law and the forms it should take would be comforting but they would also be delusive. Moral philosophy is notably inept in indicating precisely how competing moral claims should be resolved; and the infinite variety of moral claims to disobey the law makes impossible any attempt to essay even tentative resolutions for each possible conflict. For both these reasons, any plausible theory about the occasions for and limits of disobedience must be somewhat sketchy and unsatisfactory, and mine is no exception.

Part IV concerns official responses to moral claims to disobey the law. The initial chapter explores why an actor's moral perspectives might make a difference in how he should be treated and offers some general comments on how choices to accord different treatment may be made. Subsequent chapters examine a variety of ways, inside and outside the law, by which those applying the law may temper their reactions to breaches of legal duty. Among the techniques within the law are the general justification defense in criminal law and an analogous privilege in tort law, exemptions for conscientious objectors, interpretations of constitutional rights, exercises of police and prosecutorial discretion, determinations by judges and jurors about criminal sentences, executive pardon, and legislative amnesty. I also discuss official violations of legal duties to apply the law, and certain methods for deflecting the law's application that lie at the edge of what the law permits; among these latter are jury and judge "nullification" of legal rules, and perhaps some examples of police decisions not to proceed.

The discussion of techniques of amelioration by officials deals with a number of related inquiries: how far should the legal system accommodate moral claims not to comply; how is the present law and the duties it imposes on officials to be understood; what sorts of reasons might justify official noncompliance with legal duties? In contrast with Parts II and III, much of Part IV concerns legal doctrine and its theoretical implications; but much is also directed to the moral responsibilities of officials and to the requisites of a just legal order.

2

The Claims of Law

Discussions of moral duties to obey the law usually proceed on the implicit assumption that the law demands obedience. This assumption has the air of being self-evident. The law is, in part, a system of rules that proscribes and prescribes behavior. Is it not the nature of such systems to demand that people act as they are directed?

This chapter explores this preliminary assumption. Although not false, the assumption fails to engage the various senses in which behavior may be proscribed or prescribed and the more complicated ways in which one can speak of the demands of a system of rules— ways that look beyond formal texts and the sanctions they specify to the desires and expectations of people within the system. I show that the important truth of the assumption about the law's demands neither lies in the inherent logic of a coercive order of rules nor extends to everything that may be called a legal duty.

Understanding to what extent the law seriously claims obedience is crucial to an inquiry into a possible moral obligation to obey. Since a general moral requirement to obey is unlikely to be *broader* than the law's demand for obedience, plausible theories about moral obligations to obey are effectively circumscribed by the extent of the law's demands.

I will discuss three respects in which mandatory rules may do less than demand behavior they seem to require, drawing from nonlegal examples to illuminate complexities in the law. I will then turn to the question of the ultimacy of the demands the law does make.

HOW "MANDATORY" RULES MAY DO LESS THAN DEMAND BEHAVIOR THEY APPEAR TO REQUIRE

Higher Norms

Illustration 2-1:

The by-laws of a private golf club provide that "Active members may set rules of play, consistent with the official rules of golf and state law." Members vote that a field that adjoins a green and is owned by an absent landlord will be treated as in bounds. Geraldine, conscious that reliance on the rule will involve civil and criminal trespass, refuses to comply with it and relies on the bylaws' reference to state law.

The "in bounds" rule is invalid because it conflicts with a higher norm, the law of the state incorporated in the club's bylaws. Because the rule is invalid, what the club's system of rules really demands does not include what that rule's terms require.[1]

That legal systems are composed of hierarchies of norms is a familiar truth. In the United States, legislation and executive acts are invalid if they fail to conform with written federal and state constitutions; even in countries without such constitutions, administrative rules and local ordinances may be invalid under national legislation. Although citizens might be required to obey any legal rule not yet authoritatively declared to be invalid[2] the law, at least in common-law countries, is different. If his claim of invalidity is vindicated, a person who has "violated" a lower norm is considered not to have broken the law.[3] When the law affords such a privilege, we can say that it does not demand the behavior provided for by invalid lower norms.

For the purposes of this study, we may largely disregard possible assertions that a violation of international law renders the law of one's own country invalid,[4] roughly assuming that the highest norms of a country's law will recognize no norms that are superior to it.[5] This assumption reflects a correct sense in which one may say that the law claims ultimate authority within a society.

This notion of ultimacy does not entail that the law of the state is self-contained. Open-ended legal provisions, such as the constitutional bar on "cruel and unusual punishment," may need to be filled in according to moral standards external to the provisions themselves. Exactly how this is to be done is controversial, but when the materials of a rich legal tradition are not dispositive, judges must rely on either a community's social morality or independent standards of what is morally right.

These references outward do not deprive the law of ultimacy, as long as the law itself directs the references, and as long as changes within the law, including constitutional amendments, are capable of overriding conclusions reached under the external normative standards. Although the ultimacy of state law is presumed in virtually all modern states, it could be otherwise. A constitution could contain an unamendable provision that no law contravening natural law is valid; or, without such a provision, judges and other officials could simply operate on that basis. In such a polity direct claims about morality might operate as claims of unconstitutionality do in the United States. The state's law might still take precedence over the norms of other organizations within a society, but positive legal rules would be subject to an external standard against which their validity, even as positive law, would be assessed. Dominant legal theory and practice now do not make the validity of the highest legal norms depend on their consonancy with moral norms.[6]

Thus, the law of a state is ultimate in an important sense; how this ultimacy is to be understood is a complex question reserved for the last part of this chapter.

Failures to Qualify and Opting In and Out

Illustration 2-2:
To become and remain a member of the Millionaires' Club, one must keep a net worth of over $1,000,000. During the course of a year, Harriet fails to acquire that net worth because her expensive uninsured home burns down; Susan's net worth falls to $800,000 because her stocks drop sharply in value; and Francis gives $900,000 of his $1,500,000 to charity. Harriett's application for membership is denied and Susan and Francis are dropped from the rolls.

In one sense, the rules of the club require the complicated set of actions necessary to acquire and retain $1,000,000. But the requirement need not reflect any judgment that a member really ought to do that. Other members may view Harriet and Susan as having suffered bad luck, and they may admire the sacrifice of Francis,[7] who has made a conscious choice not to conform with the club's "requirement."

A look at the rules alone may not tell us whether the members really insist on behavior or treat it only as a condition of continued membership. Given the limited arsenal of sanctions available to private associations, expulsion may constitute the only response to behavior that is seriously wrong. Excommunication from a religion, for example, typically connotes a judgment more momentous than that a member's acts and beliefs have merely drifted away from the conditions of membership. To decide whether a rule's prescription is a genuine demand or only a condition of membership, we need to know a good deal about the nature and purposes of an organization and the attitudes of its members and officials.

Because people do not join modern states as they join private organizations, and breaches of legal norms do not lead to simple termination of association between the violator and the state, someone does not disqualify himself from a regime of state law by failing to comply with its norms. Choices of residence and citizenship do, of course, affect the extent to which a country's laws will apply. Immigrants and naturalized citizens explicitly "opt in"; and those who leave a country or abandon citizenship[8] alter their rights and duties in significant ways. Some behavior by aliens, such as a failure to remain in the country for specified periods, may forfeit rights of permanent residence or potential citizenship; but more generally, the idea of opting out by failing to comply concerns only particular activities regulated by law.

Choices of whether to become and remain involved, and unchosen grounds for disqualification, matter for discrete publicly controlled activities and for optional legal institutions, such as testamentary disposition of one's assets. A failure to pay a yearly fee, conscious or inadvertent, might result in loss of a state-issued hunting license or membership in a government-run recreational association. A person need not make a will, but to invoke the legal rules that dispose of property according to will, he must follow prescribed steps. If the person fails to perform the required acts, say by getting only one witness to sign rather than two, the will may not be effective but the individual has not committed any wrong from the state's point of view. The somewhat clumsy attempts to make a will, like a field goal kick that goes wide of the uprights, amount, in H. L. A. Hart's phrase, to a "nullity."[9] The state's refusal to treat those efforts as successful is not a sanction for impermissible behavior but rather a formal recognition that the actor has not managed to bring himself within the class of people who have made valid wills. Parsing the grammatical structure of a rule will not necessarily reveal its purposes and character. Some forms of "nullity," such as the invalidation of a marriage or a refusal to recognize a child as legitimate, may be employed largely to discourage behavior.[10] But the central point for our purposes is that "power-conferring" rules genuinely limited to prescribing how a person must engage the law's help do not demand obedience in any sense relevant for this study.

Acceptable Fouls and Breaches of Legal Duty

The third way that rules may demand less than they seem is more complicated and, given its crucial relevance for the law, warrants more extensive explication.

Acceptable Fouls

Illustration 2-3:

The basketball rule book makes almost any body contact a foul; but experienced players understand that referees will permit a certain amount of pushing, and they are trained to make effective use of that privilege. At certain points in a game, strategy dictates committing fouls that referees will call, and experienced players know when such fouls should be committed. As long as the fouls are not too flagrant, they are considered a normal part of the game, and no knowledgeable person regards them as a serious wrong. The "sanctions" applicable to such fouls—an out of bounds for the opposing team or foul shots—are not severe enough to stop their intentional commission; and it is generally felt that were sanctions severe enough to stop most fouls now committed, the game would be less interesting, particularly because it would reduce the chance of a losing team catching up in the final minutes.

This illustration highlights two significant practices. The first is the formal specification of proscribed behavior that reaches beyond the behavior participants in an institution expect to produce either disapproval or sanction. Why does the rule book make some actions fouls that are not treated as fouls in actual games? One reason is that some differences between what good referees call fouls and what they do not involve subtle matters of degree and context[11] that hardly lend themselves to succinct verbalization. Although rule makers might adopt some vague phrase like "inordinate pushing," they instead state a clearer (though partly false) line between what is allowed and what is not. A stated rule against all pushing may help reduce the amount and intensity of pushing that actually takes place,[12] and it curbs grounds for complaint when referees do call pushing fouls. Finally, the rules of basketball serve multiple purposes, and the simplified book rules help guide youngsters learning to play.

The second significant practice in this illustration is the implicit labeling of actions as "wrongful" by use of the word "foul," though fouling is a part of what competent players are expected to do.[13] Commission of a foul does result in some consequences harmful to one's own team, but "blame" is ordinarily inappropriate for the fouling player.

If the proscriptive language of the rule book cannot be taken at face value, how can we say what the rules *really* demand? Talk of this sort involves a simplifying anthropomorphization but what is meant is what is demanded by the people concerned with the rules—the rule makers, the referees, perhaps spectators, and, most important, opposing players, whose mutual expectations dominate informal "pick-up" games. A sharp division among expectations might make it hard to decide what "the rules demand," but when substantial commonality exists over acceptable behavior, we can speak comfortably if imprecisely in those terms.

The two practices illustrated are by no means limited to games.[14] Authoritative statements of norms that are broader than the behavior genuinely intended to be deterred or sanctioned is widespread. Parents easily find themselves slipping into that pattern of proscription, and many organizations have detailed rules that no one regards seriously. Unless one is very familiar with an institution, identifying instances in which behavior formally labeled wrong does bring on a sanction but is not really regarded as wrongful is more difficult; but some prohibitive formulations within many organizations are considered as presenting persons with a kind of free choice of whether to comply or suffer the consequences.

Acceptable Breaches of Legal Duty

Discussions of obligation to obey the law of the state commonly have in view serious criminal law provisions that are actively enforced. These present the demands of law in their starkest form, but when we consider something closer to the whole corpus of legal duties, we have less confidence about what the law requires of us.

I have already put aside power-conferring rules that do not

themselves create duties but prescribe how persons are to engage the law's assistance. Such rules apply to officials, as well as ordinary citizens, indicating how they are to exercise their authority effectively.[15] Insofar as the legal system contains norms that confer simple permissions to engage in behavior, these also do not raise issues about obedience.[16]

Once we attend to strategies of legislative design and levels of enforcement, and to the varieties of legal duties, we can see that not every aspect of what constitutes a genuine legal duty reflects a serious demand to be obeyed.

I consider, first, norms enforced by public sanctions, such as fine, imprisonment, or loss of privileges. Although these include some mandatory administrative rules, I shall oversimplify a bit by referring to them as criminal prohibitions. Roughly, a duty of this type that a court should enforce in an appropriate case[17] is a legal duty within the system of law in which the court operates.[18]

Broad Language

Illustration 2-4:

Legislators in a jurisdiction have enacted a law that says "any person who gambles for money commits a Class A misdemeanor." One group in the legislature, a majority, wished only to deter and penalize gambling organized by professionals; but, believing that a law cast in those terms would be too difficult to enforce and having confidence in the state's enforcement officials, adopted the broader prohibition whose terms where designed to reach gambling between friends as well. A handful of legislators strongly disapproved of all gambling and wanted to have private gamblers prosecuted. A somewhat larger minority disapproved of private gambling and welcomed any deterrence of it that the statute would provide; but, for reasons of efficiency and privacy, agreed with the majority's view that enforcement should be directed only at professional gamblers. Another minority voted against the act. Police and prosecutorial officials have agreed that only when strong evidence exists that someone is a professional gambler should he or she be prosecuted. Most of these officials do not think treatment of private gamblers as criminals is at all appropriate; a minority do not object to such treatment but accept the enforcement policy as a sensible response to limited resources and to the probable intent of the legislature.

This illustration is uncharacteristic in some critical respects. The percentage of acts not really intended to be stopped is a very high proportion of all acts covered by the statute; more commonly, most behavior reached by a statute is meant to be deterred and only activity on the fringes is beyond genuine legislative concern. Usually, more-over, the line between what is and what is not meant to be deterred will be less sharp than that between private and professional gambling. This illustration is also uncharacteristic in its assumption of clear views among legislators and concerned officials. Legislators will usually not have precise opinions about how much of the covered behavior they really want to stop; those responsible for enforcement, once they have decided that behavior is not serious enough to warrant the employment of their resources, will usually not pause to determine whether criminal penalties are intrinsically inappropriate. Finally, in assuming that intended coverage is clearly much broader than the intended practical effect, the example obviates a typical claim of statutory interpretation that coverage should be narrowed to conform with the preceived social evil.

Although the illustration poses the question of the law's demands in sharper form than situations in real life, nevertheless, in many actual circumstances enforcement consciously does not approach the boundaries of a norm's coverage, and most legislators do not want such enforcement or would not want it if they thought about the subject. Analysis of the illustration can illumine understanding of the more complex situations that actually arise.

What does the law demand of private gamblers—persons who would be convicted if prosecuted?[19] My basic answer follows the analysis of fouls in basketball. As long as those who made the law and enforce it do not wish to discourage private gambling, the actual operation of the legal system does not do so, and other citizens are not depending on the law to stop such behavior among their fellows, to say the "law demands" that people refrain from gambling would be artificial and excessively formal.

A conceivable objection to this conclusion is that if the law reaches the behavior and at least a few legislators or citizens want the law to affect the behavior, that should be sufficient to say that the law demands it.[20] Once one concedes that what the rules of law really demand is not determined solely by their literal terms, however, one must also concede that the views of an extremely small minority of persons connected with the rules cannot determine their demands.

If we vary some assumptions in the illustration, deciding whether the law demands that people refrain from private gambling would be more difficult. The illustration rests on the premise, widely accepted within the United States and England,[21] that prosecutors have discretion not to enforce a law against all the persons it covers.[22] What if some aspect of the law required prosecutors to proceed against all violations, and that aspect was uniformly endorsed as a standard of how prosecutors really should act? In that event, we would expect legislators to be more careful about the scope of their statutory language. But legislators might sometimes have conflicting sentiments, rather hoping that a particular law will not be enforced in all its scope but still believing in a norm of full prosecution. And enforcement officials might deviate from the general norm of full enforcement in exceptional cases. Despite legislative ambivalence, one could still say that the law, taken as a whole, demands official enforcement and demands that people not commit acts that give rise to the duty to enforce.

Altering assumptions about the views legislators and enforcement officials have about gambling can also affect analysis of the law's demands. Suppose that all the relevant officials would be pleased in principle to have criminal enforcement against private gambling but agree that resources for enforcement must go elsewhere. In that event, the criminal prohibition of private gambling is regarded as a serious matter, and we cannot conclude from the failure to enforce that the law's demands do not reach private gambling.[23] What we should say if the legislature regards enforcement as a good idea but prosecutors believe that whether or not people gamble is their own business is more troublesome. Because the legislature has adopted the law and more directly represents citizens, its views probably count as dominant, but as relevant officials become more divided in their attitudes, any attribution to the overall spirit of "the law" becomes more difficult and imprecise.

A middle course between the law's really demanding behavior and meaning to leave it untouched is of some interest. Suppose that legislators disapprove of private gambling, considering it self-destructive and a danger to the performance of family and other obligations, but also regard criminal enforcement against such private activity as inappropriate. Expecting nonenforcement, legislators include private gambling within the criminal prohibition as a symbolic expression of society's disapproval of that behavior and as a mild discouragement of it. We might then sensibly say that what the law really does is to express a preference against private gambling but without demanding that people stop.

However these more troublesome borderline instances are resolved, the central conclusion here is the following. When the written law forbids behavior that legislators do not mean really to discourage, when that behavior is consistently not proceeded against by enforcement officials with discretion not to proceed, and when that choice is based on the sense that such enforcement would be intrinsically inappropriate, then the law does not *really demand* that people refrain from the behavior involved.

Compliance or Remedy—Varieties of Legal Duties

Of legal duties that are undoubtedly meant to be effective in some way, a question may still be raised whether their aim is primarily to produce the behavior required by the duty or is equally well served by remedial satisfaction. Apart from minor fines for such matters as parking violations, this issue is not a serious one for norms of criminal law. Often cast in moral terms, these norms are meant not only to create fear of formal penalties but to provide concrete guidance about minimally acceptable social behavior, a guidance supported by condemnation of those who deviate. From the law's point of view submission to the criminal sanction is not as desirable as compliance with the law in the first place. The same may be said about provisions requiring official performance of duty. When officials are directed to perform certain actions, the aim of the rules, whether backed by sanctions or not, is to get the officials to perform those actions.

Serious questions about the relation of performance and remedy are raised by civil law duties. These duties may be roughly divided between those imposed by rules of general application and those that derive from some voluntary, contractual, undertaking.[24] Violations make one liable to another private person, typically to pay damages, but occasionally to perform an act required by a court order.[25] I shall concentrate on violations of duties that are intentional,[26] since my general subject is conscious breaches of legal duty.

Oliver Wendell Holmes attempted to distill the essence of the civil law by suggesting that it presents people with a choice of whether to obey or suffer the consequences.[27] Whatever general jurisprudential merit that position may have, it certainly fails to capture all that the civil law as a whole is designed to do.

The behavior covered by intentional torts such as libel and assault is considered wrongful. Although many torts are also crimes, a legislative choice against invoking a criminal sanction need not reflect indifference as to whether people comply or pay damages. In some jurisdictions, striking another person is criminal only if physical injury results; but it would be absurd to say that the tort law, which reaches striking that does not injure, leaves people a choice of whether to refrain from striking or to strike without injuring and pay tort damages. Civil rights statutes, in large part, establish new civil wrongs. Whether or not they involve criminal penalties, they reflect standards that legislators believe deserve compliance. For at least the core of most general civil wrongs, the law does demand that people not engage in the proscribed actions, even when private redress constitutes the only remedy.

Some civil wrongs are set very broadly, however, much like the hypothetical criminal statute against gambling. A modern statutory example may be the wide prohibition against reproducing copyrighted works on photocopying machines and computers—one that private citizens are apparently expected to violate flagrantly.[28] Analysis of what the law really demands is complicated here by private enforcement power. Many persons or companies whose works are reproduced will wish that violations not take place and a few may think enforcement worthwhile. Although potential victims do not want violation of their legal rights, we may still conclude under certain conditions that the law does not really demand compliance. When the law sets a remedy that is uneconomical to pursue in a wide range of cases, when legislators would not regard violations in this range as genuine wrongs, when most people do not understand the law as seriously aiming to restrain them, and when most victims do not so regard the law in this way either, then even though these victims might prefer that people not engage in the behavior (e.g., photocopying a chapter of a library book), and even though a court would grant some remedy if suit were brought, the law does not demand restraint.

When general duties are backed by effective remedies, the remedies are usually regarded as second best substitutes for compliance; but for duties designed to protect exclusively economic interests, the law may be indifferent between performance and full prompt compensation.[29] This idea of indifference has sometimes been thought to have more general application to contract duties.

Is Holmes's hard-bitten view that the law presents a choice between compliance and sanction apt at least for contracts? Although the fact that breaches of contract are not usually referred to as violations of law is hardly dispositive,[30] usage may reflect an attitude that breaking a contractual obligation does not have the same seriousness as violating a general duty.

Perspectives for evaluating what contract law demands include the entire law as it relates to contracts, the function of that law in society, and the expectations of those involved in that law. Some of the most important aspects of the entire law concern the law of remedies.

Doctrines that injunctive relief in the form of specific performance is usually not available, that parties cannot recover incidental damages, and that breaching parties need not disgorge gains that exceed the injured parties' expectations may be viewed as encouraging parties to breach in some circumstances,[31] much as the limited sanctions for fouling actually encourage some fouls in basketball games. The permissibility of lawyers advising parties to breach may be similarly understood.[32] Some legal doctrines, such as the wrongfulness of encouraging a breach of contract, however, suggest that breaches are genuinely wrongful and that prompt compensation is not regarded as satisfying one's duty.[33]

How the law relating to contracts functions and the expectations that law generates vary depending on kinds of contracts and relationships. For some commercial contracts, in which financial profit and loss in the particular transaction predominate, an economic analysis indicates that contractors should breach and pay damages when that is more efficient than meeting the direct contractual obligation;[34] parties may develop their expectations accordingly. But even in the marketplace, not all considerations are reducible to precise degrees of financial gain and loss; and financial profit itself, over the long haul, may depend in part on being a reliable business partner. Certainly in many personal contracts elements of reliance and trust that performance will occur are important. The terminology of "breach" and ancillary doctrines against breach may represent a kind of legal support for reliance of this kind.

These brief comments are hardly enough to settle what the law "really" demands regarding contracts. We live in a society in which goals of economy efficiency and standards of personal reliance rest in somewhat uneasy tension and in which the doctrines of the law itself emit different signals about the significance of breach. That particular issue has larger implications for the manner in which contracts and cooperative activities are, and should be, regarded. Nevertheless, we can probably conclude that for some, but not all, contracts the law, as understood in the present legal climate of the United States, is really indifferent between performance and prompt payment of loss.

The preceding discussion highlights a more general caveat. Let us suppose that for some or all contracts a party exhibits higher compliance with "the law" by performing than by breaching and promptly paying full compensation. Should we say that the law "demands" performance? The push the law gives toward performance is much weaker than the push it gives toward compliance with serious criminal proscriptions. If both are "demands," they are demands of a different dimension. We should expect the strength of the moral reasons in favor of complying with the law to vary with the strength of the law's demand for compliance; other things being equal, the moral reasons will be stronger when the law's demands are more insistent.

THE LAW'S DEMANDS AND THE LAW'S ULTIMACY

I shift now to the yet more subtle question of how the law's demands are to be taken. In what sense does the law, which recognizes no higher norms outside the law and overrides other systems of norms when its provisions are in conflict with theirs, claim ultimacy?[35]

Although a precise statement may be impossible, the issue is whether the law, in the loose sense of which I have been speaking, really seeks to displace other competing bases for action. We can recognize immediately that most individuals will not concede the law ultimate authority with respect to their own choices. In liberal societies, people tend to believe that other claims on them may occasionally make disobedience of laws morally justifiable. Does their refusal to recognize the law as the ultimate authority for the rightness of actions it requires somehow conflict with what the law as a system claims? Does their refusal indicate a weaker attachment than the law seeks? These questions might be reframed as whether the law claims ultimate authority within its own domain or claims unqualified ultimate authority. This inquiry is important because some writers simply assume that the nature of law or of modern legal systems is to *claim* ultimate authority in the stronger sense.[36] Yet, the possible truth of that assumption lies not in logical necessity but in arguable empirical facts.

I begin with an example that clarifies what I mean by the more limited claim of authority of "ultimacy within its own domain."

Illustration 2-5:
Peter tells Diana, who is the tournament director and its final authority, that a visit to his seriously ill sister will conflict with a scheduled tennis match. Diana responds: "I'm very sorry. I can't postpone the match. If you go, you will have to default, and I must fine you $100, according to the rules of our association. Of course, I wouldn't presume to advise you and will fully sympathize if you visit your sister."

In the interests of the enterprise of which Diana and Peter are both part, she prescribes these adverse consequences without intending or wishing that they control Peter's decision.[37] Those who wrote the association's rules might be of similar mind. Believing that the failure of association members to play on schedule does often occasion blame, they may have felt the need to write a rule with very narrow possibilities for postponements and avoidance of fines and with little discretion for individual tournament directors. Writing such a rule, they recognized that some blameless people would be penalized.

Despite the strong and obvious disanalogies between this example and situations involving the law of the state, which covers the lives of those subject to it pervasively and more clearly makes judgments about good and bad behavior, a similar idea of ultimate authority in one domain *could* exist for secular state authority.

Illustration 2-6:

In the midst of the twenty-second century, the world government asks for communities of volunteers to settle on Mars. The few volunteers willing to hazard the harsh conditions are members of six different religious communities, who share only a common despair over the insidious secularity of modern life. Permitted to establish an independent, sovereign government, the emigrants agree that each religious community will be largely self-contained, but that laws to govern common community life and the coercive apparatus of a state will be necessary; and that given the vast differences among the religious communities themselves, the limited functions of the state should be carried out on a secular basis. To implement these principles, the emigrants agree that legislators will be chosen from people living on Mars, but that to ensure impartiality and secularity of administration, their high executive officers and leading judges will be brought from Earth.

Each religion has a comprehensive code of behavior or supports general moral principles that have potential application to every situation; and each claims that persons should regard their religious obligations as ultimate. Thus, all understand that conscientious citizens will be guided by a sense of religious obligation in what they do. It is hoped that conflicts of legal requirements and religious obligations can be minimized, but all are aware that some such conflicts may arise. With some regret, the emigrants conclude that even in the event of conflict, public authorities should apply the secular law as written, since they distrust the ability of those authorities to determine sincerity of religious assertion and they recognize that some conscientious believers may engage in acts dangerous enough to others to make physical restraint necessary.

In the society the emigrants establish, the state would have final authority over physical force, and, for purposes of the application of that force, the law would define the ultimate standards of acceptable behavior. Yet neither citizenry nor governors would assume or encourage the idea that the law is the ultimate guide for behavior in the sense of supplanting or overriding the guidance of quite different religious beliefs.

This illustration demonstrates that state legal authority claiming ultimacy only within its own domain is conceivable. Any further claim to ultimacy as the final arbiter, overall, of the reasons for performing actions is not a logical corollary of state law. Any conclusion that the stronger form of ultimacy is, in fact, characteristic must be based on claims presently and historically made by legal systems. Any conclusion that the stronger form of ultimacy is required must be based on the practical needs of legal systems.

Exactly what sort of ultimacy the law presently asserts is elusive. Neither legal norms themselves nor the system's overall structure are very revealing; and officials and citizens may not have very refined views on what considerations potential actors should take into account. Judges imposing sentence often leave no doubt of their opinion that what the criminal has done is definitely wrong overall and would be so regarded by any decent person. Since serious crimes with harsh sanctions forbid behavior that most citizens consider deeply wrong, we may fairly conclude that an aim of much of criminal law is indeed to supplant, so far as it can, any springs of action that would lead to violation. But we should not move too quickly from judgments about serious crimes to inferences about other parts of the law.

Perhaps the supposition that the whole law claims ultimacy in the strong sense is most plausible for secular societies that lack a highly cohesive moral outlook—societies in which the law becomes a kind of secular religion. Even in these societies, however, it is doubtful that most participants in the system hope or expect that the law in all its variety will dictate the actions of those subject to it.

That an across-the-board claim of ultimacy in the strong sense is necessary for a modern legal system to prosper is also highly doubtful. For many legal rules, it may well be enough if citizens regard them seriously and take them into account along with other considerations relevant to overall choice. Whether or not a claim that citizens should always attach *some moral weight* in favor of obedience is a typical and necessary corollary of modern legal systems is a more troubling question, one postponed for discussion in Part II.

The main burden of this chapter has been to suggest that if some general moral duty to comply with law does exist, it is a duty that applies only to behavior that the law really demands, not to everything formally classifiable as a legal duty. The last section of the chapter has expressed skepticism about the idea that whenever the law *does* seriously demand behavior, it should be understood as aiming to supplant all bases for choice that might lead to disobedience.

NOTES

1. Whatever other bases for invalidity exist, will private organizations at least implicitly accept the laws of the state as limits on their own rules? Not necessarily. A dissenting religious group may self-consciously require behavior forbidden by the state in which it exists.

2. Such a practice could work with a reasonable degree of fairness only if (1) citizens had ways other than disobedience to raise claims of invalidity and (2) some accommodation were made when two legal rules *required* inconsistent behavior.

3. When the lower norm is a court's injunction, the rule in the United States does require obedience until invalidity is established. See *Walker v. Birmingham*, 388 U.S. 307 (1967).

4. Primarily derived from treaty obligations, norms of international law play an increasing role in supranational relations, especially for countries in close-knit regional associations like the Common Market. Asserted conflicts with international law do sometimes underlie claims of domestic invalidity, although the traditional practice has been that such conflicts do not affect the internal validity of laws adopted within a country.

5. As the importance of the international order further increases, persons will more often be faced with the question whether or not to obey its norms, a question that now arises mainly with respect to the laws of individual countries. As international norms apply more frequently to individuals, one possibility is that their prescriptions will actually conflict with what are treated as valid legal prescriptions within the individual's own country. Such an eventuality could, logically, occur in a single legal system, see Munzer, Validity and Legal Conflicts, 82 Yale L.J. 1140 (1973); but I assume that any developed legal system will have techniques to resolve apparent conflicts.

6. In the United States, both the view that existing constitutional standards should be interpreted in accordance with natural law and the view that natural law provides a moral perspective against which people should evaluate all positive law enjoy substantial followings, but the claim that a constitutional amendment in violation of natural law lacks positive legal authority is not often made.

7. If this strains credulity, we can imagine the even shaper example of a Fear of Flying Club whose members are dropped from the rolls when they conquer their fear.

8. In some countries acts short of an explicit renunciation of citizenship—

for example, acquisition of another country's citizenship or a vote in a foreign election—may be taken to constitute a choice to give up citizenship. But in the absence of behavior that reflects some intent to align themselves with another state, citizens do not lose citizenship, however wrongly they behave. In the United States, the Supreme Court has sharply restricted grounds on which U.S. citizenship may be deemed terminated. See, for example, *Afroyim* v. *Rusk*, 387 U.S. 253 (1967).

9. See H. L. A. Hart, The Concept of Law 29–36, 33–35 (1961).

10. Legislators may or may not have decided against employing more straightforward sanctions.

11. A common practice among professional referees is to call fouls more closely when they wish to get a rough game "under control."

12. That possibility seems more plausible for inexperienced than for experienced players.

13. To be more precise, players are often expected to try to perform actions that carry a very high risk of ending in fouls and are sometimes expected to commit fouls intentionally.

14. Nor are they present in every game. With the possible exception of footfaulting in informal play, tennis may be a game in which the formal rules are widely followed. Chess may be another example.

15. Some rules that confer power also impose duties, about which we can properly talk of obedience. Usually a rule stating the jurisdiction of a court not only gives the court authority to dispose of disputes within its terms but also instructs the court to accept cases that fit. These mixed rules, unlike "pure" power-conferring rules, are within the broad concern of this study.

16. A norm permitting open fishing at every time of year would differ from a power-conferring norm in not touching the creation of new legal rights and duties, but both norms would leave to the actor the choice of what to do.

17. I use the word *should* rather than the word *would* because some courts may enforce duties they have no legal business enforcing and may fail to enforce duties they are legally bound to enforce.

18. Many jurisdictions have a doctrine of desuetude that deprives legal norms of effect if they have lain unenforced for many years. According to this doctrine, which in fact has been given little application in American criminal law, statutes that were once valid can cease to become so without ever being explicitly repealed or implicitly overridden by contrary subsequent statutes. Although statutes that have lost effect in this way may be discovered in the statute books, these are no longer valid legal norms and they will not be enforced by courts. "Noncompliance" with them is not a real violation of law but rather is like "noncompliance" with a law previously repealed.

I do not mean to exclude by definition the possibility that some duties might really be of a criminal law type, though enforceable through very different organs than the courts. One can *imagine* citizens being required by law to shun people who perform certain sorts of wrongful acts without the interposition of any legal process for determining the guilt of the wrongdoers.

I disregard norms of this sort because they do not figure in modern legal systems.

19. The sentence in text assumes that a private gambler's constitutional attack on the law would fail. If the statutory language is clear, a challenge to the face of the state would be unsuccessful. A general enforcement policy directed against professional gamblers, who pose a graver threat to the public interest than private gamblers, is clearly permissible. The private gambler's constitutional argument that, given previous enforcement policy, the law may not be applied to him is more plausible, but under present law previous enforcement policy does not establish constitutionally permissible limits of prosecution even if the policy is longstanding and publicly stated. Someone, for example, who is outside the reach of enforcement policy and is prosecuted because of a mistaken judgment that he falls within it, may be convicted if the statute's terms apply to him. Unless the gambler could show an unacceptable motive for his own prosecution, such as his race or unpopular ideas, he would almost certainly lose.

20. In a rare passage addressing this general problem, Philip Soper (A Theory of Law 87 [1984]) says "any case in which I am potentially subject to conviction by implication means that someone cares, however slightly." Soper assumes that if nobody cares, then desuetude has eliminated the legal force of the rule. This assumption disregards the long time it takes for desuetude to occur and the point that a law may be actively enforced at the core and disregarded at the fringes. I shall discuss in Chapter 8 Soper's argument that the sentiments of individual legislators are an important moral reason to obey the law.

21. Matters are complicated somewhat in England because of the possibility of private prosecution.

22. The existence of police discretion is, as Chapter 15 indicates, somewhat more controversial.

23. Here I part company with any extreme "realist" position that legal requirements can be reduced to predictions about what officials will do if one acts in certain ways.

24. Although many rules of general application, such as the tort duty not to commit assault, apply to everyone, others, such as the duties of physicians, attach to particular positions that are entered voluntarily. As to some kinds of contracts, such as marriage and large employment contracts, the law dictates certain crucial terms. Thus, voluntary action is connected to some general duties, and mandated elements characterize many contractual relationships.

25. Willful refusals to obey these court orders may produce confinement that is designed to coerce compliance.

26. When liability is grounded on negligence or strict liability, deciding what the law demands is difficult for a reason different from those discussed in the text. The problem then is whether one can speak of behavior being demanded when only bad consequences give rise to liability and when no conscious choice to violate the law or take a forbidden risk need be present. Of

course, one can intentionally commit a wrong or undertake a risk for which negligence would be a sufficient basis of liability. Such choices are within this study, and, subject to whatever other qualifications may be relevant, we can speak of the law as demanding that people not intentionally perform those acts.

27. Holmes, The Path of the Law, 10 Harv. L. Rev. 457, 462 (1897).

28. In this instance, the result may be less a consequence of legislative design than of new technology overtaking an existing formulation.

29. By prompt, I mean immediately upon breach rather than after judgment. Because legal processes are time-consuming and expensive, a resolution that does not require the use of these processes is preferable to an otherwise similar resolution that requires them.

30. The terminology may be a product of the way *most* contract terms are set by the parties rather than by general law. However, violations of treaty obligations are often referred to as breaches of international law, and ordinary breaches of contract are at least breaches of legal duty.

31. See, generally, Restatement (Second) of Contracts, Introductory Note to Chapter 16; R. Posner, Economic Analysis of the Law, Ch. 4 (2d ed. 1977); Farnsworth, Your Loss or My Gain? The Dilemma of the Disgorgement Principle in Breach of Contract, 94 Yale L. J. 1339 (1985). Farnsworth notes that fiduciaries are held to stricter standards than breaching parties to ordinary contracts. Id. at 1354–60.

32. See ABA, Model Rules of Professional Conduct, Rule 1.2 (1983), discussed in id. at 1358.

33. J. Finnis, Natural Law and Natural Rights 323–24 (1980). Finnis concludes that the principle of the common law is that one has a real duty to perform. He relies in part on the English rule that administrators must perform contracts and on the assumption that parties could write contracts to allow performance *or* payment if that is what they wanted. In the United States, however, a rule against specifying penalties is a serious impediment to writing a disjunctive contract. For some critical American perspectives on tortious interference with contract, see Prosser on Torts 979 (5th ed. 1984); Dobbs, Tortious Interference with Contractual Relations, 34 Ark. L. Rev. 335 (1980); Perlman, Interference with Contract and Other Economic Expectancies: A Clash of Tort and Contract Doctrine, 49 U. Chic. L. Rev. 51 (1982).

34. If the contractors acted with full rationality, however, inefficient performance would not result from an enforceable duty to render such performance. The parties would agree on some compensation less than the cost of performance and greater than its value.

35. This subject is very closely related to a topic I pursue in Chapter 4, the significance of the government's legitimacy to a duty of obedience.

36. See J. Raz, The Authority of Law 30–32, 236 (1979).

37. The point here is not an indifference between performance and sanction. The sanctions involved make sense largely as a deterrent to nonperformance.

3

Moral Claims and Moral Appraisal

In this chapter, I explain what I mean by conflicts of law and morality, sketch their sources, and clarify the concepts and terminology I use to discuss them. I also provide a brief theoretical account of the nature of the particular moral evaluations that constitute the heart of the book.

WHEN LAW AND MORALITY CONFLICT

The previous chapter concluded that the law often, though not always, seriously demands behavior prescribed by legal duty. These demands commonly carry moral weight. The moral reasons to comply with law include reasons independent of it for doing what the law requires (e.g., the moral reasons against killing innocent people) and reasons that derive from the interposition of the law. At least in a society with a decent political and legal order, the law's requirement of certain behavior may be a significant moral basis for engaging in that behavior, a subject that Part II explores in some depth. The moral weight that often, or always, lies behind the law may be opposed by competing reasons on which moral claims to disobey are based. These reasons give rise to conflicts between morality and the law.

In the narrowest sense, one might say that a genuine conflict between law and morality exists only when, after all claims have been properly weighed, moral reasons require action that is contrary to what the law demands. For the purposes of my study, I discuss categories of situations that are broader than this in important respects. Given my interest in how actors *resolve* competing claims, I include potential conflicts that arise when substantial moral reasons point toward noncompliance with law. Thus, I discuss circumstances in which an actor's overall judgment is rightly that the moral claims in favor of obedience carry the day.

I treat as a conflict any situation in which the actor has good reasons for being *free morally* to disobey, and include as good reasons some that do not count as moral. When moral evaluation leads someone to conclude that he can obey or not as he pleases, no strict conflict exists with the law's demands, because the person does nothing immoral by obeying; but since his evaluation does reject the law's implicit judgment that he is *required* to refrain from the forbidden behavior, it falls within the compass of this study. Closely related to this point is the moral status of some nonmoral reasons. As I indicate later, I assume that reasons relating exclusively to one's own welfare do not establish what, morally, one ought to do; people are free morally not to pursue their own welfare. Yet if one has a substantial selfish reason for action, that reason may override a weak moral reason against the action.

Illustration 3-1:
Patricia has promised an acquaintance that she will pick him up for the theater at 7:30. Just when the time has come to leave, she receives a telephone call from a quiz show that presents an opportunity to win $30,000 if she remains on the line for twenty minutes. Patricia does not really need $30,000 but that amount of money would make her life easier. She knows that if she stays, her friend will be quite nervous and that they will be late for the play. Patricia is pretty sure an apology on her part will be accepted but, given their previous relations, she can imagine no kind of "compensation" that will actually make her being late the preferred outcome from the friend's selfish point of view.

Patricia does not have a moral duty to stay on the telephone line and try to win the money, but if she does so, the breach of her promise to the friend is morally justified.[1] When similar reasons support a violation of law, I count them as raising a conflict between morality and law.

On some occasions people will mistakenly think that they have good moral reasons for disobeying the law or that, on balance, disobedience is morally appropriate. Parts II and III concentrate on correct appraisal of moral claims; however, Part IV, which deals with official responses to moral claims to disobey, effectively regards a conflict as arising whenever those subject to the law believe that one exists.

For my purposes, a moral reason is best understood as one that relates to the well-being of others, what is owed to them or will serve their interests in some way.[2] This particular subject matter approach to morality[3] fits most comfortably with its social purpose, which is largely to allow a tolerable mutual existence by setting constraints on people's uninhibited pursuit of their own well-being.[4] This approach does not treat as moral aesthetic reasons, prudential reasons that concern self-interest,[5] and duties to God that do not implicate one's treatment of others. Although excluding religious or other duties that concern one's treatment of oneself[6] from the domain of morality departs from commmon practice, the simplifying assumption that moral reasons concern one's relations with others adequately captures the subjects of this book, especially when the power of nonmoral reasons to negate what would otherwise be moral duties is recognized.[7]

I reject any idea that the domain of morality involves only matters of great moment about which people do or should feel strongly. However social morality is divided from such normative social institutions as etiquette, the factors that people weigh in considering trivial choices often closely resemble those touching graver concerns. When a tired spouse deliberates whether or not to offer to wash the dishes, considerations of self-concern and self-sacrifice, fairness, love, and the spouse's welfare flit through his mind. To say that the choice does not concern morality would be odd.[8] Even choices to observe the rules of etiquette can be moral if one wishes (for unselfish reasons) to avoid needless hurt and offense. My rejection of a "seriousness" threshold of morality is fairly important for this study, because whatever may be true about compliance with law in the abstract, compliance with many laws on many occasions is only of trivial significance.

Morality, however, does have its limits. In some kinds of choices, people do not think in terms of the interests of others, they are not expected to think in those terms, and it would be undesirable for them to do so. A choice to select vanilla rather than chocolate ice cream may have some differential effects on other persons, but, barring some exceptional circumstances, thinking about the choice in moral terms is simply not profitable. I will treat as outside the moral domain matters that, despite their slight indirect effect on others, are not apt subjects for moral deliberation and are not treated as such by prevailing moral views.

SOURCES AND VARIETIES OF MORAL CLAIMS TO DISOBEY

Sources

Moral claims to disobey can arise from a variety of moral reasons for disobedience, as well as from religious duties and selfish interests. I will put aside for the rest of this chapter situations in which it is claimed that a nonmoral reason makes noncompliance morally acceptable and concentrate on reasons for disobedience of law that are themselves moral.

The moral reasons claimed on behalf of disobedience are nearly as extensive as the whole array of moral reasons people accept. They may be thought to be rooted in a secular morality or in some religious truth—for example, that God ensouls a fetus at the time of conception; they may be thought derived from reason, revelation, nonrational intuition, or free choice or upbringing; they may or may not be thought to fit with conventional morality; they may be thought to turn on the likely consequences of action or on the relation of an act to some "deontological" duty or moral right defined without relation to consequences; they may be thought applicable to all persons, to all persons in the actor's situation, or only to those precisely like the actor; they may be related to political and social convictions or derived from aspects of morality far removed from those concerns.

What one hopes to "accomplish" by possible disobedience may also vary greatly. A person may object to the law he disobeys, to some other law or policy, to the whole political order, or to some private organization that benefits from compliance. Or, without any such complaint, the person may believe that powerful independent moral reasons support noncompliance on this occasion. He may or may not hope to communicate some important message to others by disobeying. The aim may be to improve the political order or the laws, or achieve another desirable objective, or only to adhere to proper moral norms.

Unless one could present convincing arguments why moral claims in favor of obedience should always prevail, a proposition that is highly implausible even for decent and well-ordered societies, one could hope to resolve all the perceived conflicts of law and morality only by offering a complete moral theory with comprehensive applications. That task is far beyond this study's scope. I do comment on the strength of moral claims commonly associated with obedience and disobedience of law; but what I say is not designed to alter the vastly different moral perspectives readers will bring to many subjects. A reader persuaded by the analysis I offer has to fit its conclusions into the fabric of his or her own moral perspectives when considering the question of compliance with law.

Varieties

When substantial moral reasons support obedience to law, a defense of disobedience must claim that the reasons favoring disobedience somehow cancel, outweigh, or otherwise carry the day against,[9] both the morally grounded claims of law as such and whatever independent moral reasons favor the acts demanded by law. I have already intimated that a moral defense of disobedience may take different forms, but these merit brief systematic exposition.

Most strongly, an actor may claim that disobedience is morally required—that to obey the law would be immoral. A less strong claim is that disobedience is morally justified—that one does no moral wrong by disobeying.[10] Justified disobedience may be morally preferable though not required, or it may be morally indifferent, a circumstance that could occur if moral reasons were evenly balanced, if nonmoral reasons in favor of disobedience outweighed the moral reasons in favor of obedience, as in Illustration 3-1, or if no moral reasons attached to either choice.[11] One might claim justification in yet a weaker sense, acknowledging that obedience would be morally preferable but asserting that nonetheless one has a moral privilege to disobey. Perhaps we need not always do what is morally best but are free to pursue our own interests although another course of action might be morally preferable. For such a claim of privilege to disobey the law, "morally permissible" may be a more precise designation than "morally justified."

A person may sometimes say, "I had a moral right to engage in disobedience." Such a statement may be a different way of asserting that what the person did was morally permissible, that he did no moral wrong. But rights can have a special and distinctive sense, relating to autonomy and limits on interference from outsiders.[12] The claim to have a right is the claim that outside interference would be morally wrong. Despite occasional assertions that rights make sense only if conferred by law, plainly, social morality may include concepts of moral rights; and attempts to formulate systems of morality independent of present social morality might also include moral rights.

A sentence about moral rights in this distinctive sense is complete only if it includes, explicitly or implicitly, reference to a potential interferor and type of interference. The usual reference, and the one of primary importance for this study, is to the coercive power of the state; a person's claim of a moral right to do something is that the state is not warranted in using its coercion to compel him to do otherwise. One may acknowledge that an action would be morally wrong—for example, expressing hateful views about a racial minority—and still claim that those who engage in it have a moral right against the state to do so. One's moral rights against the state do not necessarily settle how private individuals may properly respond.[13] Even if the state should tolerate expressions of racial bigotry, individuals may be warranted in greeting bigots with disapproval and minimizing contacts with them.[14]

TERMS AND ASPIRATIONS OF MORAL APPRAISAL

This book involves analysis both of claims that people should or should not obey the law and of ways in which legal institutions may respond to those claims. These questions are not mainly legal ones; the law cannot settle whether it should be obeyed or whether its present way of dealing with moral claims to disobey is sound. Whether or not people should obey the law as such is a matter of political obligation, a subcategory of moral standards that focuses on what people owe their government or fellow citizens. Also fitting into this subcategory are some claims in favor of disobedience, for example, those found in the Declaration of Independence. Other moral questions, such as the acceptability of abortion, which might affect whether or not one should obey particular laws, fall within a wider range of evaluation. Assessment of possible government responses to moral claims to disobey involves a mix of political philosophy, theory of punishment, and more general moral considerations.

Much of this book consists of my own moral appraisals of how citizens and the government should regard claims made on them.

Tempting though it is simply to proceed with the exercise and let the reader make what he or she will of the judgments, a succinct account of my understanding may make it easier to place my views in the context of each reader's own moral perspectives. Before I embark on that account, however, I will indicate the way I deal with some complexities in standards of judgment and use of terminology.

Standards of Judgment and Terminology

Appraisal of choices may be complicated by an actor's motives, by factual mistakes, or by variant perspectives of actor and observer. When an actor does what is morally right, but does it for morally unacceptable reasons—for example, frees a slave only to cause pain to the master whom he hates—one needs to distinguish evaluation of the actor from evaluation of his course of action. Linguistic care is also needed when the actor's choice rests on a mistaken factual judgment— when the act would have been right given the supposed facts but wrong given the actual facts.[15] A moral evaluation must indicate whether what is being assessed is the quality of the act given the actual facts, the supposed facts, or facts the actor might reasonably have supposed.

Appropriate terms for judgment are also more complex when the person making a moral appraisal does not share the actor's moral premises. The appraiser who thinks an act wrong under a correct moral view but right under the actor's moral view may believe that one valid moral principle is that people should do what they think is right.[16] The appraiser will have to formulate an evaluation very carefully to capture all these nuances.

For the most part, I sidestep these complexities by assuming that actors are trying to do what is moral, are open to adoption of the correct moral position, and make accurate factual appraisals. Departures from these simplifying assumptions are indicated.

The special vocabulary with which moral reasons for performing acts are expressed causes some difficulty, at times reflecting a deeper confusion over the nature and force of a moral reason. Two central and related problems are the significance of the words *obligation* and *duty* and the difference between having a moral reason for performing an act and having sufficient reasons for doing so.

Obligation and *duty* are used in two distinctive ways. In one usage they are words at the top end of a scale that expresses the power of moral reasons in favor of an act. The scale goes from what is morally permissible, to what is morally preferable, to what one morally ought to do, to what is one's moral duty or obligation. On this scale, the distinction between "morally preferable" and "morally ought" reflects the division between supererogatory good acts and acts for which condemnation is an appropriate response to failure. When obligation and duty are present, the appropriate demand for compliance is very strong. In this usage, obligation signifies what one must,[17] or is required, to do from a moral point of view; one has, for example, a moral obligation to lift a drowning baby out of a shallow pool.

The second usage of obligation and duty treats them as concerning particular kinds of moral reasons for performing actions. An obligation is voluntarily undertaken by a promise or other action. A duty attaches to a particular position or to one's status as a human being; one speaks of the duties of judges and parents and of people generally. In this usage, one can speak of moral obligations and duties, but one can also speak of obligations and duties that are other than moral. These nonmoral duties, or obligations, may carry moral weight—"it is morally right that judges perform their legal duties"—but moral argument is needed to link the nonmoral duty to what one morally ought to do.

When obligation and duty are used in these senses, they need impart no especially strong moral requirement. One may have no obligation to lift a strange baby from a shallow pool, but the moral "ought" to perform that act will be much stronger than one's obligation to keep a minor promise. Obligations and duties of this sort may also be outweighed. If I can save the baby only by breaking a promise, I morally ought to do the act that will fail to satisfy my moral obligation. Whereas an unvarnished statement that one ought to perform a particular action reflects what one should do overall, statements about moral obligations and duties need not carry that implication and therefore may be weaker in a significant way.[18]

Distinctions of "prima facie obligations," "prima facie duties," and sometimes "prima facie oughts" are one means of capturing the difference between having good moral reasons for doing something and it being best overall that one do that thing. The term *prima facie* clearly signals that the consideration in question is one that potentially can be outweighed by competing considerations.

These terminological variations deeply infect the main subjects of this study, as evidenced by the term *political obligation*. This term has commonly been employed to apply to any theory that explains a general moral requirement of obedience by citizens to laws and political authority. In the second sense of obligation, however, a true theory of political obligation would have to assert that the moral demands of obedience are voluntarily undertaken. Social contract theory would then qualify, but some other theories would not. Theorizing about political obligations does not even quite fit the first sense of obligation, because discussion under that rubric reaches any generally applicable moral oughts to obey, not only those of great strength.

I have not adhered to a single sense of obligation and duty, believing that the inevitable price of success would be the construction of awkward circumlocutions to express distinctions that a familiar terminology could make more comfortably. Rather, I have employed the terms *obligation* and *duty* in different senses, whose meaning the context makes plain. In general, when I use duty and obligation without further indication, I mean only a strong sense of moral ought. When I talk of political obligation or obligation to obey the law, I follow traditional usage in not implying any special degree of strength; and abstract statements about an obligation or duty to obey assume that the moral reasons to obey may be outweighed by competing reasons. Sometimes I switch to the narrower, more particular use of obligation and duty, but when I do so I signal my intention clearly. Though I eschew the prima facie terminology for the most part, I deviate from this reluctance in Chapter 6 when I discuss what makes a theory amount to one positing a general obligation (in the broader and looser sense) to obey. For that exercise, the term *prima facie* is helpful in exposing what it means to have a general moral reason to perform acts falling within a particular class.

Aspirations of Moral Appraisal

I turn now to the more arduous task of explicating my sense of the moral judgments I offer. Roughly, they represent an attempt to state proper principles of public morality for modern liberal societies. By proper principles of public morality, I mean principles that should be widely accepted by members of society as regulating their mutual relations. How I understand the relation of these principles to other dimensions of morality and how I believe judgments about them can be made require brief explanation. This explanation is designed to place what follows in a larger context; but it is hardly systematic and it will not persuade those who dissent from its fundamental premises.

Much of the remainder of the book could be anchored in quite diffcrent assumptions, and its value does not rest on acceptance of the general perspective summarized here.

Not all evaluations of obedience to law require what I shall call an independent moral judgement. One aspect of moral appraisal is analysis of whether claimed derivations and analogies are sound. If, for example, citizens in a democracy are said to have implicitly promised to obey the government, one can consider whether any acts in which citizens engage with respect to the government are very much like acts normally thought to give rise to promissory obligations. If one discovers promiselike acts that citizens perform, one may conclude that the obligation to obey stands on the same footing as promissory obligation generally; if one finds a striking absence of such acts, one will suppose that whatever grounds of obligation may exist differ from promissory grounds. The process of comparison can go forward without too much worry about why promises themselves are morally binding if the premise that they are is uncontroversial.

Appraisal becomes more difficult if the acts of citizens bear some resemblance, but not a particularly close one, to promising. At this point the decision whether or not a promiselike obligation exists may be made by a judgment that goes beyond a claim that these acts of citizens are simply a subset of promises or are so close in significance that the creation of a promiselike obligation is hard to deny. This fresh judgment will be some kind of independent moral judgment that goes beyond uncontroversial assumptions about promises.

For other arguments about obedience and disobedience, in which the claimed reasons are not a subset of more general and noncontroversial moral reasons, an independent moral judgment is more evidently indispensable to evaluation. The status of these judgments is what is troublesome. At a minimum, anyone's statement of a moral conclusion amounts to an expression of his or her own ideas about moral matters.[19] One's conclusions may further reflect and be assessed against the moral assumptions of the culture in which they arise. The relevant perspective for assessment might be present dominant views or selected deeper currents of understanding, under which a temporarily prevailing view might be rejected. Some conclusions may be drawn from the logic of moral language, though I am deeply skeptical that many controversial moral conclusions can be so derived.[20]

The crucial question remains whether claims of morality can plausibly transcend particular subjects and cultures or stages of history, that is, whether one can sensibly speak of moral judgments as being correct or incorrect, true or false, in some more ultimate sense. Were moral judgments ultimately reducible to factual statements, say about what people desire, then moral judgments would be a somewhat obscure category of empirical assertions subject to similar criteria of truth and falsity. I accept the prevailing view that moral statements are not so reducible. Various traditions in moral philosophy claim that the validity of moral statements can be established by self-evidence, by canons of reason that transcend cultures, by a faculty of moral intuition that human beings share, or by reference to religious truth.

Without undertaking a close examination of the nature and limits of reason, I shall simply report my belief that some fundamental value premises, such as the badness of unnecessary suffering, cannot reasonably be rejected. Based on self-evidence and the obvious aims of having morality at all, premises like these, when related to ascertainable facts about human beings, can yield certain basic universal moral truths.[21] But unaided reason leaves many moral dilemmas unresolvable; and people's actual intuitions are too heavily influenced by culture and circumstances to produce any sure guide to what is right.[22]

My own acceptance of a kind of objectivity in ethics that exceeds what can be established by reason is based on religious premises. How these religious premises relate to objectivity in ethics is not simple. To say that "God is good," in the sense of morally good, presupposes notions of good and implies the conceptual possibility of an all-powerful Being who would not be good. Thus, we cannot simply equate any conceivable qualities or commands of God with what is morally good or right; and if we cannot do this, what help is God in determining what is morally correct? The answer is roughly as follows: If an all-powerful God loves us and seeks our welfare, it would not be *illogical* to reject as bad or treat as morally indifferent those acts God seeks to have us do on behalf of others, but it would be so odd as to be highly unreasonable. Thus, if these religious premises are granted, what is morally right will coincide with the way God consistently seeks to have us act. That is enough to ground belief in the objectivity of ethics.[23]

The previous paragraph, which inexactly summarizes traditional Christian assumptions that I share but do not here attempt to defend, does not address how someone with religious beliefs should try to ascertain ethical truth. Believers give considerably different weight to reason, inspiration (the religious analog of intuition), revelation in sacred texts, and religious authority, and that weight for many will vary according to context. Believers also differ widely over the degree to which humans are capable of understanding and expressing the purposes of God as they bear on ethical choice. What I have tried to explain is how, despite deep skepticism about people's arriving at correct moral understandings on troubling issues, I believe one can conceive of correct answers to even difficult moral questions.

How universal moral truths bear on choices in particular cultures is also somewhat complicated. Some moral statements may be universally true: love is intrinsically better than hate, happiness is preferable to unhappiness, inflicting unnecessary suffering is wrong, respecting the dignity of others is right. But other moral statements may vary depending on cultural setting. By this I mean not only that aspects of the social morality of cultures vary, but that what it is really right to do also varies.

At the level of particular actions, this point is straightforward. Suppose that in one culture, everyone expects departing party guests to say with evident sincerity that they have enjoyed themselves; in another culture frankness about the level of one's enjoyment is the norm. What should a bored departing guest say? Most people would conclude that saying "I had a very good time" would be proper in the first culture but not the second.[24] What people expect, what is taken as politeness and rudeness, can affect the degree of candor that is morally appropriate. Present capacities, as well as expectations, are important. Among people with a capacity for both forms of government, liberal democracy may be morally preferable to authoritarian rule; but for some civilizations in which no better form of government is practical, authoritarian rule is morally acceptable.

A similar point applies at a deeper level to how people look at problems and to the moral concepts they employ.[25] In a very close-knit society in which people have a strong sense of mutual identification and shared goods, a morality may work best that stresses contribution to the good of others and demands a high level of contribution. In a loose-knit society in which mutual identification is weak and people pursue disparate ends, an emphasis on rights of autonomy and on strict duties of noninterference and voluntary obligations may be best. These variations concerning moral concepts will coincide with some differences in appropriate moral choices and in the sorts of characteristics it is desirable to inculcate in people.

The view just expressed might be challenged as circular. After all, the way I have identified the two kinds of societies is hardly independent of the moral concepts that dominate them. Am I saying anything more than that for a society with strong views favoring individual autonomy, such views are appropriate? So put, my conclusion would either adopt a confused kind of relativism[26] or be highly conservative, resisting any change in moral concepts as morally bad.

To understand why this challenge would be misconceived, we can distinguish various perspectives from which a moral judgment might be made. Someone might ask the following: (1) What would be the best moral principles in an ideal society made up of people capable and willing to perform perfectly under those principles? (2) What would be the best principles for a society that is ideal except in being made up of imperfectly moral people? (3) What would be the best principles for a society at a particular stage of technological development, education, and so on, assuming complete responsiveness to proposed changes in moral concepts? (4) What would be the best principles for a society given its present attitudes and principles, and given limits to change that are inherent or themselves derive from proper moral restrictions? We might well accept principles in answer to the last question that we would judge inappropriate for any of the first three questions.

Let us suppose, for example, that people in the United States now have less cohesiveness than would be desirable for an ideal society or even for a society of its size and level of technology and education. If this is true, notions of rights and autonomy may receive more emphasis than they would under more ideal conditions.[27] The recommendation that institutions and individuals should now pay less attention to moral rights would not follow. Perhaps the lamentable lack of cohesion could be cured quickly only by morally unacceptable ideological coercion, restriction of immigration, and discrimination against religious and cultural minorities. While government and private institutions should work subtly toward developing a more cohesive society, for the foreseeable future a strong emphasis on rights may be needed to sustain mutual respect for the dignity and interests of disparate members of society. Whatever the accuracy of its factual premises, the resulting conclusion that a morality of rights is appropriate for modern American society is not circular.

I turn now to explain more precisely how I conceive proper principles of public morality. This depends on an understanding of how different levels of morality may operate within a given society. Some notions of different levels of morality are plain. Moral principles are brought to bear at different levels of choice; there are moral judgments about how one should treat family members and about proper forms of government. Somewhat different moral concepts may be suitable for these different levels—moral rights appropriately receive less emphasis within families, whose members evidence a high degree of mutual concern,[28] than they do in relations between a government and those people it rules. Different levels of morality can also involve various moral perspectives. Two persons may make similar choices from quite different moral premises. It is conceivable, though perhaps unlikely, that a society could manage with relatively little shared morality among its citizens, as long as the pursuit of sharply variant moral perspectives yielded an adequate accommodation of different interests.

I am interested in a more subtle aspect of different levels of morality—how various perspectives are employed by the same people in the same circumstances. A not uncommon example in our society involves the relationship between simple versions of Christian morality, which is perfectionist and emphasizes duty and welfare, and the morality of liberal societies, which is much less perfectionist and emphasizes rights.

Illustration 3-2:

Chris has an opportunity to apply for a position that he regards as slightly preferable to other alternatives he knows are available to him. He recognizes that his main competitor for the position would be his acquaintance Alex, who, Chris knows, will have to accept something he sees as much, much worse if he is unsuccessful. Chris applies, wins, and accepts the position, to Alex's bitter disappointment. John takes as a starting premise of Christian morality that one should love one's neighbor as oneself and regards each failure to live by this principle as falling into sin; he regards Chris's pursuit of his own slight interest at the cost of Alex's much greater interest as a moral wrong from the Christian point of view. Yet, Chris's behavior is not wrong from the standpoint of social morality, by which John largely lives. Such sacrifices may be expected in favor of family members and very close friends, but the failure to make them for mere acquaintances is not an appropriate reason for blame. John would not be willing to say that Chris "ought" to have made the sacrifice from this second moral perspective.

How can we understand John's two judgments? Perhaps he has a higher morality that he does not really live up to or expect others to follow and a lower morality that really governs his life. Or perhaps he sees his higher morality as an aspect of his relation to God and uses his lower morality for human interactions. Or perhaps he is torn between his uncertain religious convictions and the prevailing secular themes of his culture, and has not worked through to a consistent moral view. No doubt all these ways of understanding often contain a great deal of truth.

However, John could be consistent in making both judgments. He may accept Christian moral principles as those that should ideally govern people's lives not only in ideal societies but even in his own society, while also recognizing that his society is composed largely of nonChristians and people, perhaps including himself, who accept the ethical principles of Christianity but cannot be expected to live up to their demands. Because social life must be carried on among diverse groups, John may recognize the importance of having less demanding moral principles that do not rest on acceptance of a religious faith and that can be widely shared.[29] He may consider participation in the development and maintenance of such a public morality as the responsibility of everyone, even those few able to guide their own lives by the more demanding Christian morality. He may regard that public morality as what citizens should employ in their capacities as citizens and as what public institutions should inculcate. Given these perspectives, John's judgments that Chris's act is both wrong and not wrong are compatible and appropriate.

The standpoint of proper public morality is the perspective of this study, which deals with aspects of the moral principles that citizens in a modern liberal democracy should employ for their mutual relations. That standpoint does not render the religious perspective, and my brief detour concerning it, irrelevant to what follows. Beyond providing grounds for believing that moral questions, including ones of proper public morality, have correct answers, and beyond affecting the reasons for people doing what is moral, a religious perspective—at least one that includes a view of human nature, intimates what an ideal social life might be like, and assigns some values special priority—is likely to influence what one conceives as a proper public morality for a society. To that extent, my acceptance of a religious point of view may influence some arguments I advance. The arguments themselves, however, proceed without reference to religious premises and are cast in terms of secular philosophical concepts, which I take as the appropriate mode of discourse for general discussions of proper public morality in modern liberal societies.

Because the study mainly concerns choices between obedience and disobedience, the arguments emphasize the choice aspect of morality, but this selectivity is in no way meant to downplay the significance of appropriate moral dispositions. Whether one considers proper public morality or other levels of morality, moral dispositions are at least as important as the precise principles employed for particular choices. In part, the study may be taken as presupposing the virtue of being a good citizen and as analyzing some of the dimensions of good citizenship.

Relevant Moral Standards: Some Generalizations

The study's consideration of standards of proper public morality for the narrow questions revolving around obedience and disobedience of law is made against the background of a more general perspective. That perspective is displayed throughout the work, and some broad issues about ethical standards are discussed in subsequent chapters. Nevertheless, a brief summary of relevant ethical positions may help to clarify what follows.

As creatures of habit and sentiment, human beings put the interests of themselves and loved ones ahead of the interests of others. People cannot realistically be expected to be guided in their actual behavior by standards drastically out of line with their deepest sentiments and sense of themselves; such efforts, if frequent, would impose undesirable strains on their capacities. Whatever the value of holding up ideals that a few extraordinarily moral people can conscientiously strive to realize consistently, that can be employed as a basis for moral praise when satisified by others, and that may play a role in understanding human self-centeredness and divine compassion, our general conceptions of moral *demands* should be responsive to the frailties of human nature, seeking the attainable from the imperfect members of imperfect societies. In a public morality, then, a distinction should be drawn between what people morally ought to do and all that is morally preferable; a substantial range of acts of supererogation that are morally desirable but fall outside the domain of duty and ought should be recognized.[30]

Much moral education involves the attempt to encourage virtuous attitudes and characters. Room exists for adults to engage in rational deliberation and calculation when making difficult moral choices; but any general standard that expects them to face practical choices afresh with some universalist vision, such as "the greatest good of the greatest number," is unrealistic. This unrealistic quality, as Chapter 6 explores in more depth, is reduced but not eliminated by suggestions that more mundane moral principles may be useful rules of thumb or that the actors should focus on what rule, if followed, would produce the best possible results. The vision is unrealistic because it both demands such extreme submersion of one's own special interests and desires and expects a broad and dispassionate assessment.

Many moral standards that should guide education and the making of choices should be deontological, applying regardless of the consequences of particular violations. Yet such standards cannot wholly displace consequentialist considerations. Deontological standards will not dispose of some moral dilemmas, and they themselves will often be framed in a manner—"each person must give due regard to the dignity and interests of every other person"—that requires an assessment of comparative consequences in situations of choice. On occasion, a deontological standard may yield an answer, but the likely consequences are so unfavorable they rightly give an actor serious pause. Some authors have attempted to establish clear-cut and coherent frameworks for assigning places to deontological standards and consequentialist considerations, suggesting, for example, that consequential calculations can only flesh out the content of deontological standards, fill in gaps left by those standards, or override their application in calamitous circumstances;[31] however, no such neat resolution is possible. In the main body of this essay, I assume the relevance of both deontological standards and consequentialist considerations, struggling to assign reasonable weight to each in the special contexts considered. Chapter 8 in particular explores how far certain reasons for obedience that could be understood in either a deontological or a consequentialist way should be understood in one way or the other.

NOTES

1. See P. Foot, Virtues and Vices 184 (1978). The assumption that reasons relating to one's own welfare are not moral reasons may involve oversimplification of a complex problem (see e.g., D. Parfit, Reasons and Persons 318–20 [1984]; Hill, Servility and Self-Respect, 57 Monist 87 [1973]), but these complexities are not critical for purposes of this study.

2. B. Williams, Morality 88 (1972). Williams casts his discussion in terms of human well-being, impliedly prejudging the moral status of nonhuman beings in a way I want to avoid.

3. The major alternative to a subject matter approach is one that treats any reason for action that overrides other reasons as a moral one. See, e.g., R. M. Hare, The Language of Morals (1952). Compare P. Foot, note 1 supra at 181–88.

4. See, generally, G. J. Warnock, The Object of Morality (1971).

5. To the degree that one's own well-being is necessary for the well-being of others, the preservation of one's well-being does become a moral reason. In this view, suicide could be an immoral act if it left family members distraught and unsupported.

6. The problem mainly concerns proscriptions of suicide and "unnatural" sexual acts. Given the traditional assumption among people generally that these matters are a very important part of morality, it is somewhat artificial to make effect on others a crucial factor, treating adultery as an aspect of sexual morality but bestiality as a problem of nonmoral sexual norms.

7. My suggestion that nonmoral reasons can "knock out" what would otherwise be moral duties but not generate moral duties may seem paradoxical; the explanation is that although these reasons, as shown by Illustration 3-1, can establish that we do not owe some performances to others, they do not establish that we do owe performances to others.

8. One might conceivably respond that fairness within a marriage remains a moral consideration even in trivial applications. This response, however, effectively abandons any "seriousness" threshold, since my point is precisely that the same kinds of considerations that apply to momentous choices also apply to many trivial ones.

9. The notion of weighing, familiar to lawyers, undoubtedly oversimplifies how competing moral considerations are related and how moral conflicts are resolved. See, e.g., J. Raz, Practical Reason and Norms (London: Hutchinson & Co, 1975); Nozick, Moral Complications and Moral Structure, 13 Natural Law Forum 1 (1968). Raz, for example, treats moral and other norms as exclusionary, displacing a balance of reasons for and against as the basis for action. He says that whereas first-order reasons may be weighed against each other, exclusionary and other second-order reasons are canceled or limited in scope. Using this terminology, exclusionary reasons are not outweighed by competing considerations. I find any sharp distinction between weighing and canceling reasons misleading. Let us suppose, as Raz does, that an order operates as both a first-order reason and an exclusionary reason. As an exclusionary reason, it has some capacity to dictate actions, though the person subject to the order judges that better consequences would flow from disobedience of it. But if the consequences are bad enough, the order will be disobeyed. Thus, the same sorts of reasons that would weigh against competing first-order reasons and are excluded by the "exclusionary reasons" may, if strong enough, surmount the exclusionary reasons. In this essay I often talk of conflicting claims being weighed without attempting a more precise designation of how they relate to each other.

10. I pass over the paradoxical possibility, notably suggested by some theological ethics and classical tragedy, that when moral claims compete what is morally required may also be morally wrong.

11. This possibility can arise only if general moral reasons in favor of obedience do not apply to some legal duties.

12. See, e.g., R. Dworkin, Taking Rights Seriously 184–205 (1977).

13. Nor does a claim that state coercion is wrong conclude whether the state may appropriately make efforts to *persuade* people that such behavior is undesirable.

14. When John Stuart Mill discusses the acceptable reactions of others to persons who engage in self-degrading behavior, he evidences just how complicated judgments can be about how others may permissibly react to behavior that lies within someone's realm of moral freedom. J. S. Mill, On Liberty 94–99 (Oxford Univ. Pr. 1912).

15. These matters are explored more fully in Greenawalt, The Perplexing Borders of Justification and Excuse, 84 Colum. L. Rev. 1897 (1984); and Greenawalt, Distinguishing Justifications from Excuses in Ethics and Law, forthcoming in J. Law Soc. Prob. (1986).

16. One may, however, think that people bear some blame for accepting highly objectionable moral premises.

17. Stuart Hampshire has pointed out that a strong moral injunction is most naturally expressed as "you must." Two Theories of Morality 17 (1977).

18. See, generally, J. Simmons, Moral Principles and Political Obligations 8–10 (1979). Compare Raz, note 9 supra at 30, who suggests that singular ought statements usually imply that one should perform an act, all things considered.

19. When I say "amounts to," I do not mean that this is all that most moral statements purport to signify; I think it is not reasonably disputable that the "meaning" of moral statements goes beyond this. But if the more ambitious meanings of moral statements are really illusory, if there is no reality that comports with their implicit claim of objectivity, then they can in some sense be "boiled down" to statements about a speaker's reflective preferences about what people should do. If such a boiling down is appropriate, all a listener need do is compare a speaker's conclusions with his own reflective preferences.

20. R. M. Hare claims that morality connotes a universal perspective that demands that people's interests be weighed equally. See R. M. Hare, Freedom and Reason (1963); and R. M. Hare, Moral Thinking, Its Levels, Method and Point (1981). I believe that the most the nature of moral language may demand in this regard is a minimal version of universality—that anyone like the actor who is in the precise position of the actor should act as the actor should act. This minimal claim of universalization is consistent with assertions that no two moral situations are alike and that a particular actor is so specially important, his interests should count much more than those of anyone else.

21. See, generally, H. L. A. Hart, The Concept of Law 188–97 (1961); T. Nagel, The Possibility of Altruism (1970); T. Nagel, The Limits of Objectivity, in S. McMurrin, ed., 1 The Tanner Lectures on Human Values 75–139 (1980); and G. J. Warnock, The Object of Morality, especially 122–25 (1971).

22. How much moral agreement might be achieved if these influences were purged is hard to say, and whether one can even conceive of human beings not

influenced by culture is doubtful. The idea that wide objectivity in ethics could be established by an unbiased shared faculty of intuition seems unprovable and is not particularly plausible unless religious premises are introduced.

23. See J. L. Mackie, Ethics 227–32 (1977); and B. Williams, Morality 77–86 (1972).

24. An argument could be made, however, that the hypocrisy in the first culture is so bad morally that people should combat it by being completely honest.

25. See Warnock, supra note 21 at 5–6.

26. On the difference between a true relativism that denies the possibility of objective moral judgment and the view often taken by anthropologists that what is fitting for one culture may be inappropriate for another, see H. Putnam, Reason, Truth and History 119–27, 159–62 (1981).

27. See, e.g., P. Slater, The Pursuit of Loneliness (1970).

28. However, the movement for women's rights certainly indicates how more organic structures of thought can suppress the powerful interests of some family members.

29. Compare J. Rawls, Justice as Fairness: Political Not Metaphysical, 14 Phil. Pub. Affs. 223 (1985). I agree with Rawls's effort to find principles that can be accepted by persons with different religious and philosophical positions; but I believe some of the most troublesome and debatable questions of social choice cannot be resolved on the basis of shared principles alone but require reference to the unshared positions. My views on this are sketched in lectures on Religious Convictions and Lawmaking, published in 84 Mich. L. Rev. 352 (1985). A more complete account will appear in a book entitled Religious Convictions and Political Choice, forthcoming from Oxford University Press.

30. I include as an act of supererogation any act that is morally preferable but not a matter of ought or duty. For my purposes, this usage is more helpful than limiting supererogation to especially praiseworthy acts. Compare J. O. Urmson, Saints and Heroes, in A. I. Melden, ed., Essays in Moral Philosophy 198–216 (1958).

31. For discussion of the relevance of consequences in a deontological approach, see C. Fried, Right and Wrong (1978).

II

MORAL REASONS
TO OBEY THE LAW

4

Legitimate Authority and the Duty to Obey

In this part of the text, we move from an introductory exploration of the claims of law and the nature of moral judgment to the moral reasons for obeying the law because it is the law. Do we have a good moral reason for complying with a rule because it is a valid law of the state in which we reside or are citizens? Although an overall decision whether or not to obey the law on a particular occasion will also depend on independent reasons for doing what the law prescribes and on moral reasons for noncompliance, appraising reasons for obeying the law as such is an important component of the decision.

In the following chapters I discuss promissory theories of obligation, utilitarianism, the duty of fair play, and various theories that link obedience to the receipt of benefits. Each of these theories suggests reasons in favor of obedience that apply in all or some circumstances. Though I pay attention to the traditional question of whether a single source of obligation applies to all persons and all occasions of obedience, I also discuss the force of reasons for obedience that turn out to be narrower in scope.

This chapter differs from those that follow in concentrating not on substantive moral arguments but on a conceptual claim—that the concept of political authority includes the notion that those subject to such authority have a duty to obey. The chapter indicates that the conceptual claim is either wrong or not right in a way that is helpful, that it represents an unsatisfactory approach to determining the scope of a duty to obey.

After first analyzing the significance of the claim that political authority and a duty to obey are indissolubly linked, I suggest various aspects of authority and different ways in which authority may be understood. By breaking down distinguishable aspects of authority, I show that one can make sense of a concept of political authority that does not include a duty to obey. Whatever factual premises and moral arguments might be advanced in favor of including a duty to obey within the concept of political authority bear more straightforwardly on substantive reasons in favor of that duty. I conclude that concern about the concept of political authority tends to obscure rather than clarify the relevance of those arguments.

THE CLAIMED LINKAGE OF POLITICAL AUTHORITY AND THE DUTY TO OBEY AND ITS SIGNIFICANCE

Many writers on political obligation have assumed that an aspect of the concept of legitimate political authority[1] is a moral duty to obey laws issued by the authority. The idea is that one cannot acknowledge a government is legitimate and at the same time deny one has a duty to obey. Hannah Pitkin, for example, has said, "Part of what 'authority' means is that those subject to it are obligated to obey."[2] According to Joseph Raz, "legitimate authority implies an obligation to obey on the part of those subject to it."[3] Elizabeth Anscombe has written, "authority is a regular right to be obeyed in a domain of decision."[4] And Richard Flathman has suggested that if one does not understand this linkage, he does not understand the semantic rules governing the concepts of authority and law.[5]

How is this thesis to be taken? It might mean only that the definition of terms like *political authority*[6] and *legitimate government* simply includes a duty to obey. This exercise in definition is dubious but in any event, a thesis of linkage based on it would not be very interesting. What is interesting is a claim that some independent features of authority and legitimate government imply a duty to obey—that, for example, any government that is morally justified in coercing its citizens has a right to be obeyed. An example of such a claim is traditional social contract theory, which treats the right to govern and the duty to obey as arising from the same acts of consent.

The subject of Chapter 2 is significantly related to the discussion here. In that chapter we inquired whether or not an aspect of law is to make a claim to obedience. Even when such claims are made, they are not necessarily morally compelling, and when they are not morally compelling, a citizen may justifiably reject them. Here the question is whether or not a citizen who acknowledges his government is generally justified in coercing its subjects must also accept a duty of obedience. Justified coercion is a minimal condition of what one means by legitimate government; the duty to obey is what follows if that duty invariably attaches to legitimate government. Doubts about the comprehensiveness of the law's claim to obedience circumscribe the likely scope of such a duty. If a good government adopts valid laws whose scope is much broader than any expected compliance, a conclusion that the government is legitimate presumably would not acknowledge a duty to obey that reaches further than official hopes about obedience.

Why would a joinder of authority and a duty to obey matter? A showing that legitimate authority and an obligation to obey are always linked would not establish that anyone actually has a duty to obey.[7] Perhaps on examination we shall find, as Robert Wolff claims,[8] that no legitimate governments exist. Nor would a linkage necessarily affect the arguments for whether people have a duty to obey; legitimate government might rest on precisely those bases commonly suggested for a duty to obey.[9] Nonetheless, the joinder could be significant in at least three different respects.

It might yield a kind of presumption about the duty to obey. Some people may implicitly acknowledge the legitimacy of their government but doubt that they have a duty to obey. Whether their coming to understand that the justification for government coercion implies a duty to obey will move them toward acceptance of the duty or toward doubt about the justifiability of the coercion may depend on the strength of their initial convictions; but if most people are quite firm in believing their governments are morally warranted in coercing, the linkage between legitimate government and the duty to obey, when recognized, will support belief in a duty to obey. In a somewhat more complex way, the linkage might have a similar effect for scholars and others who take widespread convictions on ethical questions as evidence of what is ethically correct.[10] If a duty to obey necessarily follows from legitimate government, then the belief of the great majority of people that government is justified in coercing subjects would serve to confirm the existence of the duty.[11]

A second matter of importance concerns the apparent weight of arguments for legitimate government and a duty to obey. Some claims might have much more obvious relevance for legitimate government than for a duty to obey. For example, the assertion that life would be horrible in the absence of government bears plainly on whether or not, at a minimum, the best possible form of government is legitimate. Were the linkage to duty to obey acknowledged, we could see that the reason favoring the best government's legitimacy would also be a reason for the subjects of that government having a duty to obey—a point that might not have been clear initially.

A third way in which the linkage could be important is in construing the import of voluntary undertakings by which people establish or accept institutions of authority. One source of legitimate authority, for example, is consent. We might find instances in which people rather clearly consent to a government's legitimacy without saying anything about a duty to obey. If a duty to obey is logically linked to legitimate authority, the consent to legitimacy would carry with it an implied promise to obey, much as traditional social contract theory has assumed.

Standing alone, the claim that authority and a duty to obey are linked cannot establish either that government is legitimate or that people should obey; for all the preceding reasons, however, the claim could affect our outlook on political obligation.

AUTHORITY WITHOUT A DUTY TO OBEY

In this section, I try to identify common major elements of the concept of political authority, including a duty to obey. I then inquire which of these elements are essential for any idea of legitimate government and suggest that the duty to obey is not among them.

Aspects of Political Authority

The idea of legitimate political authority is associated with at least seven elements:

1. Persons with political authority are justified in issuing certain kinds of directives to those they govern.

2. They are justified in using force to induce compliance with these directives.

3. Other persons in the society are not warranted in issuing the kinds of directives appropriate for political authority,[12] and they also lack the right to employ coercive force on behalf of their wishes.[13]

4. The governed should pay attention to the directives of the persons with authority.

5. The governed should not interfere with the exercise of force by those with authority.

6. The governed should cooperate with enforcement efforts.

7. The governed should obey the directives of those with authority.

If the question of what distinguishes a legitimate government from a well-organized band of criminals were posed, these features of legitimate authority might be mentioned.

One can sensibly distinguish a proper government from a band of robbers without conceding a duty to obey the government. Not every kind of legitimate practical authority[14] carries such a duty. In nonpolitical and imaginary political settings we can easily conceive of authority existing without such a duty. Although these settings differ from actual political societies in important respects, the general possibility of authority without a duty to obey has crucial implications for political authority as we know it.

Authority Without a Duty to Obey

Illustration 4-1:
Five business partners decide that spending a summer vacation together would be fun. To simplify planning and forestall undue diversion from business efforts, they assign one partner, Ann, responsibility to look into possibilities and make suggestions while the other partners concentrate on firm affairs. If a suggestion of hers appeals to the other four, that will be fine; but all understand that no one need take the vacation if he or she does not prefer it to a vacation alone.

Among the partners, Ann has authority to develop common vacation plans. Similar efforts by other partners will be inappropriate. Each partner should consider carefully any plans Ann puts forward; none need look at plans proposed by another partner in violation of their agreement. No partner need accept any of Ann's plans, and none is expected to submerge his or her own interests in a desirable vacation.[15] Although Ann's authority, unlike that of a government, involves no right to coerce, the example shows that we can speak meaningfully of practical authority when others are not under a duty to do what the person in authority suggests.

One instance of legitimate and coercive practical authority that is not accompanied by an obligation to obey arises in the relationship between parents and very young children. Parents may compel their children to do things that others may not compel them to do. Although parental authority over young children concerns the relationships of parents to outsiders, it also helps justify actions of the parent when those are challenged by the child after he or she matures.[16] If an older child expresses dismay over something his parents did when the child was young, the parents might respond, "Well, we thought that would be best and we were the ones who were supposed to decide."[17]

A still sharper illustration of a similar kind of authority occurs if Beth, with full mental capacity, authorizes Carol to do something to her later, while Beth is asleep, unconscious, or wildly irrational. Carol's authority, conferred by Beth's consent, will be exercised under circumstances in which Beth has no duty to obey because she is physically or psychologically incapable of obeying. If these illustrations involving subjects incapable of obeying or perceiving a duty to obey[18] seem too remote, I turn to practical authority over persons who can perceive duties.

Parental authority over older children is one variety of such authority. Most family upbringing links legitimate parental authority with a child's duty to obey, and children typically feel some such duty, although it usually weakens as children mature and relationships with parents become more reciprocal. Before concluding too quickly that parental relationships with older children support the linkage of authority with a duty to obey, we should consider a conceivable attitude of an older child.

Illustration 4-2:
Doris, a sixteen-year-old, thinks the following: My parents can tell me to do things that no one else can tell me to do. The way our society is organized, parents need to be given powers over children, and in my rational moments I don't resent the power my own parents have to influence my behavior. Since I want their love and the things they give me, and I believe lying is wrong, I usually do what they tell me. Often I think what they say is right. Still, I have seen enough other parents and children to think that my own parents have a lot of rotten ideas about what is good for me and for others. So I really do not suppose I have some general duty to do what they tell me.

Doris recognizes the moral legitimacy of her parents' authority in a significant sense, but without conceding a moral duty to follow their directions. Although such disrespect of parental views may rarely be combined with such easy acceptance of parental authority, Doris's attitude is certainly not absurd;[19] and, although most parents aspire to greater confidence in their judgment, many families might survive tolerably well if teenage children held Doris's point of view, particularly if the children conceded the appropriateness of parental inquiry about their activities and placed a high value on telling the truth.

Is such a limited sense of authority possible in the political realm?

Illustration 4-3:

In a small society technology produces an amazing device that permits a user to know what changes in legal norms are warranted, to ascertain the legality of all individual behavior, and to impose appropriate civil or penal consequences. The device is subject to extreme abuse in the hands of someone untrustworthy. Members of the society agree that only one device will exist, and that all legislative, executive, and judicial functions will be concentrated in a single director, to be elected by the assembled society for a one-year term. Former directors are ineligible for the office and a new director's first job is to discover if the outgoing director has acted properly.

In these highly fanciful circumstances, an honest director would be exercising legitimate political authority. Because of the device's effectiveness, society would be viable even if citizens did not recognize any moral duty to comply with the director's rules. The people in such a society would have a clear sense of legitimate political authority without necessarily accepting a corresponding moral duty to obey the authority. In that context at least, a coherent moral view could include acknowledgment of legitimate government without acceptance of a moral duty to obey.

THE ELEMENTS OF POLITICAL AUTHORITY AND ACTUAL SOCIETIES

Central and Peripheral Aspects of Authority

I now return, with these examples in mind, to the seven aspects of legitimate political authority that I suggested earlier. The warrant to issue certain kinds of directives is undoubtedly part of the essential core of political authority. This warrant is what has been called a "justification right"; the government asserts the justification in the face of a possible claim that it is doing something morally wrong.[20] The justified use of force to induce compliance with directives is similar, though its status is different in one respect. We could imagine a society in which human beings were so altruistic, or in which informal restraints of social opinion were so effective, that physical coercion was unnecessary. In such a society, persons with authority to issue directives for the entire society might lack justified enforcement power. This, indeed, is perhaps the most comprehensible notion of what society would be like if the state were to "wither away," as Marx supposed. Given human beings as they now are or will be in the foreseeable future, however, the authority to coerce is an essential aspect of legitimate government in a large complex society.

The notion of political authority implies some exclusivity. More than one person or organization may have authority to do something—parents, for example, share authority over their children—but to say that one person has authority to do something means that some others lack the right to do that thing.[21] To acknowledge that a government is legitimate is to concede that it may issue directives and engage in exercises of enforcement that would be inappropriate for other persons and organizations. Such an acknowledgment therefore involves acceptance of a duty not to do those things that are appropriately reserved to government officers. To this extent, the minimal notion of political authority includes a claim by the government and those who support it against usurpation of its functions by others.[22]

The first three elements of political authority, just discussed, are sufficient to differentiate a legitimate government from an invader's army of occupation[23] or an extremely powerful criminal syndicate. Because the foreign army is committing a moral wrong in trying to control people's lives, subjects have no duty to accept its use of force and are morally justified in trying to supplant it. Prudence and concern for the welfare of others may often dictate observance of the army's directives, but the subjects will not concede that their issuance is justified.

Consideration of a government's rules and noninterference with its enforcement efforts, the fourth and fifth elements of political authority, are not quite at the core of that concept as are the government's justification rights and the duty not to usurp, but imagining a concession of legitimacy that does not include them is difficult. If the enforcement efforts of political authorities were as foolproof as those of the director and his device in Illustration 4-3, subjects would not need to regard themselves as under a *moral* duty to consider the state's rules or to refrain from interfering with enforcement. Prudence alone would dictate those actions, because disregard of the rules would lead to one's punishment; and attempted interference would be futile. Given actual circumstances, however, a person could not reasonably say that the government acts appropriately in making and enforcing rules but that he is morally free to disregard the rules and interfere with enforcement.[24] Interference, say in preventing a police arrest, is not identical to usurpation, since the interferor need not attempt to take on functions of the government; but a general privilege to interfere would not be consonant with the moral appropriateness of the enforcement efforts. Similarly, claiming that one is free not to pay any attention to the government's morally appropriate directives would be odd.

This conclusion about the duties to consider directives and not interfere with enforcement does not settle the scope of the two duties. Has one a duty to consider *all* government directives that are applicable to one's behavior, to refrain from interference in *all* situations,[25] or may these duties be more limited? My comments below with respect to a duty to obey suggest why I think only the more limited scope of these duties follows from the government's legitimacy.

Possible moral duties to cooperate in enforcement and to obey occupy a more questionable status than the duties of consideration and noninterference. If government enforcement were quite effective, the government might do without a claimed right to the help of citizens; and help may sometimes misfire or have destructive effects on relations between citizens. In a family situation, for example, a mother may discourage one son from informing on another, telling him to mind his own business, although the mother certainly would not brook one son's interference with her efforts to punish the other. Further, if enforcement were reasonably effective and citizens felt themselves to be under fairly powerful independent moral restraints from doing serious harm to their fellows, a sense of a duty to obey rules just because they issue from legitimate political authority might not be needed.[26] Thus, duties of obedience and cooperation are less central to the concept of political authority than other elements, and we can imagine acknowledgments of legitimacy that would not include them.

Factual Premises That Underlie the Claimed Linkage
of Authority and the Duty to Obey

If the concept of legitimate authority does not include as a core element a duty to obey, and an acknowledgment that political authority is legitimate need not carry the assumption of such a duty, why has the linkage of political legitimacy and a duty to obey seemed so plausible? The answer lies in premises about the importance of government and the requirements of effective government and in the implications of those premises for individual duties.

The first underlying premise is that humans need government. If government were unnecessary, an idea of legitimate government might still exist, but we would be undisturbed if an account of individual duties rendered such governments highly vulnerable.

The second premise is that a sense of duty to obey is necessary to ensure the survival or effective working of legitimate government. The bare necessity of obedience itself is not sufficient to establish this premise. Even in our fanciful society governed by the director with a magical device, a fair degree of obedience would be required for society to be viable. Here, the absence of a need for a sense of moral duty to obey derives from the ability of sanctions to guarantee obedience. Some actual governments, including foreign occupation forces, may be able to terrorize the governed sufficiently to get effective obedience without a sense of duty to obey, but these governments will not be conceded legitimacy by most who attend to these matters. That some actual governments can succeed without a sense of duty to obey does not establish that legitimate governments can do so. Perhaps some of the very features that may render a government legitimate, such as a substantial degree of personal liberty, will tie the government's success to its subjects' sense of duty. And even if some legitimate governments can survive without a sense of duty, they might support a tolerable life for citizens less effectively than if a sense of duty were present.

If government is necessary for social life, if a sense of a duty to obey is necessary for legitimate government to work effectively, and if morality embodies standards that allow human beings to live tolerably well together, the conclusion follows that individuals have some duty to obey. So viewed, the linkage of legitimate political authority and a duty to obey is seen to rest on empirical premises about what is needed for effective legitimate government. The point is implicit in the discussion of Elizabeth Anscombe, who writes, "Authority arises from the necessity of a task whose performance requires a certain sort and extent of obedience on the part of those for whom the task is supposed to be done."[27]

If the crucial empirical premise behind the linkage of legitimate authority and a duty to obey concerns the need for the duty, the question immediately presents itself whether the premise is well founded and, if so, how far it reaches. Ascertaining what sorts of attitudes subjects of governments deemed legitimate actually have would be a start. If legitimate governments in stable societies survive without a wide sense of duty to obey, that would show that the obedient attitude is not always essential to the continued existence of such governments, though this attitude might still be viewed as something that will *improve* life under any legitimate government. If the obedient attitude is present in societies with legitimate governments, we could conjecture about the effects of its dissipation.

Why the Linkage of Authority and a Duty to Obey Does Not Assist in Determining the Scope of the Duty

The nature of this empirical inquiry leads us to take care about the precise nature of the attitudes necessary to effective government. Let us suppose that some sense of duty is needed for effective government. Must citizens have a sense of duty to obey all laws in every situation, or is some less inclusive sense adequate?

Someone who begins with the assumption that the duty to obey simply follows conceptually from legitimate government will suppose that any act of the legitimate government generates the duty. Taking account of the conclusion of Chapter 2, he may concede that the duty to obey does not attach to directives of legitimate authority insofar as neither officers nor citizens expect or hope for obedience.[28] More significantly, he may also grant that because of faulty procedures or substantive injustice, some acts of an *otherwise* legitimate government are not acts of legitimate political authority, and carry no duty to obey based on their being acts of legitimate authority. What this person will not say is that an act intended to affect behavior that derives from legitimate political authority can fail to carry a duty to obey.

Yet the empirical perspective reveals the possibility of just such a category. Some government directives, for example, certain parking regulations, that are within the realm of legitimate authority and are enforced may have their purposes adequately served without a sense of duty to obey. Once we understand the empirical underpinnings of the assertion that legitimate political authority implies a duty to obey, we see that it becomes an open question how widely that duty need be conceived.

Our examination of the claimed conceptual linkage of political authority and a duty to obey has produced some important conclusions. The conceptual linkage is not of the powerful logical sort that has been supposed. Rather, it rests on empirical premises and on a normative approach that derives duties from the necessities of social existence, an approach more fully explored in Chapter 8. Even if the linkage is accurate in the sense that any acknowledgment that a government is legitimate implies acceptance of some moral duty to obey some of its directives, the linkage does not aid us in fixing the scope of the duty.

Any assertion that an acknowledgment that a government is legitimate automatically implies a duty to obey all its directives would be patently false. Within the traditions of natural law and social contract, ample room exists for claiming that some acts of otherwise legitimate political authority are outside the scope of authority, are illegitimate, and carry no right to be obeyed. Anyone wishing to deny this conclusion must employ substantive arguments, not rely on implications of the concept of legitimate authority.[29]

Once this point is granted, we can see that asking whether a government is legitimate in general or in particular actions is hardly the most helpful way to decide the nature or scope of a duty to obey. We need rather to examine the claimed substantive reasons for obedience. Within that more fruitful inquiry, the moral status of the government may make an important difference; but it is not always determinative.

NOTES

1. Perhaps "legitimate authority" may be redundant, but I employ the phrase to make clear that I am talking about political power that is not only accepted but is normatively justified in some sense. Compare William McBride's suggestion in The Fetishism of Illegality and the Mystifications of "Authority" and "Legitimacy," 18 Ga. L. Rev. 863, 874 (1984), that "'authority' denotes nothing further than the idea of possessing the ability ('power') to coerce and of exercising that power when such possession and exercise are considered acceptable by some other person." A critic could, of course, recognize that a government had "authority" in this sense without conceding that its exercise of power was at all morally legitimate.

2. Pitkin, Obligation and Consent—II, 60 Am. Pol. Sci. Rev. 39, 40 (1966).

3. Raz, Authority and Consent, 67 Va. L. Rev. 103, 117 (1981).

4. Anscombe, On the Source of the Authority of the State, 20 Ratio 1, 3 (1978).

5. Flathman, Political Obligation 89–90 (1972). See also Beran, In Defense of the Consent Theory of Political Obligation and Authority, 87 Ethics 260 (1977).

6. Plainly the term *authority* must be qualified or limited in some way if a duty to obey is to be plausible, since the kind of "authority" an expert has— what has been called authority as a personal characteristic (see Anscombe, note 4 supra, at 2)—clearly involves no duty to comply with the expert's recommendations. Richard DeGeorge distinguishes executive authority from nonexecutive authority, including in the latter category epistemic authority, authority based on competence, and authority based on personal authenticity or excellence. The Nature and Limits of Authority 22, 42–43 (1985).

7. See Flathman, note 5 supra at 99, 104–105.

8. Wolff, In Defense of Anarchism (1976).

9. See A. John Simmons, Moral Principles and Political Obligations 42–43 (1979).

10. Such a position is consistent with belief that the great majority of people may be mistaken concerning some moral questions.

11. One needs to say a little more about the content of the beliefs. If everyone thinks some legitimate government exists but half think only liberal democracy is legitimate and half think only communism is legitimate, the universal belief that some government is legitimate might not provide strong evidence that either liberal democracy or communism is legitimate.

12. Some kinds of directives, such as a specification of one's tax liabilities, appropriately emanate only from government sources. Other kinds of directives, such as prohibitions of willful killing, may also appropriately issue from other sources, such as church authorities; what distinguishes political authority in these areas are directives about the methods of enforcement, including the use of coercive physical force.

13. Some forms of physical coercion are permitted to parents and others with supervisory responsibilities over children.

14. As I have already indicated (note 6 supra), to acknowledge someone as an authority in the sense of being an expert would not, of course, imply any duty to obey. What I wish to show is that even what may be called "practical authority" need not carry with it a duty to obey. Various senses of authority are perceptively explored in Raz, Authority and Consent, 67 Va. L. Rev. 103, 106–118 (1981). See also R. DeGeorge, note 6 supra.

15. Someone who wants to vacation with the other partners may end up settling for a less than optimal location, but that will be because he or she prefers a joint vacation at that place to a single vacation at the most desired place.

16. These comments are meant to deflect the possible criticism that a special sense of authority is involved here, one that essentially concerns

parents and outsiders, rather than the relation *between* parents and child. Clear examples of this special sense of authority are authority over zoo animals or parks. The text tries to show that parental authority over young children cannot be so reduced.

17. Of course, the existence of authority would not fully justify the parents' action if it were based on seriously faulty judgment, but part of an adequate justification would include the claim of authority, and one possible ground of complaint on the child's part would be met.

18. I draw this distinction because young children have a capacity to obey before they can perceive a duty to obey.

19. G. J. Warnock, The Object of Morality 44 (1971), has suggested more generally that "one may accept a rule—that is, admit that it *is* a rule and even that it is wholly proper that there should be that rule—and yet think, consistently and reasonably, that one need not comply with it."

20. See Ladenson, In Defense of a Hobbesian Conception of Law, 9 Phil. Pub. Affs. 134, 139–41 (Winter 1980); Sartorius, Political Authority and Political Obligation, 67 Va. L. Rev. 3, 5 (1981); Smith, Is There a Prima Facie Obligation to Obey the Law? 82 Yale L. J. 950, 975–76 (1973). John Simmons correctly suggests that the term *right* is not required here to convey the central idea of justification. Simmons, Voluntarism and Political Association, 67 Va. L. Rev. 19, 23 (1981). Compare Richard DeGeorge's distinction between performatory executive authority and imperative executive authority, note 6 supra at 63.

21. A broader sense of authority includes any legal or moral right to do something. In this sense, everyone may have authority to help the poor. But only the government may help the poor by spending money that comes from payments coerced from subjects.

22. See Sartorius, note 20 supra at 5. The generalization in the text does not establish what amounts to usurpation or whether or not what would otherwise be usurpation can be warranted if the government is ineffective. Private vigilantes might argue that private punishment is either an appropriate supplement to state activity or at least justifiable when the legitimate government performs inadequately.

23. In some circumstances, a foreign army of occupation may temporarily exercise legitimate authority, as when it has fought a just war, the government of its enemy has collapsed, and conditions are not yet propitious for creation of a new government; the legitimacy of the army's power might be recognized by some subjects of the enemy state. That is not the sort of example I have in mind in the text.

I pass over the questions raised when remnants of legitimate authority combine with an occupying power to enforce basic criminal provisions that remain unchanged.

24. See Simmons, note 20 supra at 24.

25. I mean here only whether or not there is a prima facie moral duty not

to interfere in all situations. Even if such a duty existed, it might on occasion be outweighed by other considerations.

26. One can imagine, as in the family situation, a duty to obey without a duty to cooperate, but the reverse is implausible. The main purpose of most compulsory norms of criminal law is to prevent the behavior in question; enforcement against an offender is a second best alternative. If a subject has a moral duty to cooperate fully that includes turning himself in and confessing, must he not also have a duty to refrain from the behavior in the first place? And if the subject has a moral duty to *help* the government enforce the law against others, the duty's basis must be a moral responsibility to help reduce unpunished criminal behavior, which would also encompass a duty not to commit unsanctioned violations himself.

27. Anscombe, note 4 supra at 6. See also id. at 9. Anscombe apparently does not recognize the distinction I have drawn between needing obedience and needing a sense of duty to obey.

28. He might, of course, collapse this category of norms one does not have a duty to obey into a category of illegitimate norms, discussed in text, claiming that governments never legitimately adopt norms broader than the behavior they seek to control. That view is overly simplistic, as the analysis in Chapter 2 suggests.

29. I do not deny the possibility that one might carefully formulate a notion of legitimate political authority such that every directive of legitimate authority would carry a duty to be obeyed. But, in that event, the concept of legitimate authority would itself have to be framed with reference to the relevant substantive arguments concerning a duty to obey.

5

Promissory Obligation: The Theme of Social Contract

For most of the history of liberal democracies, the dominant theory about why citizens are obligated to obey the law has been social contract. According to a traditional version of that theory, a person is obligated to obey the law because he has consented to the government in a manner that includes a promise to abide by its decisions. In English-speaking countries, including the United States, it is John Locke's account of social contract[1] that has been most influential; as recently as 1970 a leading academic lawyer could speak of his theory as "the only modern rival for the doctrine that power proceeds from the barrel of a gun."[2]

This chapter deals with social contract theory insofar as it stands for genuine claims about consent and promise. The aim of the chapter is to outline the present and potential place of promise as a source of obligation to obey the law. That effort requires pursuit of a number of different but related topics. I first sketch the basic social contract theory and its tie to political liberalism. After exploring varieties of consent and promise, I conclude that many persons do apparently have promissory obligations to obey laws and other rules but that on no plausible account have all or nearly all citizens or residents of liberal democracies promised to obey. I next try to identify more carefully the persons who have undertaken to obey in a promiselike way and inquire whether their apparent obligations are vitiated by some defect. Finally, I discuss the possibility of liberal democracies consciously making greater use of promise as a source of obligation.

SOCIAL CONTRACT THEORY AND PROMISES TO OBEY

The main question that traditional social contract theory tries to answer is how a government can justly have coercive powers over free individuals. The answer, in familiar words, is that governments derive their just powers from the consent of the governed. People agree to the authority of government because the alternative of life without government would be much worse. This consent to government most directly involves acquiescence in actions of the government that are within the sphere of the authority conferred. Although the last chapter shows that such consent need not logically carry an undertaking to comply with what the government demands, the traditional social contract view is that acceptance of the government's authority does involve a corollary agreement to obey.[3] Thus, the thrust of social contract theory is to make a person's relationship to the state, or to fellow citizens, like that of a promisor: he has made something like a promise to obey the law.

This view conceives a person's obligation to obey as based on an autonomous commitment to act in accordance with the law; the limitation on what one can do is self-chosen. A promissory theory of why one should obey the law, therefore, involves moral obligation not only in the broader sense generally employed in this essay, but also in the narrower sense of moral constraints that are voluntarily undertaken.

Social contract theory connects to liberalism in two important ways. Although Hobbes's endorsement of authoritarian rule[4] and Jean Jacques Rousseau's proposal of what might be called democratic totalitarianism[5] show that social contract accounts of political legitimacy need not invariably support liberal democracy, the prevailing Anglo-American theory, drawn from Locke, has contemplated a government limited in its authority to the purposes that underlie its existence and constituted according to the periodic expression of wishes by its citizens. In this conception, a promise to obey is not unqualified; its force depends on continuance of democratic processes and on the government not exceeding its proper powers. In a deeper sense, social contract theory is a reflection of a liberal conception of human nature that emphasizes freedom and autonomy.

Although theories differ on exactly why promises carry moral force, promise is widely regarded as the clearest way in which people voluntarily assume moral obligations. By promising to perform an act, a person may generate a moral requirement that did not previously exist or may (as when one promises to do what is already a moral duty) supplement independent moral reasons for doing the act. The moral force of promise is sometimes thought to depend on the existence of a social convention of promise keeping, but mutual understanding of the significance of promise language, which could exist between two people aware of conventions of promise in another society, is sufficient to create moral obligation.[6] In any event, since both the apposite linguistic conventions and the social practice of promise keeping exist in modern society, the power of promises to generate moral obligations is undisputed.

That conclusion does not settle whether promises to do morally wrong acts carry any force, a problem I discuss later, nor does it tell us how great the moral force of promises is. On the latter subject, I shall accept the common assumptions that any undefective serious promise does carry substantial moral force and that breach of even the most clearly unconditional promise can sometimes be morally appropriate. If I foolishly say, "On absolutely no account will I fail to be there," and then find myself in the unexpected position of having to choose between showing up and saving ten lives, I should save the ten lives.[7]

EXPRESS, TACIT, AND IMPLIED PROMISES

One can be obligated in the way promissory theory assumes if one has made a promise or engaged in a promise-like act, and the promise is not undercut by duress or some other vitiating condition. Assessment of the idea that citizens have promised to obey the law demands a careful appraisal of the ways in which promissory obligations can arise.

Instances of express and tacit consent are fairly straightforward. Suppose a law school dean tells Faith, a prospective teacher, "Our practice is that faculty members teach whatever subjects the dean assigns." If Faith responds, "That's all right with me," she has explicitly agreed to comply with the practice. But promises are not always express. If the dean explains the practice and says, "If I don't hear to the contrary, I'll assume you have no objections," Faith has tacitly agreed by remaining silent and accepting a faculty position. When a person expressly or tacitly promises, he has actually signified commitment. As long as no misunderstanding exists about the nature of his words or acts,[8] the force of the commitment is plain.

Beyond clear instances of tacit promise, we move to murkier waters, where both the proper terminology and the force of one's actions become more troublesome.

Illustration 5-1:

The dean simply describes the practices of the law school to Faith without asking for any indication of her agreement to them. Two years later, Faith objects vociferously when the dean asks her to teach Torts. Although not denying that, given her background and the school's needs, Torts would be a reasonable course for her to teach, Faith objects that she does not want to teach Torts. The dean responds, "You impliedly agreed to follow our practice of dean assignment when you accepted the job."

What would the dean's statement about implied agreement mean? The dean might mean that both he and Faith understood that when a job applicant is told conditions of employment and does not object, the acceptance of the job really *signifies* agreement to the conditions. In this view, the dean would be claiming that Faith had tacitly promised to comply. But the dean might mean something different—that even though Faith's accepting the position did not signify agreement to the condition of dean assignment, her course of action committed her in some way to comply with it.

One claim of this sort is that a person's actual agreement to one thing represents a logical or moral commitment to something else.

Illustration 5-2:

A mother tells her twelve-year-old son he can attend a local college basketball game. She remarks on the evening of the game, "Be home by 10:00." He responds, "You said I could go to the game; it won't be over until 10:45 and it takes fifteen minutes to get home; so you've already agreed I can stay out until 11:00."

Assuming that leaving in midgame is not a serious option, the mother's original permission committed her logically to the 11:00 hour, even if she did not realize that at the time.[9] The moral connection between what someone did agree to and what it is claimed he impliedly agreed to may be represented by a person's sharing an apartment with a friend. In the absence of an explicit disclaimer before the friend moves in, the original tenant may impliedly have consented to the friend's having visitors, since it would be morally wrong to deny that liberty to a friend with whom one shares an apartment.

Whether Faith was committed logically or morally would depend on the circumstances. If Faith, without reading the stated rules governing the school, had signified acceptance of them, and these rules included the practice of dean assignment, she would logically have committed herself to accept the practice though not consciously agreeing to it. If she had initially expressed a willingness to do whatever was in the school's interest, the dean might argue that she was morally committed to accept dean assignment. Since some fortunate law school teachers are not subject to the dean's discretion about teaching assignments, Faith's acceptance of the job alone probably would not represent either a logical or a moral commitment to accept the practice.

The dean's assertion about implied consent might instead amount to a more complex claim that Faith's failure to raise any objection when she could have and her acceptance of the job bind her morally to accept his assignment. The dean's position would be strongest if three factors coalesced. The first involves Faith's state of mind up to the time she accepted the job. Faith may have acquiesced in the stated conditions even if she never agreed to observe them. (Exactly what state of mind a person need have in this respect is sometimes a tricky question, since some matters are so routine they are not explicitly considered. If a tennis player's actions presuppose the relevance of the usual rules—serving behind the baseline, attempting to hit the ball in court, and so on—we might say he intends to play by the rules even if he has not addressed his thoughts to the question.) The second factor is the reasonable belief of others about Faith's intent. If others at the law school believed and had good reason to believe that Faith acquiesced in dean assignment, the dean's claim of implied consent is strengthened. Reasonable belief depends substantially on factual likelihood, but the moral relationship between teaching law in a faculty and having the dean assign one's courses is also relevant. The closely related third factor involves the locus of responsibility for clarifying matters. If accepted conventions would require Faith to express a nonacquiescent state of mind, then her silent acceptance of the job can have a significance it might not have if everyone understood that no one is bound to a practice like dean assignment unless he signifies consent. When all three factors are present—subjective unexpressed acquiescence, reasonable belief in acquiescence by others, and conventions placing the burden of expressing nonacquiescence on the individual applicant—then implied consent is clearly present.

None of the factors, alone, appears sufficient to generate implied consent. If the conventional burden was on the dean to elicit an expression of consent and others did not reasonably think Faith had acquiesced, the fact that her unexpressed state of mind was acquiescent would not amount to implied consent. If others reasonably supposed she was acquiescent, but she in fact was not and the dean had failed to carry his burden of finding out, she would not have impliedly consented. And if the conventional burden was on Faith, but she had neither acquiesced nor been reasonably thought to do so, she would not have impliedly consented.

When two of the factors are present, the outcome is more debatable. Suppose, first, that Faith did acquiesce and others reasonably thought she did, although the dean failed to discharge his burden of finding out. The dean would have a strong argument that since she and others were proceeding on the assumption that she acquiesced, she was bound to comply. Similarly, if her state of mind was acquiescent and she had failed to indicate to the contrary, and conventions were quite clear that it was her responsibility to do so, she may be bound although others, knowing her character, doubted she was really willing to go along.

The most interesting case may be one in which Faith never intended to acquiesce but others reasonably supposed she had and conventions placed on her the burden of indicating nonacquiescence. This case raises the question of whether one can ever impliedly consent without being willing to acquiesce.[10] Plainly, if Faith assumed the burden was on her to indicate nonacquiescence and remained silent only because she thought she would not be offered the job if she said she was unwilling to accept assignment by the dean, she has intentionally misled others about her state of mind, and that is enough for implied consent. If she was negligent about her responsibilities, at fault for her unawareness of the relevant convention, she may also be bound to act as if she had consented, although here it becomes somewhat arbitrary whether one says "she did impliedly consent" or "she is bound to act as if she impliedly consented." Her present obligations may at this point be partly determined by a fourth factor—the degree to which others have detrimentally relied on her acquiescence. If the school's hiring of her or taking other steps depended on the assumption that she accepted dean assignment, it is evident that she is bound.

Detrimental reliance, an essential element in the legal doctrine of promissory estoppel, plays a particularly critical role if Faith's failure to follow the convention is innocent and not her fault, for example, because she comes from another culture where it is always up to the dean to ask about acquiesence to practices. If the school has not relied on her acquiescence, she can fairly resist being bound on the basis of an innocent mistake that has caused no harm; but if the school has reasonably relied, she may be bound not to shift the damage for her innocent failure onto the school. Although some of these variations leave uncertainty about the precise boundaries of implied promise, this uncertainty is warranted both by our loose understanding of the concept and, more important, by genuine doubts about what is necessary at the edges to trigger normative obligations like those accompanying promise.

At the outer boundaries of implied promise, notions of fair play, discussed in Chapter 7, may figure more importantly than promise; and it may not matter greatly in which vein some situations are described. But we need to be aware of the possibility that as one moves from express to tacit to implied consent, not only do opportunities for misunderstanding about what conduct signifies increase, but the *force* of obligations undertaken may diminish somewhat. If Faith accepts the dean's claim that she impliedly consented, she might still say, "That's not the same as actually promising." Some people who knowingly mislead others into thinking they agree to do something may nonetheless balk at saying so explicitly. Although such hesitation might reflect a wish not to lie about one's present state of mind, it may also indicate a sense that explicit promises carry more force.

Even claims of implied promise rest on some act of Faith that is asserted to be the basis of her obligation to comply; these claims are thus distinguishable from claims based on hypothetical consent or agreement. Some versions of social contract theory purport to describe what institutions *would be* agreed to by people: actual people, people rationally pursuing their own self-interests, or imaginary people denuded of some human characteristics.[11] These theories, of which John Rawls's original position is best known,[12] do not depend on the special moral force of promises or consent; rather, they reveal independent reasons why an institutional scheme is morally supportable, showing that it is fair or promotes the interests of all or most people.[13] The fact that I might have agreed to some practice under certain circumstances does not itself establish that I have actually undertaken any obligation to comply,[14] and claims based on hypothetical agreement are thus outside the scope of this discussion.

ARE PROMISSORY UNDERTAKINGS A GENERAL SOURCE OF OBLIGATION TO OBEY THE LAW?

For a promissory theory of political obligation to be persuasive, people must have undertaken a promissory obligation to obey the law. I now turn to examine whether some or all people have undertaken to obey some or all laws through actions that amount to a promise in one of the senses examined in the previous section.

Typical social contract theories envision some stage at which people agree to set up a government with a certain form. Room for disagreement exists over whether historical events like the Mayflower Compact or the adoption and ratification of the federal Constitution represent a voluntary creation of government consented to by the governed. In the case of the Mayflower Compact, the government created by agreement was ultimately subsidiary to the British government; in the case of the Constitution not all citizens participated in the representative processes by which the new government was created and not all those who did participate acquiesced. In any event, for a genuine promissory theory of obligation, the status of these historical events is largely beside the point. A particular person, right now, can be obligated only if that person has undertaken to obey. Our ancestors do not have the capacity to agree and promise for us, even if they have acted with the welfare of succeeding generations in mind. Their voluntary agreements may be some evidence that had we been in their shoes we would have agreed to the same things, but the argument based on such evidence is one of hypothetical consent and promise. It concerns what we would have promised in hypothetical conditions, not what we have actually undertaken to do.

The crucial question for any promissory theory is whether people now alive have promised to obey the law. For this purpose, whether a government was actually created by a process involving consent or originated through an exercise of force is not central. What counts for an individual is whether he or she has promised to obey; neither the unanimous agreement of those originally subject to the legal order nor the agreement of most of one's fellow citizens can obligate an individual who has not agreed.

Some people do expressly promise to obey at least some laws. Many elected officials and some appointed officials take oaths of office; and some professionals, including lawyers, take oaths when they enter their professions. These oaths, I suggest below, concern official or professional performance; they do not directly commit one to general law-abidingness. Naturalized citizens take oaths with more inclusive import. They promise to "defend the Constitution and the laws of the United States" and to "bear true faith and allegiance to the same."[15]

Most citizens make no such express promise. True, the large majority of Americans have said the Pledge of Allegiance, but that is vague in content,[16] usually said as a matter of rote, and recited mainly in childhood. Whatever force a pledge like this *might be given*, presently it does not constitute a serious promise to obey. A Law Day speaker who swears faithfulness to the law may have promised his listeners that he will obey; and more informal remarks may have a similar effect, but relatively few members of liberal societies go about telling others of their generalized commitment to be law-abiding.

If most citizens have agreed to obey the law, the agreement must be tacit or implied; but the grounds for such agreement are very hard to find.

The most frequent assertion about consent in liberal democracies is that by participating in the government, citizens acknowledge its legitimacy and agree to obey its laws.[17] Participating directly in the deliberations and voting of small groups, such as faculties or student councils, may be understood in this manner. A person who was not willing to comply with the outcome would be expected to withdraw or at least state an unwillingness to be bound. Someone who participates without any disclaimer may reasonably be understood to be bound by the result in the same manner as someone who explicitly agrees to accept the majority's decision.

The application of this approach to citizens of liberal democratic states faces substantial obstacles. We may note, first of all, that voting could not amount to consent in states such as Australia, where people are actually required to vote. More significantly, in states where voting is optional a good many citizens never exercise their privilege, so a theory of obligation based on voting (or any other form of active participation in government) will omit substantial numbers of citizens, as well as alien residents who are not allowed to vote.[18] Thus, voting or other forms of voluntary political participation cannot underlie a fully general theory of obligation that would reach all residents or even all citizens. Despite these obvious limitations of the theory, if uncompelled voters have implicitly promised to obey the law, a powerful and broad ground of obligation exists. Unfortunately, the argument for such an obligation fails.

Certainly voting in an ordinary election does not involve any explicit promise; the voter engages in no undertaking. Nor is it plausible to suppose that voting amounts to tacit consent, in the sense of a clear, though nonverbal, indication of an accepting attitude toward the government and its laws. In the United States and many other countries, avowed revolutionaries are permitted to vote; no one takes their efforts to manipulate the political processes as showing their approval of the government. Ordinary citizens are not told authoritatively that voting, by which means they express preferences for some candidates over others,[19] counts as approval of the government and a promise to obey its laws; no established social convention treats voting in political elections as a signification of agreement.

What remains is a possible argument about implied consent and promise—that although voting does not actually signify agreement to comply with law, it puts an individual in the normative posture of one who has agreed. Although any attempt to evaluate this argument fully is plagued by uncertainties concerning the boundaries of implied promise, I will outline and criticize two of the forms in which it might be developed.

The first form relies heavily on the mental attitude of the person who votes, claiming that if the voter believes the privilege of voting carries duties of compliance, then voting constitutes an implied promise to comply.[20] Assuming, as I have suggested, that voting does not actually signify consent, it may be asked how voting itself figures in this form of the argument. Unless the claim is that voting generates justifiable expectations in others, a possibility that lies at the heart of what I will treat as the second form of the argument for implied promise, the role of voting must be to focus the voter's mental attitude. Were this its exclusive significance, presumably everyone with the requisite mental attitude would be bound whether he or she had voted or not. This conclusion fits well with the idea expressed by some political scientists that for many people *not* voting reflects acquiescence with the present state of affairs, and that such people will choose to vote only when they become disturbed with existing or prospective government officials. A mental attitude alone, however, is not enough on which to ground a promise-like obligation to obey, as I have already suggested.

A further difficulty with this argument concerns the mental attitude most voters are likely to have. Until relevant empirical evidence is obtained, we must rely on our intuitions and informal sources of information. These lead me to conclude that most voters do not think very precisely about what obligations the privilege of voting carries.[21]

Many may have some vague sense that they owe, in return, some duty to acquiesce in the results of the political process; but this sense typically falls far short of a perceived obligation to comply with every law, or even every just law, that eventuates from the officials elected.

Building on the notion of promissory estoppel, the second form of the argument from implied consent asserts that, since a person would act unfairly by voting and declining to be bound, others are justified in assuming that voters who are silent are willing to be bound and the act of voting alone is enough to obligate.[22] This version of the argument also has powerful difficulties. The direct argument that fairness requires obedience to law is considered in Chapter 7, but I shall here assume an element of unfairness in someone's voting and not submitting to responsibilities of citizenship. The steps from this premise to a conclusion about implied consent, however, are strained.

One problem concerns what others might reasonably assume about the voter's willingness to be bound. The kinds of acquiescent attitudes that different people have toward their governments vary greatly, as do their ideas of what sort of behavior is unfair. When the act of voting is so far removed from the decisive deliberations and decisions that yield legal norms, an assumption that a voter is willing to comply with all laws would not be warranted.

Other difficulties inhere in the supposed mechanisms through which a promise to obey is implied. In the ordinary situation of implied promise, the person who is bound acts in a manner known to those toward whom he is obligated, he has forfeited an opportunity to disclaim the obligation, and others have relied on his behavior. In modern urban settings, a person's decision to vote may or may not be known to those outside his family, depending on how much he talks about his political behavior. At the polling place, he meets mostly strangers, though a few acquaintances may be voting at the same time. The fact of his voting is recorded, of course, and some unfamiliar local election official has checked off his name; but no significant government official is aware that he has voted.

Occasionally people do make statements about what their actions regarding voting signify. As Peter Singer notes, radical American opponents of the Vietnam War publicized their refusal to vote in the 1968 presidential election.[23] They said they did not wish to confer legitimacy on the political process and urged others to follow their example. We can certainly imagine other groups publicizing the fact that their participation in an election does connote acceptance of the results. But what can be done by the ordinary person who is not politically active but is highly alienated or wishes to qualify any commitment otherwise implied by voting? Is he supposed to tell his friends and neighbors exactly what his vote means or write a letter to the government? No one in the government is expected to deal with such matters and many friends and neighbors simply would not care precisely what one's attitudes about voting are. Thus, although anyone is *free* to make a disclaimer, it is not a serious option for many people. And the absence of that as a serious option severely compromises what can reasonably be inferred from the failure to disclaim.

The government's actions are not affected by what individual voters conceive as their obligations of citizenship; and it is highly doubtful that any individual's attitudes toward government and the law are altered by the simple fact that someone else has voted. Whether or not others loosely assume that a voter is willing to be bound, they do not rely on that assumption in their own lives. No one else is worse off because a person has failed to disclaim a possible implication of his vote. Detrimental reliance is not a necessary condition of implied consent; but when it and any subjective acquiescence are absent, a failure to disclaim could generate an obligation only if the chance to disclaim and its significance were readily apparent in the society. Neither condition is met in the context of voting.

The strongest argument for obligation deriving from voting is one that combines what I have treated as the first and second forms of the argument. If *both* the voter and others aware of his act of voting understand his vote to carry a duty to comply, then voting may have that effect even if it does not actually *signify* an undertaking to comply. Even in the cases meeting these requisites, however, it is probably unusual to have anything as precise as an implied promise to obey all laws.

The other familiar arguments about tacit and implied consent rely on residence and receipt of benefits. Remaining in a country certainly does not amount, as Locke supposed,[24] to tacit agreement to obey the laws.[25] People stay in homelands because of language, culture,[26] job, friends, and family; their inertia hardly indicates approval or acceptance of government and laws.[27] Nor is this, alone, enough to lead others to suppose any commitment to obey has been undertaken. The old bumper sticker message "America: Love It or Leave It" is an appeal; it does not reflect common understanding of what remaining in the United States means.

Although apparently conceding this much, Harry Beran has urged that continuing in residence after one reaches majority does generate an obligation to obey the law.[28] He argues that by remaining in the state people do understand that they "accept full membership" in the community; that acceptance is taken by Beran to imply an obligation to obey because such an obligation is an aspect of the moral significance of full membership and one would fail to realize this only through negligence. Beran's theory can be understood as a variant of the idea that consent to one thing logically or morally implies a commitment to something else of a sort that one initially does not recognize. To establish that an adult resident was negligent in not recognizing that full membership carries a duty to obey, Beran would need to show that full membership does carry this significance. Much of the next three chapters of this book casts serious doubt on the proposition that being a good citizen necessarily means conceiving oneself as under a duty to obey all laws. But there are more straightforward objections to Beran's approach.[29] As people continue in residence, neither they nor their neighbors assume that their doing so is accepting full membership; and, as with the case of voting, they are presented with no realistic way to disclaim such an understanding. Failing to leave the country does not usually amount to tacit or implied consent to any obligations of citizenship.

Any conclusion about agreement to obey based on receipt of government benefits would be similarly misfounded. Residents have no choice about many benefits; for example, they cannot refuse the general security afforded by police and military protection. Even as to benefits voluntarily taken, the claim of tacit or implied agreement has a fatal flaw. People continue to receive benefits from the state that they could refuse even when their preferred government is overturned by domestic revolution or foreign invasion. Receiving benefits from the state does not indicate acceptance of a regime and its laws, as starting a game of tennis indicates acceptance of the standard rules, nor is it understood to do so by others.

The arguments about implied promise based on residence and receipt of benefits are less plausible than the argument based on voting. We must conclude that most citizens do not have a promise-like obligation to comply with all laws that issue from the government.

WHO HAS UNDERTAKEN TO OBEY THE LAW?

Though promise is not a general source of obligation to obey the law, it is a source for some people at least with respect to some laws. In the next section, I will examine the significance and force of explicit and formal undertakings such as oaths. Here I consider what other acts and attitudes may generate promissory or related obligations to obey.

Even if they do not take oaths of office, people who voluntarily assume positions of official responsibility have tacitly or impliedly promised to perform their duties in accordance with the rules that govern the exercise of those duties. If taking office does not itself amount to signifying one's willingness to comply, then the new office holder's silence is the basis for legitimate expectations on the part of others that he will perform the duties of the office.

May promise-like obligations exist when neither an oath nor a definite acceptance of official position is involved? The claim that they may is strongest when someone, such as a Law Day speaker, publicly pledges himself to observe the law. A pledge of this sort may not be accepted by particular individuals in the manner that most promises are accepted,[30] but because it is designed to influence those who hear it and may be relied upon in some remote way,[31] the promise carries moral force. More informal comments that express or imply a com mitment to obey laws could also carry some force. For this purpose, a statement about the obligations one already conceives oneself to be under—"I think every citizen is bound to obey the law"—would not suffice; but an actual undertaking—"I commit myself to obey"— would create a binding obligation to those who have received the communication.

Can a mental attitude alone be the source of some obligation to obey the law, if not an obligation based on promise? In the starkest case, one might simply determine that he will obey every law or assign a substantial moral weight in favor of obedience. A more typical attitude would be somewhat less precise, involving respect for one's government and a disposition to obey its laws. Joseph Raz has argued that this attitude of "practical respect" for the law can underlie an obligation to obey.[32]

We need to begin by inquiring what the basis for such an attitude might be. If the attitude represents nothing more than the recognition of all the valid arguments for obeying the law, then the attitude itself would seem to add nothing to the force of these arguments. Suppose, instead, the attitude reflected only a mistaken assessment of the force of reasons for obeying the law. Again, the attitude would not constitute an independent obligation to obey the law (except in the general sense that people should do what they *think* is morally right); and once the person understood that his assessment of reasons to obey the law was mistaken, he should feel free to abandon his prior attitude and its practical consequences.

The claim that the attitude can have force is strongest when the attitude is freely chosen, that is, when it is adopted by a person who does not think he is morally compelled to take that point of view. Raz has in mind just such a conscious choice to give to the government more obedience than independent moral principles require. He draws an interesting analogy to friendship. A person is not morally obligated to have friends, but if he does have them, he has obligations to act toward them in certain ways. Raz suggests that similar obligations to comply with law can arise from an attitude of practical respect for law.

Scrutiny of the proposed analogy creates doubt that one's attitude alone is enough to underlie an obligation to obey. The force of moral obligations of friendship derives largely from the mutuality of expectations that arise as people become friends. Sometimes, before a relationship has developed very far, one person may *regard* another as a friend, though neither person has yet treated the other as a friend.[33] Does that attitude alone give rise to obligations? Perhaps a person's free choice of character and commitments does affect what he really ought to do. There may be some virtue, perhaps moral virtue, in sticking to certain choices once they have been made even if choices could have been made differently and even if no one else is relying on them. This position is probably unsound for discrete choices of action: a woman who makes an uncommunicated New Year's resolution to donate money to one charity and ends up donating the money to another is probably not less praiseworthy than a similar woman who carries out the initial resolution. But deeper choices of character and commitment may carry moral force even when freely entered into in the first instance.

If some moral ought does lie behind freely chosen uncommunicated commitments, it is a much weaker ought than derives from communicated commitments and mutual expectations. When a person with the attitude of practical respect for the law has acted toward others in a way that communicates his attitude, the expectations he creates may well be a source of obligation, though reliance on those expectations will be much weaker and more diffuse than the mutual reliance of friends. In this form, implied consent becomes the basis for obligation that derives from the attitude of practical respect.

Any moral force that derives directly from an attitude of practical respect or its communication to others will be limited in scope to its actual coverage. Persons who perceive no independent obligation to obey the law may be unlikely to adopt an undifferentiating attitude of practical respect. Rather, they may identify areas of blindness, invasion of personal domain, overregulation, and so on in which they do not respect the government and would not freely choose to put themselves under an obligation to obey that does not already exist. In short, their approval of the government may be selective, much as many older children give considerable respect to elder authority figures in some domains and virtually none in other domains. Thus, even for those who make free choices and communicate them, attitudes of compliance may not constitute the general source of obligation toward all laws that social contract theory has traditionally posited.

THE FORCE AND SIGNIFICANCE OF PROMISES TO OBEY

The conclusions that most citizens have not undertaken to obey the law generally but that some citizens have undertaken to obey at least some laws leave us with two important questions. What is the force and scope of the promises that officials, professionals, and some citizens have made? Should consensual bases of obligation be more widely employed? These questions are explored in this and the succeeding section.

Not everything that looks like a promise creates a binding obligation. As the law of contracts suggests, a promise may lack moral force because of the conditions in which it is given or because of some defect in its terms. As far as the law is concerned, a promise either has force or it does not;[34] moral judgments can be more subtle, recognizing the possibility that conditions may diminish the force of a promise without eliminating it altogether.

Conditions

I will look first at the circumstances of the promise. If the person making a promise is not able to understand its significance, or is incapable of rational judgment, or is forced by a very unpleasant and unfair alternative, the promise is without effect.

None of these conditions vitiates the typical oath of office, or the tacit promise to perform that officials make simply by taking their offices. No one has to hold public office and office holders understand the duties they are undertaking. Society is justified in trying to obligate officials to perform responsibly, and the demand that one who chooses such a position agree to perform its duties does not amount to anything like duress.

Matters may be a little less clear-cut when we turn to the prospective lawyer. He or she has invested a lot of time and money in preparing for that career. A refusal to take an oath to support the law may mean loss of an opportunity to practice. Here, the alternative is much more forbidding than in the case of the office holder. Yet, society has a strong interest in the responsible performance of professional duties, and the practice of a profession is a kind of privilege. One has ample warning what is expected when one embarks on training for it. Conditioning the privilege on a stated willingness to perform professional duties is not duress.

The same conclusion applies to the oath of naturalized citizens. A country is undoubtedly under some moral constraints in how it chooses who to permit to be residents and citizens. Strong reasons support the admission of some prospective residents, such as spouses of citizens and those who have cooperated with war efforts of the government; and it may be, as Michael Walzer suggests, that a healthy political order should permit most permanent alien residents to become citizens.[35] In the United States citizenship makes one eligible for a limited number of jobs that aliens may not occupy and gives additional security against deportation, but most legal rights of citizens are also enjoyed by alien residents. Even if the government is morally required to offer resident aliens the chance to become citizens, its decision to extend that opportunity only to those who agree to comply with law does not amount to duress toward those who would like to become citizens.

The situation may be different when persons reasonably fear they will suffer serious harm if they do not agree to obey. Conscripted soldiers in the United States have traditionally taken a "step forward" that represents a promise of allegiance, conscripted jurors take an oath to perform conscientiously, and subpoenaed witnesses must swear to tell the truth. A soldier may rightly perceive that a determined refusal to assent may lead to jail; and some jurors and witnesses fear similar consequences if they refuse to promise. What is the status of promises made in such circumstances?

Putting aside the possible religious significance of an oath to God, the answer will depend on the state of mind of the oath taker and the fairness of the conditions under which the oath is extracted. I shall assume that the choice facing a soldier or prospective juror or witness is not so disturbing that he is rendered incapable of rational choice; the person deliberately chooses to take the oath. That the alternative itself if forbidding is not by itself enough to deprive a promise of its force; a person's consent to an operation and the accompanying implied promise to pay for it carry force, even if they are given in response to a diagnosis that imminent death is the likely alternative.[36] But the threat facing the soldier is different; it has been created by the very institution that seeks his promise. Granting that a government can morally conscript citizens and penalize them for failing to fulfill duties, can its use of vastly unequal bargaining power to compel a person to promise to fulfill the duties actually increase the force of the person's obligations to do so?

I shall attack this complex and troublesome question by initially addressing the less difficult variations. Let us first imagine a soldier or subpoenaed witness who thinks the government's compulsion is fair and who freely gives the requisite oath. When I say he freely gives the requisite oath, I mean he would be willing to promise to perform his duties even if no negative consequence attached to his refusal to promise. Such a person might not have served without the government's compulsion, but finding himself conscripted, he thinks he should perform the role as demanded and is willing to promise to do so. His promise is not extracted under duress because he gives it without regard to the sanctions for refusal. At the other extreme we can imagine someone who correctly thinks that his government's compulsion is unfair and its demanded performance immoral and who would be unwilling to promise to perform the duties were not a serious sanction the only alternative. In that circumstance the requisites of duress—that is, strong and improper pressure producing an unfree choice—are present and the promise is without force.[37]

The intermediate situations are more debatable. Suppose the promisor rightly understands that the government's original compulsion and the demand for a promise are fair, but he would be unwilling to promise unless the demand for his promise was also backed by compulsion. In this case the government has done nothing wrong, yet the promise is offered only to avoid an unpleasant alternative that the government has created to extract the promise. We might initially be inclined to think the government could never justifiably extract a promise under this sort of compulsion; but its doing so generally may lead to a somewhat higher level of performance of important public duties and allow a greater degree of trust between actors and government officials regarding the performance of compelled duties. Given the longstanding swearing of compelled witnesses and the generally accepted use of affirmations of truthfulness on tax forms, we should hesitate to conclude that all forced undertakings are of no effect, especially since our social life is probably somewhat enhanced if people assume they do have force. Quite possibly, however, compelled undertakings have *less* effect than undertakings given under freer conditions.

Does the promise have force if the promisor wrongly thinks government compulsion to promise is unfair? We can imagine the circumstance under which the promisor commits himself, only because of compulsion he regards as wrongful and later is persuaded that the compulsion was appropriate. Such a person should probably regard himself as bound, having consciously given a promise that he recognizes would have had force if he had understood more fully the conditions of its utterance. This conclusion, however, does not determine what view an outsider should take at the time the promise is given. Unless others have relied on the promise to their detriment, the fact that the promissor believes he is promising only under pressing and unfair conditions is probably enough to deprive the promise of moral force.

I have implicitly assumed in all this discussion that whether or not one intends at the time to keep a promise is not critical to its force. Certainly this is true in ordinary settings, and I see no reason it should be different here.

This lengthy discussion shows just how difficult it is to identify instances of duress when government compulsion leads to promises to obey; but I have suggested that the critical elements are the presence of compulsion that is, or is perceived to be, unfair and the fact that a promise would not have been given without the compulsion. Deciding what amounts to unfair compulsion, of course, leaves great latitude for disagreement.

Terms

A second basis for believing a promise to be without force is some defect in its substance: the terms may be part of an unfair exchange, require more than can reasonably be expected, or demand the commission of immoral acts.

Not every binding promise need involve an exchange at all. If someone freely decides to commit himself to perform an act benefiting others, his promise has force even if he expects nothing in return. But when promises to do something are given in return for benefits to be received, a gross unfairness in the exchange may undermine the force of the promise. In some circumstances, the question of fairness of terms may be hard to distinguish from the question of duress, but the basic inquiry concerning terms is whether or not the promisor gets a fair return for what he gives, not whether the promisee acted fairly in trying to elicit a promise.[38]

If one looks at the exchange of benefits and burdens, the oaths of officials, lawyers, and naturalized citizens are fair; those who take the oath receive as much as they promise to give.[39] From the standpoint of almost all prospective witnesses, telling the truth and promising to tell the truth are preferable to going to jail, so the concern about these compelled promises goes to the legitimacy of the government's establishing the grounds of exchange, not to the balance of benefit and burden. A similar conclusion applies to the compelled oath of conscripted soldiers.

Different aspects of the terms of many oaths are troubling and bear on both their force and their reasonable interpretation. These aspects are breadth and duration. John Simmons has suggested that the promise of naturalized citizens may be understood as one "to obey all valid laws."[40] If so, the promise covers all of a society's laws for the rest of a citizen's life. That is quite a promise. Certainly the citizen will not fully keep his promise, because everyone breaks the law on occasion; very likely, the citizen will face at least some circumstances in which the force of the promise will conflict with his sense of moral duty.

Rolf Sartorius has made the claim that people cannot reasonably be held to a promise that covers a vast variety of laws for a long period of time.[41] Before we swallow that claim too readily, we should note that in its overall impact on people's lives, a promise to obey laws is, as Sartorius recognizes, not more constraining than the marriage contract; most of us subscribe to that at least once, and we think it has force. The single promise to take someone "in sickness and in health" covers unforeseeable contingencies whose effect those making the promise can scarcely comprehend. Sweeping promises do have force, but the analogy to marriage promises helps illustrate the truth that lies behind the objection to such promises. External conditions and one's own attitudes and beliefs can change drastically over time. People are much less to blame for abandoning commitments when circumstances have altered radically.[42] An *irrevocable* sweeping promise may well lose moral force slowly over time,[43] and it carries more force for expected situations than for unexpected ones.

Another way of dealing with this problem is to suggest that long-term promises carry implied exceptions for changed circumstances. We can certainly imagine circumstances in which the answer to a claim that one is bound by a promise is that the situation at hand simply was not conceived at the time of the promise. A person asked to obey a very wicked law might respond that when he promised to obey a country's laws he never imagined a law of this sort could ever be adopted. The possibility of implied exceptions is important and will often aid in giving a reasonable construction to apparently unqualified promises. Sometimes, though it may often be hard to say just when, the correct analysis is that the promise, properly understood, does not apply rather than that its force is diminished or is outweighed by stronger countervailing reasons.

Implied exceptions, however, do not cover all the difficulties of changed circumstances. Often when one makes a promise, one is consciously aware of the possibility of variant circumstances and promises to be faithful regardless of their dimensions. The marriage contract is a striking example; one whose spouse suffers a debilitating physical illness that drastically alters a relationship cannot plausibly say the marriage promise did not cover this contingency. One of the purposes of many promises is to commit one against a possible change in one's present perspectives and desires. For this reason, the implied exception approach works particularly badly if all that is involved is a change in the outlook of the promisor, not in the external circumstances he faces. Yet people do change over time, and their undertakings of times long past should not exercise too great a restraint on their development. The idea of diminishing force often better captures this normative judgment than the idea of an implied exception.

Even if we put aside the problem of unforeseen circumstances, a promise to obey all laws will certainly be broken. Could a conscientious person subscribe to such a promise? People recognize that the obligation of a promise may be overridden, so when they make one they implicitly acknowledge that something may require them to break it. But honest people do not make unqualified promises if they are sure they will break them.[44] A thoughtful person cannot sincerely promise to obey all valid laws on all occasions.[45] That in itself is strong reason to construe the vague oath of naturalized citizens in some weaker sense, as a promise to support the legal order generally and comport oneself as a law-abiding citizen, or conceivably as a promise always to assign some moral weight to one's legal duty.

The oath of an office holder is less sweeping than the oath of a naturalized citizen. It concerns obedience to the laws that control performance of official duty and only while the official is in office. The oath may not be explicitly limited in these ways, but a present or past official who engages in illegal acts of prostitution or overreports charitable deductions on his income tax is not thought to have violated his oath of office.

Although an official may not have a chance to retract the oath, he may resign if his legal duties conflict with conscience. For those reasons, the power of the oath does not lessen over the term of office; and the oath should reasonably be understood as covering compliance with all official legal duties. These conclusions do not settle two very important matters—how one's legal duties are to be understood and whether or not an official is ever justified in violating his oath while staying in office; these subjects are dealt with in Part IV.

The lawyer's oath is limited like that of the official but extends in time like the oath of the naturalized citizen. Like the resigning official, the lawyer may stop practice if he finds that performing his role conflicts with moral duty; but for most lawyers such a choice has momentous consequences. With respect to lawyers, I will illustrate the problems regarding the force and meaning of an oath with a specific example.

Illustration 5-3:

Larry is approached by a group of people who plan to demonstrate against the use of civilian nuclear power at a local facility. They want to make sure that no one gets hurt, but they also want to commit a crime for which they will be arrested. Larry is a former member of the county attorney's office who is well versed in the criminal code and police department practices during demonstrations. He is not himself opposed to the use of nuclear power but respects the conviction of the demonstrators and believes their actions are proper in a democratic society. He also thinks he has it in his power to minimize the possibility of violence by carefully planning with them a trespass that will remain peaceable but will result in arrest. Larry believes that if he does engage himself to this degree, he will be guilty, under the state's criminal law, of aiding and abetting the trespass, and he fears he will also run afoul of standards of professional ethics.[46] He wonders whether he will also violate his oath as a lawyer if he helps plan the trespass.

The answer may well depend on the precise language of the oath or preliminary undertakings.[47] If Larry has promised to comply with the law and with rules of professional ethics, his having taken the oath will constitute a substantial moral reason against giving the advice. In some jurisdictions, however, what an applicant has promised may be subject to a more flexible interpretation. In Georgia, for example, one taking the oath swears that he will "justly and uprightly demean [himself] according to the laws, as an Attorney, Counsellor and Solicitor."[48] Though the oath might be read as barring every conscious illegal act in one's role as a lawyer,[49] Larry, by his own lights, would be acting justly and uprightly, technically breaking the criminal law in order to prevent violence and serve the broader aims of the legal order. Perhaps this oath is flexible enough to permit his behavior.[50]

One possible defect in a promise to obey the law is that it may require the commission of immoral acts. It has often been suggested that a promise to do what is morally wrong is not binding.[51] Unless a regime were so wicked that obeying the law would be wrong a high proportion of the time, the claimed lack of force of promises to do wrong would not infect one's whole undertaking; a general promise to obey would ordinarily be binding but would lack force on those occasions when obeying the law would be wrong. I will consider the claim on this assumption, suggesting that a promise to do an individual wrong is not always without force and that, in any event, promises to obey are quite different from promises to do individual wrongs.

In typical examples illustrating the lack of force of promises to do wrong, the initial promise is an obviously unjustified promise to perform a very bad act. If Pat promises to help Frank kill an innocent person, then obviously Pat should not carry out her promise; and such an example inclines one to suppose that the promise has no force at all. But we would be mistaken to conclude quickly that promises to do wrongful acts never have force.

Illustration 5-4:
Frank is a lifelong friend of Pat. Frank has been deeply hurt by Gloria's breaking up with him. Frank pleads with Pat to lie to Gloria that Frank is really interested in someone else. Pat tries to dissuade Frank from his plan to deceive Gloria, but Frank is insistent. Pat finally promises that if Frank does not change his mind she will tell the lie. All along Pat has regarded Frank's course of action as morally wrong and she subsequently concludes that despite the claims of friendship she should not have agreed to help him. But she feels a hesitancy to desist now that she has promised.

In this illustration Pat faces a difficult choice at two stages. Although Frank's wish to deceive Gloria is not morally justified, the moral bonds of friendship may be strong enough that Pat should assist Frank if she cannot deflect him from his plan. Whatever the proper initial choice, at the second stage Pat's promise is in place. I am not sure how much can be provided in the way of defense, but my own sense is that in this context, given the relative nonseriousness of the wrong and the close ties between Pat and Frank, the promise carries normative force.[52] How this conclusion bears on analysis of the promise to kill is difficult. One might suppose that the promise to kill has some slight force that is simply far outweighed by the moral reasons not to kill. But we might say that promises to do wrong can have force only if reliance on them by the promisee is reasonable; in this respect the promise to kill and the promise to tell a minor lie are qualitatively different.

The promise to obey the law is different from both these examples in important respects. The promise covers a class of actions most of which are morally required, or at least morally appropriate, and a small minority of which may be morally wrong; often the promisor will lack acquaintance of facts that would make possible confident assessment of the morality of a particular act of obeying the law. Given the value of a consistent pattern of behavior that does not demand close assessment of individual instances, a promise to follow such a pattern may have force in its occasional immoral applications even if a separate promise to conform to the law on a single occasion when it would be immoral might not have force. When the promise is not sufficient to justify doing what would otherwise be wrong, it may still be enough to require the actor to pursue an alternative course that does not require breaking the promise. The oath of office, for example, might affect whether an official should resign rather than breach a legal duty that requires a wrongful act.

This discussion is hardly dispositive on the force of promises to do what is wrong; however, it shows both that if a regime is generally just, the problem of wrongful applications does not undermine the force of the promise for other applications and that a promise to obey may well have a normative force on some occasions when the act of obedience would be wrong in the absence of the promise.

POSSIBLE EXTENSION OF PROMISSORY OBLIGATIONS TO OBEY

Having suggested that many citizens make no promise-like undertaking to obey the law, I have also argued that some do engage to obey in a general way and others promise to comply with laws relating to special duties. I have concluded that such promises ordinarily have moral force and constitute a substantial moral reason for obedience. The

degree to which obligations in any society depend on voluntary promises is subject to change, and promises to obey the law could loom as
more or less important in the future than they are now.

Given their present relative unimportance, I will ask whether expansion of their significance would be warranted. An expansion in
promise-like undertakings could occur over time as informal conventions shift, establishing tacit or implied promises where none existed
before; but I shall focus on the more straightforward courses of the
government's demanding or requesting people to make explicit promises to obey or its clearly stating that certain acts will be construed as
amounting to such a promise.

Whether or not the government could elicit a greater number of
explicit or tacit promises with moral force depends on the conditions
under which they would be given and the fairness of their terms.
Suppose the government either expelled native-born citizens who refused to promise to obey or deprived such persons of all benefits of
government that are capable of being taken away. The severity and
unfairness of these sanctions would render promises to obey without
force for persons who gave the promise to avoid these harms. The
same conclusion would also be reached if the government, instead,
announced that continued residence or acceptance of benefits would
be *taken* as a promise to obey.[53] But if the government conditioned the
privilege of voting on a promise to obey, or announced that voting
would be so understood, neither duress nor unconscionability of
terms would infect the result. People can live comfortably without
voting, and a promise to obey is reasonably connected to the privilege
of voting. If the government simply requested people to make periodic
affirmations of continued willingness to obey, without conditioning
any benefit on the affirmation, anyone who voluntarily offered the
promise would also be bound. Many might, of course, be influenced
by subtle and not-so-subtle social pressures to go along, but unless
these were extreme, they would not undermine the force of the promise. In sum, there are steps a government might reasonably take to
make promise a more important source of obligation than it now is.
What effect such steps might have on the actual level of law-abidingness is highly uncertain, but many people might hesitate more to break
the law if they thought they had promised not to do so.

Yet, there are very powerful reasons to oppose such a program. We
have seen that an unqualified oath to obey all laws on all occasions is
not one that can sincerely be given by thoughtful persons. Finding
language that is less absolute but clear in its significance and compre-

hensible to ordinary persons is virtually impossible. We would be left with some vague undertaking to be law-abiding. Although such an oath might lead some people to take law observance more seriously, others would be offended by having to subscribe to it. Reliance on oaths of this breadth trenches on values of free belief and expression, and the pressures toward social conformity of which it smacks have unplesant symbolic overtones. Further, extensive use of oaths and promises risks devaluing the currency. A child whose parents continually demand promises of conscientiousness—"Will you promise to do your homework and not watch T.V. while we are out?"—will begin to take promises less seriously. The same is undoubtedly true for adults. Insistence on promises can also have the undesirable effect of under-emphasizing the significance of other bases of duty to obey the law. It is unfortunate if people begin to think all or most moral duties are matters of promise.[54] The benefits and costs of more extensive promises to obey are certainly subject to debate; however, my own conclusion is that outside the context of an alien's shifting his basic political loyalty, such promises should not be elicited from ordinary adults in a liberal democracy.

PROMISES TO PRIVATE INDIVIDUALS AND GROUPS THAT CONFLICT WITH PATTERNS OF OBEDIENCE

A chapter on promise and obligations to obey the law should not close without brief mention of the two-edged character of promise. Just as promises can create substantial moral reasons to obey, they can also create substantial moral reasons to disobey. Except in the context of cooperative criminal endeavors and large-scale political and social protests that involve lawbreaking, explicit promises to disobey the law on particular occasions are relatively rare, but undertakings of personal and group loyalty are not.[55] Some such undertakings never require action that violates the law, and with others the promisor may reasonably claim he never intended his broad promise to cover illegal acts. But this will not always be the case. Some organizations face predictable conflicts with the law; one need only think of the history of many religious sects. People who promise to support such organizations are aware that their group loyalty may require violations of law. Promises of assistance to family members or friends may have similar import when the promisor knows that the person to whom he promises has been breaking the law. Promises of group and personal loyalty are, of course, subject to the same sorts of qualifications and limitations as promises to obey the law, but there is no good reason to suppose that such promises will always be without moral force on every occasion when they require violation of law.

NOTES

1. J. Locke, Two Treatises of Civil Government.

2. E. Rostow, The Rightful Limits of Freedom in a Liberal Democratic State: Of Civil Disobedience, in Rostow, ed., Is Law Dead? 39, 48 (1970).

3. On the conceptual distinction between consent and promise, see A. J. Simmons, Moral Principles and Political Obligations 75–77 (1979); and Raz, Authority and Consent, 67 Va. L. Rev. 103, 120–22 (1981). Although Raz recognizes that in certain situations consent need not involve the undertaking of an obligation, he says (mistakenly, in light of the analysis in the previous chapter) that "consent to a political authority is the same as a promise to obey it." Id. at 121.

4. T. Hobbes, The Leviathan.

5. J. J. Rousseau, The Social Contract.

6. As long as the promisee understood the kind of commitment the promisor was making, that would be a sufficient basis to give the promise force. Defeat of the justified expectations of the promisee without any good reason would come close to the kind of moral wrong done by telling a lie. See G. J. Warnock, The Object of Morality 105–10 (1971), who asserts a tighter connection between veracity and keeping promises.

7. The promise may leave me with some residual moral responsibility to apologize or try to make up the promisee's loss in some way, but I should not carry out its initial terms.

8. When the person to whom a promise has purportedly been given misunderstands the actor's intent, determining whether or not a promise exists is more troublesome. This problem is discussed later in connection with implied promises, but it is worth saying a few words about mistakes over actual significations of commitment. If the "promisor" has not intended to promise and could not reasonably have been thought to do so, no promise exists, whatever the "promisee" may suppose. When the "promisor" has intended to promise but the "promisee," though "receiving" the communication, does not realize its significance, the promise does exist and the "promisee" can take advantage of it when he comes to realize its significance. The difficult cases are those in which the "promisee" reasonably understands a promise to exist, but the promisor has not so intended his words or actions. Here, neither the idea that promises must be voluntarily given (see J. Rawls, A Theory of Justice 345 [1971]) nor the idea that promises can arise through negligence (see P. Soper,

A Theory of Law 65 [1984]) is quite right as far as moral responsibility is concerned. Without doubt, the objective significance of one's words or acts can bind at law just as if one intended to promise. No doubt, also, if one's negligence caused another reasonably to rely on one's apparent commitment, one would have a moral duty to rectify the situation in some way. But the person who can honestly say, "I'm terribly sorry; I really didn't intend my words to be taken in the way you did, though I can see the misunderstanding was entirely my fault," may well not have a moral obligation to do exactly what the "promisee" understood the commitment to be, especially if the promisee has not relied on the commitment to his detriment. Even then the "promisor" may owe the "promisee" *something* because of the latter's disappointment, but what he owes need not be identical with the scope of the apparent commitment.

9. Of course, her retraction of the original permission in light of what she now knows would not be illogical.

10. John Simmons addresses this question in Consent, Free Choice and Democratic Government, 18 Ga. L. Rev. 791, 802-7 (1984). See note 8 supra for an analogous discussion in the context of express and tacit promises.

11. In attempting to draw a sharp analytical distinction between theories of genuine consent and theories of hypothetical consent, I do not mean to suggest that all traditional theorists fall clearly into one category or the other or that a theory resting on genuine consent cannot be profitably reinterpreted in terms of hypothetical consent.

12. John Rawls, A Theory of Justice (1971).

13. The point is forcefully made in R. Dworkin, Taking Rights Seriously 150-53 (1977).

14. A conceivable exception to this principle may occur when there was an actual occasion, say a meeting, at which I would have consented and actually planned to consent but for some fortuitous reasons that disturbed the ordinary course of events—say my car failing to start—I did not consent. Then, the fact that I would have consented may possibly put me in a position similar to that of those who did consent.

More broadly, what I as an individual would have agreed to may affect what it is fair now to do. Imagine that some parents agree with Phyllis that she will give physical instruction to their children for twenty dollars a day each over a period of three weeks. No mention is made of missed days. A child misses a day because of a family visit. His parents and Phyllis agree that neither payment or nonpayment is indicated by the original agreement and that neither resolution is *intrinsically* more fair than the other. Phyllis, however, says she would not have agreed to the arrangement if this possibility had been considered and missed days were to be unpaid, and the parents acknowledge that they would have agreed to pay for missed days if the subject had arisen. What these parties would have agreed to if the subject had come up has a bearing on what is now fair even if it establishes nothing about what *generally* would be fair for persons in this sort of arrangement.

15. 8 U. S. C. § 1448 (1976).

16. "I pledge allegiance to the flag of the United States of America, and to the Republic for which it stands, one nation, under God, indivisible, with liberty and justice for all." Apart from the question of what attitudes toward law are consistent with allegiance, a point briefly considered below in connection with the naturalization oath, there is the further question of how far one's undertaking is qualified if one thinks disobedience will promote liberty and justice.

17. See, e.g., J. Tussman, Obligation and the Body Politic (1960); and J. Plamenatz, Consent, Freedom and Political Obligation (2d ed., 1968).

18. Professor Tussman recognizes this difficulty and suggests that some adult citizens will remain "political childbrides," governed, like minors, without their own consent. Tussman, note 17 supra at 37.

19. See Cohen, Liberalism and Disobedience, 1 Phil. & Pub. Aff. 283, 311–12 (1972); Simmons, note 10 supra at 800.

20. Speaking of what he calls tacit consent, Tussman says that an "act can only be properly taken as 'consent' if it is done 'knowingly,' if it is understood by the one performing the act that his action involves his acceptance of the obligations of membership." Obligation and the Body Politic at 36.

21. Compare Simmons, note 10 supra at 801.

22. See P. Singer, Democracy and Disobedience 51–56 (1973).

23. Id. at 54.

24. J. Locke, Second Treatise of Civil Government at 98–99 (1960).

25. This ground, of course, has conceivable application to residents only if they are able to emigrate.

26. The plausibility of Socrates' claim that remaining in Athens created an obligation to submit to the punishment of that city-state (see Plato, The Crito) rests largely on the existence of other city-states nearby with the same language and similar cultures.

27. As Jeffrie G. Murphy has pointed out, the question whether continued residence can be taken as tacit consent is not the same as whether explicit consent given in order to continue residence would have moral force. Murphy, Consent, Coercion and Hard Choices, 67 Va. L. Rev. 79, 92 (1981). Murphy suggests that Hume's famous response to Locke that a poor peasant or artisan has no free choice to leave his country (D. Hume, Of the Original Contract, C. W. Hendel, ed., David Hume's Political Essays 43, 51 [1953]) may be understood either as an answer to the claim about tacit consent or as a claim that even explicit consent would not be binding.

28. See Beran, In Defense of the Consent Theory of Political Obligation and Authority, 87 Ethics 260 (1977).

29. A more expansive critique is provided in Simmons, note 10 supra at 802–9.

30. See C. Fried, Contract as Promise (1981).

31. Philip Soper, note 8 supra at 69, suggests that others will not rely to

their detriment on a person's undertaking to be law-abiding, because they have ample prudential grounds, based on sanctions, to comply. But a person may be confident he can break the law with impunity; if he complies because a respected friend has promised to obey the law, he has relied to the apparent detriment of his selfish interests.

32. J. Raz, The Authority of Law 250–61 (1979).

33. What I have in mind are situations in which someone feels a personal bond toward another met in professional situations or at parties, although the actual relationship between the two has not yet proceeded beyond the purely professional or social. The person may *feel* like a friend toward the other while recognizing that the relationship is not yet a friendship.

34. The law does distinguish between contracts that are totally void and those that are voidable at the option of a party. Also, available remedies may be regarded as reflecting some judgment about whether a certain class of promises has greater or lesser force.

35. See M. Walzer, Spheres of Justice 31–61 (1983).

Since some aliens have much more pressing reasons to become residents, than to become citizens once they are residents, the argument that to condition their residence on an oath to obey would constitute duress would be more powerful than the analogous argument about the grant of citizenship.

36. See generally Murphy, note 27 supra at 83–88.

37. Even this point is debatable. One might argue that the best moral practice is one that always attaches some moral weight to a promise. J. L. Mackie has suggested that, in some contexts at least, even promises of hostages to pay money to their criminal captors have force, because the practice of keeping such promises leads to better treatment for hostages. J. L. Mackie, Hume's Moral Theory 104 (1980).

38. The sentence in text glosses over some complicated problems. If individuals are really autonomous and aware of the relevant facts, who but each individual is most competent to assess the balance of an exchange? How could a rational and fully informed individual agree to an exchange that would (*ex ante*) give him less than he receives? And even if actual individuals do not always make rational decisions about exchanges, in a liberal society should there not be a strong presumption in favor of their capacity to do so? On such premises as these, worry about the fairness of terms can be translated into worry either about the adequacy of the promisor's information and the rationality of his choice or over the fairness of the promisee's eliciting the promise in the way he did. A faltering swimmer who promises to give $100,000 to the only person capable of saving him gets as much as he promises to give, but the promisee has imposed unfair conditions of choice. It is a genuine question, therefore, whether the fairness of an exchange of benefits and burdens is relevant to the force of a promise except insofar as it indicates something about the appropriateness of the conditions under which the choice was made; an agreement like that made by the drowning swimmer can be

understood as defective in either respect. In contracts law, many "unconscionable" terms are subject to a similar analysis.

39. Jeffrie Murphy suggests that the monopolistic position of the government, its unequal bargaining power, and the vagueness of terms of a contract with citizens might undermine the force of an undertaking to obey (Murphy, note 27 at 91–92). But he fails to note that the government has no means of penalizing someone for a faulty interpretation or indeed of enforcing the contract at all. A breach of law may be penalized but it is not penalized more seriously because one has promised to obey. The citizen's effective freedom to disregard the terms of the "contract" makes it seem a good bit less "unconscionable."

40. Simmons, Voluntarism and Political Associations, 67 Va. L. Rev. 19, 34, n. 28 (1981).

41. Sartorius, Political Authority and Political Obligation, 67 Va. L. Rev. 3, 13 (1981).

42. The doctrines of frustration of purposes and impossibility allow relief from contractual obligations when circumstances turn out very differently from what the parties expected. Of course, in contract law a change in attitudes and beliefs by one of the parties is not a basis for relief.

43. This point is tricky regarding the marriage contract. Although the original promise may lose force over time, duties based on detrimental reliance may increase in force.

44. One might argue that it is all right to make an unqualified promise if you know you are going to break it only in a small percentage of the instances it covers. At least in circumstances when one has some control over the scope of the promise, that does not seem correct. If I am asked to promise never to drink alcohol again, and I know I plan to drink on rare occasions, I should say: "Well, I am willing to promise to drink only rarely."

45. Perhaps if one has no control over the language of a promise and must simply choose between promising or not, one is morally justified in promising to do more than one is willing to do if one is willing to do most of what the promise encompasses. The *force* of the promise, which represents a commitment made to someone else, is probably not affected by this mental reservation.

46. The Model Rules of the American Bar Association, Rule 1.2, and the Code of Professional Responsibility, Disciplinary Rule 7-102(A)(7), forbid assisting a client in conduct that the lawyer knows is criminal.

47. In some jurisdictions, applicants for the bar answer questions about their willingness to comply with professional rules.

48. Georgia Rules Governing Admission to the Practice of Law B-19 (1984).

49. Whether this oath itself reaches the standards of professional ethics depends on whether they are understood to be laws. That question would be critical if what Larry considered doing was a violation of professional ethics but not of any ordinary law.

50. If the oath is so understood, someone who expects to give such assistance after becoming a member of the bar could sincerely take it.

51. E.g., A. J. Simmons, Voluntarism and Political Associations, 67 Va. L. Rev. 19, 36 (1981).

52. See generally Warnock, note 6 supra at 109, 116.

53. Simmons, note 10 supra at 809–18, has a much more extensive discussion leading to this conclusion.

54. Jonathan Bennett has made this point in correspondence with me.

55. See, generally, M. Walzer, Obligations: Essays on Disobedience, War, and Citizenship 7–16 (1970).

6

Utilitarianism: Consequential Reasons for Obedience

Within the Western liberal tradition, utilitariansim has been the main competitor to a promissory view of political obligation. Although recent emphases on rights and justice have eroded the hold of utilitarianism on American social and legal thought, the utilitarian phrase, a balancing of interests, still sums up a widespread sense of how social problems should be resolved. I turn now to utilitarianism, to see whether it provides a more convincing account than promissory notions do of why people generally should obey the law.

Some distinctive differences between social contract theory, as I have thus far interpreted it, and utilitarian theory bear significantly on their evaluation in relation to obeying the law and on what one can hope to accomplish in a single chapter. Utilitarianism is a complete theory of substantive morality in a way that promissory theory is not. If utilitarianism is a correct theory, then obedience to law should be treated as other sorts of moral choices; the morality of any kind of act will depend on whether or not it will promote consequences more favorable than those produced by some alternative. Under utilitarian theory, other sources of moral duties are either illusions or are derivable in some way from utilitarian grounds.[1]

When we evaluated promissory theories of obligations to obey, we began with an assumption that ordinary promises have moral force and inquired whether or not the citizen makes something like a promise to obey. Since a utilitarian account of obeying laws is no different from a utilitarian account of other moral issues, evaluation demands judgment about the overall merits of utilitarian theory. Although I do not shirk such judgments in this chapter, a comprehensive and systematic appraisal of utilitarianism is beyond my aims. I concentrate on relations between utilitarianism and obedience to law, offering my reflections about the broad utilitarian approach in more summary form only.

Under strict utilitarianism, what is right depends completely on what will promote the good; all moral reasons for action ultimately reduce to favorable consequences. One may believe, however, that favorable consequences are always, or sometimes, good moral reasons for performing actions even if other kinds of reasons are also relevant. Under this view, a consequential account of obedience to law could coexist comfortably with deontological reasons for obedience. On some occasions, consequential reasons would supplement or oppose the force of deontological reasons; on other occasions, if deontological reasons do not reach every choice about obedience, consequential reasons alone might be relevant. We therefore need to inquire whether such reasons are important aspects of decisions to obey or not even if they do not encompass the whole of morality.

A troubling conceptual question infects discussion of a utilitarian account of obedience to law: is such an account one theory about obligation to obey or an alternative to such theories? The doubt on this score is a compound of at least two uncertainties.

One uncertainty involves generality. Theories of political obligation have typically been thought to apply to every instance of law observance, or at least every instance involving just laws within a just society. On some occasions disobedience of such laws may have no harmful consequences or may have a balance of consequences that is favorable. Can a theory be one of obligation to obey if it concedes that obedience should be determined solely by a balance of consequences and that the balance will sometimes work against obedience? That issue implicates a broader problem about the nature of prima facie moral obligations that is addressed after the basic outlines of utilitarian approaches and some implications of act utilitarianism are explored.

The second uncertainty concerns the nature of the moral force of consequential reasons to obey. If such a reason applies and is not outweighed or canceled by some contrary reason, do we say that someone is under an obligation or duty to obey and ought to obey? This question does not arise with a promissory theory. Someone who has promised to obey is obligated to obey and, in the absence of an overriding contrary reason, ought to obey. But, as I have suggested in Chapter 3, sometimes when only favorable consequences are involved, we may hesitate to say that a person is obligated to promote those consequences or even that he ought to do so. Contributing $500 to charity may be morally better than spending the same amount at expensive restaurants, but the contribution may represent what is called a supererogatory act rather than what a person "ought" to do. Serious analysis of the moral force of consequential reasons to obey is reserved for the last section of the chapter.

ACT UTILITARIANISM AND RULE UTILITARIANISM

Any utilitarian account makes the morality of an action turn on consequences, but it may matter a great deal for the problem of obedience whether the focus is on individual acts or on a broader class of acts. According to the familiar version of utilitarianism called act utilitarianism, the proper choice to obey or disobey depends on which course will produce better consequences in the particular instance.[2] Other versions of utilitarianism involve two stages of application. The prospective act is fitted into a general class of acts, and the proper choice depends on whether performance of acts in that class is desirable or undesirable. One approach of this sort is called utilitarian generalization: the rightness of an act depends on what the consequences would be if everyone in a similar situation acted in the same way. Another approach is rule utilitarianism: the rightness of an act depends on whether or not it can be justified by a moral rule that would have desirable consequences if accepted.[3] I will concentrate on act utilitarianism and rule utilitarianism, because I believe they adequately raise the major distinctions for my purposes.

The initially stark differentiation between act and rule utilitarianism may be somewhat misleading. No genuine act utilitarian will suppose that individuals should undertake extensive calculations each time they perform an act with moral significance; to do so would take too much time and energy. In the practical moral life, frequent reliance on "rules of thumb" such as "lying is wrong" is appropriate. Nor does an act utilitarian neglect the realities of habit and imitation. One consequence of an act will be how it influences a person's own future choices and the choices of others; and these may be best channeled if generally desirable standards are observed. Another reason for paying attention to such standards is the individual's recognition that he may not be very objective in weighing likely consequences in a particular instance.

If act utilitarianism is capable of recognizing the importance of standards of behavior, rule utilitarianism can accommodate the idea that most moral rules, like "lying is wrong," have exceptions. The relevant rules would simply carve out necessary exceptions. Indeed, it has sometimes been doubted that rule utilitarianism is really practically distinct from act utilitarianism.[4] Whether it is or not depends on the level of generality at which the rules are cast. If a rule utilitarian allows an indefinite number of qualifications to simple rules based on any features of a situation that could affect consequences, his universe of immensely complex rules and applications may dissolve into the act utilitarian's direct evaluation of consequences for each case.

This "collapse" into act utilitarianism can be avoided by insistence on a certain level of generality. One kind of generality concerns the breadth of classes of instances in which one should behave in such a way. Another kind of generality involves the position of other actors; a person might have to ask whether it would be desirable for everyone to break a law, rather than whether it would be desirable for him or her to break it, given the compliance of others.

If moral rules are to be general, an action in conformity with a rule may be "right" even though violation of the rule on that occasion would predictably produce better consequences. When asked why moral rules must be general, the rule utilitarian claims that the wide practice of rule utilitarianism will produce better results than the wide practice of act utilitarianism. As children develop their moral capacities, they need to be taught relatively simple moral rules, and reference to such rules by adults leaves less room for misjudgment. Because our moral vocabulary does and should depend somewhat on the needs of our particular social order, the rule utilitarian thus offers a reasonable account of why behavior according to a rule that is both teachable to and applicable by real persons should be considered right, even if other behavior would promote better consequences in the particular instance. This is the proposition that divides the rule utilitarian from the act utilitarian, who believes that it can never be morally right to perform an act that one knows will have less favorable consequences than an alternative.

Before proceeding to analysis of utilitarianism and obedience to law, I need to make two other clarifications. The first is relatively minor and reiterates a point briefly discussed in Chapter 3.[5] Whether acts should be judged on the basis of foreseen consequences, foreseeable consequences, or actual consequences has always been a perplexing terminological point for an act utilitarian.[6] Since any prospective actor must do the best he can on the basis of estimations available to him before he acts, and since the appraisal of him as an actor should depend on what he knew or could have known, the tangle over terms has not been of real practical importance. I shall simply avoid it by assuming that, in the main, actual consequences do not deviate from predictable consequences.

The second clarification is more important. I am using *utilitarian* here as a word to cover any theory that makes consequences the determining factor in an act's morality, thus disregarding important variations among theories that are undoubtedly utilitarian or consequentialist and including some theories for which the label utilitarian is controversial. Bentham, the father of modern utilitarianism, made happiness the test of welfare; but a theory is utilitarian in my sense even if the good to be achieved is defined quite differently, and even if principles of allocation constrain pursuit of the maximum amount of that good.[7] Thus, theories that people should aim to maximize satisfaction of rational desires,[8] or to create "the greatest love possible" in any situation,[9] or to satisfy peoples' preferences equally count as utilitarian in this broader sense. I certainly do not wish to deny that for many purposes, it will matter tremendously exactly which consequences are to be promoted and how they are to be distributed;[10] but for theoretical questions of obedience to law, similarities among consequentialist positions are much more important than these differences.

In the pages that follow I consider three basic criticisms of utilitarian theories about obedience to law. The first is that a utilitarian approach fails to capture all that people feel, and properly feel, about their responsibility to obey the law. The second criticism is that the whole enterprise of people deciding on balances of consequences is misconceived. The third criticism is that because utilitarianism calls for too much in the way of concern for others, simple consequentialist reasons in favor of obeying the law are often inadequate to make obedience a moral requirement. In the first two of these discussions, I begin with a rather straightforward act utilitarian account and then inquire whether or not revision along rule utilitarian lines could resolve important difficulties. Because my treatment of the first criticism concerns the particular relation of utilitarian theory to obedience to law, it is disproportionately long; its exploration also includes comment on whether utilitarian accounts are theories of obligation to obey the law or alternatives to such theories.

UTILITARIAN STANDARDS AND EXISTING AND ARGUABLY PROPER ATTITUDES TOWARD LAW

Practical Implications of an Act Utilitarian Attitude

How would a consistent and disinterested application of utilitarian standards comport with most people's sense of when they should comply with legal duties? A high degree of noncorrespondence would show, at least, that utilitarianism cannot explain present attitudes toward the law. A committed utilitarian might claim that such a divergence would indicate how far present attitudes should change, but many others would regard the noncorrespondence as some evidence that conscious utilitarianism would fail to yield the morally best set of attitudes about obeying the law. For this reason, the possibility of noncorrespondence warrants careful investigation.

One might initially suppose that, in principle, a standard of judging each act in terms of the balance of its consequences would render the whole structure of legal rules and legal rights vulnerable. But a moment's reflection shows why this is not so. Given their limited knowledge and understanding and their selfishness, human beings need fairly clear rules to govern many activities. They also need the support of authoritative adjudicators and centrally organized sanctions to ensure that the rules are observed by those who might benefit from breaking them. Legal rules, and the rights they create, help establish for a society what one citizen can expect of another, and typically they mark occasions for the intervention of public force. Legal norms are necessary for personal security and to create clear domains of personal autonomy; and legal rights, especially of property and contract, are essential for economic planning of any complexity. The usefulness of previously established and generally applicable norms governing classes of circumstances and conferring rights is much too obvious to be denied by utilitarians.[11]

The utilitarian considerations that underlie the establishment of a legal system would govern the actions of a self-consciously act utilitarian official. Operating within a system in which strong expectations are desirably created, he would have powerful reasons for satisfying them. He would want to avoid the resentment, insecurity, and retaliation that occur when individuals are denied the enjoyment of institutionally created expectations; and he would not want to damage the system that creates those expectations by flouting its rules. An official would often suppose that the outcome prescribed by a legal rule is a more reliable guide to general welfare than his own cursory calculations might yield; but even when convinced that the outcome prescribed by a legal rule is indifferent or somewhat undesirable, judged apart from the existence of a rule, he would usually believe that the benefits of his conforming to the rule were sufficient to require that course.

Similarly, for the act utilitarian citizen, no slight advantage to himself or others could justify a violation of law that would disturb institutionally created expectations and cause resentment. If the citizen assumed that obedience to law was ordinarily desirable, further reasons for observance of legal rules in more doubtful cases would lie in the benefits of habits and examples of obedience. A simple illustration is the corrosive effect of initially safe disobedience of some traffic laws. As people became accustomed to "beating" red lights on the street corner where I live, the time between when the light changed to red and drivers stopped got longer and longer, until pedestrians and cars relying on the green in the other direction were really endangered. (Only a citywide enforcement effort halted this disturbing downward spiral.)

Yet another consequentialist reason for citizens to obey, one emphasized by Philip Soper, rests in the feelings and attitudes of those with responsibility to make and enforce laws.[12] People whose response to the good faith efforts of officials to exercise authority is to refuse compliance may show the officials a lack of respect that will cause unhappiness and disappointment. Officials frequently do not regard disobedience in such a personal way, but undoubtedly such feelings are sometimes present, and officials who become discouraged enough may cease to perform effectively.

All these reasons suggest that an act utilitarian approach taken self-consciously by an official or citizen would produce very strong reasons for observing the law in many instances. Still, such an approach may be seen as failing to capture a reflective moral attitude that good laws have a moral claim on us that goes beyond the negative consequences of disobedience. David Lyons has suggested that people assume that legal rights created by good legal rules have "moral force"—that is, a power to determine the moral justifiability of actions *independent* of the effect that observing such a right has on considerations of welfare.[13] Lyons's point might be generalized to include legal rules that do not guarantee legal rights.

What Is an Obligation to Obey?

One way of putting Lyons's point is that people believe they have an obligation to obey the law that an act utilitarian does not recognize. I want to pause over the terminological question. What is at issue is a prima facie obligation, one that may be outweighed but that applies to every law, or every just law. But this clarification still leaves open a number of possible senses of prima facie obligation.

One possible sense, analogous to legal usage about evidentiary burdens, concerns the assumption that should be made in the absence of further information or argument about whether obedience is right or wrong. In this sense, one might assume that lawful behavior is morally desirable unless contrary reasons suggest themselves. A utilitarian living within a generally good system might well subscribe to this proposition, believing that obedience of most laws most of the time is desirable. But this proposition has negligible practical importance, because one will never identify an act as a violation of law and nothing else; understanding other features of the act, one will be able to perceive moral reasons for and against performing it. Therefore, in contrast to cases of undiscoverable fact, this sort of initial presumption cannot determine whether or not one should obey.

A related sense of prima facie obligation might be that when one's estimate of probable consequences leaves one uncertain about a desirable course of action, one should observe the law.[14] Because we often cannot be confident about overall effects of disobedience, accepting an obligation in this sense would have great practical power. Could an act utilitarian accept this sense? He might distrust his own powers of calculation, and believe that the law often provides a better guide than his own assessments of desirable action. What he could not accept is that, apart from a gross generalization about likely desirable consequences, there was yet another reason to obey the law if the consequences appeared uncertain.

A third conceivable sense of prima facie obligation is that in every instance of a class of acts, at least one reason exists to perform the act. If this were all that were required, the condition would be met for utilitarian theory if every choice to obey the law involved at least one desirable consequence. Whether this condition can be met is debatable, but perhaps the concern about official feelings[15] or, more plausibly, the concerns about habits and example do apply to every instance of law observance. Even if the condition could be met, however, it seems clear that this is not enough to constitute any ordinary sense of prima facie obligation.

The difficulties are two: (1) having *a* moral reason to perform each act in a class of acts does not seem sufficient to make performance prima facie preferable, and (2) not every moral reason, when applicable, underlies a duty or obligation to act. Soper, drawing from M. B. E. Smith, observes that every murder may make some contribution to the overpopulation problem, but that does not establish a prima facie obligation to commit murder.[16] We cannot have a prima facie duty to do what it is always, or almost always, wrong to do on other grounds. Further, as Soper observes in connection with forcible demands by robbers for money, we do not have a prima facie duty to do what is wrongly demanded of us.

Do we have a prima facie duty to do something there is always *a moral reason* for doing and that would not be an independent wrong or represent a submission to a wrongful demand? The account is still too broad. I do not have a prima facie obligation to vote Republican in every election, or to give money to every poor person I pass, although there may always be at least one good moral reason for performing each of these acts. A problem illustrated by the voting example is that one good reason will always exist against voting Republican as well. When some moral reasons are always lined up on each side, we do not say one has a prima facie obligation both to do that sort of act and not to do it. A second problem concerns the moral force of a reason to act. Speaking of a general obligation to obey the law, one has in mind at least some minimal notion of ought and blame. The idea is that if, without any countervailing reason, a person disobeys the law, he has done something wrong for which a degree of blame is appropriate. The illustration of donations to the poor shows that a general moral reason that applies to a class of acts need not carry this force.

Of the notions of prima facie obligation considered thus far, we have concluded that the third notion, having *a* moral reason to obey the law in every instance, is not a plausible rendering of the idea of prima facie obligation.[17] The first idea—that one begins with an initial presupposition in favor of obedience—is one an act utilitarian could accept but has little or no practical impact. The second idea—that one should resolve doubtful instances in favor of obedience—is one that might be accepted by an act utilitarian but only on consequentialist grounds.

A final sense of prima facie obligation is that obedience of law carries some moral weight independent of consequences. Were this so, in cases in which all the consequences of obedience and disobedience were equally balanced, or the consequences of disobedience marginally were favorable, obedience of law would be the morally appropriate course of action. It is in this sense that, as Lyons observes, the straightforward act utilitarian does not concede that the law has moral force. If *this* is what is meant by an obligation to obey the law, simple act utilitarianism does not support such an obligation.

Act Utilitarianism and Prevailing Attitudes Toward Legal Duties

I turn now to the substance of Lyons's claim that people do recognize an obligation, or moral force, in this sense and that act utilitarianism fails to account for it.[18] It is much less clear than Lyons supposes that most people believe the law generally has such moral force. Public officials responsible for policing and prosecuting violations of the law often do let minor, technical violations go without intervening. Necessary allocation of resources is a partial explanation, but some violations are so trivial that proceeding against them would be inappropriate even if ample resources were available or enforcement cost the government nothing.[19] Such an attitude may be taken not only when the violations do not directly impair the legal rights of others, but also when they do, as in the case of an isolated trespass against someone else's land. Imagining instances in which the rules of law are thought to have no moral claim on adjudicative officials is harder, but the utilitarian may respond that cases get to adjudication only when someone cares a good deal about application of the rules and that, because of the publicness of their performance, adjudicators need to be consistently faithful to the law.

When we think carefully about ordinary people's attitudes toward the law as it applies to them, we recognize that many persons do not suppose a substantial moral question is raised by unnoticed trespassing on the land of another or by breaking a (good) law against speeding at hours when driving that speed is not dangerous.[20] And, of course, many people feel no moral qualms about breaking laws they think foolish or intrusive on private domains. Reflection on these examples leads to skepticism over whether most people actually believe in a kind of moral surcharge in favor of obedience of every law, or even every good law, on every occasion of possible violation. And that skepticism largely undercuts any supposition that for most laws utilitarianism is grossly at odds with present attitudes.

The practical problems with application of an act utilitarian approach are most severe with respect to laws that impose general obligations—tax regulations, currency and customs restrictions, and similar laws. General obedience to such laws is often critical to the provision of public goods, but individual violations do not make an observable difference; no one is directly hurt. And many sorts of violations are unlikely to be discovered. In such circumstances, people may conclude that no harm will be done by undisclosed import of a prohibited item or that their use of money owed in taxes will be better than the use the government would make of the same money.

Of course, such judgments will often be rationalizations of self-interest, but sometimes they will be correct.[21] Present attitudes toward tax liabilities and import restrictions no doubt vary greatly among societies and in relation to particular legal duties. But if the moral force of these collective legal obligations depends on the usefulness of an individual's contribution in relation to the contributions of others[22] it would rest on a shaky moral foundation. Here, at least, the act utilitarian approach is out-of-line with how law-abiding citizens conceive their moral duty.

Rule Utilitarianism and Its Implications

Does rule utilitarianism comport better with existing or proper attitudes toward law? Whether or not rule utilitarianism would include a general duty to obey the law would turn on the exact level of generality at which the relevant moral rules were best cast. That would depend in part on the nature of the political order and the kinds of legal rules a society had; but whatever these features looked like, one proposing a rule utilitarian account would have to deal with some general theoretical problems that warrant mention and summary treatment. Such an account must suggest how the relevant rules are chosen—whether an actor should pay attention only to existing moral rules, to ideal moral rules, or to moral rules that have a chance of acceptance within his own society. Such an account must also indicate how moral rules should treat the likely compliance or noncompliance of others.

We may begin with the basic proposition that for a rule utilitarian, the basis for judging a possible rule is its prospective contribution to desirable consequences. That, not some independent value of fairness, will be the standard for judging whether or not a rule should refer to the likely compliance of others. Certainly it is possible to conceptualize a rule in the following form: "Do not walk on the grass unless enough other people are avoiding the grass so that your walking will not do any damage." A rule utilitarian would ask whether such a rule would yield desirable consequences, saving the grass and allowing some pleasurable and unharmful walking on it. He might well conclude that a rule in this form would be too difficult for individuals to apply and that its broad acceptance, combined with imprecise applications, would endanger the grass. Further, those who refrained from walking on the grass might resent those enjoying a "free ride."[23] So the more rigid moral rule, "Do not walk on the grass," might well be the best one from a rule utilitarian perspective, though it would preclude some harmless walking on the grass. We can now see clearly how a rule utilitarian account would deal with taxes, accepting a rigid moral rule in favor of paying taxes that would preclude individuals from weighing alternative uses of funds in particular cases. General acceptance and adherence to that rule might well produce better overall consequences than general acceptance and attempted adherence to a more flexible rule.

Desirable consequences are also the standard by which a rule utilitarian should judge a proposed rule in light of its present acceptance. The easiest case is an ideal rule that is also presently accepted; the rule utilitarian will certainly endorse that rule. Also easy is a presently accepted moral rule that does not produce desirable consequences; the rule utilitarian will reject it. The hard situation is one in which a presently accepted rule makes some contribution to overall welfare, but acceptance of another rule would be preferable.[24] Perhaps now we need to distinguish between rule utilitarianism as a theory for social reform and rule utilitarianism as a theory for individual choice. Someone who is mainly trying to influence the attitudes of others should undoubtedly encourage acceptance of the better rule, unless the relevant population is incapable for some reason of accepting it or the dislocations and unhappiness caused by the change would outweigh the benefits of its acceptance. The difficult question concerns the individual making a choice to act when his act will have minimal effects on the attitudes of others. If the benefits of following the better rule do not depend on the actions of others, then that is the rule that should guide the person. However, if compliance with that "rule" accomplishes no good at all given the acceptance by everyone else of a different rule, following it has no point. If everyone else walks across land where grass could grow if nobody walked, a particular individual lacks any good reason to refrain from walking there himself.

The problem of choosing behavior when not everyone is willing to cooperate in achieving the best consequences has been examined with great subtlety by Donald Regan.[25] He proposes, as an alternative to both act utilitarianism and rule utilitarianism, a principle of co-operative utilitarianism: "What each agent ought to do is co-operate, with whoever else is co-operating, in the production of the best consequences possible given the behavior of non-co-operators."[26] A sensitive rule utilitarian would adopt something like Regan's approach in choosing the rule to guide his behavior,[27] though paying attention to the formulation of a generalizable and teachable rule to a degree that Regan's formulation may not reflect.

To determine whether or not to accept a moral rule that all laws, or all just laws, should be obeyed on all occasions, the rule utilitarian would have to consider the consequences of accepting such a rule compared with the consequences of a more flexible approach, making whatever adjustment is appropriate in light of the fact that some people will not adhere to what ideally might be the best rule. What result the rule utilitarian would arrive at is an open question;[28] but he *might* settle on some rule that supports general observance of law. Would such a rule utilitarian accept an obligation to obey the law in a sense that an act utilitarian would not?

The answer is clearly "yes." If the best moral rule would prescribe observance of law, the rule utilitarian would say that obeying the law is morally right even when the balance of consequences of particular acts of observance would be unfavorable. This does not mean the rule utilitarian would say that obeying the law would always be morally correct. The rule in favor of obedience might conflict with some other moral rule whose force would be stronger on the particular occasion and, conceivably, the moral rule in favor of obedience could also be outweighed by very powerful reasons of self-interest. What is crucial is that the rule utilitarian would recognize a reason for obedience that did not reduce to a balance of consequences on the particular occasion. That may be the sense of moral force of which Lyons talks and is perhaps the most straightforward sense of prima facie obligation. If that sense is accepted, then at least sometimes obedience to law will be morally right even though disobedience would produce better consequences.

We have seen that rule utilitarianism does square better than act utilitarianism with any assertions that people do, and should, believe legal claims generally have a moral force that reaches beyond consequences in individual instances. More particularly, rule utilitarianism can more comfortably endorse the view that people should have such feelings about tax laws and related norms concerning public obligations, whose violation hurts no one directly.

This conclusion about rule utilitarianism, however, raises a crucial question about its plausibility. If desirable consequences are the standard for judging possible rules, how can it ever be right to follow the rules when one knows that breaking them will produce better consequences? Any response that introduces the notion of fairness to others who comply reaches beyond desirable consequences, and I will postpone its treatment for the next two chapters. The genuinely consequentialist response is that the practice of thinking and talking about such actions as right supports the desirable rules and thus has desirable consequences.

Since the very meaning of moral concepts may properly depend on what will serve social welfare, the rule utilitarian does have an adequate response to the apparent paradox about terminology.

What is less clear, however, are the practical implications of the rule utilitarian's theory for a person who is aware of all these complexities and is confident that others will not know of his act. If such a person is firmly convinced that a wrong action (one not in conformity with the best rule) will produce more desirable consequences than a right action (one in conformity with the best rule), and this judgment includes a realistic appraisal of all the possible effects of his nonconformity on the attitudes and behavior of himself and others, then it is highly doubtful that rule utilitarianism provides an adequate reason for not breaking the rule. Because the rule utilitarian's concept of what is morally right can itself be seen as serving utilitarian objectives, it is a genuine moral question how he should choose when it will serve those objectives not to do what is right in a particular instance.

Neither the rule utilitarian's definitional stipulation nor a publicity requirement that moral rules must be publicly stated and defensible resolves this substantive question. One might talk about fairness or a notion that acting on the basis of principles different from those one defends undermines integrity, but the first of these steps, and perhaps the second, would take one beyond utilitarian evaluation.

Thus far I have spoken of act utilitarianism and rule utilitarianism as sharply divergent alternatives. I have briefly mentioned the possibility that a rule utilitarianism cast in terms of highly complex and particularized rules might "collapse" into act utilitarianism; but I now want to focus on a version of act utilitarianism that moves in important ways toward rule utilitarianism. Offering an account that is presaged in the work of Henry Sidgwick and other utilitarian theorists, R. M. Hare has met criticism of an act utilitarian point of view with suggestions that act utility plays only a limited role at the level of practical moral thinking.[29] According to Hare, act utilitarian thinkers and educators recognize that most people, including themselves, should make ordinary moral decisions intuitively; they also recognize that sound general dispositions and feelings need to be inculcated. The substantive principles consonant with those dispositions would not be departed from "without strongest grounds." More systematic act utilitarian perspectives would be reserved for appraisal of moral intuitions and the resolution of instances when intuitions conflict. Thus, in the great majority of instances, people might properly follow their intuitions that observing the legal rights of others and obeying the law are things they morally ought to do, without ever engaging in any sort of utilitarian calculation. In emphasizing the tentativeness and restraint with which people should turn to act utilitarian calculations, Hare provides a particularly sophisticated account of the role of guiding principles that are more deeply set in people's moral dispositions than the phrase "rules of thumb" suggests.

Does Hare recognize a general obligation to obey the law? In acknowledging the possible value of an intuition that one should obey the law without worrying too much about consequences, he joins the rule utilitarian. But Hare apparently does not agree that an act may be right even though the actor correctively perceives it will have less desirable consequences than an alternative act.

The conclusions of this section may be briefly summarized. Tension does exist between a straightforward act utilitarian account of obedience to law and any sense that laws, or just laws, have moral force on all the occasions of their application. Since it is doubtful that people do assume all just laws have such moral force, the act utilitarian account may not be widely incompatible with existing and proper attitudes toward law; but it does appear genuinely disturbing when applied to laws imposing obligations that do not implicate the rights of individuals and whose violations cause no direct harm. Unlike the act utilitarian, the rule utilitarian can support a general obligation to obey laws or broad classes of laws and can provide a clear theory of why meeting tax and related obligations should be considered morally right. More complex act utilitarian accounts, like that of Hare, can also go a substantial distance in this direction.

DIFFICULTIES IN APPLYING UTILITARIAN STANDARDS

Whatever its correlation with present or desirable attitudes about obedience to law, utilitarianism cannot be an acceptable theory about this subject if it is inherently flawed. One pervasive objection to utilitarian theory is that interpersonal calculations of welfare are impossible, even in theory.[30]

What is often not recognized is the extent to which this objection, if correct, undermines not only a straightforwardly consequentialist morality, but also other familiar moral positions. Many who have refused to accept utilitarianism have acknowledged that *one* duty humans have is a duty of benevolence,[31] a duty that should be followed when no other moral standard would be violated. Many have also acknowledged that deviation from ordinary moral standards is appropriate when the overall consequences are harmful enough.[32] Further, the *application* of nonutilitarian standards is often not free from interpersonal calculations of welfare. For example, if one aimed to apply a standard that people should show each other decent concern, what does the standard indicate about the appropriate level at which a stereo set should be played at various times of day in an apartment building with one-room apartments and very thin walls? One would undertake some weighing of the comparative benefit of enjoyment of music at various decibel levels with the harm of disturbing those in adjoining apartments.[33] No doubt, what decent concern requires may be more complex than a simple weighing of the welfare of the persons involved, since compliance with justified expectations of the quiet one can expect may be independently important. But these expectations themselves are likely to be grounded on some rough and socially shared sense of a balance of harms and benefits.[34]

Once we recognize how often nonutilitarian moral positions share the assumption that interpersonal calculations of welfare are possible, we may doubt if any plausible moral question can do entirely without them. We can also see that no one is rigorously skeptical about this possibility when facing practical moral questions; people have little difficulty concluding that one person's loss of life is worse than another's sprained ankle. None of these facts, of course, proves that the assumption is correct, and its soundness may depend to a degree on how the ultimate standard for weighing burdens and benefits is conceived; but I shall suppose that interpersonal calculations of welfare have enough meaning in enough situations to sustain the diverse moral theories and practices that depend on them.[35]

The theoretical claim that interpersonal calculations are possible does not establish that they can be carried out with a reasonable degree of accuracy. One problem is ignorance of future events; humans are often unable to tell what consequences, especially remote ones, will result. But rules of thumb are highly useful in cases of uncertain consequences, and a system of morality may work reasonably well, even though the correct applications of relevant standards are sometimes uncertain, as long as individuals employ the standards in good faith.[36] The worry about individual calculation does not rest on ignorance alone, however. It reaches human selfishness and powers of rationalization. People have a marvelous capacity to convince themselves that what is in their own self-interest is also in everyone else's interest. Telling people to decide moral questions on the basis of an open-minded weighing of all relevant consequences may invite them to rationalize pursuit of their own ends.

Although personal bias may also creep in when someone tries to decide what moral rules should be followed, the opportunities for unconscious special pleading are much less under a rule utilitarian approach than under a straightforward act utilitarian one.[37] This comparative advantage comes at a price, however. An emphasis on rules risks inability to resolve many moral issues and infidelity to common moral experience, much of which involves weighing of loose competing principles.[38]

THE UNREALISTIC DEMANDS OF UTILITARIANISM

Any moral theory that makes overall welfare the ultimate standard for how individual choices among possible acts "ought" to be made exhibits a fundamental defect, whether overall welfare is mediated by general rules or not. Such a morality asks too much of people, at least if it purports to set standards that most people are really expected to live up to rather than to announce an ideal to which the most saintly among us may aspire.

As I suggested near the end of Chapter 3, a public morality that talks of duties and strong oughts must be rooted in what is realistically possible for humans, and most people are not capable of according the same weight to the interests of strangers as they do to their own interests and the interests of those they love.[39] Nor do most people, in their nonperfectionist moments,[40] feel they have failed morally when they pursue their own interests at the cost of the much stronger interests of strangers. This difficulty severely threatens a utilitarian account of obedience to law.

Before discussing the implications of this judgment, I want to discuss some possible defenses of utilitarianism against my charge that it is unrealistic as it relates to obeying the law. One response is that utility is actually best served by people not aiming to promote general welfare. Another is that an aim to promote the general welfare would be desirable and that asserting a duty of that sort is also desirable. The third response would be to acknowledge that promoting general welfare is often not a duty but to claim that obedience to law is a duty.

Utilitarians have not been blind to the realities of human relationships and motivation, and their theories are meant to be responsive both to people's special positions and to their limited altruism. First, utilitarians do not recommend that actors disregard ties such as family relationships. Imagine a parent who rigorously adheres to act utilitarianism in personal judgments. The parent recognizes that his own child has less need for a vacation than other children; yet he may still appropriately spend his money on his own child's vacation. The choice can be justified because the parent's efforts for his own child will help support a sense of love and security that the parent is incapable of creating in strangers. Although utilitarianism undoubtedly allows some special consideration to those to whom we are closest, most people afford consideration to themselves and their loved ones far greater than could be warranted by a self-conscious equal universal concern for all human beings. Thus, the problem of limited altruism remains.

Utilitarians of all stripes have understood that people are often motivated by objectives other than promotion of general welfare.[41] Such motivations pose no problem as long as they exist compatibly with the broader utilitarian objective. The extreme version of compatibility is the "invisible hand" assumption that overall welfare will be promoted best if people simply pursue the concerns that matter most to them.[42] Assured of such compatibility, an individual could recognize that the moral act is the one that best promotes overall welfare but rest comfortably in the belief that following his own inclinations will have that effect.

At the superficial level at least, any such view is subject to the crushing objection that general welfare would obviously be better promoted if people exhibited a higher degree of concern for remote strangers. In a world in which differences in wealth and privilege are as extreme as they are, an unselfish sharing of resources by the fortunate could make a great difference in the lives of many less fortunate. If all those with a net worth of over $100,000 regarded themselves as under a duty to give half their wealth to the poor and performed that duty, the world would be a better place. Thus, belief that people's untutored inclinations uniformly serve the general welfare is highly implausible.

This conclusion, based substantially on the diminishing marginal returns of wealth, might be resisted by a more subtle defense of the invisible hand benefits of selfishness. Generous attitudes in rich people generally might be correlated to other dispositions that would impair general welfare, such as a lack of drive necessary for high productivity. At a deeper level, then, the widespread existence of the generous attitude might have overall harmful effects. Alternatively, the urging of generosity might prove unfortunate because generous attitudes are not widely attainable and their attempted cultivation and encouragement might lead to useless frustration and resentment. Whatever the merit of these defenses of selfishness, each suggests an odd distortion of utilitarianism at the level of individual choice. Suppose a wealthy individual is considering donating half his money to the poor. He believes that widespread adoption of generous attitudes might be harmful but is confident that his own generosity will accomplish much good, will not render him less productive, and will not infect others by example (he might donate anonymously). Under an act utilitarian theory he ought to make the donation, and it would be a peculiar form of rule utilitarianism that would proscribe his donation because general acceptance of such a duty, highly desirable in itself, would have subtle negative effects on other desirable attitudes. Similarly, if the individual himself knows he would not suffer frustration and resentment at making the gift, the fact that others might suffer if they conceive themselves as under a duty to make similar gifts would not appear to be a good reason for him to refrain. As utilitarian arguments, claims about linkages of attitudes or impracticability seem more relevant to education and other social teaching than to individual choice by persons who are self-consciously utilitarian.

The defense of selfishness may better be understood as criticism of individuals thinking in self-consciously utilitarian terms. So far in the discussion of utilitarianism we have assumed that reflective individuals should believe that their common moral notions are compatible with overall welfare, and that utility is the appropriate standard against which to test possible individual actions or rules of action and to resolve difficult conflicts. That is, we have assumed utilitarian theory recommends that individuals consider utility an ultimate standard of proper action. But a different sort of connection is possible. Perhaps overall welfare will best be promoted if individuals conceive of moral oughts in nonutilitarian terms, though institutions, such as criminal punishment, should be designed to bring people's selfish interests in line with general welfare.

Were the arguments against the duty of generosity so understood, the resulting theory would cease to be utilitarian for purposes of this study. Whether or not publicity is an inherent condition of all *moral* principles that apply to social relations,[43] my concern is with principles of public morality that guide individual behavior and form the basis of claims by fellow citizens. A theory that uses an ultimate utilitarian standard to judge practices, institutions, and attitudes but recommends wholly different criteria for the self-conscious moral choices of individuals does not count as utilitarian in this sense.

The second response to my conclusion that utilitarianism is unrealistic in demanding too much remains more faithful to a thoroughgoing utilitarian theory. This response admits that much more embracing generosity is both desirable and unattainable but asserts that urging people that their duty lies along these lines will have overall positive effects. In this view, the criticism of being unrealistic is deflected with the claim that having standards of duty few people are capable of actually satisfying may itself be desirable. Because we are familiar with forms of Christian morality that assert people have duties that far exceed the capacity or willingness of most people to perform, we know that such a use of moral concepts is neither inconceivable nor obviously wrongheaded. No conclusive refutation of this defense of a utilitarian standard of duty may be possible; but the difference between personal moral aspirations and a shared public morality is critical here. When one is talking about a shared public morality, the language of "duty" and "right" is, as I have suggested in Chapter 3, better reserved for those acts people are really expected to perform.[44]

The third response is to try to accommodate the distinction between "ought" and mere moral preferability within the bounds of a utilitarian theory and to assert that obeying the law falls within the realm of "ought." It is doubtful that simple act utilitarianism can comfortably achieve such an accommodation. Under that theory an individual might well feel an increasing stringency as the consequences of his acts become more momentous, but often the consequences of law breaking are not momentous. There would be no reason from a simple act utilitarian perspective always to treat obeying the law as a matter of "ought" or "duty" and to regard most other opportunities to promote welfare as not involving "ought" or "duty."

Rule utilitarianism is somewhat more promising in this respect. No doubt, rule utilitarianism can differentiate between kinds of desirable behavior that should be treated as duties, involving blame for failure to perform, from other kinds of desirable behavior that should not be so regarded.[45] That differentiation concerns the blaming and approving behavior of outsiders. But what of the actor himself; should he seriously aim always to perform the best act or to follow the rule whose observance will produce the best acts? J. O. Urmson writes, "No doubt from the agent's point of view it is imperative that he should endeavor to live up to the highest ideals of behavior that he can think of, and if an action falls within the ideal it is for him irrelevant whether or not it is a duty or some more supererogatory act."[46] Contrary to the gist of this thought, many people, I suspect most, are quite willing to settle for doing less in their own lives than is optimal from a moral point of view. They are relaxed in the moral rigor they demand of themselves just as they are relaxed in the moral rigor they expect of others. Quite apart from blaming others, a rule utilitarianism that tried to accommodate this reality would require principles relating to what people really ought to strive to do and weaker principles of moral preferability. And if rule utilitarianism were to assert a duty to obey the law, it would have to include obedience to law in the former category. A sufficiently sophisticated form of rule utilitarianism might both develop a category of morally preferable supererogatory acts and explain why, on consequentialist grounds, obedience to law should be treated as a matter of duty rather than supererogation. Any approach of this sort would be likely to rely heavily for its classification of obedience to law on the considerations addressed in the following two chapters, though more on *feelings* of fairness and less on fairness itself than my discussion does.

Because my aim is not to try to work out all the possible implications of novel forms of utilitarian theory, I now revert to my initial conclusion that familiar forms of utilitarianism do not provide a satisfactory account of moral duty, because they unrealistically bring too much behavior within that range. This objection to utilitarianism is bolstered by the now familiar objection that, by creating a general duty to promote overall welfare, it makes individuals hostages to the purpose of others, forcing them to deviate from their own projects whenever external circumstances make overall welfare more likely to be promoted by another action.[47] In one of Bernard Williams's examples, a chemist with a strong objection to war research might be led by utilitarian principles to take a job doing just such research, when he knows declining the job would lead a zealous proponent of such research to take the job. This downgrading of an individual's own projects, and his or her own moral feelings, involves an unacceptable denial of individual integrity.

We are now ready to explore the implications of the conclusion that people do not have a general duty to promote overall welfare. This conclusion does not undermine either the idea that welfare in some more indirect sense underlies a duty to obey, a subject pursued in subsequent chapters, nor the idea that desirable consequences are often good moral reasons for obeying the law.

Exactly how desirable consequences might figure in this resepct is shown by considering three categories of situations in which an actor must choose what to do independent of any specific moral obligation or duty that imposes a requirement of action.[48] In one category, consequences are so trivial or indeterminate apart from one's own preferences that one appropriately does not think in moral terms at all. In another category, the consequences are so momentous—for example, the death of a stranger one could easily save—that a failure to promote desirable consequences would be a failure to do what one "ought" or "must."[49] In the intermediate third category, consequences are important enough to make it appropriate to think about an act in moral terms and to say that promoting the favorable consequences is preferable to not promoting them. But their promotion would be considered a supererogatory act, an act that it would be morally preferable for someone to do but not an act that one "ought" to do. Doing the act is met with praise but failure to do the act is not met with blame. Many situations in which more favorable consequences would be promoted by one act than by others fall into this category. The existence of this third category reflects the freedom and autonomy of human agents[50] and represents a sort of liberation from the notion that every choice of moral relevance is governed by duty.[51]

When important reasons of consequence support obedience to law, we can at least say that these are good moral reasons to perform the act, reasons of the sort that apply generally to supererogatory acts and that would make obedience morally preferable in the absence of countervailing reasons. Whether the consequences of ordinary citizens disobeying the law *as such*, apart from more obvious harmful consequences of an act that happens to be in disobedience of law, would ever be momentous enough in themselves to throw obedience into the second category, the category of "ought" or "must," is dubious; however, the consequences of disobedience might occasionally push within that category a choice that is already on the border on other grounds.

A conclusion that obedience to law might usually be a matter of performing only a morally preferable supererogatory act remains perplexing. Whatever the precise attitudes people in our culture have toward the law, most of them do feel obedience to law is often a serious issue that concerns duty or obligation in the sense of a strong moral ought, not just some combination of weaker reasons that point to the moral preferability of obedience. Because utilitarianism in any of its ordinary versions assumes that we always "ought" to do what promotes desirable consequences, familiar utilitarian theory does not explain why failing to promote the general welfare by disobeying law is regarded as more serious than countless other forms of failing to promote the general welfare.

NOTES

1. A notable example of such a derivation is John Stuart Mill's discussion of justice in his essay on Utilitarianism (1863). See also H. Sidgwick, The Methods of Ethics 421–25 (7th ed., 1962).

2. See, generally, Smart, An Outline of Utilitarian Ethics, in J. J. C. Smart and B. Williams, Utilitarianism: For And Against 1–73 (1973).

3. See, e.g., Brandt, Toward a Credible Form of Utilitarianism, in H.-N. Castaneda and G. Nakhnikian, eds., Morality and the Language of Conduct 107–43 (1963). As this article, among others, reveals, any simple statement of a rule utilitarian position, such as that provided in the text, is bound to obscure complexities and to conceal divergences among rule utilitarians over exactly how the appropriate test for rules should be formulated. Brandt's own final formulation shows how much more involved a standard is likely to look after

the complexities are addressed: "An act is right if and only if it conforms with that learnable set of rules the recognition of which as morally binding—roughly at the time of the act—by everyone in the society of the agent, except for the retention by individuals of already formed and decided moral convictions, would maximize intrinsic value." Id. at 139.

4. See D. Lyons, Forms and Limits of Utilitarianism (1965); R. Wasserstrom, The Judicial Decision (1961).

5. See Chapter 3, Standards of Judgment and Terminology.

6. Smart, note 2 supra at 46–49, has a clear discussion of this issue and adopts a terminology that distinguishes the forms of evaluation. One feature of the problem is whether, when acts unpredictably produce bad consequences, an actor should be said to be justified or excused. I comment on that in Greenawalt, The Perplexing Borders of Justification and Excuse, 84 Colum. L. Rev. 1897, 1907–12 (1984), concluding that when appraisal is concentrated on the actor, the term justification is more appropriate.

7. In his introductory book on ethics, William Frankena treats a theory that introduces distributive limits as no longer purely utilitarian. W. Frankena, Ethics (1973). In A Theory of Justice (1971) at 25, John Rawls also assumes that a principle of distribution disqualifies a theory from being utilitarian.

8. See id.

9. See J. Fletcher, Situation Ethics 96 (1966).

10. Though in my usage here, a theory that said "Distribute desirable consequences equally" would still be utilitarian, a theory that said "Promote desirable consequences only for those who deserve them morally" would not be utilitarian, if "moral desert" involved the introduction of a nonconsequential notion of what is morally right action. The reason for this distinction is that the second theory, unlike the first, would demand nonconsequentialist moral appraisal.

11. See, e.g., R. Sartorius, Individual Conduct and Social Norms 56–73 (1975).

12. P. Soper, A Theory of Law 75–90 (1984).

13. D. Lyons, Utility and Rights, in J. R. Pennock and J. W. Chapman, eds., Nomos XXIV, Ethics, Economics, and the Law 148 (1982).

14. See Honoré, Must We Obey? Necessity as a Ground of Obligation, 67 Va. L. Rev. 39, 47–48 (1981).

15. See Soper, note 12 supra.

16. Id. at 85. See Smith, Is There a Prima Facie Obligation to Obey the Law? 82 Yale L. J. 950, 965 (1973).

17. I believe, however, that Soper's theory may adopt just this weak sense of prima facie obligation. In addition to the pages cited in note 12, see Soper, The Moral Value of Law, 84 Mich. L. Rev. 63 (1985).

18. Many of the thoughts presented here are developed more fully in a response to Lyons in Greenawalt, Utilitarian Justifications for Observance of Legal Rights, Nomos XXIV, note 13 supra at 139.

19. In Chapter 2, I have suggested that in some of its reach, the written law

may not pose a serious issue of compliance, because compliance is not really expected. One might by extension say that failure of officials to enforce the law sometimes does not pose a real question about nonenforcement. However, there is some behavior that the law seriously seeks to prevent, but against which using the full engines of enforcement would still be inappropriate. One thinks, for example, of minor cheating on income taxes.

20. By calling the law good, I mean not only that the speed limit is generally appropriate but that the law is not defective in failing to make an exception for hours when few people are around. There is a limit to how much such rules can sensibly be tailored to variant conditions.

21. One might talk about the long-term corrosive effects of nonpayment and the many ways in which the incidence of nonpayment are communicated to others, but these utilitarian arguments rest on doubtful factual premises. I do not mean to deny that actions with imperceptible effects on a large number of people can be wrong (see D. Parfit, Reasons and Persons 75–82 [1984]); but the taxpayer may claim that the good effects of his use of the money outweigh the bad effects of its unavailability to the government, and the violator of customs laws may claim that no one is harmed if his use of the item is benign and he would not have bought a similar item domestically.

22. It might be stipulated that a person cannot consider the likelihood that others similarly situated and with similar preferences will comply with substantive standards that have general application. See M. Singer, Generalization in Ethics (1961). Under this stipulation, the principle "It is all right to evade taxes if one's own use of money will have better consequences than the government's use of it" would not be acceptable, if one's ability to use money better depends on the government's having collected enough money from others to provide vital state services. Such a stipulation may be appropriate, but it requires either a move to rule utilitarianism, considered later, or the introduction of some independent moral value relating to fairness.

23. This reason comes close to a fairness reason, because it concerns resentment from perceived unfairness; but as long as the focus is on the negative qualities of resentment, the reason remains a utilitarian one.

24. See, e.g., Brandt, note 3 supra at 118–19.

25. D. Regan, Utilitarianism and Co-Operation (1980).

26. Id. at 124 (emphasis omitted).

27. See H. Sidgwick, note 1 supra at 423–509.

28. Richard Brandt, a leading rule utilitarian, has suggested the absence of a prima facie obligation to obey the law. See Brandt, Utility and the Obligation to Obey the Law, in S. Hook, ed., Law and Philosophy 43–49 (1964). See also Soper, note 12 supra at 62; Smith, note 16 supra at 968–69.

29. R. Hare, Moral Thinking, Its Levels, Methods and Point (1981); Hare, Utility and Rights: Comment on David Lyons's Essay, in Nomos XXIV, note 13 supra, at 148.

30. Although I have phrased the point in terms of welfare, the same

problem arises if desirable consequences are formulated in many other ways as well.

31. See, e.g., W. D. Ross, The Right and the Good 21 (1930).

32. See, e.g., C. Fried, Right and Wrong 10–11 (1978).

33. See Ronald Dworkin's acknowledgment that what amounts to being fair to one's fellows may turn on a weighing of benefits and harms. A Reply by Ronald Dworkin, in M. Cohen, ed., Ronald Dworkin and Contemporary Jurisprudence 247, 264 (1983).

34. A possible position is that no standard that transcends cultures exists for weighing harms and benefits, but that a person has a moral duty to apply standards of his own society. Under this view, a broad consequentialist approach to moral decision might be feasible, but the necessary assessments might have no correctness beyond a particular culture.

Another claim that might be made is that questions involving adjustments of interests can be decided in terms of economic efficiency, determined by willingness to pay. In theory, no outsider would have to weigh harms and benefits to different individuals. However, if the standard of judgment is present willingness to pay, it is unclear why the present distribution of income and popular levels of understanding should largely determine resolutions of such conflicts; and in practice market imperfections often make confident answers about efficient allocation impossible. If the standard of judgment involves an ideal distribution of resources, and people with full information making rational judgments about what will serve their needs, then relevant questions seem not very different from ones cast directly in terms of overall welfare.

35. A utilitarian approach could survive a moderate skepticism whether some questions involving competing interests have any correct answers. If one set of consequences could not be said to be preferable to another, then an individual would be morally free to act in a way that would bring about either set of consequences.

36. Teachers cope with similar difficulties when they grade essay exams.

37. Utilitarian generalization and cooperative utilitarianism (see note 25) also reduce these opportunities by their emphasis on behavior in which many people may engage. Since they do not stress the teachability and general acceptance of moral standards, attempts to apply them might lead to somewhat more special pleading than attempts to apply rule utilitarianism, but they do not suffer the drawbacks of rule utilitarianism's overemphasis on rules.

38. See G. J. Warnock, The Object of Morality 61–70 (1971).

39. See J. L. Mackie, Ethics 129–134 (1977).

40. A serious Christian may view his self-aggrandizement as a continual falling into sin; but most serious Christians continue to overweigh their own interests in everyday life without intense psychic pain.

41. See, e.g., Mills, Ethical Writings, in J. Schneewind, ed., at 292–93 (1965).

42. See B. Mandeville, The Fable of the Bees 31, 157 (1962).

43. See, e.g., K. Baier, The Moral Point of View 196 (1958); J. Rawls, A Theory of Justice 133 (1971). For utilitarian theorists who acknowledge the possibility that the best standards for action should not be publicly advocated, see Sidgwick, note 1 supra at 489–91; P. Singer, Practical Ethics 180 (1979).

44. John Mackie has a succinct and persuasive discussion of the point. Ethics, at 131–32. Mackie does not really consider the possible benefits of a perfectionist morality within a serious religious community, in which admission of one's moral imperfection is importantly related to one's sense of a relationship with God and fellow human beings. I assume that Mackie's skepticism about any possible value would extend to that context, but mine does not.

The point made in the text and discussed by Mackie is closely related to John Rawls's supposition that any acceptable morality must not impose undue strains of commitment. A Theory of Justice 176, 498–500 (1971). Rawls's major objection to utilitarianism as a principle of social justice is that it demands too much of the worse off to justify their misfortunes on the basis of benefits to the better off. But one might also say that serious demands that anyone sacrifice his or her own interests to serve the general welfare impose strains of commitment that are too great.

45. See, e.g., Urmson, Saints and Heroes, in A. I. Melden, ed., Essays in Moral Philosophy 198–216 (1958).

46. Id. at 214.

47. See B. Williams, A Critique of Utilitarianism, in J. J. C. Smart and B. Williams, Utilitarianism: For and Against 97–117 (1973).

48. See J. S. Fishkin, The Limits of Obligation 10–23 (1982). In the text I pass over the complication introduced by imperfect duties defined so that I might be "required" to give some money to charity but am left free morally to decide to whom to give the money.

49. James Fishkin raises disturbing questions about any general supposed obligation to save strangers at slight sacrifice, pointing out that if I have a duty to spend fifty dollars to save a life, I may have a duty (or succession of duties) to donate virtually all my income for famine relief. Id. at 68–73.

50. See D. Heyd, Supererogation 166–76 (1982).

51. S. Scheffler, The Rejection of Consequentialism 62 (1982).

7

Fair Play

If neither promise nor desirable consequences yields a satisfying account of why most citizens ought to obey the law, perhaps their receipt of benefits is a source of obligation. Acceptance of the benefits of a political order might be thought to underlie a duty to obey the law based on fairness or gratitude owed to one's fellow citizens or one's governors. In this chapter I will concentrate for the most part on an obligation of fairness owed to one's fellows, and not worry too much about whether the outer edge of that obligation overlaps with a duty of gratitude. At the end of the chapter, I will comment briefly on the possibility of a duty of fairness toward one's governors and on the relevance of duties of gratitude.

The fair play theory of obligation is that citizens who take the benefits of a society have a duty of fairness to their fellow citizens to abide by the rules of the common enterprise. Without positing a highly artificial notion of consent, this theory still grounds the responsibility to obey on a person's voluntary acts, his acceptance of benefits. The resulting obligation produces an "ought" to obey that could not be created by desirable consequences alone. The attractiveness of the theory is that it suggests a powerful duty to obey, while avoiding the implausibility of promissory notions and the weak force of reasons based exclusively on desirable consequences.

Many traditional social contract theories can profitably be reinterpreted as suggesting a duty based on fairness to fellow citizens; but C. D. Broad may have been the first to suggest explicitly that a duty of fairness may require one to contribute to a cooperative scheme even when the contribution is not necessary to achieve the scheme's objectives. In a 1916 article largely critical of arguments from false universalization, that is, arguments that one should not perform an act if the consequences of everyone's performing the act would be bad, Broad concluded that arguments about a fair distribution of burdens do have force when cooperative schemes produce benefits for a group of people.[1] In 1955, H. L. A. Hart indicated the implications of this idea for obedience to law.[2] Suggesting that political obligation is intelligible only if understood as different from other right-creating transactions such as consent and promising, Hart made the following statement:

> When a number of persons conduct any joint enterprise according to rules and thus restrict their liberty, those who have submitted to these restrictions when required have a right to a similar submission from those who have benefited from the submission.[3]

John Rawls developed this basic idea more fully in a 1964 paper.[4] Considering a mutually beneficial and just scheme of social cooperation, whose advantages could be obtained if almost everyone cooperates in a manner requiring sacrifice or restraint on liberty, but whose advantages could be enjoyed by those who do not cooperate as long as they are few, Rawls claimed the following:

> Under these conditions a person who has accepted the benefits of the scheme is bound by a duty of fair play to do his part and not to take advantage of the free benefits by not cooperating.[5]

Rawls conceived of the political order of a just society as being such a scheme of social cooperation, with constitutional procedures for enacting laws as a fundamental part. Citizens who have accepted the benefits of a just constitution have, he contended, an obligation to obey the laws enacted under it.

In this chapter I suggest that the duty of fair play applies to many more political orders than Rawls recognizes, but its import is not to create a strong duty to obey all laws on every occasion of their application. I begin with a clear illustration of the duty and comment briefly on some of its central features. I then indicate the major difficulties in understanding the duty as it applies to the nonvoluntary relationship between citizen and state. I consider the relevance of benefits that are not voluntary, of ignorance about how benefits are provided, of the injustice of a political order, and of the attitudes of those whose contributions sustain a scheme of cooperation. Finally, I address the subtle question of the scope of the duty.

THE DUTY IN ITS CLEAREST FORM

Illustration 7-1:
Having been left a hard tennis court by the builder, all the residents of a new housing development agree that upkeep will be provided by residents who use the court, paying fifty cents for each hour of use. The Monroes then move in. Before they purchased the property, they consistently told the seller and development officials that they objected to the scheme and were unwilling to promise either to pay their share or to refrain from using the court. After moving in, they repeat that they do not consent to the scheme because use is not worth fifty cents an hour to them. They would nevertheless like to use the court when no one else is doing so. Their use would not add at all to the cost of the upkeep.

May the Monroes, morally, use the court without paying at all or paying less than the fifty cent rate? If we put aside long-term indirect effects, utility would be served by their doing so. Yet, the other residents, worried about the difficulties of setting any sliding scale of fees, may fairly decide not to reduce the price for the Monroes. In that event, the Monroes must choose between paying fifty cents for each hour they play or not playing. If they voluntarily accept the benefits of this scheme of mutual cooperation—benefits conferred by the willing payments of others—then they must adhere to the rules of the scheme.[6]

This example illustrates how the duty of fair play can require actions not covered by either a principle of consent[7] or simple calculations of utility. The scheme in this example is undeniably cooperative. It has been voluntarily agreed upon, it is fair, and participation in it and acceptance of its benefits are voluntary. Though people enter the scheme because of its benefits, they carry their share of the burdens partly out of a sense of duty to fellow participants. At least when those conditions are met,[8] a person who decides to accept the benefits of the scheme has a duty of fair play to comply with the governing rules.

APPLICATION TO POLITICAL COMMUNITIES AND THE LAW

Writers who have suggested that a duty of fair play to one's fellows underlies one's obligation to obey the law have implicitly drawn an analogy between political society and the tennis court scheme; the sacrifices of other citizens that benefit us are the source of our responsibility to comply with the rules that govern our life together. The sacrifices of other citizens mainly take the form of respect for rights and transfers of resources needed to finance government. The duty of fair play requires similar sacrifices by us.

The duty of fairness in relation to obeying the law can be understood at a number of different levels. At the most concrete, one can think of specific legal obligations, such as stopping at red lights. If other drivers benefit me by obeying the rule that requires stopping, I may have a moral duty to do the same. At a more general level, one can think of groups of laws, such as traffic laws, or branches of law, such as the criminal law. I may have a duty to comply with particular laws from which I receive no benefit if there is a broader and related class of laws whose observance by others does produce benefits for me. Finally, one can think of the entire legal order; as long as I benefit from the observance of many laws, I may have a duty to comply with every facet of the legal order.

Acceptance of Benefits and Participation

A radical difference separates the tennis court scheme from every political order. In even the most voluntarist political orders, those in which the fair play duty has seemed most relevant,[9] neither participation nor the acceptance of many benefits is voluntary. Many important legal duties do not depend on the voluntary acceptance of benefits and many benefits cannot be refused.

Some benefits provided by the state *are* accepted voluntarily; one may or may not use a state park or museum for which a fee is charged.

Other benefits, such as military and general police protection, constitute public goods that are open,[10] available to everyone whether they want them or not and regardless of their actions. Still other benefits, such as basic education, involve action by recipients but that action is compelled. Finally, some benefits may be refused, but the state's control over options leaves little real choice; people may not have to call the fire department when their homes are burning, but the state's monopoly over firefighting forecloses other possibilities for relief.

In the political context, acceptance of the few benefits for which one has a really free choice is not sufficient to ground an obligation to obey all or most laws. So, the basic question is whether receiving benefits that are not genuinely voluntary can give rise to the duty of fair play. Because the question arises most starkly in connection with open and compulsory benefits, benefits one is unable to refuse, I will consider it in that context; but the analysis is also relevant to benefits, such as firefighting, that are "chosen" in less than free conditions.

When someone really does not want a benefit, its unavoidable receipt cannot give rise to a duty of fair play to contribute one's share.[11] If military defense is viewed in isolation, a pacifist who abhors such defense does not have a duty of fair play to contribute his share, even if the defense in fact is highly valuable to him as well as his fellow citizens.[12] But many open benefits are welcomed by most citizens. If someone is delighted to receive a benefit, understands the cooperative scheme by which it is supplied, rightly regards himself as a member of the group properly called upon to contribute toward the benefit, and believes that his required share is fair, then that person may be in the same position as someone who has genuinely chosen to receive a benefit he could freely refuse.[13]

Later, I will discuss in some detail the significance of understanding the cooperative scheme and the problem of unfair shares, but here I need to say a few words about being delighted to receive benefits and the stipulation that one rightly regards oneself as a member of the group properly called upon to contribute. Being pleased to receive benefits involves not only preferring to have the benefits rather than no benefits at all but accepting those benefits as substitutes for alternative benefits that might have been provided. If a cooperative scheme provides a beautiful neighborhood rather than decent roads, someone who cares intensely about decent roads and knows decent roads could have been provided instead may not regard himself as under a duty to contribute to the beautiful neighborhood even though he prefers it to an ugly neighborhood. In making the point that acceptance of benefits is partly a matter of comparison, I do not mean to suggest that people who get less than their first choice of benefits have no duty of fair play at all; much will depend on how much they like the benefits they do get and how strong their preference is for alternative benefits. In subsequent discussion I will largely disregard this comparative perspective, assuming that desired benefits are those people would want even if they could choose between them and alternatives.

What it takes for someone rightly to regard himself as a member of the group properly called upon to contribute is more complex. We can imagine a situation in which one is very happy to receive a benefit, but because of the motives of those providing the benefit or their remoteness from the person benefitted, he has no duty of fair play toward them. If the workers of a foreign country accept lower wages to produce cars at a lower price, and I am able to purchase for $8000 a car for which I would have been willing to pay $9000, I owe no duty of fair play to the workers. Part of the point here is the incidentalness of the benefit conferred on me; the workers have made this sacrifice to improve their own economy, not to save foreigners money. But it may also be relevant that no past close association has existed between the foreign workers and myself; we are not parts of the same community.

What makes one a member of the group that is properly called upon to contribute? When benefits may be freely accepted or rejected and the scheme fairly treats acceptance of benefits as placing someone within the group bound to contribute, then one's act of accepting the benefits puts one within that group and generates the duty of fair play. This was the situation with the Monroes and upkeep of the tennis court. When benefits are open, one's placement in the group may be more complicated. It may depend on a pattern of continuing relationships that makes one a member of the community. If burdens are reasonably cast on members of the Columbia Law School faculty or on U. S. citizens, I am a member of both these groups, regardless of the attitude I take toward the particular scheme under which the burdens are imposed.

On some occasions, when one's connection with the scheme is somewhat tangential or the appeal for contribution itself leaves room for some self-definition by persons from whom contributions are sought, one's being a member of the group to whom any duty of fair play applies may depend on one's own attitude toward the scheme. Suppose I would prefer paying $100 a year to losing public television programs. If I further approve the scheme by which all viewers are solicited for contributions and I understand that no programs would be aired without those contributions, I may have a duty of fair play to contribute something.[14] But if I believe that public television should be supported exclusively by government funds, commercial advertising, or wealthy patrons, I may not be under such a duty.

The Import of Ignorance

In the clearest instances of the duty of fair play, the relevant facts are grasped by all and the person subject to the duty does not diverge from other contributors in judgments concerning the fairness of the scheme. Here, I investigate the significance of someone's being unaware of important facts or wrongly believing that the scheme is unfair to him.

I begin with a problem concerning when a person acquires relevant information. Ordinarily, the duty of fair play relates to a continuing enterprise in which one's present and future acts are based on assessment of how one's fellow participants have acted in the past and on expectations of how they will act in the future. In fact, Rawls talks at one point of the duty to obey the law as depending on "our intention to continue accepting the benefits of a just scheme."[15] John Simmons points out that one may have a duty of fair play to pay for benefits already received even if one does not intend to receive further benefits;[16] but, if the benefits are open, Simmons says, they must be taken "willingly" and "knowingly" for the duty of fair play to arise, the knowingly standard requiring "an understanding of the status of those benefits relative to the person providing them."[17] If Simmons means to suggest that the understanding must coincide in time with the receipt of benefits, he is mistaken.

Illustration 7-2:

The Monroes move into the housing development with no awareness of the tennis court scheme described in Illustration 7-1. Believing that use is free and that the builder is paying for the upkeep, they use the court for a month. Their ignorance of the actual scheme for upkeep is the product of a neighbor's dog taking from their doorstep a notice setting out the terms of the system. At the end of the month someone comes around to collect. The Monroes acknowledge that they think the scheme is fair, that they would have agreed to it if asked, that their use of the court was well worth the money to them, and that their misunderstanding did not affect their frequency of use or other expenditures.

Under these conditions, the Monroes should recognize that they have a duty of fair play to pay their share for past benefits. Although the illustration involves benefits one is free to refuse, the conclusion also applies to open benefits. If one achieves a recognition that open benefits one has welcomed could not have been provided without the contributions of others like oneself, one may have a duty to contribute for past benefits received. The same may also be true if the recognition involves understanding that something one previously regarded with indifference is really a valuable benefit.

Exactly how to describe the person who would be under a duty of fair play if he recognized facts he does not yet recognize is troublesome. The terminological quandary is related to the familiar problem in moral theory, discussed earlier, of how to characterize actions that derive from a mistaken view of the facts,[18] but the fair play notion gives the problem a special wrinkle in this context. Although we must qualify the thought by explanatory phrases, we may say that a person acted wrongly when his act was the product of excusable ignorance, but we cannot say that a person acted unfairly if he was excusably ignorant of the facts that would make the action unfair.[19] Thus, regarding past events, a person would not be said to have violated a duty of fair play if he or she was unaware of the facts that gave rise to the duty. But if someone were speaking to the same ignorant person about what he should now contribute, he might well say, "You *have* a duty of fair play." The explanation of the duty would cover the facts that give rise to the duty. If the relevant facts are reasonably straightforward, their presentation will eliminate excusable ignorance. We then face a somewhat unusual circumstance in which the explanation of the moral duty actually generates the duty.

How should someone speak about the present status of a person who is not involved in the conversation? How shall I speak of ordinary citizens who are extremely unlikely to read this book? Here delicate judgments are required. Two of these judgments concern the actual extent of people's factual knowledge and how much and what sorts of knowledge are necessary to generate the duty of fair play. We will return to these matters later. Another delicate judgment involves placing blame for ignorance. That may depend partly on the sort of ignorance involved. If people are blind to the contributions of their fellow citizens, we may think they are being unfair in refusing to open their eyes to what makes their life tolerable. On the other hand, if ignorance is of the benefit of some expensive undertaking like the space program, we may think that the government should carry the burden of informing citizens of its importance. When people are not to blame for their ignorance, we may say that they lie under a potential duty of fair play that will typically come into effect when they have adequate information.

Even this conclusion needs qualification in one respect. If a factual issue crucial to the duty is highly complex and the individual is, after careful thought, unconvinced by the information and arguments presented, then he does not lie under a duty of fair play even if adequate efforts to inform him have been made. A pacifist who is convinced that all military efforts are counterproductive in the long run and therefore military expenditures do not benefit him is not under a duty of fair play to contribute, even though he may be factually mistaken about the value of the benefit and may have been provided adequate information on that score.

The import of mistaken normative judgments is sometimes different from that of mistaken factual judgments. If someone is aware of relevant facts about benefits conferred but does not grasp the implications of those facts for his own responsibility, then he lies under a duty of fair play. Duties of fairness, like other duties, do not depend on one's actually perceiving what fairness requires if one is aware of the facts that make certain actions required by fairness. We do not hesitate to say someone has violated a duty of fairness or acted unfairly when he is morally insensitive to what fairness requires; though such condemnations do not seem quite apt when a conscientious person fails to understand the dimensions of a duty, we nonetheless suppose that the duty applies.

Other kinds of normative mistakes, however, may relieve one of the duty of fair play. Suppose a pacifist accepts all the facts put forward for military defense, but believes that the use and threat of force are absolutely wrong. The "benefit" of defense is, on normative grounds, not one he wants. Even if *this* normative position is mistaken, he lacks a duty of fair play to contribute for something he does not want. Normative mistakes that are remote from the requirements of fairness itself are relevant in the same way as factual mistakes.

Nonvoluntarist and Unjust Political Orders

Once we accept the idea that the fair play duty can apply to benefits not voluntarily received, we can see that the power of the duty is not limited to voluntarist and just political orders.

Illustration 7-3:

Constance lives in a village occupied by an invading army. To deal with the village's severe water shortage, the army's commander sets strict limits on use of water and requires each citizen to transport a certain amount of water each day from a stream that is one mile away from the village. Constance thinks both the invasion and the commander's peremptory imposition of the scheme are unjust, but she regards the compulsory aspect of the scheme and the allocation of benefits and burdens as fair. She knows that cheating by a few people who fail to bring water or make excessive use of it will not undermine the system; she also knows that most people will observe the restraints out of a sense of fairness to their fellow villagers.

Constance has a duty of fair play to her fellows not to cheat. Her duty arises out of their cooperative behavior that confers on her the benefits of water use. The point of this example can be generalized to whole political orders and their laws.

Illustration 7-4:
A militaristic neighbor conquers a small democratic country, Pastoria, to render its own borders more secure. Wishing to keep the Pastorian population as sympathetic as possible, the invaders keep all basic laws in place. Revenues are spent much as before, and the invader finances its military forces and governing apparatus from its own treasury.

The Pastorians owe no moral duty to the new government as such, but what of their duty to their fellow citizens concerning laws that establish mutual restraints and impose financial burdens for public programs? The duty to one's fellow citizens should not shift radically when, through no fault of theirs, the government has suddenly become illegitimate. In fact, after invasions or internal takeovers by autocratic regimes, the basic rules of criminal and civil law of previously democratic societies often do not change very much. The bulk of German criminal and civil law did not change radically under Hitler or during allied occupation, and the Communist countries of Eastern Europe still have criminal and civil codes that are not very different in their proscription of acts that threaten personal security from the codes that have long existed in civil law countries. It would be surprising if the moral duties of citizens with respect to these laws lapsed suddenly with the change in political power. Regarding these kinds of laws, a reflective citizen who had lived *all his life* under a morally illegitimate government might still recognize the fairness of his share of burdens borne.

Both the water hauling scheme and laws protecting personal security benefit participants in obvious ways. But we are ready now to see that the duty of fair play can arise even if a scheme as a whole confers no benefits on the participants.

Illustration 7-5:
The water to be hauled by villagers in Illustration 7-3 is to be consumed exclusively by the invading troops. If insufficient water is brought, villagers will be shot at random. Many villagers haul water not only to save themselves but to protect their fellows, including Constance.

As long as Constance receives and accepts this life-saving benefit of the cooperative effort, she has a duty of fair play to do her share.

This last illustration has important implications for what renders someone an appropriate member of the group making the contribution and for the outer limits of a duty of fair play. Suppose the invaders are unaware of Constance's existence and she could escape from the village without danger. She would prefer that the water hauling scheme not exist at all, and in that sense she is not voluntarily involved in it. Nevertheless, if she has always been a member of the village, and is so identified by herself and others, she may rightly feel she has a responsibility to carry a share of a burden imposed on the group of villagers including herself. If the burden is to be borne by villagers, she is appropriately a member of that group.

Interestingly here, as long as she is a member of the class other villagers seek to benefit, she may have a duty of fair play, even if the possibility of escape makes her capable of doing without the benefit.

One limit of the duty is tested if we imagine that Constance alone among the villagers is aware that because the invaders have underestimated the number of villagers, the amount of water brought when everybody does his or her assigned share is more than is needed by the invaders, who mistakenly think that some villagers are making extra trips. May Constance simply stop hauling water, which she knows is contributing to an unnecessary surplus? If Constance can relieve the burden more generally, by setting up a plan by which different villagers get days off, she should do that. But perhaps telling the other villagers of the surplus will run too high a risk that the invaders will find out, and increase the total amount of water demanded. If Constance has a good moral reason not to inform the other villagers, and her own failure to haul water will not be noticed by them, and thus will not undermine morale and cause resentment, perhaps the duty of fair play does not require her to do something that serves no useful purpose from the villagers' point of view. Her fortuitous and exclusive knowledge may place her in a unique position, different from that of the other villagers. This tentative conclusion suggests how greatly ordinary notions of fair play depend on general agreement among contributors about what contributions are to be or on either shared knowledge of free-riding opportunities or a realistic possibility of spreading relief from excess contributions. When none of these conditions is present, there may be no duty to contribute in the way that others are doing.

John Rawls suggested that a cooperative scheme must be just for the duty of fair play to arise.[20] We have seen that, to the contrary, a scheme that is unjustly imposed on an innocent population may give rise to a duty of fair play. This conclusion yields a certain irony. Imagine that Constance is subject to an inappropriate scheme, one that employs compulsion when only voluntary adherence would be morally acceptable or one that promotes ends, such as aiding the invader, that no participant should have to serve. If the scheme has been freely decided upon by most of those contributing to it, in one respect it has less power to generate a fair play duty than if the scheme is imposed by an invading army. When most of those contributing adopt the scheme, they are the ones who are imposing unfairly on others whose contributions are demanded, and that unfair imposition may preclude the generation of a duty of fair play; when the scheme is imposed by outsiders, the bulk of participants have done nothing wrong to those whose contribution is demanded, and the duty of fair play to the bulk of participants is not undermined. (In another respect, explored later, the legitimacy of the process by which a scheme is adopted can enhance the claim that one has a duty of fair play to obey.)

A different way in which a scheme can be unjust is by unfairly exploiting nonparticipants to the advantage of participants. Slavery and unfair restraints of trade are examples. Assuming that one participant benefits from the cooperation and restraint of other participants, does he have a duty of fair play to contribute his share? One possible answer is that one can never be obligated to do what is wrong; but I have suggested in the chapter on promissory obligation that that answer is wrong; and if promises to do wrong have some moral weight, so also may obligations of fair play arise for schemes that involve moral wrongs. Of course, the morally proper response may be never to accept benefits from an immoral scheme, but if one does immorally choose to accept the benefits or has done so in the past, one may lie under a duty of fair play to other participants to do one's share in the future.

The claim here is not, of course, that one should, on balance, make the contribution; the duty of fair play may be outweighed by other moral responsibilities. Indeed, we should expect in the case of an isolated scheme to do wrong that the duty of fair play would rarely be strong enough to dictate a contribution to the immoral scheme.

The answer may become more complicated when the wrongful activity is only one of the many relations in which people are joined. Illuminating examples involve activities of countries that promote national interests at the unjust expense of populations outside their borders, when those activities involve restraint and sacrifice by citizens of the country whose interest is served. The citizen who realizes the injustice can be faced with an immensely troubling question of whether or not his duty to his fellow citizens outweighs the moral reasons not to promote the injustice.

The Attitudes of Other Participants

The duty of fair play exists for someone who accepts benefits under a cooperative scheme. One essential aspect of such a scheme is that the contributions or restraint of others provide a benefit that the person wants. Is that enough, or must the others be making their contributions with a certain attitude? Must they be acting in a cooperative spirit or at least with a degree of disinterest?

Selfish reasons for entering a cooperative scheme do not undermine a duty of fair play;[21] the tennis court example shows that. But it is highly doubtful if a duty exists when others *observe* the rules only because of their fear of sanctions or other interferences with self-serving interests.

Illustration 7-6:
Two distrustful strangers meet shortly before both are to be attacked by marauding outlaws. Each realizes that, whatever the other does, he will have a better chance to live if he runs away, as long as coordination is not possible. Each also realizes that if both stay and fight, they will both have a better chance to live than if both run away. The diagram indicates the possibilities.

CHANCES OF SURVIVAL

	A runs	*A stays and fights*
B runs	A—25% B—25%	A—10% B—90%
B stays and fights	A—90% B—10%	A—60% B—60%

The strangers distrust each other so completely that neither is willing to count on any agreement to stay and fight; but they do agree that they will simultaneously chain each other to their posts, and they do so. Neither is counting on the other's sense of obligation and each knows that the other is not counting on him. B has managed to effectively chain A, but A has botched the job. B realizes in the midst of the attack that he can manage to run away.[22]

Since neither stranger has asked for or counted on the other's self-restraint, B probably has no duty of fair play to stay. The duty of fair play arises when the self-restraint of most participants flows from a sense of what is owed to others, and that sense is absent here. True, A has shown B the minimal respect of not pulling his gun on B and chaining B while he, A, remained unchained. But this degree of restraint from doing a wrong to B, which B has already reciprocated, would not seem enough to ground a duty for B to stay and protect A. More generally, if all initial agreement does is to produce an effective engine of sanctions, a model not far removed from Hobbes's idea of the creation of government,[23] and if compliance flows *solely* from fear of sanctions, participants do not have a duty of fair play to each other.[24]

The law of unjust enrichment provides an interesting analog for this moral question. The legal question is whether, when one person's pursuit of his own aims confers incidental benefits on another, the second person has a duty to contribute or to compensate the first for these efforts. Traditionally the indirect receipt of benefits produced by the self-interested actions of others has not been a source of a duty to pay, but Philip Soper points to contrary authority involving lawyers' fees, and suggests that one's moral duty may be broader than one's legal duty.[25] No doubt, uncertainty about the value of benefits someone has taken no positive steps to acquire does point in this direction. This uncertainty, which prevails if benefits and costs are not purely monetary, is a strong reason against any general rule of legal recovery; but the difficulty of outsiders calculating benefits has little bearing on the moral duty of a person who does regard a benefit as well worth the share he might pay.[26] On the other hand, rather different reasons suggest that a moral duty might be less extensive than one's legal duty.[27] Recovery for lawyers' fees might be mainly a utilitarian technique for encouraging suits when many people suffer small similar losses and problems of coordination and prospective free riding discourage litigation unless those who do pay for it are assured of contributions from others who benefit. If this were the basis for the legal rule, it would have little bearing on the moral duty of the incidental beneficiary who has not intentionally manipulated the situation to his advantage.

If purely self-interested compliance with rules is not enough to give rise to a duty of fair play, what sorts of motivations are adequate? Most clearly qualifying is the sense among participants who comply with rules that they are involved in a cooperative scheme and they owe restraint to their fellow participants. But as long as the participants restrain themselves from some sense of duty and recognize that those who stand to gain are their fellow citizens, that should be sufficient to generate a reciprocal duty of fairness to comply. It should ordinarily be enough, then, if fellow participants restrain themselves out of a sense of duty to the government, or out of a sense that independent moral reasons make contrary behavior a wrongful violation of moral rights, or even out of a deeply engrained "habit" of social morality in which are embedded views about the limits of self-aggrandizement. In sum, while a prudential fear of sanctions is not a motive for restraint that triggers a reciprocal fair play duty, other, broadly "moral," motives that involve some notion of sacrifice of self-interest are sufficient.

This conclusion lays the groundwork for a brief examination of the attitudes most people have about why their fellow citizens observe rules and contribute to the government. Our earlier discussion suggested that an individual actually lies under a duty of fair play only if he or she understands the critical facts that give rise to the duty or is to blame for not understanding those facts. John Simmons bases a profound skepticism about the application of the duty of fair play to political communities largely on his conclusion that many citizens regard benefits "as purchased (with taxes) from a central authority, rather than as accepted from the cooperative efforts of our fellow citizens."[28] This view gives tax payments an unwarranted centrality and constricts too narrowly the kinds of motivations of others that give rise to the duty of fair play. What is plausible in the position concerns the scope of the duty of fair play more than its existence.

Because Simmons is mainly concerned with a general obligation to obey all laws, he may be thinking in terms of some overall package of benefits; but certainly if we focus on discrete collections of law-related benefits, the view that they are purchased with taxes is unrealistic. Everyone benefits from observance of rules that prohibit personal violence and define and protect personal property. Since the state is usually not able to repair fully damage done in violation of those rules, it clearly matters to us whether people refrain in the first instance from assaulting us or stealing our property. Because taxes obviously do not directly buy such restraint, the idea that this crucial benefit is purchased by taxes must be that the taxes purchase enforcement mechanisms and that the fear of sanctions and other motives for restraint that enforcement produces do not involve the kind of sacrifice that could generate a duty of fair play. Contrary to this assumption, most people do restrain themselves partly out of a sense of duty, and I have argued that this is sufficient motive to give rise to the duty. Any person blind to the sense of duty of fellow citizens would be to blame for holding that perception, and the duty of fair play would exist despite this ignorance of relevant facts.

For benefits that are more plausibly "purchased" with taxes, a citizen needs to ask why other people pay their taxes. With the exception of such things as license fees, no one person's taxes directly buy the benefits that person receives. If other citizens pay taxes exclusively out of fear of punishment, then a person has no duty of fair play to pay his own taxes; but if others pay partly because of a sense of moral duty, then a fair play duty to pay is generated. We can now see that the idea that people "purchase" benefits with taxes is ambiguous in its implications. If a sense of duty helps explain why others pay their taxes, what the purchase idea establishes is not the absence of a duty of fair play, but a duty that is limited to tax paying. Any premise that many people conceive that benefits are purchased with taxes appropriately leads to skepticism over the existence of a duty of fair play in political communities *only* if all important benefits are so understood and the predominant motivation for paying taxes is conceived as fear of enforcement, *and* a person is not to blame for holding these two views. I doubt that many people do, after reflection, hold either of these views and my own contrary assessment leads me to conclude that those who do hold the views are to blame for holding them.

THE SCOPE OF DUTY

The nonvoluntary nature of political orders and of many of the benefits they provide does not prevent duties of fair play from arising, but it does drastically affect their scope. For a number of reasons, the duty is considerably more limited than a duty to obey all laws on all occasions.

General Noncompliance

The first and most obvious point is that many laws are not obeyed by most people. In many localities in the United States, laws against jaywalking and driving over fifty-five miles an hour on highways come immediately to mind. In some societies, pervasive violation of currency restrictions and tax liabilities occurs. Since the duty of fair play requires only that one contribute one's fair share, it does not demand that someone comply with legal norms that are flouted by everyone else.

More generally, what many people may expect of themselves and others may be a hard-to-define tolerable level of observance, with some rules disobeyed to some extent some of the time. Consider the quantifiable matter of taxes. Suppose Paul learns that people on the average do not pay five percent of the income taxes they owe, that most people avoid between two and ten percent and are aware they are doing so. Whatever Paul thinks about other moral duties (he may regard lying on a tax return as immoral), he does not have a duty of fair play to carry a heavier burden than others are doing. But at least some very conscientious people are paying their prescribed amount of taxes and doing so out of a sense of duty; what of Paul's duty of fair play to them? It may matter here how high a percentage the very conscientious are and what attitudes they have. The greater their number, the more one may have a duty to respond to their behavior. If the very conscientious are led to believe that by complying with the legal requirements they are exactly fulfilling their intended share of the burden, then anyone who supports the system that encourages their ignorance may owe them the same level of sacrifice. If people who pay their legally prescribed amounts realize they are paying more than their intended *share*, their choice of full compliance may not create a reciprocal duty in others.

Thought about legal rules that are generally not observed exposes the practical significance of the concern that the duty of fair play is really not a theory about obligation to obey the law as such. The concern most broadly expressed is that the duty arises out of the actions of others rather than the rules themselves. As long as most people take the rules to define what is appropriate behavior and comply with the rules, this concern seems little more than a quibble; the rules are determining what the sacrifices of others are and lay the parameters for the duty of fair play. But when people generally do not comply with the rules, we can see that the rules no longer set what is required by fair play.

Fair Shares and the Import of the Duty of Fair Play

Even when most other people are complying with the law, a person may think that the duty of fair play does not require his compliance. I will examine three broad kinds of situations in which this may be so: when a person thinks the law gives rise to no duty in general or in a particular application; when a person thinks noncompliance will meet whatever duty would be met by compliance; and when a person thinks that his prescribed share is too great. The initial discussion of these matters will focus on particular laws or groups of laws; only in a final subsection will I inquire about the possible application of a duty to obey all laws because of the broad compliance of other citizens with laws in general.

The appropriateness of individual judgment on these matters is largely a consequence of the nonvoluntary nature of political orders.[29] Faced with the tennis court scheme, the Monroes had to decide whether to participate or not, and if they did participate they had to contribute their prescribed share. Since they could choose to take the benefits or not, they were not morally free to redefine the nature of the scheme in the way they preferred. Because in political communities people are neither free to refuse most benefits of government nor to escape most legal duties, the "scheme" does not have the take it or leave it character of the tennis court. As our example of the pacifist shows, people considering the force of their moral duty need not accept the judgments of the community about what count as benefits; nor need they accept the community's judgment of how much a fair share is or of how to contribute that share.

Belief That No Duty Arises

A person may think that part of the law is wholly illegitimate.[30] For example, Paul, who has "deviant" sexual inclinations, may believe that laws forbidding sexual acts among consenting adults do not involve mutual restraint for mutual benefit, but rather satisfy the moralistic bent of some people at the expense of a minority of which he is a part, severely inhibiting strong desires that help define his very personality.

In part, Paul's challenge is that the majority has no wish to commit the acts involved anyway; though they may suppose the acts are morally wrong, they lack any inclination to commit them and thus need exercise no restraint themselves. This much might also be said of the laws against forcible rape,[31] since most people have no wish to commit that act; but other features distinguish rape laws from the laws against consenting sexual behavior. There can be no doubt that the interests protected by the law against rape warrant protection; few rapists would themselves like to be subject to violent sexual assault. We can be rather sure that even if most people had some inclination to commit rape, there would still be a law against it. For these reasons, the person who would like to commit rape must still consider the laws against it to be proper, and should view those laws as part of a package of restraints against personal violence that do operate for mutual benefit.

Paul, who wishes to commit consenting sexual acts, may take a different view of the laws that restrain him. If he lives in a liberal society, or himself accepts liberal principles, he may strongly doubt that the interest such laws protect are even legitimate,[32] and he will certainly believe that if most people had serious inclinations to commit such acts,[33] the laws against them would disappear. Unlike the prospective rapist, he may suppose that those laws are not a proper part of a package of restraints that overall is reasonably fair to him. Believing that the laws are fundamentally unjust, he may think they generate no duty of fair play to comply.

With respect to other sorts of laws, neither their general legitimacy nor their actual coverage may be challenged, but someone may think they generate no duty of fair play on certain occasions. The tennis court scheme shows that the duty of fair play can be violated though no one is actually harmed by the Monroes playing and not paying rather than not playing; but even such violations involve a person's "taking advantage" of the sacrifices of others—sacrifices needed to confer the benefits—without making a similar sacrifice. Some violations of law need not involve either harm to others or taking advantage in this manner. Ruth, who breaks a thirty-mile-per-hour speed limit at 4:00 A. M., or trespasses far from anyone's sight, may believe that it would be perfectly all right if everyone acted in the same way. She is indifferent to whether others forbear from such acts, since their forbearance confers no benefit on her.

It might be argued that Ruth's conclusion either rests on an assumption about the law's impropriety as applied *or* mistakenly neglects the benefits of the forbearances of others from individual judgment. If Ruth strongly believed that the relevant speed limits should be much more flexible, she might think some instances of coverage to be definitely erroneous (illegitimate would be too strong a word here); but she may well suppose, instead, that clearness of notice and simplicity of enforcement justify general rules that cover some occasions when observance of the rules is actually not warranted by their purpose. In the concrete context, she may think no exception should be made to the thirty-mile-per-hour speed limit, although sometimes driving over that speed is safe.[34]

Ruth's acceptance of the appropriateness of the law as written does not necessarily imply that she thinks she benefits from other individuals declining to exercise their own judgments about what is safe driving. She *might* think that general and rigid rules, if widely observed, do produce that benefit; and if she thought that in connection with the thirty-mile-per-hour speed limit, she might have a duty of fair play not to exercise her own judgment. But she might, consistently with her belief about simple enforcement, think that for many situations individual judgment is a safe guide and be happy to have others exercise it; in that event, the duty of fair play to obey the speed limit would not arise for those situations.

Meeting the Duty of Fair Play by Noncompliance

On some occasions a person who accepts the existence of a duty of fair play and the fairness of his share may suppose that he can fully satisfy his duty without complying with the rules. In the most obvious cases, someone may believe that acceptance of punishment will satisfy all the aims of a system of restraint. Joan may accurately report her income but openly refuse to pay taxes, knowing that the government will be able to exact from her enough to cover the taxes owed and its enforcement expenses. Such behavior does not involve a genuine failure to contribute her share of taxes.

In other circumstances, a person may acknowledge that disobedience does produce some adverse effects that the law is designed to avoid but think that the overall effect will be to benefit fellow citizens. Suppose Joan trespasses at a nuclear weapons facility, fully expecting arrest and conviction. Few other citizens will think that she has treated them *unfairly* by violating the law if she sacrifices her immediate interests for their long-term welfare, undertaking a burden that is much more onerous than what they are called upon to do by the law. And even if others should happen to regard following the rules as required by fairness, Joan need not accept that perspective.

The Duty of Fair Play and Unfair Shares

Individuals might welcome the benefits they receive from a scheme, understanding that the restraint and contributions of others make those benefits possible, and yet think that they are being asked to carry an unfair share of the burdens. What would their duty be if their share was unfair, and how might they arrive at the judgment of unfairness?

The basic answer to the first question is that one's duty is to contribute a share that would be fair. John Simmons suggests that the duty of fair play does not arise at all if people "believe that the benefits received from the governments are not worth the price they are forced to pay."[35] His supposition that many people have precisely this attitude is one basis for his conclusion that "citizens generally in no actual states will be bound under the principle of fair play."[36] I will indicate later why I think this particular supposition itself is implausible, but here I want to explore its implications.

Simmons assumes that acceptance of benefits includes belief that they are worth the price, but if the benefits are open and separated from the process of contribution, a person could welcome the benefits while thinking the demanded contribution too high. If the benefits are attainable only because of the contributions of others, the person who rightly thinks he is being charged too much is bound in fairness to contribute a fair amount. In making acceptance of benefits necessary for the duty and treating acceptance in the political context as including belief that the benefits are worth the price, Simmons arbitrarily constricts the scope of the duty of fair play as it relates to law.

We can imagine at least three arguments that might be employed to defend Simmons's position as it applies to the balance of benefits and burdens, or, more generally, to unfair shares.

First, if the scheme is grossly unwarranted or unfair, one may have no duty of fair play to support it even if one receives some benefits one welcomes.[37] Such a judgment, which would require an estimate of available alternatives, might well be made, but it hardly applies to every case in which one thinks that benefits are not worth the price or that one's share is otherwise unfair.

A second defense of the Simmons position would be that if the issue is either-or—observance of the rules or not—and the duty of fair play does not demand observance, then, practically, the duty is of no effect. The problem with this argument is that it misconceives the nature of many obligations that derive from law. With tax obligations, a crucial part of a citizen's duties to the state, the issue is more or less, not either-or. A person whose only complaint is that the benefits are worth half of what he or she is charged has a duty of fair play to pay at least half. Even with more ordinary disobedience of law, such as speeding or petty theft from one's employer, questions arise about how often and how severely one will violate legal rules. The duty of fair play can have importance even if it does not require strict compliance on every occasion.

The third defense is that Simmons is interested in a duty of fair play that requires compliance with every law on every occasion. I agree that if the benefits of government are not as great as the burdens or if one's demanded share is unfair, then one does not have *such* a duty; but to focus exclusively on such a powerful form of the duty of fair play is wholly to miss its significance in many circumstances.

One's judgment about whether one is being asked to contribute a fair amount to some cooperative scheme will involve evaluation of a number of highly complex factors. Here I content myself with exploring these factors, not trying to provide concrete guidelines about how one would reach an overall judgment of unfairness. One standpoint of appraisal undoubtedly is a comparison of total benefits and total burdens. Unless a person is an anarchist or believes that his society is extremely repressive toward him, he will probably conclude on due consideration that the total benefits he receives from government and law exceed the total costs of his required contribution.[38] Life without law and government would, after all, be extremely rudimentary and highly insecure, if indeed we can even imagine it over any extended period of time.[39] In light of this, Simmons's supposition that many people think burdens outweigh benefits is puzzling; and, in the absence of a thoroughly worked out anarchist position, anyone who holds that view in a reasonably fair society is to blame for failing to give minimal reflection to the matter.

A second standpoint of appraisal is a comparison of marginal benefits and marginal costs. A person may think that the benefit–cost ratio would be much better under a different sort of government, one that could provide similar benefits at much less cost or add other benefits, at little cost, that his own government fails to give. A dissenter in a Communist country may believe, for example, both that economic benefits could be provided at less cost and that a non-Communist government could afford important political liberties now denied. Some people believe that beyond a core of virtually invaluable services, what their government does is wasteful or counterproductive.

In the United States, a significant minority of the population may hold this view about military expenditures. Imagine Nora, who pays $4000 a year that goes to military purposes. Believing some degree of deterrence essential to preserve the country in its present form, she regards her first $1000 in tax money as buying protection for which she would be willing to pay $10,000, were the cost that high. But she views the next $3000 spent as wholly wasteful or adding very little to the level of security. "Is the total benefit to you of defense worth the $4000?" "Yes," she responds. "Is the added benefit of defense worth your last $3000?" "No," she answers. People who think a minimal state is essential to security but object to many state functions[40] may well have a similar attitude about the whole package purchased with their tax dollars.

Someone who thinks marginal benefits are priced much too high will suppose that a better government could provide equal or superior benefits at lower cost. He will conclude that the contribution demanded of him is too high, and, at least if he holds his fellow participants partly responsible for the mistaken choices, he will also conclude that his fair share is less than what is demanded.

Another perspective is comparative—one's own share of benefits and burdens compared with those of others. One might be satisfied with the package of total and marginal benefits given for one's contribution but still object if others one regards as relevantly similar are paying less for the same benefits, or getting more benefits for the same costs, or getting a higher proportion of the benefits they care most about.[41] In the absence of widespread, blatant, and obviously indefensible favoritism, any stand on appropriate comparative resource contribution will require controversial and difficult judgments about distributive justice and the comparative value of benefits. It will be a rare person who thinks his or her share is completely fair in relation to every other member of society. Many will suppose that they fare better than they should vis-á-vis some parts of the population and worse than they should vis-á-vis others. Anyone who thinks his own share is roughly what it should be will have a duty of fair play owed to those less or equally fortunate to contribute that share.[42]

Thus far I have avoided the problem of people on whom special burdens are placed, burdens such as criminal penalties or highly dangerous military service. If one violates a duty of fair play to obey the law in the first instance, the duty may extend to submission to an appropriate penalty, even though the penalty involves a burden much more onerous than other people have to bear. The implications of a fair play theory of punishment need not be developed in detail for us to see that special burdens imposed because of previous violations are fair in principle. Highly dangerous military service for draftees is more troublesome. Without any wrongdoing or voluntary choice to pursue that course, a soldier may be required to sacrifice his life for his fellow citizens. How can that be a fair distribution of burdens? The answer lies in an *ex ante* appraisal of risk. If a country occasionally needs a draft and the draft is fair, each citizen (or male citizen) faces a risk that he will be drafted at some point and required to put his life in grave danger. *Ex ante* this risk is widely shared and the chances that any individual will actually find himself a draftee in grave danger are slight. The benefits of government and law are worth the costs, including this risk discounted by its unlikelihood. The draftee who finds himself called upon to expose himself to grave danger may view his compliance as called for by the duty of fair play if the *ex ante* risk is reasonable and the process by which he was placed in that position is fair.

Fairness of Shares and a Fair Political Order

My discussion of fairness of shares has thus far proceeded without reference to the fairness of the process by which benefits and burdens are assigned. I have briefly mentioned freedom of expression but only as one kind of benefit, not as a condition of a fair political process. I want now to ask what difference a fair process should make to one's evaluation of fairness of shares of burdens and benefits. I shall assume that a process that encourages open discussion and grants participants equal voice and influence is most fair. Such a process can affect judgment about one's share in a variety of ways.

Unless a majority has ganged up on a minority and virtually disregarded its interests, a process that is fair in the way I have described provides an important check on one's independent judgment about fairness. We must all recognize how biased we are in assessing our own claims; if we get what we initially think is short shrift from a process that is fair, we have cause to wonder whether we have misestimated our own claims in comparison with those of others. I am not invoking a skeptical view that no standard of fair shares exists other than what is arrived at by a fair process; rather, I assume that a fair process is more likely to produce a fair distribution of shares than decision by a few individuals or a narrow ruling class, and that individuals, realizing this fact, have more reason to revise their initial opinions about what is fair when their claims are rejected in a fair process than when they are rejected by an unfair one.

If one's interests are fairly considered and represented, that in itself may reduce the unfairness of the share that results. A draft limited to males provides a concrete example. Let us suppose that with modern warfare, adequate reasons apart from existing cultural prejudices do not exist for restricting combat duty and conscription to males.[43] A man legally subject to the draft may believe the system is unfair because it makes his risk of being drafted and of being placed in grave danger double what if would be if women were also subject to the draft. His knowledge that the limitation to men was approved by predominantly male legislatures in which interests like his were adequately represented may not remove his sense of unfairness, but it should temper it. What this illustration shows is that unfairness is not exclusively a question of what one gets and gives in comparison with others but is directly affected by the degree of consideration that has been given to one's interests and the attitudes of those finally responsible for deciding on benefits and burdens.

In at least one respect, a fair political process can make a claim of unfairness *stronger* than it would otherwise be, a point that is closely related to the earlier discussion of how the duty of fair play can arise when a scheme is unjustly imposed on participants. Nora's objection to her share of taxes is that the marginal benefits are inadequate, vast sums of money being squandered on unnecessary military hardware. If the military budget has been endorsed indirectly by most of the population, Nora can rightly conclude she is being improperly put upon by her misguidedly militaristic fellow citizens, though they are making similar sacrifices themselves. If an unpopular military dictator has imposed the expenditures on an unconsenting populace, Nora may feel that she owes it to her fellow citizens to contribute her fair proportion, though she believes all are being made to pay too much.[44]

A fair political process can affect the significance of unfair shares in two ways. Such a process may make unfair allocations of benefits and burdens more easily correctible; someone who is aware that unfair allocations are likely to be temporary may have stronger reason to contribute his prescribed share in the meantime than someone who thinks his unfair position is intractable. Further, shares of political opportunity and influence are important in their own right. A person who judges his own political share to be fair or disproportionately large may regard that as a kind of counterbalance to perceived unfairness of other sorts of shares when making an overall evaluation of benefits and burdens. Unfairness of tax burdens, for example, may loom as less significant overall if one has at least a fair share of political power. At the extreme, it might be thought that a fair share of political power is overwhelmingly important in relation to other matters and that one who has that share has no legitimate claim that his duty of fair play is diminished by unfairness in other kinds of shares. Such a view would either involve an overestimate of how likely fair political shares are to produce fairness in other respects or reflect an unwarranted assumption about the comparative significance of political participation and other aspects of people's lives.

Among large political orders, vast differences exist in the fairness of processes by which benefits and burdens are allocated, and these differences should affect assessments of the fairness of shares in the ways indicated. In even the fairest political orders, large variations in power and influence exist, so that in each modern society there are many people who can rightly claim they have less than a fair share of political participation.[45] These people lack a basis for tempering judgments that they are otherwise being treated unfairly and that this unfairness affects the scope of their duty of fair play.

Maintenance of Law in General

A critic might fairly comment that much of this chapter misses an important point by speaking of discrete benefits and burdens and not focusing on the legal system as a whole. All citizens benefit from the observance of law by other citizens, and one aspect of the duty of fair play may be to do one's share to maintain an overall fair system of law observance.[46] Viewed in this way, the duty may seem to reach all the laws of a society and to be a potential source of a general obligation to obey. In a small group setting, at least, such an argument would have considerable force. If the organization of the group is fair overall, noncompliance with rules in one domain could reasonably be viewed as unfair to those who observe the rules in other domains.

This perspective could alter one's view of some of the situations I have previously discussed. Suppose that Nora thinks her taxes are disproportionately high in comparison with those of other people, but she regards the distribution of political power and general principles of law observance as fair. She might now view her failure to pay her prescribed share of taxes as a failure to do her fair share in regard to the political system itself. Similarly, Joan's conclusion that she can satisfy all the reasons for compliance by declaring her tax liabilities and passively allowing the government to collect may also be subject to reexamination. By openly disobeying the law that requires her to pay, Joan may be failing to satisfy the overall objective of law observance. Even the claim about morally illegitimate laws might now look different; fair play in terms of general law observance might require compliance with occasional improper laws.

The fairness duty to maintain the legal order overall will apply only if the system overall is reasonably just. Here may lie the roots of the assumption by Rawls that the duty of fair play itself will apply only to just political orders. Although the duty to fellow citizens to maintain the legal order may typically be much weaker than duties that arise out of distributions of benefits and burdens more narrowly understood, it still is a significant aspect of the duty of fair play in fair political orders.

Nonetheless, the duty of fair play still falls considerably short of creating an obligation to obey all laws on all occasions. Citizens have a fair play duty only to do as much as their fellows; since most people do disobey many laws, no one has a fair play duty to do better in terms of law observance than they do. Further, if some sorts of violations, like driving over thirty miles per hour at 4:00 A.M., would do no harm even if everyone engaged in them—neither direct harm nor harm to law observance when it matters—an individual does not have a fair play duty to avoid the violations. Nor does the aspect of law observance really undermine Joan' claim that she is not violating a duty of fair play when she fails to pay her tax. Although Joan is failing to satisfy one reason for initial compliance, she is also subjecting herself to monetary penalties and a possible jail sentence, and she is doing so in an attempt to benefit her fellow citizens by highlighting the injustice of public expenditures. Because she is making a greater sacrifice than others, she may feel she is contributing as much as, or more than, her prescribed share, although she is not doing so in the legally prescribed way. Given the nonvoluntary nature of the political order, she is free morally to decide *how* to contribute her share, and she can still maintain that she is fully meeting her moral responsibility not to take advantage of others.

Finally, the substantial unfairness of even the best political orders affects the practical import of this wider duty to maintain the legal order. Those who have neither a fair share of political power nor a fair share of other benefits will not have a duty of fair play to do as much as their more favored fellows to maintain the overall system.

FAIR PLAY AND GOVERNMENT OFFICIALS

The duty of fair play has been widely conceived as being owed to fellow citizens, but we can imagine the possibility that it would be unfair to those in authority to disobey the law. Indeed, one way of understanding Philip Soper's argument that we should not break the law because doing so will cause disappointment and frustration among government officials[47] is that we owe these officials a duty of fair play.

This version of the duty of fair play has some force at the level of small associations when people exercise authority out of a sense of duty to promote a common enterprise.

Illustration 7-7:
Ten friends decide to form a basketball team for a local recreation league. They ask another friend, Walt, if he will agree to be their coach, with responsibility to schedule practices, decide on lineups and substitutions, and plan defenses and simple offensive plays. Walt, who lacks any ambition to coach the team, agrees for the sake of his friends and carries out these responsibilities.

If the team members fail without good reason to show up for practice or refuse to come out of a game when Walt directs, they are acting unfairly toward him as well as toward their teammates. (Because they are also breaking an implied promise, this would be one of the many occasions in which the duty of fair play overlaps with a promissory obligation.)

This duty of fair play toward persons with authority may have a limited scope in the context of a legal order. Persons do often find themselves in a personal relationship with particular officials, such as welfare officers and public school teachers. If those officials put themselves out on behalf of a citizen, the citizen may have a duty of fair play to comply with the official's directives. But when one contemplates disobeying a general law in a way not connected to any particular official, the idea of fair play to officials is stretched too far.

The problems concern both the reasons for performance of official duty and what might amount to an unfair response by citizens. The taking of public office does not usually involve the kind of restraint or sacrifice of self-interest that ordinarily triggers a duty of fair play. Though some officials seek their positions from a sense of duty, most officials occupy their positions because they desire to have them. Many feel that a job that serves others is particularly worthwhile and rewarding; their attitude is somewhat unselfish, but the officials who have that attitude do not regard themselves as making sacrifices when they take office. The performance of official duties is more complex, often involving a mix of wishing to do a job well, desiring recognition, and wanting to serve others effectively. On particular occasions, the latter motive may predominate, and a sense of duty to the public may also figure in an official's refusal to take improper advantage of his or her position, say by accepting a bribe.

Officials expect a certain amount of disobedience of laws, and some of their jobs actually rest on that disobedience. Lawbreaking can hardly be an unfair act toward police officers and criminal court judges generally. And the connection between law violation and the official performance of legislators and high executive officials seems too remote to consider in terms of fair play. Acts that frustrate their performance or undermine their effectiveness may be unfair to officials, but most kinds of violations of law do not fall into this category.

In sum, fair play to officials could hardly underlie a broad obligation to obey all laws on all occasions. While it may on some occasions add something to the notion of fair play to fellow citizens, it usually figures less prominently.

GRATITUDE AND ITS RELATION TO FAIR PLAY

One possible source of a duty to obey the law is gratitude. Gratitude has been little discussed as a moral duty in recent literature and is sometimes treated as mainly a matter of etiquette; however, John Simmons, drawing from older philosophers who took the duty very seriously,[48] argues persuasively that when someone greatly benefits us we may have a genuinely moral debt to discharge, requiring actions that go well beyond expressions of thanks.[49] Like the duty of fair play, the duty of gratitude is based on the receipt of benefits; the relationship between the two duties is subtle. I will briefly explore that relationship, before examining the relevance of gratitude to obedience of law and concluding that it is not of great significance.

The duty of gratitude might be thought in a particular circumstance either to have the same scope as the duty of fair play or to reach further than that duty. In the event of identical coverage, the duty of gratitude might be merely another perspective for looking at the same obligation prescribed by fair play, adding no special moral force; or the duty of gratitude could take on independent practical importance by strengthening the force of the reasons to do an act or designating more precisely what act was to be performed. The duty of fair play is grounded in part on appreciation that others are playing their parts in a cooperative scheme out of a sense of duty; if the actions of others do not go beyond this in some respect, to speak of a duty of gratitude would simply be to reiterate an aspect of the duty of fair play. But if the person doing his or her duty does so in an especially caring manner or has chosen to undertake particular duties because of deep concern for others (one thinks of many underpaid nurses, for example), then responsive feelings of gratitude are appropriate; and a duty of gratitude might genuinely reinforce one's own responsibilities to do one's share.

Duties of gratitude, as Simmons points out, are among the least specific in designating what acts are required.[50] People who owe such duties are typically free to determine what acts will express their gratitude. Although it might mandate a kind of good will that is not a component of fair play, a duty of gratitude would not yield a more specific designation of what acts to do than fair play does.

The main practical importance of a duty of gratitude depends on its reaching circumstances not covered by the duty of fair play. Both duties arise when others have voluntarily conferred benefits that, on reflection, one values and does not mind receiving in the way they have been conferred.[51] The acts that trigger the duty of fair play are performances of responsibilities in a cooperative scheme; distinct duties of gratitude arise from acts that go beyond these in some way. The most obvious instances are those in which someone else does much more than is required by duty, an act of extraordinary generosity, for example. But the bare performance of certain moral duties, such as saving the life of a drowning swimmer, may also create debts of gratitude.[52] If one person confers a very specific benefit on another when doing so is not his specially defined social responsibility (the rescuer is not a paid lifeguard) and is particularly praiseworthy, then the person benefited may owe a debt of gratitude, though the person conferring the benefit had a moral duty to do so.

In some situations, the distinction between a duty of fair play and a duty of gratitude may depend on how clear social conventions are about appropriate performances by the persons involved. To show how a duty of gratitude can arise from performance of a moral duty, Simmons uses an example of a person who damages his car driving a gravely injured person over rough roads to the hospital. If it were clearly understood in society that drivers had to take gravely injured people to hospitals and that the injured should pay for damage to the drivers' cars, then the duty to pay would be one of fair play rather than gratitude. Even though one would not know in advance what responsibilities one might end up having, the arrangement could still be seen as a cooperative one, designed to minimize for each citizen the risk of dying because no one would drive him or her to a hospital.

The duty of fair play has generally been seen as arising only if one is subject to reciprocal obligations at the time one receives benefits; however, our examination of initial ignorance casts this limit into question. We have seen that a person initially ignorant about benefits or the way they are provided can, upon acquiring the relevant facts, have a duty of fair play to pay for benefits received in the past. This notion may be extended to people who are incapable of understanding or of contributing when they receive benefits.

Illustration 7-8:

It is clearly established in Bunwate that parents have highly specific duties toward young children and that mature children have highly specific duties to infirm parents who have earlier performed their parental duties. Peter and Paula have performed their duties, and have done so partly in the expectation of subsequent compliance with the social convention by their children. Upon reaching adulthood, Christopher and Claudia realize how greatly they have profited from their parents' care, count that benefit much more than the burden on them of caring for their parents in their years of infirmity, and approve the social convention.

In this setting, one might well speak of the children's duty in terms of fair play rather than gratitude.

Whether gratitude or fair play is the appropriate language for this sort of situation is itself somewhat arbitrary; and if, as I have suggested, the duty of fair play relates partly to specificity of expectations about how those benefited will behave, the line between the two kinds of duty is bound to be blurred. Having chosen to construe fair play somewhat broadly, I now turn to the possible significance of a duty of gratitude that goes further and bears on whether one should obey the law.

The duty of gratitude could be seen as owed to the government or to fellow citizens. Conceivably, the beneficiary of particular acts of law observance that show him special concern might have a duty not to violate the legal rights of the person conferring the benefits, a duty that either reinforces or goes beyond the scope of the duty of fair play. But generally law observance is not especially praiseworthy nor does it appropriately engender feelings of gratitude, and one's duties to a broad class of fellow citizens are better understood in terms other than gratitude.

What of a duty of gratitude toward the government? The idea is that since we have received extensive benefits from it, we owe it a duty of gratitude that is satisfied by our obeying the government's directions. That such a duty can exist is certainly the import of the Crito, in which Socrates asserts that one reason he should not escape punishment is because of gratefulness to the "laws" of Athens, which have reared and educated him.[53]

Simmons doubts whether duties of gratitude can be owed to institutions.[54] He reasons that if an official does only what is required, no debt of gratitude arises; if the individual goes beyond the call of duty, then the debt of gratitude is toward him or her and not to the institution. Though he recognizes that individuals do feel debts of gratitude toward institutions such as colleges, Simmons thinks they are mistaken.

Simmons's skeptical position rests on an overly rigid distinction between institutions and the people that make them up. Certain institutions perform at a level that is higher than one could reasonably count on for an institution of that sort. At some colleges teaching is taken especially seriously and the professors take more time to prepare and improve their teaching styles than is common. At these schools, such diligence is regarded as a matter of duty among faculty members. Do the students who benefit have any debt of gratitude? They may not be able to single out individual faculty members who are owed gratitude, yet together with their predecessors the faculty has created a level of performance that is well above an acceptable level. Even when a student identifies a particular teacher as deserving a debt of gratitude for his or her extraordinary diligence in teaching students, certainly one appropriate responsive action is to be highly conscientious about institutional responsibilities, such as preparing for class and contributing to discussions.

These notions might be extended to gratitude for the particularly valuable acts of government officials, but the duty of gratitude would still have relatively little importance for observance of the law. The first reason is that, as already suggested, most official acts are ordinary performances of duty, not appropriately the subject of gratitude. The second reason is the indeterminateness of obligations of gratitude. If we owe our government gratitude for the special excellence of our political order, we should respond with some contribution to that

order; but that might take many other forms than meticulous observance of legal requirements.[55] At most, one could say that if a duty of
gratitude of this sort does exist, carefully complying with legal norms
would be one appropriate way to satisfy it. Such a duty could then be a
good reason for obeying the law on many occasions, though not one
that creates a particular obligation to act in such a way.

FAIR PLAY AND OTHER REASONS TO OBEY THE LAW

The duty of fair play is significant source of moral duty to obey laws,
although it does not support a general obligation to obey all laws and
its precise contours for the complex responsibilities imposed under a
legal order are debatable.

The relationship between this duty and other reasons to obey the
law are illuminating. In some circumstances the duty of fair play
overlaps with and *reinforces* a promissory obligation. A promissory
obligation is stronger if it also involves doing one's part in a cooperative scheme, and one's obligation to act fairly toward other participants is strengthened by a promise to do so. Our review has suggested
that the duty of fair play also reaches many situations in which no
express or implied promise is to be found.

The duty of fair play requires some actions that would not be called
for by a simple utilitarian theory. One way of looking at the duty in
those settings is that it sets distributional limits on the allocation of
burdens and benefits, demanding a fairer distribution of fewer total
benefits than a less fair distribution of a greater total. The duty also
bears a stronger and more positive connection with utilitarianism. The
most telling objection to a utilitarian account of obedience is that we
really do not have an unremitting moral responsibility to promote the
general welfare; we are often free to pursue our own interests at the
likely expense of the greater interests of others. The duty of fair play
shows why if others have restrained themselves for our benefit, our
attention to their interests is a matter of duty or obligation, something
we strongly ought to do. Whatever may be true about unselfish violations of law that are thought to benefit fellow citizens, violations that
are selfish or that promote the interests of a small subgroup or the
interests of persons outside the society do conflict with the duty of fair
play if they involve "taking advantage" of the restraints of the large
body of fellow citizens.

NOTES

1. Broad, On the Function of False Hypotheses in Ethics, 26 Intern. J. Ethics 377 (1916).
2. Hart, Are There Any Natural Rights?, 64 Phil. Rev. 175 (1955).
3. Id. at 185.
4. Rawls, Legal Obligations and the Duty of Fair Play, in S. Hook, ed., Law and Philosophy 3 (1964).
5. Id. at 10.
6. John Simmons uses a very similar scheme, involving a community well, for similar purposes. A. J. Simmons, Moral Principles and Political Obligations 126–27 (1979).
7. In most hypothetical cases in which the duty of fair play seems most clear, a plausible argument that a person is bound by express or implied consent can also be made. If the Monroes had simply moved into the development without comment on the scheme, it might be argued that they had impliedly consented to abide by all practices within the development of which they knew or could have learned. The caveat about their consistent rejection of the scheme is meant to meet this possibility. In any event, the main purpose of a clear case of the duty of fair play is to establish a standpoint from which variations can be considered. Even if the clear case involves some overlap with obligations of consent, that purpose would not be undermined. As subsequent discussion shows, the outer reaches of the duty of fair play include many situations for which no plausible consent argument could be mounted.
8. Rawls talks of cooperative schemes whose advantages depend on almost everyone's cooperating. Legal Obligation and the Duty of Fair Play, at 10. As John Simmons indicates, the duty of fair play can arise even if the success of the scheme does not depend on contributions by a high percentage of those who benefit and are supposed to contribute. Simmons, supra note 6 at 106. A scheme may be inefficient if it calls for contributions much in excess of what is needed to make it work, but if the share of contributions is fair, the duty of fairness arises nonetheless. Imagine, for example, that a plot of grass that is endangered will be saved if only forty percent of the residents henceforth desist from walking on it. If the cooperative scheme is that no one walk on the grass, and virtually everyone observes the rule against walking on the grass, every resident has a duty of fairness not to do so.
9. Rawls presupposes a constitutional democracy (Rawls, supra note 4 at 5) and speaks of "a mutually beneficial and just scheme of social cooperation" (Id. at 10). According to John Simmons, "[o]nly political communities which at least appear to be reasonably democratic will be candidates for a 'fair play account' to begin with." Simmons, supra note 6 at 136–37.
10. See, generally, E. Ullmann-Margalit, The Emergence of Norms 50 (1977); J. Rawls, A Theory of Justice 267 (1971).
11. Robert Nozick illustrates the point with ingenious examples. Anarchy, State and Utopia 93–95 (1974). See also Simmons, note 6 supra at 126–34 and

D'Amato, Obligation to Obey the Law: A Study of the Death of Socrates, 49 U. S. C. L. Rev. 1079, 1103–8 (1976).

12. Because of other benefits the pacifist receives, he might have a duty of fair play to pay his overall tax assessment, part of which goes for military expenditures.

13. See Simmons, supra note 6 at 132.

14. This conclusion may not hold if the issue is whether the money is to go to public television or another charity for which the need is greater. Perhaps the conditions I have specified are enough to make it unfair to take advantage of contributors by pursuing one's self-interest without considering the needs of public television but not enough to make it unfair to make equivalent sacrifices for other charities. Perhaps the fact that the scheme envisions voluntary contributions is sufficient to allow a beneficiary to weigh the need of public television against other needs.

15. Rawls, note 4 supra at 10.

16. Simmons, note 6 supra at 107.

17. Id. at 132.

18. See Chapter 3, Standards of Judgment and Terminology, and Chapter 5, Express, Tacit, and Implied Promises.

19. We might say, however, that "he did an act that was unfair."

20. Rawls, note 4 supra at 9–10. Simmons, note 6 supra at 109–14, effectively criticizes this limitation.

21. Simmons, note 6 supra at 172, says the duty of fair play can arise "even if the individuals' reasons for making the sacrifice [are] purely self-interested. . . ."

22. The illustration closely resembles the Mortarmen's Dilemma, discussed in E. Ullman-Margalit, note 10 supra at 30, as one variety of prisoners' dilemma.

23. See T. Hobbes, The Leviathan.

24. Ullmann-Margalit suggests various ways in which this sort of dilemma may be resolved to achieve the desirable response of both persons staying and fighting. Note 10 supra at 30–38.

25. P. Soper, A Theory of Law 70–73 (1984).

26. Id. at 73.

27. I here exclude from consideration a moral duty that *arises* because the legal duty is created. In this context, the use of the legal analogy is meant to help reveal what is an independent moral duty.

28. Simmons, note 6 supra at 139. Simmons asserts that many other citizens do not willingly accept benefits in the sense of thinking that the benefits are worth the burdens. That basis for skepticism about the duty of fair play is discussed in the text accompanying notes 35 and 36. Correspondence from Simmons reveals that, to a large extent, the point on which we disagree is the range of motivations by others that can give rise to the duty of fair play. He insists on a much stricter sense of *cooperation* than I do.

29. I use the word *largely* because a voluntary scheme may be *so* unjust

that one can, morally, take advantage of the benefits without complying with the rules. If the community requires blacks to pay twice as much as whites to use the tennis court, and the Monroes are the only black family wishing to play, they would not violate any duty of fair play if they report and pay for only half as many hours as they actually use the court. Indeed, it may be doubtful whether they have any duty of fair play at all to a group that has discriminated so sharply against them.

30. See Smith, Is There a Prima Facie Obligation to Obey the Law?, 82 Yale L. J. 950, 958 (1973), who claims that "virtually every legal system contains a number of pointless or even positively harmful laws."

31. I am considering "rape" here as synonymous with forcible sexual assault, disregarding traditional definitions that make it a crime that can be committed only by males against females who are not their spouses.

32. The basic claim would be that a liberal society should not preclude some people from acting merely because others feel disquiet about the acts. See, e.g., J. S. Mill, On Liberty; and H. L. A. Hart, Law, Liberty and Morality (1963). Whether or not such feelings are legitimately protected is a complex question in its own right; and those who support laws against consenting sexual acts among adults may also make arguments about physical and mental health, the protection of children, and the preservation of family life. The discussion in the text is meant to illustrate a perspective about laws that would bear on one's sense about any fair play duty, not to resolve whether some or all prohibitions on consenting sexual acts are actually illegitimate.

33. By "serious inclinations" I mean here conscious desires that people are strongly tempted to satisfy, not suppressed desires that may be unconscious roots of intolerance and prohibition.

34. More strictly, safety is comparative. What the person will think is that driving in excess of the speed limit on some occasions is no less safe than driving within the limit on most occasions.

35. Simmons, note 6 supra at 139. Simmons treats this attitude as relevant to whether benefits have been accepted voluntarily. Given the rule that one must pay taxes in full, he likely sees payment as an either-or matter. The possibilities of selective payments and of cheating on declarations give many people the practical opportunity to pay less than the amounts they legally owe.

36. Id. See text accompanying note 28 for another basis for his skepticism about the duty in the political context. Simmons recognizes at other points in his book (e.g., id. at 159) that the less fortunate may have duties to give some support to the law, though less than what the more fortunate should give.

37. See, e.g., Milner Ball's suggestion that the systemic injustice of modern states is so great that citizens lack an obligation to obey the law. Ball, Obligation: Not to the Law But to the Neighbor, 18 Ga. L. Rev. 911, 914, 921 (1984).

38. An exception to this generalization is a wartime soldier on a highly dangerous mission. Below, I explore the problem such situations raise in connection with comparative shares.

39. The sentence in the text does represent rejection of anarchist positions. I do not attempt to rebut those positions nor to explore complexities such as whether or not a legal order could exist without centrally organized coercive sanctions.

40. See R. Nozick, Anarchy, State and Utopia (1974).

41. An example would be a person in an unfree society who gets the same economic benefits for the same costs as others but who cares deeply about liberty of speech and recognizes that most of his fellows do not care at all about that. He might perceive himself as suffering a kind of comparative deprivation.

The text is not meant to cast doubt on the proposition that some differences in shares of burdens and benefits may be warranted and be so understood. For example, the rich may appropriately be asked to pay a higher proportion of their income in taxes than the poor.

42. What of the rich leftist who thinks his own share of taxes is much less than it should be? The duty of fair play would not seem to require that one do more than the share prescribed by the rules of the cooperative scheme, even if a better scheme would prescribe a greater share.

43. In *Rostker* v. *Goldberg*, 453 U. S. 57 (1981), the Supreme Court case upholding the restriction of draft registration to males, the constitutionality of a statutory ban on combat duty for women was a premise from which all the opinions began.

44. If the only consequence of her not paying her share of the unnecessary excess will be a slight decline in military expenditures, she may not have any duty of fair play to contribute that share, since it does not purchase benefits she wants; but if the consequence will involve penalties for other citizens, as in Illustration 7-5, or a shifting of burdens to other citizens, she may have a duty to pay all her prescribed share.

45. The term *unfair* is sometimes used to imply correctibility. Quite possibly, differences in power and influence are unavoidable in a large political order. If so, those with less than an equal (or ideally appropriate) share are not necessarily being *treated* unfairly. Nevertheless, someone uncorrectibly subject to political inequality does not have the reasons discussed in the text to alter his or her judgments about other unfair shares.

46. Peter Singer, in Democracy and Disobedience 42–75 (1973), suggests such a view but concludes that in modern liberal democracies many people do not have a fair share of influence.

47. See Soper, note 25 at 75–90.

48. Simmons, note 6 supra at 160–70, discussing, among others, Plato, Ross, Hume, Kant, and Sidgwick.

49. Id. at 163–83.

50. Id. at 167–68.

51. Simmons provides a much more detailed account of the conditions that bring duties of gratitude into play in id., at 170–83.

52. Id. at 179–81.

53. Plato, The Crito, 50d–51d. But see Olsen, Socrates on Legal Obligation: Legitimation Theory and Civil Disobedience, 18 Ga. L. Rev. 929 (1984), who carefully develops an argument that Socrates does not endorse the position he ascribes to the "laws" of Athens.

54. Simmons, note 6 supra at 187–88.

55. See Smith, note 30 supra at 953.

8

A Natural Duty to Obey:
Benefit, Need, and Duty

In this chapter, I explore theories of obligation to obey the law that may loosely be grouped as theories asserting a natural duty to obey. After briefly explaining why theories of natural duty are important and how they differ from other moral bases for obedience, I try to show the strengths and weaknesses of particular arguments about a natural duty, what features unify apparently disparate approaches, what assumptions need to be made for an account based on natural duty to succeed, and how far the range of a plausible account reaches.

A natural duty is one that arises because one is a person or a member of a society or because one occupies some narrower status, such as being a parent. Because such duties do not depend on voluntary actions that bring one within their reach, their application is potentially broader than duties based on promises or fair play. In contrast with utilitarianism, theories of natural duty may explain why obedience to law is a genuine duty, not just a question of morally preferable action, and why obedience may be called for though no untoward consequences will flow from disobedience.

One of the critical features of a natural duty to obey the law is that the triggering conditions of the duty do not involve appraisals of consequences in individual cases. The duty is understood as the natural duty not to lie. One need not appraise the likely consequences of telling a particular untruth to decide that the duty not to lie applies. (I do not mean to suggest that consequences will necessarily be irrelevant to whether, all things considered, lying is called for; the duty may be outweighed by sufficient favorable consequences of lying. But one knows that the duty not to lie counts for something even if lying will do no harm.)

A second feature of a natural duty to obey is closely related to the first; the duty has at least some power to overcome a balance of favorable consequences. Again, if one has a duty not to lie, one should not lie when one estimates that slightly better consequences will result from lying than from telling the truth. At the extreme, a duty might be thought absolute with respect to desirable consequences, "trumping" the most powerful considerations of consequence; but all it needs to count as a duty is to have *some* trumping capacity.

The third critical feature is the appropriateness of blame for failures to perform. If, without an excuse, one fails to perform a duty, one is blameworthy.

The theories that I group together in this chapter are traditional natural law, John Rawls's natural duty to support just institutions, Anthony Honoré's duty based on necessity, Philip Soper's duty not to injure those exercising authority, and John Mackie's independent duty to obey. Each of the theories posits some reciprocal relationship of benefit and duty, the benefits given by the government underlying the duty to obey. Like utilitarian approaches to obedience, these theories assume that government is valuable and that obedience contributes to its effectiveness. Like the duty of fair play, these theories emphasize benefits conferred on citizens, though paying less attention to particular balances of costs and benefits and to attitudes about benefits.

These theories rest on diverse foundations, and a plausible challenge to my whole enterprise is that I am treating similarly theories whose underlying bases are radically different. I try to demonstrate that the points of commonality are great enough to warrant common treatment.

My initial investigation of each of these five theories about obedience to law involves both exposition and criticism and eventuates in a drawing together of the common threads. My subsequent exploration of the critical assumptions that are necessary to support a natural duty to obey leads me to conclude that such a duty does exist but does not reach even all applications of just laws under just regimes. Finally, I turn to unjust laws and unjust regimes, claiming that for application of the duty no sharp line can be drawn on the basis of the justice of a law or a regime.

FIVE THEORIES

Traditional Natural Law

By traditional natural law, I mean the longstanding position in moral and legal theory that human law is in some sense derived from moral norms that are universally valid and discoverable by reasoning about human nature or true human goods. Rooted in Greek and Roman ideas, this view has dominated centuries of Roman Catholic thought. Given its most influential systematic explication in the writings of St. Thomas Aquinas,[1] it remains the prevailing Catholic position and is accepted in various forms by many others of different religious persuasions. In this chapter, I will concentrate heavily on the account given by John Finnis in his Natural Law and Natural Rights,[2] a comprehensive and sensitive modern exposition of this traditional view. This concentration no doubt obscures important divisions among natural law theorists,[3] but since what unites them is, for our purposes, much more important than what divides them, the gain in clarity of analysis is warranted.

According to natural law theory laws are rules for the common good, the common good embracing the good of individual members of the community.[4] Human beings need authority to coordinate activities of any complexity as well as to guide those who are ignorant and to curb antisocial selfish inclinations.[5] Political authority, necessary to promote human flourishing, is a natural institution to promote the common good.[6] Because individuals have a duty to promote the common good, they have a duty to support those who exercise political authority and to obey valid laws. As Finnis puts it, one aspect of action for the sake of the common good is being a "law-abiding citizen" and to be a law-abiding citizen requires obeying the law even when one does not see an independent reason to do what the law requires.[7] Although the moral obligation to obey each law is "variable in force,"[8] the reasons that justify creating laws that are "relatively impervious to discretionary assessments" are "reasons that also justify

us in asserting that the moral obligation to conform to legal obligations is relatively weighty."[9]

Implicit in the idea of the common good is a notion of reciprocity.
The promotion of the community's common good involves the promotion of the good of each member.[10] Thus, in being a law-abiding
citizen, someone is contributing toward the effectiveness of an institution that is necessary for his own welfare. The duty to obey the law is
related to the benefits the existence of law confers on him. These
involve both the intrinsic good of social relations and goods that the
citizen can pursue on his own if given protection, respect and support.

Two distinctive features of traditional natural law theory are its
"realism" about the origins and survival of actual political authorities
and its stringency about what counts as a law carrying a moral
obligation to obey. Recognizing that many governments originate in
force and treating effectiveness as the most critical ingredient of authority, natural lawyers have claimed that the obligation to obey can
arise under all sorts of governments.[11] Particular laws, however, that
are not addressed to the common good, or suffer other defects that
make them unjust, do not generate the moral obligation that follows
from just laws.[12] As we will see later, natural law posits a different
reach to the duty to obey than each of the other theories I discuss.

A fundamental question concerning a natural law duty to obey is
whether or not an underlying assumption about self-evident human
goods or the teleology of human beings is maintainable. This chapter
skirts that question, but its examination of the other theories of
natural duty supports the idea that the receipt of benefits as a member
of a community generates a duty to contribute to the good of the
community by obeying its rules. Whether or not the duty to contribute
to the common good by obedience arises if obedience on a particular
occasion will not contribute to that good is a troublesome problem
reserved for subsequent examination.

A Natural Duty to Support Just Institutions

John Rawls, in A Theory of Justice, departs substantially from his
earlier fair play account of political obligation. A duty of fair play, or
fairness, is still treated as important for the mostly better-placed
members of society who "gain political office and . . . take advantage
of the opportunities offered by the constitutional system,"[13] but Rawls
now considers a natural duty to promote and support just institutions

as the general moral basis for obedience to law in a nearly just society.[14]

Principles of Justice in the Original Position

Although I will claim that Rawls's natural duty can be detached from most of what he says about substantive principles of justice, the duty is presented as an aspect of a comprehensive theory, and I begin by placing it, however briefly, within that theory. As one aspect of his ideal theory of justice, Rawls claims that the natural duty to support just institutions fits with conclusions about justice in social institutions. Suggesting that the principles of justice for a liberal democratic society are ones that would be chosen in an "original position" by persons under a veil of ignorance about their places in society, natural talents, particular interests and emotional propensities,[15] Rawls argues that people in the original position would reject utilitarianism as the operative principle for judging social institutions,[16] choosing instead the principle that inequalities are acceptable only if they are to everyone's advantage, that is, only if those who get less than others still get more than they would under more egalitarian conditions.[17] For societies capable of fulfilling the basic wants of individuals,[18] all of three more specific and now familiar principles of social justice would be applicable: (1) the priority of equal liberty, (2) fair equality of opportunity, and (3) the allowance of differences in wealth and organizational power only if these serve the interests of the worst-off class of society.[19]

These principles of social justice provide the background against which natural duties of individuals would be determined. Rejecting utilitarianism as an appropriate guide for individual action,[20] persons in the original position would wish to guarantee just institutions effectively, and would accept among natural duties a duty to create and support just institutions. Rawls's most precise statement of this duty is as follows: "first, we are to comply with and to do our share in just institutions when they exist and apply to us; and second, we are to assist in the establishment of just arrangements when they do not exist, at least when this can be done with little cost to ourselves."[21] Because just political institutions will include a principle of majority rule, and majority votes are bound to produce some results that minorities regard as unjust, putting up with such laws is the price of effective majority rule.[22] The duty to support just institutions will include a duty to obey even laws that are unjust, as long as they "do not exceed certain limits of injustice."[23] Rawls's account of natural duty is one aspect of a constructivist theory that uses shared premises of liberal democratic cultures to determine principles that would be chosen in an initial position of equality.[24]

Though they are embedded in a unified and complex theory, the essential arguments that Rawls presents for a natural duty to bolster just social institutions would have force even if justice in social institutions were conceived differently.[25] Imaginary beings in anything like an original position would want principles of moral duty that would help maintain just and desirable[26] social institutions.[27] Because the original position analysis is designed to draw out the reflective moral intuitions of actual people about justice, actual people would, if Rawls is right, acknowledge a duty to support a political order that is just.

The Natural Duty in Nearly Just Societies

What relevance does such a theory of natural duty have for members of societies who judge their institutions to be less than ideally just? That would seem to depend on the degree of injustice, the potentialities for greater justice, and perhaps the relation between injustice and the members of society whose possible duty is involved. Since Rawls develops the natural duty in a section of the book that deals with disobedience in nearly just societies and treats that general problem in a way markedly similar to his treatment in earlier articles concerning modern liberal democracies,[28] we may conclude that he thinks the citizens of such societies lie under the natural duty.[29]

In judging the degree of injustice that would obviate the duty for some or all citizens, one would presumably need to consider the feasible set of alternatives. If the institutions of society A and society B fall substantially short of ideal justice, but in society A, the present institutions, because of historical conflicts and class resentments, are about the best that can be achieved, whereas in society B the institutions represent a sharp and reversible deterioration from much better institutions, a natural duty to support existing arrangements might apply in society A but not in society B.

Contemplating a society that accepts proper principles of justice that benefit everyone, Rawls does not emphasize the reciprocal dimension of his natural duty, but a duty to support institutions that are generally just might well be weakened if the unjust features of those institutions worked regularly to one's disadvantage. Within fairly just political orders, the strength, or existence, of the duty for particular individuals may depend partly on whether those individuals are, overall, gainers or losers from injustice. If, for example, the political order in the United States still operates with substantial unfairness toward Native Americans, their duty to support the political order may be less than that of the average citizen.[30]

Content of the Duty to Support Just Institutions

Having suggested the possible relevance of a natural duty to support just institutions in nearly just societies, I turn to the nature of the duty, the situations that it reaches, and a particular criticism leveled against it as a basis for obedience to law. I want, first, to disentangle compliance with the rules of just institutions from other weaker or more controversial aspects of the duty that Rawls explicates.

We can identify three different elements of the Rawlsian duty: compliance with just institutions that apply to us, doing our share in those institutions, and promoting just institutions that do not exist. The compliance element is the only one comfortably viewed as involving a strict moral duty, a duty that requires the performance or nonperformance of specific acts and whose application does not depend on likely consequences. The duty to assist in the establishment of just institutions that do not exist cannot plausibly be understood as a duty to contribute to every enterprise promoting more just institutions. Rawls considers beneficence in the realm of supererogation rather than duty;[31] if he is right that we do not always have a duty to support the welfare of others at our own modest expense by contributing to each worthwhile charity, it is unlikely that we have a duty to contribute to each effort to enhance justice. Even if one were to think of a weak "imperfect" duty that could be satisfied in various ways, the moral reasons for promoting just institutions would not require choices of specific acts. And such a duty would certainly not demand aid to efforts that were predictably bound to be wholly ineffective.[32]

Similar qualifications can be raised about any duty to "do our share in just institutions," at least when our share is not as precisely defined as in the civic responsibility to vote. Moreover, that aspect of the duty is subject to an independent objection. Rawls's own emphasis on doing one's share reflects a belief that participation in public affairs is an aspect of good citizenship and the good life. The benefits gained from the political order might be claimed as grounds for a positive duty to participate actively; however, such an assertion collapses if one considers alternative altruistic life-styles. A person who withdraws from public life and devotes himself to medical research or to prayer for humankind, trying to better the human predicament in ways quite different from active political participation, is not violating some duty to his fellows.

The duty to obey the law is different from these other two parts of the duty to support just institutions. Not depending on a controversial positive duty of political participation, it can rest on a negative duty not to do anything unjust or undermine just arrangements; it can yield clear directions for choice in particular instances; and its application may reasonably be understood not to depend on whether particular acts of disobedience will have bad consequences. Circumscribed to include only compliance, the duty to support just institutions that apply to us resembles the natural law duty to obey the law.

The existence of pockets of injustice within generally just political orders presents a kind of conceptual barrier to understanding the duty to support just institutions as including a general duty to obey the law. The underlying substantive difficulty is this: most actual political processes are unfair in important respects, most pervasively in the preponderant influence of the rich and powerful, but also in such details as the ability of powerful committee chairmen in the U.S. Congress to see that benefits go to their own localities. These imperfections partly undermine the more just aspects of the political order. A person who refuses to comply with some law that directly derives from those imperfections, or who disobeys some other law to expose the imperfections, may take the view that his aim is not only to discourage individual unjust outcomes but also to *improve* justice in the processes by which decisions are reached. Even if actors limited their considerations to support of just institutions, compliance with law would not always be morally preferable to noncompliance.

Whether this conclusion is consonant with saying that the duty to support just institutions generates a *general* duty to obey depends on how the conclusion is framed. If we said simply that, on balance, the duty to support just institutions sometimes tips in favor of disobedience, the duty to comply would not sound general.[33] If, instead, we looked at the duty to obey as separate, and perhaps acknowledged that disobedience has some tendency to undermine the society's just political institutions, we could conclude that the duty to comply remains in force, though it is outweighed on the occasion by the need to enhance the justice of political institutions in some narrower respect. I shall assume that the duty to comply can be so understood and that the possibility of competing claims within the rubric of support of just institutions does not itself undercut the notion of a general duty to obey.

Rawls's assumption that the natural duty to comply provides a genuine alternative to obligations based on voluntary undertakings has been challenged by John Simmons, who objects to Rawls's view that we have a special duty when just institutions *apply* to us.[34] He points out that a moral duty of support usually does not arise simply because an institution—say a professional association—purports to apply to us; we must voluntarily accept the application of the institution before such a duty arises. If voluntary acceptance were needed to generate the natural duty to support just institutions that apply to us, the duty would be much less general than Rawls supposes and would actually collapse into obligations arising from voluntary acts. On the other hand, were the duty to be understood as not depending on voluntary acceptance, an institution's forcing itself upon us would not be morally relevant and we should have as much duty to support just institutions that do not apply to us as those that do.[35] Simmons pointedly concludes that citizens would then have no special duty to support the just political institutions of their own countries over the just political institutions of other countries.[36]

At least as far as obedience to law is concerned, Simmons's challenge is not apt. The duty to obey may exist even if everything he says about the failure to establish a special duty to one's own government is correct. A duty not to undermine just institutions may well reach our relations with the governments of other countries when we visit those countries or have other relations with them.[37] And, even if in principle our duties to other governments do not stand on a different basis from our duties to our own government, citizenship or chosen residence could make a powerful difference to the precise import of those duties, since one's particular status reasonably affects what can justly be demanded and expected.[38]

Moreover, we have strong reason to suppose, contrary to Simmons's basic theoretical claim, that special duties can be generated by application of institutions that do not involve voluntary acceptance. His examples draw on institutions that virtually everyone assumes should not morally be applied without such acceptance. But there are other institutions to which people believe compulsory application is morally appropriate—notably the family (up to a certain stage in life) and the state. As I will explore further in connection with Tony Honoré's claim about a duty based on necessity, when the nonvoluntary application of an institution is morally appropriate, it may give rise to duties that do not relate to institutions that do not apply.

These focused inquiries about Rawls's natural duty to support just institutions leave us with a more general question: Does the duty to obey depend on likely or possible effects on just institutions, or must one obey the law whenever the rules of the just institutions demand it? Neither every refusal nor every known refusal to adhere to the norms arrived at by majority rule threatens the principle of majority rule.[39] Though Rawls often talks of violations of the duty as if they will really undermine just institutions, he also conceives of the duty as meeting the requirements of a traditional theory of political obligation, one that posits a general duty of citizens to obey the law. Because Rawls makes no mention of the possibility that noncompliance with laws might fall outside the natural duty if it has no predictable effect on just institutions, and because of Rawls's broader adherence to Kantian ethics, we can assume that Rawls understands the duty to apply in a way that does not depend on factual evaluations in particular instances;[40] however, whether or not that way of conceiving the duty is persuasive is as troublesome and important a question here as with respect to traditional natural law and the theories I will now proceed to discuss.

Necessity as a Ground of Duty

Tony Honoré has suggested that the duty to obey laws arises out of necessity.[41] He claims that certain relationships give rise to special duties in the absence of any voluntary act: an uncle has a duty to see to the care of an orphaned nephew; a woman made pregnant by a rape and unable to have an abortion has a duty to care for the child. The basis for the duty of the person deemed to be suitable to render care or supervision is the "need for an individual, a thing, or an institution to be cared for or supervised."[42] The state is required to take care of native-born citizens; its relationship to them is nonvoluntary, based on necessity. The individual has a corresponding duty to comply with the requirements of his fellow citizens represented by the law. Rather than positing any general theory about true or valid claims of morality and political morality, Honoré tries to establish the connection between the debated duty to obey and a more generally accepted duty.

Honoré's general argument that duties of care can arise because of special nonvoluntary relationships is persuasive. These responsibilities arise because physical proximity or convention places individuals in the position of being counted on to render care; the individuals have genuine moral duties to satisfy those expectations.[43] In theory, the special position of being a citizen could, in like manner, lead to one's being counted on in ways that would create a moral duty; but Honoré's progress from his plausible premises to his conclusion that citizens have a prima facie duty to obey all laws is less than compelling. To distill the potentially sound elements of Honoré's account, we must reject some of what he actually says.

The main argument Honoré makes in favor of the duty of necessity moves from the obligations of those who become alien residents to the duties of native-born citizens. A noncitizen impliedly consents to obey "because he knows that the state and its citizens would not agree to his coming or remaining except on the condition that he agree to abide by its laws."[44] The native-born citizen, who the state is actually obligated to care for, must have at least as substantial duties toward the state.

Honoré is mistaken about what can fairly be supposed about resident aliens. Entry for residence may imply a general attitude of compliance to law, but given uncertainty and disagreement about morally required and morally ideal attitudes toward the law, any attempt to sum up a general consensus knowable by citizens and immigrants about the attitude immigrants should have toward the law is bound to fail.[45]

The remainder of Honoré's argument is also crucially flawed. Though native-born citizens generally have obligations as powerful as those admitted by the state, states can strike bargains with outsiders that impose obligations not rightly imposable on citizens. For example, a state with too many doctors might reasonably condition an alien doctor's immigration on agreement to practice in a remote area, even though requiring native-born doctors to practice in that area might be an unacceptable constraint on liberty.[46] Because citizens may not have all the duties that can result from a bargain between the state and aliens who seek to be residents, the latter's supposed duties do not settle the duties of citizens.

Another simpler argument intimated by Honoré fits better with the general thrust of his essay. The basic idea is that the state is in the position of badly needing the citizen's support reflected in compliance with law; the citizen's duty to comply flows out of the state's need, and the performance of its own duty to care for the citizen. Unfortunately, powerful disanalogies exist between this application of the "duty of necessity" and the "ordinary" examples from which Honoré draws. In the latter, a discrete person needs help, and if the individual with the "duty of necessity" to provide it fails, someone is likely to suffer. This model may apply to laws that protect important rights of individual citizens, such as the right to bodily security. Since a single violation defeats the state's aim of protection, the state really does need everyone's compliance. As to such laws, however, one might speak more directly of a moral duty not to violate the justified expectations of individuals, including expectations generated by legal rights; so reference to the state's need seems superfluous, unless the point concerns some broader effects of violations.

The notion of necessity to comply fits much less well with other laws. As to some, failure to comply by one individual may not interfere with the state's positive efforts at all (one person evades the draft or customs laws), *unless* the state's *need* is conceived to include fairness in allocation of the burdens it imposes. As to other laws, a failure to comply may have some extremely slight, *de minimis*, overall effect (e.g., one's failure to pay $10,000 in taxes increases the national debt by that amount). For both of these sorts of laws, no single individual's compliance is really "necessary." Nor is his compliance "necessary" in regard to "rights-protecting" laws if one thinks of the broader purposes that concern the state rather than damage to the individual victim.

If necessity seems too strong a word for each citizen's compliance with law, the state does need general obedience if it is to function effectively; the benefits conferred on individual citizens by the state may well be sufficient to generate some duty to comply with its rules. On this point, Honoré's theory links to traditional natural law and Rawls's natural duty of justice. Since Honoré puts his theory forward as one that supports a prima facie duty to obey the law generally and in all societies,[47] it is broader than traditional natural law in reaching unjust laws and broader than Rawls's approach in reaching unjust regimes. Honoré's account of an obligation to comply that does not leave citizens free to assess whether compliance with particular laws, and compliance on particular occasions, contributes to the needs of their fellows sharply poses the question of how persuasive nonconsequential versions of this sort of duty to obey are.

Respect for Officials Exercising Authority

Philip Soper, like Honoré relying on reflective moral judgments rather than presenting a comprehensive theory of morality, has developed an account of obligation that marks an interesting variation on some of the themes discussed so far.[48] Soper urges that, since coercive government is necessary for human beings, those who try to govern in the interests of their subjects are not committing a moral wrong against them. Subjects should respect the good faith efforts of those with authority, and a crucial way to show this respect is by obeying their directives. Subjects have a prima facie obligation to obey the law because those with authority care about whether or not the law is obeyed and they deserve respect.

An analogy to the family drawn by Soper helps to clarify the approach.[49] A sensitive daughter in a good family recognizes the need for parental authority and understands that her parents are trying to exercise their authority in her interest. Because her refusal to comply with their directions will cause them disappointment or unhappiness, the love, or at least respect, that she feels for her parents provides an important moral reason to do what they direct. This reason covers the many situations in which her disobedience will adversely affect her parents' self-interest only by causing psychological pain.[50]

For the citizen, "[a]cknowledgment of the value of law arises out of rational appraisal of one's own self-interest in the maintenance of a coercive social order."[51] If that person's interests are taken into account along with those of other subjects, and officials have a good faith belief in the justice of the system, then, according to Soper, the person owes respect to the officials exercising authority.[52] Obeying the law is one important way to show respect. Recognizing that the conditions he sets will be met by most modern governments, Soper argues that the "respect" reason for obedience applies even to a regime the citizen regards as substantially unjust as well as to unjust laws within a just regime.[53]

At first glance, Soper's choice of respect for officials appears odd for a general theory of obligation. In most circumstances, the success of the project in which an official is engaged is a much more powerful reason to comply than possible affront to officials.[54] Soper does not deny this; he does not contend that respect for officials is uniquely powerful as a source of obligation. Its significance lies in its breadth. Soper realizes that compliance will often not matter to the success of the endeavor, but in his view respect is always implicated and therefore can underpin a general obligation to obey the law on every occasion of application.

We may profitably broaden Soper's account to include respect for citizens who are also contributing their parts to the maintenance of law;[55] violations of law may be an affront to them as well as to officials exercising more specific responsibilities within the legal order.

To succeed as a theory of general obligation, Soper's approach must meet two possible challenges. One challenge is that showing respect is too weak a reason to be a duty. Soper apparently does not wish to claim that showing respect for officials is a duty in some strong sense, only that it is a good reason for obeying the law. On this interpretation, his notion of a prima facie duty is very weak. I have suggested in Chapter 6 that we do not ordinarily conceive of a prima facie duty as existing just because a moral reason exists to perform each act in a class.[56] Even if performance of most acts in the class, such as contributing to charities would be morally preferable, a person may not be under a prima facie *duty*, he does not have a duty to perform every morally preferable action. If respect for officials and law-abiding citizens is a weak moral reason for obedience that, standing alone, puts obedience only within the zone of supererogation, a person is free to disregard it without being subject to blame, even when no competing moral reason exists. On this interpretation, Soper's theory is much less stringent in its constraints on citizens than other theories that citizens have a general duty to obey.

An effort might be made to meet this difficulty by claiming that what we owe officials and law-abiding citizens is much stronger than what we owe those who solicit for charities. Such a claim would emphasize that officials and citizens are performing a designated role in a scheme that includes us and is for our benefit, that *this* involvement on our behalf puts us under a duty to show respect for their efforts. Such a claim brings us to an emphasis on reciprocity as the source of duty and would make Soper's theory much closer to the other three approaches we have examined than it initially appears.

A second challenge to Soper's theory is that the respect reason does not apply to many instances of violations of law. Many violations will not affront anyone because they remain secret; many other trivial or technical violations that are known also cause no affront to any individual.[57] Understood as a theory about causing disappointment and resentment in actual individuals, the theory falls short of providing an argument about consequences that reaches every instance of law violation.[58] Soper can meet the challenge of nonapplication to many instances of law violation only if respect for officials can be cast in a deontological way that does not depend on the likely consequences of a particular violation, a problem that, as we have seen, also affects the other theories discussed.

An Underived Obligation to Obey the Law

Another possibility, offered by John Mackie, is a duty to obey the law that is not derivable form any more basic, more general, moral principle.[59] Believing that conventional morality desirably includes a prima facie obligation to obey that cannot be derived from any body of philosophically plausible moral principles, Mackie says that the obligation should be conceived as an independent one.

Under Mackie's more general theory,[60] which denies that objective moral prescriptions exist, humans should develop[61] moral prescriptions that will serve their purposes. Moral norms are needed to resolve situations in which one person's self-interest dictates violation of practices that, if generally observed, would promote the welfare of all. Notions of reciprocation are much more effective psychologically than any principle of universal benevolence of the sort posited by utilitarianism.[62] The norm that one has "a prima facie obligation to obey the law as such is a further, though more extensive, reciprocal norm, like those that prescribe gratitude and loyalty to friends, collective action or forbearance, and honesty about property."[63] Though not derivable from any more general norm, the obligation to obey is significantly connected to other moral principles and might be defended in part in terms of a "coherence" justification that draws from other norms of reciprocation. Like the other theorists discussed in this chapter, Mackie begins with the desirability of law and law observance and seeks to draw out a nonconsequential principle that one is obligated to obey the law on every occasion of its application. Like Honoré and Soper, Mackie does not place unjust regimes or unjust laws outside the bounds of the duty.

The Common Threads

Each theory of a natural duty to obey that I have explored rests on the importance of government for human life and the need of government to be obeyed. Each, with varying degrees of explicitness, posits some reciprocal relationship of benefit and duty, the benefits given by the government underlying the duty to obey. Like the duty of fair play, these theories emphasize benefits conferred on citizens; they differ from that duty in placing greater emphasis on the *need* for obedience, in paying less attention to particular balances of costs and benefits, and in not making the duty depend on attitudes one has about the benefits received. Like utilitarian approaches to obedience, these theories assume that government is valuable and that obedience contributes to its effectiveness. With the possible exception of Soper's approach,[64] they differ from utilitarianism in claiming a stronger source of obligation than the simple accomplishment of good consequences. They also differ in not making application of the obligation turn on the likely consequences of particular violations.

Although the theories vary significantly in their underlying fundamental assumptions about the nature of political morality, the steps by which they arrive at the duty to obey are remarkably similar. In each, obedience is positively valued because it contributes to an essential social objective. Mackie relies on the logic most straightforwardly, but it is also found in Honoré's notion of necessity. Soper emphasizes respect, but the duty to show respect by obeying derives form the value of law.[65] Natural law theory does not claim that obedience to law is self-evidently good or an obvious aspect of human nature; rather, obedience is needed if humans are to accomplish their true purposes or achieve the goods that are self-evident. In Rawls's account, the contractors in the original position do not begin with obedience, the duty to obey is a means to support the effectiveness of just institutions.

In each theory, then, the good consequences of widespread obedience underlie the duty to obey.[66] Yet each theory, Soper's possibly excepted, supposes not only that the duty is more stringent than whatever moral reasons ordinarily exist to promote good consequences, but also that the duty comes into play even when, predictably, disobedience will cause no harm and obedience will achieve no good consequences. These two steps—from consequential reasons to a duty of some stringency and from consequential reasons to a nonconsequential duty—are the subject of the next section.

A GENUINE DUTY CONCEIVED IN NONCONSEQUENTIALIST TERMS

Should the reason for obeying the law—whether it be to support the common good, to support just institutions, to maintain necessary authority, or to show respect for officials and law-abiding citizens—be conceived as giving rise to a nonconsequential duty to obey the law on all occasions? The response that such a duty exists requires a positive answer to each of five narrower questions, which I consider in turn: (1) Should the underlying reason to obey be understood as giving rise to a moral "ought" rather than something relevant to moral preferability that will often leave a choice to do the better act a matter of supererogation? (2) Should a person conceive the reason to obey as having some power to trump a balance of consequences in favor of disobedience? (3) Should a person deciding whether to obey have to disregard whether others who are similarly situated are likely to obey? (4) Should a person have to disregard the practical acceptability of everyone who is similarly situated disobeying the law? (5) Should a person take as the relevant unit for consideration all laws and all applications, or narrower classes of laws and applications? All the questions but the first concern whether a duty to obey the law should be understood in nonconsequential terms. Lying behind each of the five questions are more abstract and pervasive theoretical problems about the substantive content of ethics, about how one judges between competing claims about how moral duties should be formulated. Although these background problems are implicated in every question, they are raised most sharply in connection with the fourth question and I address them explicitly in that context.

The Realm of Duty and Ought

The first threshold the claimed duties in this chapter must surmount is why the reasons they present should be viewed as giving rise to moral "oughts" rather than regarded simply as relevant to morally preferred supererogatory acts. Promoting desirable consequences is often praiseworthy, but the failure to do so is not a subject of blame. What answer, if any, may be given to the person faced with a choice whether to obey who says: "No doubt, my obeying will have good consequences, promoting the common good, helping the government work, strengthening just institutions, and avoiding affront to concerned officials. But if I need not devote most of my resources to charity, why ought I to obey?"

The correct answer to this query lies in the notions of reciprocation on which each theory relies more or less explicitly. The crucial point is that the demand is being placed on us under a necessary scheme in which we are fairly involved and whose aim in part is to benefit us.

The nature of what is promoted and the presence of demands on us are not, themselves, sufficient to place us under a moral duty. If I can promote the common good or just institutions in a remote country by making a financial contribution to a political organization within that country, I have no more duty to do so than to contribute to a hospital within the country; barring extreme need, these possibilities both fall within the zone of supererogation. Nor would a moral "ought" arise if the country passed a law requiring all foreigners with a certain level of income to make a prescribed contribution; a demand by a remote organization that does not benefit me cannot turn my assistance into a duty. Were I the indirect unintended beneficiary of the country's internal economic policies—say a consumer who ends up paying less because of an export subsidy—I would still have no duty to contribute

in return. The situation may not even be changed fundamentally by
my being one of those whom an organization does seek to benefit. If a
government freely gives money to relieve a drought in another country, the beneficiaries may have some vague duty of gratitude,[67] but the
donating government is not in the position of being able to create
duties with specific content.

The crucial components for a duty to comply with demands are that
benefits are combined with my being, in some sense, a member of the
community that the organization mainly serves, that I am someone
that the organization has a duty to benefit, that the organization's
demands are properly placed on people like me regardless of their
voluntary adherence, and that the effectiveness of the organization
depends on people like me complying with its rules.[68] The notions of
reciprocation that these conditions embody lie close to a formulation
of the duty of fair play, differing mainly in that they do not depend on
the attitudes the person has about the benefits he or she is receiving.
That these conditions can generate a moral "ought" or duty even in the
absence of willing acceptance of benefits is supported by the broad
theoretical analysis presented in the later section on the acceptability
of noncompliance.

Capacity to Trump a Balance of Consequences

That the duty to obey can sometimes "trump" a balance of consequences favorable to disobedience follows closely from what has just
been said. A typical aspect of a moral duty owed to someone is that one
should perform the duty even when somewhat more favorable overall
consequences will result from nonperformance. If the consequences
are bad enough the duty may give way, but the duty has power to
offset at least weak considerations of consequence. The duty that
citizens have to obey the law, based on reciprocation, should be kept,
even when modest advantages flowing to oneself or others from disobedience might indicate that disobeying would have overall better
consequences.

Can One Consider the Likely Compliance of Others?

One aspect of conceiving the duty to obey in a nonconsequential way
is that a potential actor is barred from considering the likely compliance of others. Such a preclusion has often been understood to rest
on a moral principle of generalization: "If the circumstances of the

case are such that the consequences of everyone's acting in that way in those circumstances would be undesirable, then the act is wrong, and it is irrelevant that the consequences of one person's acting in that way in those circumstances would not be undesirable."[69] To understand the force of this principle, we need to delineate its scope and the kinds of situations to which it applies.

Initially we need to narrow the principle a bit to exclude three sorts of situations. The principle is of no help when an actor must choose between two alternatives and general conformity with either alternative would be highly undesirable.[70] The principle is not relevant when someone considers a course of action, such as celibacy, that most people have no desire to follow;[71] one does not need to restrain himself from his preferred course of action if the self-interested acts of others will more than meet general human needs. Nor should the principle be conceived to apply when an overall harmful act is already so widespread that one's engaging in it does no added harm. If everyone else's walking has destroyed the grass, one ceases to have a duty to avoid crossing the plot on which grass once grew and might grow again if everyone stopped walking there. In contrast, the generalization principle may be offered as an answer to the person who says, "It is all right if I disobey the law because almost everyone else is obeying." The answer takes the familiar form: "But what if everyone did that?"

In many situations, the principle of generalization will not be the only argument against disobedience. If a violation involves a known infringement of an individual right, harm is being done regardless of the compliance of others. If noncompliance, say failure to pay a tax, makes a slight negative difference to the government's budget overall, one's own act of disobedience will have undesirable consequences, even though they may be hard to trace. In some circumstances, disobedience up to a certain threshold may do no harm, but disobedience beyond that threshold is seriously harmful;[72] if an actor is not sure if the threshold has been reached, the risk that his or her disobedience will exceed it is a strong reason to obey. Finally, arguments about bad habits and examples need not rest strictly on a generalization principle, since those arguments urge that one's apparently harmless act may have subtle and indirect undesirable consequences.

Reliance on generalization is decisive when plausible arguments about the act's harm are wholly lacking or require bolstering.

Illustration 8-1:

A law prohibits pollution of rivers. Peter knows that if everyone for whom it would be convenient discharged a particular substance into the river, the water quality would suffer; but he also knows that most others will not break the law and that his own discharge and the discharges of the few others breaking the law will not undermine the quality of the water *at all*.[73] Peter is confident he can keep his own discharge secret from others and that, in that event, it will cause no harm whatsoever.

The principle of generalization renders the discharge wrongful despite its harmlessness.

This principle has sometimes been offered as a, or the, central truth of ethical thought,[74] one supported by Kant's fundamental principle that one must act according to principles that one could universalize.[75] A minimal notion of universality, implicit in ethical language and thought, however, does not establish the principle of generalization as it applies to practical choices. That minimal notion does bar claims based on particular names and places. I am not allowed to do something simply because of who I am, *unless* being who I am makes me different, from a moral point of view, from other people;[76] if my situation is identical with that of someone else, I am under the same moral constraints as the other person.[77] What this minimal notion of universality does not preclude is Peter's taking the following position: "Any person who knows that the compliance of others will render his own discharge harmless is morally free to make it." Because Peter's moral standard, which makes the likely compliance of others part of the morally relevant conditions of his own situation, satisfies the minimal notion of universality, something more is needed to show its unacceptability.

It might be suggested that denial of the principle of generalization is somehow incoherent. The idea is that if Peter can justify his noncompliance on the basis of the compliance of others, then each of the others could do the same, and everyone could disobey, bringing about the harmful consequences. But this claim of incoherence is mistaken. Peter *knows* that not everyone will assess the situation just as he does; he takes as a matter of fact the responses and likely responses of others. Anyone in the same circumstance could morally make a similar assessment, but each person doing that would also know that most people's patterns of behavior will be set for the short-term future. If more people do start to make the discharges, then discharges may become harmful; but *until* they do so, or predictably are about to do so, any potential discharger may make the same moral assessment as Peter and engage in the discharge without bringing about harmful consequences. The claim that the principle of generalization is incoherent is circular; the claim's crucial assumption, that a person should not employ a perspective of moral evaluation that leads to the result it does only because he knows that others similarly situated are not making the same evaluation, turns out to be the principle of generalization the claim is meant to support.

The principle of generalization may be grounded in the impracticality of moral principles that make duties turn on the harm of one's own act in light of the compliance of others[78] and on fairness.[79] In the next subsection, I will explore how arguments of impracticality can be formulated; I need only mention here that grave dangers of self-serving evaluations would almost certainly infect moral standards like that proposed by Peter. The idea of fairness lying behind the principle of generalization is that it is unfair for me to get an advantage that people just like me, from the moral point of view, are foregoing.

In terms of fairness, both the celibacy case and a case in which all others are already making the discharge are revealed as fundamentally different from the case in which the restraint of others makes my potential act harmless. In the celibacy case, no one *need* exercise restraint, and in the excess discharge case no one *is* exercising restraint. The purpose of generalization is very close to the duty of fair play. The principle of generalization is broader than the duty of fair play; its application does not depend on one's willing acceptance of benefits or on mutual expectations about restraint that characterize cooperative schemes,[80] but the moral premises of the two norms are similar.

The Acceptability of Noncompliance by All Those Similarly Situated and the Bases for Determining Moral Standards

Establishment of the generalization principle alone does not settle that a duty to obey the law should be conceived in nonconsequentialist terms. A person contemplating disobedience may claim that if everyone similarly situated disobeyed, no harm or tendency toward injustice would occur. Such a claim would most clearly arise if the law was highly unjust, but that situation is put aside here. A law might instead be exceedingly trivial without being unjust in the usual sense, and a person might conclude that widespread disobedience of that law would have no negative effect. I will focus on what is perhaps the more common case of a law that has many applications that are important and some that are not. Consider the examples posed in Chapter 7 involving Ruth, who is a sober driver considering at 4:00 A.M. whether or not to exceed a thirty-mile-per-hour speed limit that she thinks may safely be exceeded by any other sober driver at that time; or is a hiker in the woods wondering whether or not to walk on someone's posted land, believing that similar unseen violations by others would do no harm. Unlike Peter in the pollution illustration, Ruth can define her situation in a way that makes no reference to whether others in like circumstances actually do comply; she can contend that, regardless of the degree of compliance by others, her disobedient act and others like it will do no harm. Ruth can also claim, as Chapter 7 indicates, that she is not taking advantage of others.

If Ruth can make those judgments, what reason is there for her to think she has a duty to observe the law on occasions like these?[81] She might question whether the basic ground for obedience, for example, promotion of the common good or support of just institutions, has any moral weight when the ground clearly does not apply. Put more abstractly, her question is as follows: How can a moral reason that derives from the desirable consequences of most acts in a certain class turn into a nonconsequentialist duty to perform every act in the class?

One possibility is that the duty to obey is itself presently understood by most people as applicable regardless of any likely harmful consequences. In fact, attitudes toward law are complex and ambivalent and it is doubtful one could capture any general understanding. In any event, a finding that people believe in a general duty to obey might cast some sort of burden on those who would reject this view, but that finding alone would not be sufficient to withstand moral criticism that a true, or better, conception of the reasons to obey would be formulated in terms of likely consequences in particular instances.

Another possibility for understanding the duty in a wholly nonconsequentialist way is that it derives from some broader and accepted nonconsequentialist duty or fits closely with a number of related nonconsequentialist duties. The theories outlined here do not rest on a claim that a duty to obey can be derived from some uncontroversial more general duty,[82] although the line between a derivation and a coherence justification is by no means distinct. As Mackie's work most sharply suggests, the relationship between a citizen and the state is not quite like other relationships. Arguments about a duty to obey often proceed by drawing some analogy to another sort of relation. Honoré, for example, talks about necessity as a source of duty in family relations, and Soper draws on family relations to illustrate the duty to show respect for those in authority. It will often be somewhat arbitrary whether at the end of one's efforts one posits a general duty, for example, necessity, and says that the duty to obey the law is a subcategory of that duty, or one says, as Mackie does, that related and complementary duties exist in various spheres.

Someone who bases the argument for a duty to obey on its coherence with other accepted duties might claim that a nonconsequentialist understanding fits best with the understanding of the related duties. One way to resist this sort of "fit" argument would be to concede the crucial linkage between obedience to law and other duties, but urge that all of them would be better understood in at least partially consequential terms. A different response would be to detach the duty to obey the law from the duties to which it has been related. Let me provide a specific illustration in terms of Soper's analogy to the family. When people have a close personal relationship, failures to obey the directions of those in authority are likely to lead to covering lies and restrained communication. For this reason, the duty to obey even of teenage children might best be conceived as one that does not rest on predictable consequences in particular instances. But most undiscovered violations of law do not subtly damage any personal relationships between actors and officials, so this particular reason for a deontological duty is much weaker in that context. Thus, one willing to concede that respect in the family gives rise to a deontological duty might resist the extension of that conception to respect for officials.

A final way to argue that the duty to obey is nonconsequential is to claim that, considered by itself, that conception of the duty is superior to a consequential one. What exactly constitutes superiority and how is it to be established, if it is not based on "fit" or on present understanding of the duty to obey? A person might urge that revelation shows that God has instructed us to conceive our duty to obey the law as applicable regardless of likely harm; but such forms of argument are not an appropriate means of justifying conceptions of public morality in a pluralist society. A person might claim that shared intuition directly establishes such a duty. None of the positions summarized in this chapter rests on either revelation or direct intuition. They are based, rather, on the assumption that the relevant moral norms will be most effective in promoting human good if they are understood in nonconsequentialist terms. Mackie explicitly advances such a standard as the criterion for judging moral positions; and Rawls's device of the original position works to a similar effect.[83] Honoré relies in part on the supposed ill effects of people not believing in a prima facie obligation to obey,[84] and Finnis, in his exposition of natural law, tries to show how moral principles promote the common good.[85]

To say that a norm will be most effective if cast in nonconsequentialist terms is to say something other than that it would be most effective if followed perfectly;[86] the norm must also be one that will have actual appeal to human beings and is capable of being complied with sufficiently to make the results under that norm preferable to those that might be achieved under an alternative.

The argument that a nonconsequentialist understanding is preferable to a consequentialist one could be made in various ways. The clearest argument is one that shows that a consequentialist understanding would be obviously self-defeating in some significant respect. Finnis offers such an argument about promise-keeping.[87] Imagine that people decided to keep promises only if doing so would be beneficial, or would at least satisfy the psychological expectations of the person to whom the promise was given and of other concerned persons. Such an attitude might lead people to break promises with relative freedom when only the promisor and promisee knew of the promise and the promisee has died[88] or would be unaware of the breach. But if people know that promises are freely broken in these settings they will know that promises made to them that must be carried out in such contexts will not be very reliable. The practice resulting from these attitudes will deprive them of confident expectations and will therefore substantially undermine the benefits that promises afford to those who wish to control future events indirectly.[89] A consequential attitude toward keeping promises[90] will thus seriously erode the social benefits of the institution of promises.

A consequentialist understanding of a duty might fall short of this sort of logical difficulty and still be self-defeating in a practical sense. Something along these lines might be said in defense of both the generalization principle and the idea that a duty can "trump" competing consequences. Given people's uncertainty about how others similarly situated will act and about when dangerous thresholds are reached, and given their propensity to underestimate the harm of their own individual actions, a broad principle that people should consider the likely compliance of others might consistently lead to inadequate levels of compliance when widespread compliance is needed. The same propensity to underestimate the harms of self-serving actions helps to explain why a duty should be understood as requiring compliance even when one judges that the balance of consequences favors noncompliance.

One can make both these sorts of arguments about the self-defeating character of a consequentialist understanding without reference to particular features of a society or its stage of history; but we reach much more difficult terrain in deciding what conception of the duty will best promote human good when we address circumstances in which everyone similarly situated could disobey the law with no ill effect. Here, resolution most plainly turns on how many of these circumstances there are, how clearly they can be identified, and how great the damage is from misidentification. If these circumstances are few and difficult to identify and people strongly incline to think that acts they would like to perform fall into this category, then a nonconsequential understanding will work better.

On the other hand, if legal regulation of life is so pervasive that many instances of violation have no harmful tendency (i.e., would not do harm even if engaged in by everyone similarly situated) and if people can and do identify those instances with a high degree of accuracy, a consequentialist understanding will be most sound. An overall judgment about a preferred understanding will rest on the extent of legal rules and the degree of disinterestedness and acuity of the population. One thinks, for purposes of comparison, of norms urged on children; parents will be much more likely to build consequential elements into norms urged on older children, "Do this only if. . . ," than into norms urged on younger children, "Never do this." A population that well understands various aspects of law and its benefits might appropriately be able to rely on a standard that is more consequential than a less well informed population.

If one were trying to evaluate what sort of standard would work best, one would also have to consider present attitudes about the duty to obey and linkages with related duties. A certain cost in uncertainty and instability would be involved in shifting from one sort of understanding to another, so it might be better for a society to maintain its present understanding than shift to one that would be slightly better but for these costs. The duty to obey the law could not be viewed in isolation. Suppose a consequential understanding of when the duty applies would work best there if viewed alone but people could not compartmentalize to this degree, and acceptance of such an attitude toward obedience to law would erode desirable nonconsequential understandings about related matters.[91]

The last few passages may suggest a conscious manipulation of notions of duties that is unrealistic, much in the way that Mackie's talk about inventing morality is unrealistic.[92] But that is not their intended import. I am not concerned directly with what people in a position to influence moral thinking should do; rather I am trying to answer what it means to say that one conception of a duty is correct or superior to another. And when a duty of proper public morality is claimed to rest on benefits to human beings, I see no way short of an inquiry as complex as the one I have suggested for assessing its scope. Even this inquiry omits a crucial and difficult element—how large is the community that counts? Some limited moral notions might be particularized in terms of individual countries, but since we are all part of a larger intellectual community with a shared moral discourse,[93] one's inquiry would have to attend to the institutions, practices, and attitudes within that larger community.

I have sketched the outlines of an adequate theoretical answer to the question of how a duty that depends on the generally desirable consequences of obeying the law might best be cast in nonconsequentialist terms. Because the answer bears a resemblance to rule utilitarianism, I should briefly note how the approaches in this chapter differ from it. At least in most versions of rule utilitarianism, actors within the society consciously think in terms of what rules of action, if followed, will have desirable effects. The theories we have examined explicitly or implicitly assume that social life will be benefited if the basic duty to obey the law is conceived by actors in terms that do not depend on desirable consequences. The morality publicly announced and taught would not refer to appraisal of consequences as the standard determining whether or not that duty exists. The reference to overall desirable consequences would come in only at the level of inquiry as to whether moral principles conceived in nonconsequentialist terms are sound, and that would not be an inquiry in which most people would engage. Although rule utilitarianism might be presented in a way compatible with this approach, it would have to drop any notion that ordinary people should address moral questions with a consequentialist perspective.

Classes of Laws and Applications

The theoretical adequacy of a line of argument for a nonconsequential duty does not itself show that a duty to promote the common good or support just institutions underpins a duty to obey the law on every occasion of its application or that such a duty should be understood as a separate duty of reciprocation. Unless the claim is put in terms of benefits to the rest of our moral notions, the theories in this chapter could establish such a duty only if certain factual predicates are joined to the broad theoretical base. It must be true that more limited beliefs about a duty to obey would result in an inadequate level of compliance. Given the other reasons that have been suggested in this book concerning why many people have duties to obey many laws, and given all the occasions in modern societies with highly complex and technical legal norms when disobedience of law will not inflict harm on others, have an undermining effect on just institutions, or take advantage of others, a general duty to obey is probably not needed to sustain adequate compliance.[94]

Lest too much turn on individual calculation, one might understand the duty as one to comply with laws of the state directed toward what are the state's proper ends, including security, liberty, justice, and welfare,[95] when one's compliance and that of one's fellows may reasonably be thought necessary to success. Such a duty would have important nonconsequential elements, incorporating the generalization principle, and having some power to outweigh a competing balance of consequences; but it would not reach evidently foolish laws or applications of laws when general noncompliance plainly will not interfere with the state's legitimate ends.

I have been assuming in the preceding discussion that the duty to obey is conceived to be at least moderately strong. That is the assumption of all the theories in this chapter with the exception of Philip Soper's. The assumption, however, obscures yet another complexity: the relation between the coverage of a duty to obey and the strength of the duty. Suppose, on the one hand, someone said that all he meant by a general duty to obey was a moral duty of however slight strength in favor of obedience, one that might give way in many cases to very slight, including selfish, reasons to disobey. Violation of such a "duty" would warrant only slight blame, and even that would be appropriate only in the absence of competing reasons. If the general duty resolves itself to such a minimal "ought," one might very well concede a general duty to obey all laws, the concession amounting to little more than that basic ideas of reciprocation provide some rather vague reason for obeying the law. If, on the other hand, a general duty to obey is put forward as a moderately strong moral "ought"—one that can be overridden only by substantial reasons in favor of disobedience—then there is good reason to resist the assumption that such a duty is implicated whenever we must choose whether to obey the law or not.

Our inquiry has indicated just how complex the notion of a general obligation to obey the law is. I conclude that no such general obligation exists if the obligation is taken in its traditional sense as at least a moderately strong ought. Yet, a natural duty to obey does exist; and it requires obedience of law in some circumstances in which no other valid theory of obligation generates a duty to obey.

THE LIMITS OF A NATURAL DUTY TO OBEY

The discussion thus far has assumed that a duty to obey may be outweighed by competing reasons. The injustice of a particular law or of the government overall can undoubtedly function in this way, supporting a reason for disobedience that may override a duty to obey. The issue for this section is whether injustice more directly establishes a limit on the natural duty to obey itself. If such a limit is sound, the original duty may be understood not to reach these situations of injustice at all. Whether the natural duty reaches an unjust law or regime is, in part, a substantive moral issue, but one that also involves tricky problems of conceptualization. I consider, first, whether a duty that would otherwise be applicable extends to unjust laws, and then turn to the problem of unjust regimes.

Unjust Laws

Three of the theories of natural duty, Honoré's duty of necessity, Soper's duty to show respect, and Mackie's independent obligation to obey the law, are claimed by their proponents to reach both unjust laws and unjust regimes. Rawls's natural duty to comply with just institutions concerns only nearly just constitutional orders but reaches unjust laws within these orders. The natural law theory of a duty to obey to promote the common good does not place critical emphasis on the justice of a political order but is claimed to be inapplicable to unjust laws.

If, within an acceptable political order, an unjust law is adopted, why should there be any moral reason to comply with it? The answer we get from Honoré, Mackie, and Rawls is fairly simple. Citizens will have a hard time drawing a line between just and unjust laws, and if they perceive their duty to obey as reaching only just laws, they will end up disobeying many just laws that they think are unjust.[96] Further, the entire legal system has great value for social life, and disobedience of even unjust laws will have a tendency to undermine the effectiveness of law and of fair political processes, if these exist. On abstract grounds similar to those just discussed for not permitting citizens to judge the consequences of particular acts of disobedience, these theorists urge that, as far as the original duty to obey is concerned, citizens should not conceive of a sharp division between just and unjust laws. The injustice of a law may provide reasons strong enough to disobey, but these reasons will *outweigh* the duty to obey, not eliminate it altogether.

Soper's emphasis is on the good faith of officials. If they are performing the valuable task of governing and try to govern in the interests of all the people, they are owed respect for their efforts even when they perform occasional injustices. Whether, as Soper apparently assumes, this reasoning reaches injustices that the officials recognize as such is dubious,[97] but it does explain why showing respect constitutes a moral reason to obey when the injustice of a law is not recognized by those who adopt and enforce it.

In contrast with the position that the duty to obey attaches to unjust as well as just laws stands the traditional natural law view, capsulized in the somewhat misleading phrase that "an unjust law is not really a law." As we shall see, that view is a good bit more complex than is often recognized, but it does deny, in some sense, that the duty to obey the law reaches unjust laws.

The most familiar passage on this subject is one from Aquinas, and it provides a good starting point for analysis:

> . . . Laws framed by man are either just or unjust. If they be just, they have the power of binding in conscience. . . . Now laws are said to be just, both from the end, when, to wit, they are ordained to the common good,—and from their author, that is to say, when the law that is made does not exceed the power of the lawgiver,—and from their form, when, to wit, burdens are laid on the subjects, according to an equality of proportion and a view to the common good.

> On the other hand laws may be unjust in two ways: first, by being contrary to human good, through being opposed to the things mentioned above:—either in respect of the end, as when an authority imposes on his subjects burdensome laws, conducive, not to the common good, but rather to his own cupidity or vainglory;—or in respect of the author, as when a man makes a law that goes beyond the power committed to him;—or in respect of the form, as when burdens are imposed unequally on the community, although with a view to the common good. The like are acts of violence rather than laws; because as Augustine says (De Lib. Arb. i.5), *a law that is not just seems to be no law at all.* Wherefore such laws do not bind in conscience, except perhaps in order to avoid scandal or disturbance, for which cause a man should even yield his right. . . .

Secondly, laws may be unjust through being opposed to the Divine good: such are the laws of tyrants inducing to idolatry, or to anything else contrary to the Divine law: and laws of this kind must nowise be observed. . . .[98]

According to Aquinas laws may be contrary to human good not only when they are directed at objects other than that good but also when they exceed the lawmaker's authority and when they impose unequal burdens. Because a "law" that exceeds the lawmaker's legal authority will not usually be considered a norm requiring obedience within a legal system,[99] we may put that kind of defect aside. We may also assume that inequality of burden connotes a substantial injustice about comparative burdens and benefits. Not each small deviation from an ideally just distribution can reasonably be enough to make a law unjust and not binding in conscience. Finnis adds another criterion of injustice: not treating people as capable of self-direction by failing to afford them an opportunity to understand and comply with the law.[100] And we might add from the natural rights tradition that an important category of unjust laws is gross violations of conscience.[101]

The question that concerns us does not arise when some higher, constitutional, standard renders invalid a statute or administrative rule that is unjust in some respect; such legislation fails to be law within the legal order itself. The issue is whether a law that meets all the criteria of validity within a legal order[102] and yet remains deficient from the standpoint of justice fails to raise the duty to obey.

Although Aquinas quotes Augustine to the effect that an unjust law "seems to be no law," he does not suggest that it is ineffective for all purposes[103] or that it may be totally disregarded. In contrast with a law that is opposed to Divine good and may not be observed, a law that is contrary to human good does not bind in conscience, "except perhaps to avoid scandal or disturbance. . . . " Aquinas himself does not explicate this cryptic qualification, but reflection indicates a variety of relevant moral considerations that the law may generate. One kind brought to mind by the words "scandal or disturbance" concerns the desirability of avoiding disruption of the social fabric. If the government is generally just and disobedience of an unjust law would threaten its stability, that would be a strong reason for compliance.

Unjust laws can also affect morally proper behavior by rendering others subject to legal sanction. Imagine a law requiring racial separation that a member of the dominant white racial majority rightly believes is unjust.[104] This person realizes that members of the oppressed black minority are hesitant to discourage overtures by whites with whom they have contact, and he also recognizes that officials learning of proscribed racially mixed gatherings inflict severe penalties on blacks and do little to whites. The fact of the law and its enforcement significantly alter the moral responsibilities of a prominant white person toward the blacks with whom he or she might associate.

We must conclude that elaborating the distinction between just and unjust laws cannot possibly resolve all questions about the moral appropriateness of compliance or disobedience. In his careful treatment of the subject, John Finnis accepts this judgment, but nevertheless contends that unjust laws "simply fail, of themselves, to create any moral obligation whatever."[105] Finnis first qualifies the situations in which unjust laws do not create moral obligation; people are bound to obey otherwise acceptable laws that have been adopted from unacceptable motives, and they are also bound to obey laws that are unjust in their distribution of burdens as long as the distribution is not unjust to them.[106] Other unjust laws do not create moral obligation; there may be moral reasons that relate to the common good for obeying, but these are "not based on the good of *being* law-abiding. . . ."[107] The gist of Finnis's position seems to be that because a proper kind of law promotes the common good, a law that fails in this respect cannot generate the duty to be law-abiding.[108]

Despite a terminological difference, Finnis has conceded much of the moral substance in the arguments of Honoré, Mackie, Rawls, and Soper; but one practical divergence of moderate significance remains. While Finnis acknowledges that reasons concerning the stability of the whole system may create a duty to obey, apparently a citizen faced with an unjust law may decide if disobedience will actually threaten the law as a whole. He or she is thus permitted on such an occasion a consequentialist evaluation of the duty to obey, and may disobey if harmful consequences will not occur. The other theorists posit a nonconsequentialist duty to obey even when a law is unjust.[109] To consider this issue carefully, we need to repair to three elements of a nonconsequential duty suggested in the last section: (1) genuine duty rather than simple moral preferability; (2) applicability regardless of whether bad consequences are likely to occur in the particular instance; and (3) power to trump competing considerations of consequence.

Principles of reciprocation for benefits that law and government confer generally are sufficient to generate a duty to obey, making unwarranted disobedience blameworthy rather than merely a failure to do what would be morally preferable. The injustice of a particular law does not automatically remove the reasons for obedience or alter the basic relationships that make obedience a matter of duty. If obedience to an unjust law is morally preferable to disobedience for the sorts of reasons that underlie the duty to obey in cases of just laws, obedience remains a requirement of duty.

Whether or not the duty should be viewed as applicable regardless of the likely consequences of disobedience is more troublesome. Let us assume, first, that an actor regards a law as clearly unjust and is correct in that judgment. Obedience to an unjust law will usually, if not always, constitute a kind of support for that law.[110] Obedience will also support the law more generally, which one has a duty to do in a nearly just society. If one has a duty to support just institutions *and* a duty not to support injustice, these two duties come into conflict in the instance of an unjust law. An actor can satisfy one duty only at the expense of the other.

A sensible approach to this dilemma is to attend to the likely consequences of what one does, and gauge whether an act of obedience will in fact have the beneficial effects regarding the common good and just institutions that usually flow from obedience to law and will promote the particular law's injustice. Roughly, what would otherwise be viewed as two duties that apply independent of consequences might be treated as canceling each other out, leaving the actor to weigh the effects of his actions. If, in terms of justice or common good, only beneficial or only harmful consequences would flow from obedience, the actor's duty would be determined accordingly. In the event of a mix of consequences, both duties would still carry some power; in the absence of other considerations, overall duty would depend on whether, overall, justice or common good would be served by obedience.

One might conceptualize this conclusion by saying that in the event of a clearly unjust law, the natural duty to obey should be viewed in a partly consequential way, its application resting on likely actual damage to the common good or just institutions.[111]

If the natural duty to obey has some power to override ordinary considerations of desirable consequences, it would retain that power in this setting. That is to say, if justice overall would be furthered by obedience, one might have the duty to obey despite a balance of welfare consequences favorable to disobedience.

A defender of a nonconsequential account of the duty to obey might claim that my assumption of clear injustice is unrealistic, that part of the point of a nonconsequential duty is to deal with uncertainties and disagreements over whether particular laws are just. Relying on the analysis in the last section, he could urge that a nonconsequential view of the duty is a substantial guard against misjudgment. The implications of this position for cases of perceived clear injustice are somewhat cloudy. Presumably people do have a natural duty to avoid supporting injustice that applies when the law permits someone to support injustice or not. It would be logically possible to suppose that the moral duty simply terminates when the law *demands* an act of support, but given all the injustices that have been demanded by laws in even fairly just societies, the idea that the duty terminates in the face of the law seems implausible. If that is so, an actor who believes that a law is clearly unjust finds himself in the dilemma of having conflicting duties. Resolution would then take something like the course outlined.

The worry about misjudgment may still apply to cases of uncertainty. Perhaps actors should view themselves as under a nonconsequential duty to obey when they are not firmly convinced that a law is unjust.

In a broad sense, I have supported Finnis against the other theorists in the view that application of the duty to obey unjust laws is different from its most forceful application to just laws. But in the previous section, I have already rejected the idea that the duty applies forcefully even to all laws that are not subject to a defect of justice. I have argued that, given the many trivial, foolish, and overbroad laws and the many circumstances in which disobedience, even if widespread, will not undermine the serious aims behind laws, a natural duty to obey does not apply on every occasion of application of even just laws. Thus, I agree with the other theorists opposed to Finnis who argue that, in terms of a duty to obey, no sharp distinction exists between unjust laws and all just laws.

The absence of such a distinction is further shown by a richer analysis of the character of just and unjust laws. Laws that are just in their general terms may have some unjust applications. Do these create the natural duty in its most powerful form because the law as a whole promotes the common good, or do they not create that duty because the particular feature in question is defective? Laws could often have been better drafted to avoid their unjust features; but sometimes laws are drafted as well as they can be, given the appropriate limits on proliferation of exceptions and the needs of enforceability, and yet produce morally unjust results in some cases. Do these laws, wholly appropriate as written, create the strongest kind of natural duty? Presumably, Finnis would answer "yes"; but these further subtleties about what it means for a law to be unjust reinforce doubt that a radical difference in the duty to obey depends on whether a law, as written, does or does not pass the test of justice.

The injustice of a law is highly relevant to whether people should, on balance, obey it, and injustice can directly affect whether the duty to obey is conceived nonconsequentially; but the borderline of just laws does not mark a prominent and rigid boundary in the duty to obey.

Unjust Regimes

On the question whether a duty to obey the law ceases to exist if a regime as a whole is unjust, Rawls opposes the views of the other theorists of natural duty. They claim, with minimal qualifications in the case of Soper,[112] that the duty exists in all political orders. Rawls, focusing on the duty to comply with just institutions, suggests that the duty applies only within just political orders. Since Rawls's ground of duty is different from, and narrower than, that proposed by other theorists, and the nature of the duty to obey may affect its application to unjust regimes, the respective positions are not necessarily irreconcilable.

I will first concentrate on a duty to obey that derives from the necessity of government and the need to promote the common good. Here, we may distinguish between laws as they settle coordination problems and as they lend support to the government in power. Most laws will serve both functions, but one function or the other is likely to predominate. Traffic laws and laws restraining personal violence mainly concern coordination and restraint within the society; a law forbidding citizens to criticize the government or to listen to foreign broadcasts mainly bolsters the government. My discussion of the duty of fair play in Chapter 7 suggested that that duty applies even when the source of authority for law is an unjust regime, as long as the distribution of burdens and benefits among citizens is fair. I used the ordinary criminal law, which may shift very little as regimes change drastically, as a practical illustration in the political context. The same illustration may be used here to show that some laws that concern coordination and restraint can generate a natural duty to obey even when a regime is unjust in another respect. Only the existing government is actually in a position to resolve coordination problems; if it does so in a fair way, reasons for obedience related to the common good apply.

The conclusion is different when one focuses on laws whose function is to support the government. If the regime is unjust, a citizen does not have a duty to those who govern or to fellow citizens to keep the regime in power. This stark formulation requires some clarifications and qualifications, which I will introduce by examining what I call the argument from anarchy.

The argument begins with the premise that any government, or almost any government, is better than anarchy, the absence of government. Citizens who live under even a very bad government are getting something of significant value, and they have a duty to preserve this valuable institution. I will not pause to examine in depth the proposition that even a very bad government is preferable to anarchy,[113] a proposition with which I agree.[114] The crucial flaw in the argument lies elsewhere. Anarchy may exist for brief periods in turbulent societies, but it is not a feasible long-term option for modern human beings. The only realistic alternative to a very bad government is some other government. If we assume that the worst possible government is better than anarchy, it still is worse than any feasible option. Its value and claim to preservation must be judged in terms of feasible options, not in terms of a social state that is not practically conceivable.

What I have said about anarchy points the way to how the overall injustice of a regime should be regarded as affecting a duty to obey government-preserving laws. For this purpose, justice is comparative. If we grant that liberal democracy is a preferable form of government to other possibilities that now manifest themselves, we must recognize that not every society is ready for and capable of maintaining that form of government. What is a good government for a particular society must be judged in terms of what is possible for that society. And obedience to support a government must be judged in terms of likely changes. If one knows that the only government likely to replace the present one will be more unjust, that is a strong reason to support the present government. One must also take into account the dangers of violence and instability in deciding whether to disobey in the hope that a better government will emerge. For laws that mainly support the government, the duty to obey turns very much on context, on the degree of injustice and practically feasible options.

Many laws are mixed, serving a coordination purpose and supporting the government. One's duty to obey can be divided between these two respects and analyzed in the terms indicated above.

I need say relatively little about Rawls's duty to support just institutions. The application of that duty must also be understood in comparative terms. If one's society has a constitutional order that is as just as one could hope for in that society, then a duty to support just institutions should reach compliance with its laws. The application of the duty must also attend to subparts of political orders. An oppressive regime might have relatively just administration of ordinary criminal laws. Especially if change in government is not likely, a duty to support just institutions might well require compliance with subparts of the legal system that are just.

The overall conclusion is that the natural duty to obey does not apply only to just regimes and that the relevance of injustice must be assessed in light of context and alternatives. This conclusion complements my conclusion in this and prior chapters that the "moral legitimacy" or justness of a government is no guarantee that its laws carry a duty to obey in all applications; the discussion here indicates that the moral *illegitimacy* of a regime is no guarantee that its laws generate no duty to obey.

NOTES

1. T. Aquinas, Treatise on Law, from Summa Theologica.

2. J. Finnis, Natural Law and Natural Rights (1980).

3. I am not confident that Finnis's position represents the dominant view on each point I discuss; and it may well be that some other positions within the natural law tradition can avoid particular criticisms I offer. I also have no view on how Aquinas himself is best to be interpreted on points that divide those who consider themselves followers of his.

For readers familiar with modern legal philosophy, I note that the views of Lon Fuller and Ronald Dworkin accept too little of the traditional position to count as natural law theories in the sense I use here.

4. See Aquinas, note 1 supra, Of the Essence of Law, Second Article; Of the Power of Human Law, Fourth Article.

5. See Finnis, note 2 supra at 231–32.

6. See id. at 245–52.

7. Id. at 314–17.

8. Id. at 318.

9. Id. at 319.

10. See Alasdair MacIntyre's reference to the "notion of the political community as a common project. . . . " After Virtue 146 (1981).

11. Finnis, note 2 supra at 246–52.

12. See id. at 351–66; Aquinas, note 1 supra, at Of the Power of Human Law, Fourth Article. Augustine, and other members of the early Christian

church, tended to take a more absolute view of the duty to obey political authorities. See H. Deane, The Political and Social Ideas of St. Augustine 89–91, 142–52 (1963).

13. J. Rawls, A Theory of Justice 333–55 (1971).

14. Id. at 344.

15. The devices of the original position and veil of ignorance are designed to draw out principles that we would accept in reflective equilibrium, a point at which discrepancies between our general moral principles and our intuitions about particular moral conclusions are reconciled after they are adjusted to fit with each other (id. at 48–53). The conditions of the original position are also set on the basis of a reflective equilibrium that reconciles their apparent appropriateness with the appropriateness of the results they yield (id. at 20). In writings since A Theory of Justice, Rawls has clarified the status of the conditions of the original position and of the principles derived from it. These are not claimed to rest on any universally valid theory of human nature or rational choice, but rather on the "basic intuitive ideas that are embedded in the political institutions of a constitutional democratic regime and the public traditions of their interpretation." Rawls, Justice as Fairness: Political Not Metaphysical, 14 Phil & Pub. Aff. 223, 225 (1980). The agreement in the original position represents a conception of persons as "free and equal." Rawls, Kantian Constructivism in Moral Theory, LXXVII J. Phil. No. 9, 515, 552–54 (1980).

16. A Theory of Justice, at 60–90. Rawls claims that those in the original position will want to ensure that their welfare will not be sacrificed for the welfare of others. They will also recognize that in actual societies public acceptance and approval of the utilitarian principle would generate frustrations and resentments that could be avoided by acceptance of the "difference" principle, which imposes less onerous strains of commitment and is more stable. Id. at 176–83, 498–500.

17. I understand Rawls to claim that this "more general conception of justice" (id. at 62) would be accepted in the original position during the process by which the parties arrive at more specific principles.

18. Id. at 542–43. At an earlier stage of development, liberty might not be given priority.

19. Id. at 60–90.

20. Id. at 333–42. One ground for the rejection of utilitarianism at the level of individual choice is the poor fit between it and a nonutilitarian theory of justice.

21. Id. at 334.

22. Id. at 350–62.

23. Id. at 351.

24. See note 15.

25. Rawls indicates that "it would be possible to choose many of the natural duties before those for the basic structure without changing the principles in any substantive way." Id. at 110.

26. I add the word desirable here to cover the possibility that persons in an original position might opt to have a government promote a particular conception of the good, making judgments that did not involve justice between persons, as it is usually understood.

27. A separate principle of this sort might not be needed, however, if utilitarianism were selected as the appropriate principle for justice in social institutions.

28. See especially Rawls, Legal Obligation and the Duty of Fair Play, in S. Hook, ed., Law and Philosophy 3 (1964). The ground of the duty has altered, but the reasons why the duty applies to unjust as well as just laws remains essentially the same.

29. All of these democracies fall short of Rawls's principles of justice in what they actually accomplish and in what are taken as guiding principles, but they do approximate these principles in important respects. The duty to support existing institutions may generally be stronger in societies that are *more* just.

30. See, generally, Ball, Obligation: Not to the Law But to the Neighbor, 18 Ga. L. Rev. 811, 912–14 (1984); and Olsen, Socrates on Legal Obligation: Legitimation Theory and Civil Disobedience, 18 Ga. L. Rev. 929, 961–64 (1984).

31. Rawls, A Theory of Justice, at 109, 117.

32. Possibly actions might be required that themselves would have no measurable effect but, taken together with similar actions, would have a positive effect. See, generally, D. Parfit, Reasons and Persons 75–78 (1984).

33. David Richards, Conscience, Human Rights, and the Anarchist Challenge to the Obligation to Obey the Law, 18 Ga. L. Rev. 771, 784 (1984), casts the natural duty of justice in this way.

34. A. J. Simmons, Moral Principles and Political Obligations, at 147–52 (1979).

35. Though Rawls is evidently thinking mainly of people who will be reached by just institutions, he is not clear whether the duty to help establish just arrangements that do not exist extends to just arrangements that will not apply to us even when created. Simmons assumes that Rawls posits a general duty to promote just institutions whatever the scope of their application but that Rawls thinks this duty is weaker than the duty to support just arrangements that apply to us. Simmons himself concludes that, unless the arrangements have been voluntarily accepted, the duties are of equal force—indeed, are reducible to a single duty to promote just institutions. Id. at 154.

36. Id. at 155–56.

37. One might say that the political arrangements of those countries apply to us to the extent of our relations with them.

38. Rawls talks of a natural duty to render aid that applies generally (Rawls, note 13 supra at 114); but it does not follow that when a rescue must be made an ordinary beachgoer should regard his responsibilities no differ-

ently from a designated lifeguard. Assuming that a compulsory draft for military service is morally acceptable, a country may reasonably demand service of residents but not visitors.

39. We can even imagine a society in which law observance is so widespread that actors who commit peaceable disobedience and then submit to punishment might actually strengthen the political processes by increasing sensitivity to issues of justice; and this might be true even if their own claims of injustice are ill-founded or trivial.

40. Compare Richards, note 33 supra at 784, whose account of the duty is otherwise close to Rawls's but who asks if obedience will actually advance and not retard justice.

41. Honoré, Must We Obey? Necessity as a Ground of Obligation, 67 Va. L. Rev. 39 (1981).

42. Id. at 51.

43. David Lyons suggests that these duties derive from a more general duty to help others in need. Lyons, Need, Necessity and Political Obligation, 67 Va. L. Rev. 63, 70 (1981).

44. Honoré, supra note 41 at 58–59.

45. Of course, a particular society might meet this challenge by communicating to alien residents more precisely what is expected of them, though the chapter on promissory obligation suggests the vagueness that is likely to inhere in any general oath.

46. With native-born prospective doctors, the state might make a similar bargain by agreeing to pay the expenses of medical education in return for such an agreement.

47. See id. at 48. Honoré does not deny that the duty to obey can be outweighed, but he supposes that it has some force in every instance.

48. See P. Soper, A Theory of Law 75–90 (1984); see also Soper, The Obligation to Obey the Law, in R. Gavison, ed., Issues in Contemporary Legal Philosophy: The Influence of H. L. A. Hart (forthcoming Oxford Univ. Pr.). I provide a more extensive analysis and criticism in Greenawalt, Respect, Fair Play, and the Obligation to Obey, in id.

49. A Theory of Law, at 77–79.

50. Putting the point this way falsifies the strong sense of identification that many parents feel toward their children. Reduced to the practical level, Soper's theory reaches a parental directive to do homework as well as a directive to set the table.

51. The Obligation to Obey the Law at 35.

52. Id. at 26, 44.

53. Id. at 32–33.

54. Soper illustrates his theory with a lifeboat passenger who awakens to find someone (not an officer) in de facto control. Soper stresses as a reason to comply with directives "the impact on the person who stands in front of me trying to do his best to accomplish ends thought to advance the interests of the

group as a whole, including myself" (A Theory of Law, at 80). How little the feelings of the person exercising de facto authority count here in comparison with the success of the endeavor!

55. Soper concentrates on officials because their acceptance of rules is a minimal condition of law, see Obligation to Obey the Law at n. 37, and Soper wants to tie an obligation to obey to what counts as law. See Greenawalt, note 48 supra at n. 18 for criticism.

56. See Chapter 6, What Is an Obligation to Obey?

57. These points are explored in greater depth in Greenawalt, note 48 supra.

58. One might talk of remote likelihoods that someone will be affronted, but if that is sufficient to support utilitarian reasons for obedience, then the likelihood of creating a bad habit or bad example to others is a much more straightforward utilitarian reason that will apply in every case.

59. Mackie, Obligations to Obey the Law, 67 Va. L. Rev. 143 (1981).

60. Outlined in id., the theory is more fully developed in J. L. Mackie, Ethics (1977).

61. Mackie talks of "inventing" moral prescriptions that serve human purposes. But the idea of invention should not be taken too literally. People tend to develop moral principles that will make life in society tolerable, and the relatively small minority that understand the relation between human needs and moral principles may sensibly promote those that are useful in a more self-conscious manner.

62. This is not Mackie's only objection to utilitarianism. See J. L. Mackie, Ethics, at 125–48.

63. Mackie, note 59 supra at 153.

64. As indicated earlier, it is doubtful if Soper himself intends any stronger sense of obligation, but if he does not, his sense of duty is weaker than that ordinarily employed.

65. Although the importance of the task in which officials are engaged generates the duty of respect, Soper's argument for the duty does not explicitly rely on the need for obedience. Given all he says, the duty might come into play even if society would be unaffected by widespread disobedience. Thus, I may be unfairly stretching Soper's own account by including him among theorists who make the *contributions* of obedience to an essential social objective critical. We could interpret, or transform, that account, however, to emphasize the long-term harmful effects if officials are not given respect.

66. See note 65 supra for a qualification about Soper's duty to show respect.

67. Of course, if such contributions are a slight step toward rectifying an unjust global distribution of wealth, gratitude may not be called for.

68. I do not address some of the subtle questions concerning the minimal involvements necessary to make one a member of the community on whom demands are properly placed. Perhaps if I am visiting another country, and the law of that country undertakes to protect the personal property of visitors

in the same way as it protects the personal property of residents, I have a natural duty to comply that extends at least to laws protecting personal property.

I am dubious that even the conditions indicated in the text are enough to generate a strong duty to show respect to officials, especially since most officials occupy their positions for largely self-interested reasons.

69. M. Singer, Generalization in Ethics 137 (1961). Singer actually calls this a generalized principle of consequences, which he distinguishes from a broader principle of generalization. The distinction is not important here. Some difficulties with any broad version of the generalization principle are illuminatingly discussed in J. Fishkin, The Limits of Obligation 97–146 (1982).

70. See M. Singer, note 69 supra at 72, discussing "invertible" situations. If desirable consequences *depend* on different people doing different things, the principle offers no guide for individual choice. Edna Ullmann-Margalit observes that these situations are not true "prisoners' dilemma" problems and that it is the latter to which the generalization principle applies. The Emergence of Norms 57–58 (1977).

71. Because everyone's remaining celibate would mean the termination of the human race, it would be better if everyone tried to have at least one child than if everyone tried to have no children; but as long as the self-interested inclinations of others lead them to have children in excess of the number that would be ideally desirable, the prospective celibate commits no moral wrong by refraining from having children. See H. Sidgwick, The Methods of Ethics 487–88 (7th ed., 1962); and K. Baier, The Moral Point of View 209 (1958). The principle of generalization is relevant only if the number of others who, apart from their sense of restraint, would like to engage in the act is great enough so that negative consequences would occur if they all did engage in the act; therefore, the principle may not apply if others obey only because they fear getting caught disobeying a rule.

72. See D. Lyons, Forms and Limits of Utilitarianism 63–75 (1965).

73. This is a threshold example in which the actor is sure the particular threshold has not been passed.

74. See, generally, Singer, note 69 supra. I address this claim as it relates to principles governing practical choice. I do not consider whether at some higher level the principle of generalization limits the kinds of approaches to moral choice an individual could claim are sound, precluding the assertion that moral principles are sound for him if they could not be employed by others.

75. "Act only on that maxim whereby thou canst at the same time will that it should become a universal law." Id. at 9.

76. An extreme existentialist might say that a determination about what a person should do has no conclusive bearing on what anyone else should do; however, he probably would not deny the proposition in the text, but rather assert a moral uniqueness of each individual and situation that precludes

judgment that two situations requiring choices are essentially similar, or argue that moral principles yield no correct choice even in the initial situation.

77. See J. L. Mackie, note 60 supra at 83–90.

78. See, generally, Ullmann-Margalit, note 70 supra at 53–60. She assumes that moral norms designed to resolve the difficulties of prisoners' dilemma situations will include a generalization principle.

79. In his treatment of claims about the relevance of universalization, C. D. Broad found many to be ill-founded and argued that those that were well-founded rested on fairness. Broad, On the Function of False Hypotheses in Ethics, 26 Intern. J. Ethics 377 (1916).

80. One is tempted to say that the principle of generalization does not require a cooperative scheme, whereas the duty of fair play does. But my analysis of the duty of fair play suggests that at its edges it reaches schemes that are cooperative only in a broad sense.

81. Of course, she might quickly concede a prima facie duty in the weak sense of a starting presumption that would operate until she saw that the basic ground of obedience did not apply.

82. Mackie says explicitly that the duty is not derivable from other duties, and Rawls speaks of an independent natural duty. Finnis, Honoré, and Soper each relate their duty to obey to some broader duty, but either the broader duty is itself dubious or the derivation is by no means obvious.

83. The import of his analysis is to persuade us that the natural duty to support just institutions is the best moral principle to protect just institutions. His specification that principles of morals must be ones that can be publicly announced and taught also supports the conclusion that the true principles are those that will work best for people.

84. Honoré, supra note 41, at 42–44.

85. Finnis, supra note 2, at 297–350.

86. Recall from Chapter 6 the criticisms that act utilitarianism is too difficult a standard to follow and that all versions of utilitarianism make greater demands on people than they can plausibly be expected to accept.

87. Finnis, supra note 2, at 298–308. See also G. J. Warnock, The Object of Morality 33–34 (1971).

88. I pass over here the reality that many people who believe in an afterlife will suppose that promisees who have died are capable of being disappointed or angered.

89. It is doubtful *how great* an effect such attitudes would have on the institution of promises. One consequence would be fewer secret promises with more promises being made in front of people likely to know if they are violated.

90. I am talking here about the basic obligation to keep a promise, not whether that obligation can be outweighed by strong competing consequential considerations.

91. If, for example, Alasdair McIntyre is right that virtues such as truth and courage must be exercised without regard to consequences if they are to

produce what he calls "internal goods" (see After Virtue 185 [1981]), an argument might be mounted that moral duties generally will best be conceived in nonconsequential terms.

92. See note 61.

93. Obviously the *degree* of sharing is strongly affected by language, geographic location, economic development, and particular cultural traditions.

94. See Dauenhauer, On Strengthening the Law's Obligatory Character, 18 Ga. L. Rev. 821, 825 (1984), who suggests that "exaggerated claims concerning the duty to obey a provision of the law have the effect of weakening that duty."

95. See Pennock, The Obligation to Obey the Law and the Ends of the State, in S. Hook, ed., Law and Philosophy 77, 79–81 (1964).

96. They will, of course, also obey some unjust laws that they think are just; but these laws would be obeyed if they conceived their duty as reaching all laws, just and unjust. The obedience of unjust laws raises different questions than the disobedience of just laws; hence, I do not focus on it in this discussion.

97. In his book, supra note 48, Soper emphasizes the good faith of officials with respect to the overall political order; but if an individual is confident that the good faith of officials does not extend to a particular law or segment of the laws, why the individual should show respect by obeying that law or laws is not clear. To take a practical example, an individual within a system he or she regarded as acceptable might think that officials act in good faith with respect to most laws but that when it comes to laws limiting sexual acts among adults, officials willfully impose their own blind prejudices or pander to the prejudices of a narrowminded minority of voters. I do not understand why respect for officials in other contexts should require obedience to these laws if the individual's appraisal is correct. In a subsequent article, The Moral Value of Law, 84 Mich. L. Rev. 63, 75 (1985), Soper intimates that there may be no good reason to obey a particular law if the "good faith" of the officials is lacking as to it.

98. T. Aquinas, Treatise on Law, from Summa Theologica, Of the Power of Human Law, Fourth Article, Whether Human Law Binds a Man in Conscience? Though Aquinas quotes Augustine in this passage, the latter took a more absolute view of the duty to obey. See H. Deane, The Political and Social Ideas of St. Augustine 89–91, 142–52 (1963).

99. "Ultra vires" laws are not typically treated as if they never existed, but usually someone who refuses to comply with such a law is not considered to have done anything illegal. The notable exception to this principle in American law concerns disobedience to injunctions whose substance exceeds a court's power. The rule requiring obedience seems to be a compound of the perceived need to protect the authority of courts and the existence of techniques to get invalid injunctions vacated fairly quickly. See, generally, *Walker v. Birmingham*, 388 U.S. 307 (1967).

100. J. Finnis, Natural Law and Natural Rights 353 (1980).

101. See Richards, Conscience, Human Rights, and the Anarchist Challenge to the Obligation to Obey the Law, 18 Ga. L. Rev. 771-77 (1984). One might, of course, say that any unacceptable violation of conscience is not a promotion of the common good; but one would need to recognize that some violations of conscience are reasonably thought to promote the welfare of the majority.

102. The issue is most straightforward in a legal order, such as that possessed until recently by Great Britain, in which no higher standards of validity exist. British constitutionalism has been altered in this regard by adherence to European conventions under which British laws may be reviewed by supranational organs. Even in the days of parliamentary supremacy, the law of Great Britain included standards of fairness and justice to *interpret* legislation; such interpretations, of course, could be overridden by clear parliamentary mandate.

103. The point is emphasized in Finnis, note 100 supra at 363-66, who most helpfully relegates to its proper subsidiary position the dispute over whether an unjust law is really a law.

104. Any system that accepts racial separation is almost certainly disqualified from being an "acceptable" system, at least at this stage in history. One can imagine more debatable illustrations of the same point that would apply to systems that are acceptable overall.

105. Finnis, note 100 supra at 360.

106. Id. Finnis apparently has in mind unjust shares of otherwise acceptable burdens, as might exist in an unfair tax schedule, rather than a system that burdens people in a wholly illegitimate way, as in slavery. His conclusion that those who benefit from burdens that are too light have a duty to obey shows how far notions of reciprocity underlie his ideas of promotion of the common good.

107. Id. at 361.

108. Finnis himself employs the complicated terminology of a "legal obligation in the moral sense." Id.

109. Soper suggests (A Theory of Law at 75-90) that his duty to show respect may be understood in either a utilitarian or a deontological way, but he inclines toward the latter understanding.

110. If someone submitted to a law in a manner that plainly indicated a sense of moral outrage at what the law demanded, the act of obedience might not be supportive of the law.

111. Alternatively, one might say that the duty in a nonconsequential form still has relevance, because it does the work of canceling any nonconsequential duty not to support injustice.

112. He says that government must at least take into account the interests of all citizens (though not necessarily in fair proportion) and be believed by officials to be just. Quite possibly the Union of South Africa and the Soviet Union, for example, qualify under these criteria.

113. A serious discussion of that subject would require, among other things, a careful appraisal of what one means by anarchy, of the elements of ordinary government that would necessarily be absent. Roughly, I have in mind the absence of organized coercive sanctions. I believe that small groups of people with common goals and small "primitive" societies can manage without such sanctions but a modern large society cannot.

114. I doubt, however, that an extremely wicked government, such as that of Nazi Germany, is preferable to anarchy.

III

THE LIMITS OF JUSTIFIABLE DISOBEDIENCE

9

Resolutions Among Competing Moral Grounds: The Absence of Clear Priorities

Part II of this book explored basic grounds for a moral duty to obey the law as such. Though the analysis has failed to yield any single ground of duty to obey all laws, or all just laws, on every occasion of their application, it has established multiple grounds for obedience in various circumstances.

In Part III, I turn to the claims to disobey outlined roughly in Chapter 3 and inquire as to how a person may resolve conflicts between these and moral reasons for compliance, including independent moral grounds to do what the law demands and whatever grounds for obeying the law as such apply. I also discuss possible limits on the occasions for and tactics of disobedience, including the troubling question when, if ever, violent acts of disobedience are warranted. The investigations in this part lead to rejection of many sharp lines that have sometimes been proposed as dividing the morally permissible from the morally impermissible. Although decisions concerning whether and how to disobey the law often involve delicate judgments that cannot be captured by rigid categorizations, some signposts to identify critical features do exist.

Resolutions of conflicting reasons could lead a person to various conclusions about his moral responsibilities. He might think he "ought" to obey the law or "ought" to disobey, and the "ought" might be perceived as one of greater or lesser stringency.[1] Alternatively, he might think he is morally free to obey or not. I do not mean to refer here to cases in which a person is uncertain what duty he has, as frequently as those may occur, but to cases in which he reaches a positive conclusion that his choice is not covered by a duty in either direction. That could happen if he did not think any of the moral reasons on either side, taken alone or together, established a moral "ought," or if he thought such considerations on one side were somehow canceled out by considerations on the other side, leaving him to choose between acts. A prima facie duty to obey might be canceled by a competing duty or by some special moral right that carries a freedom to disobey. Belief that one has a freedom to obey or not would not necessarily imply that a choice was morally indifferent, but if one of the alternatives was morally preferable, it would be a matter of supererogation rather than "ought."

This chapter mainly examines some abstract possibilities for resolving clashes of considerations. I explore in turn the possibilities that the duty to obey has priority over all else, that the duty has priority over utilitarian considerations and perhaps future-regarding considerations of justice, and that individual rights take priority over the duty. This substantive discussion is preceded by a brief elaboration of the difficulties of moral appraisal by outsiders that builds on some comments in Chapter 3.

CHOICES OF ACTION AND APPRAISALS OF OTHERS

Because I focus primarily on the person who must decide whether or not to obey a law, I want to highlight some of the complexities that affect the move from someone's making a decision about obedience to an outsider's appraisal of that choice.

Illustration 9-1:
Rachel reads in the newspaper that a large group of people have trespassed at a civilian nuclear power plant, protesting the development and use of such power. Rachel carefully thinks through the competing claims and decides that it would be morally wrong for her to engage in such a trespass. She is asked by her friend Sophia whether she thinks that the demonstrators have wrongly disobeyed the law.

What steps must Rachel take to go from her evaluation as a potential demonstrator to her evaluation of those who have demonstrated? Rachel might, of course, be hesitant to pass judgment on the demonstrators if her own conclusion was uncertain or concerned only moral preferability rather than "ought"; but I shall assume that Rachel's conclusion is certain and is about duty, not a weaker degree of moral preferability.

Four barriers, at least, still lie between her own conclusion and a simple response that "the demonstrators were wrong to disobey the law." Two barriers involve clarification.

Chapter 3 mentioned the familiar idea that a person is often to be praised for acting upon conscience even when the moral conclusion that his or her conscience reaches is mistaken.[2] Unless Rachel knows enough about the demonstrators' convictions to pass a judgment on both act and actors,[3] she will have to indicate carefully to Sophia that she is appraising only the morality of the action, not also offering moral praise or blame for the demonstrators.

Rachel must also deal with a certain ambiguity in Sophia's question: is Sophia asking for an overall judgment about the demonstrators' acts or a more particular judgment about their choice not to obey the law? If Rachel knows that her opinion of civilian nuclear power coincides with that of the demonstrators, but she considers the claims of law to be more weighty than they do, she can say both that the demonstrators acted wrongly overall and reached a mistaken conclusion about obeying the law. But if Rachel regards civilian nuclear power as much less of an evil than the demonstrators do, she might conclude that the trespass would be morally justified given the demonstrators' beliefs about civilian nuclear power but not justified given the actual facts. In this event, she should tell Sophia that the act is wrong because of a misappraisal of civilian nuclear power, not because the demonstrators have wrongly weighed the claims of law against competing claims. Relying on brief squibs of news on television or in newspaper articles, most outsiders will lack any precise notion of the demonstrators' reasoning, and, of course, the demonstrators themselves may come to the same practical choice from varying perspectives. Were Rachel to suffer this typical infirmity of outsider ignorance, her careful response to Sophia might be, "What they did was morally wrong, but I don't know whether they mistakenly assessed facts relating to nuclear power or mistakenly weighed moral claims about obedience to law."

The final two barriers go beyond clarification to the substance of

Rachel's evaluation. If an act would be morally wrong for her, it would be morally wrong for anyone similarly situated; but the trespassers may not be similarly situated. Insofar as balances of benefits and burdens are relevant to the duty to obey, differences in objective circumstances could affect the justifiability of obedience. Perhaps the use of nuclear power casts special burdens on those who live near the sites of power plants or on younger people, who are more likely to suffer the long-term effects of inadequate disposal of radioactive wastes. If Rachel is elderly and lives far from any site, she might be wrong to disobey, though disobedience might be justified for those at greater risk.

Not only may objective circumstances of this sort matter, but also individual acts and attitudes may be significant. For a promissory obligation, whether or not Rachel herself has undertaken to obey will matter; for the duty of fair play, her particular attitude, perhaps never revealed, toward benefits and burdens will count. Thus, she may have a duty that someone who is otherwise in identical circumstances may not have. Reliance on other sorts of duties may allow Rachel to judge the acts of the demonstrators without knowing such facts about them; but she might find herself unable to assess the morality of each demonstrator's action without knowing his or her present attitudes and the history of his or her various undertakings.

None of these difficulties precludes appraisal of the disobedient actions of others; however, they do indicate how tricky it can be to move from a judgment about one's own potential action to such an appraisal. I now shift from this set of complexities to the substantive resolutions that a potential actor must make, inquiring whether clear rules of priority can be established.

DO DUTIES TOWARD THE STATE TAKE PRIORITY?

Though rarely defended by academic writers on obedience to law, the idea that duties to the state have an absolute or near-absolute priority is one that often infects popular discussions of the subject. This view, which has roots in Christian and classical thought, reflects both the importance and the power of the state. Jesus's injunction to "render unto Caesar what is Caesar's"[4] and St. Paul's claim that, because political authority is instituted by God, "every person [should] be subject to the governing authorities"[5] have often been taken as demanding uncritical submission to civil authorities.[6] Although Christians through the ages have had very different interpretations of the relevant biblical passages[7] and of the citizen's obligations to the state, the basic premise that political authority is ordained by God has been one basis for assigning the claims of the state a high priority.

The Aristotelian idea that the state is the highest form of human community, one essential for human flourishing, has similar implications; with some modification, this idea has been transformed into a central aspect of the Catholic tradition through the writings of Aquinas. The undoubted necessity of the state, the inclusiveness of its control, and the immensity of its coercive force help bolster the view that its claims are highly important. Further, belief that the state itself makes a moral claim to priority (a subject discussed in Chapters 2 and 4) and that it acts properly in overriding other claims when it enforces the law is sometimes thought to lead to the conclusion that the citizen, at least in a just state, should accede to this claim of priority.

Were a powerful basis to support the view that obligations to the state take absolute priority, or do so with highly limited exceptions, we could comfortably conclude that obedience to law should win out over competing moral claims. But, if we put aside religious assertions based on Scripture—which, in a pluralist culture, are not a proper basis for developing a shared public morality—we discover the absence of any compelling reason for placing moral claims to obey the law on a higher, qualitatively different, level than other moral claims.

That the state employs a coercive force that is not available to other organizations is not by itself a reason for its demands to have a specially high moral status nor is the fact that, *within the law*, the claims of law take priority. There may be good reasons why the state typically treats the demands of law as overriding competing demands (Part IV suggests some important qualifications to this assumption); but the viability of a political order need not depend on individuals' submerging other moral demands in the face of state claims. Even if the state asserts that its demands have moral as well as legal priority, individuals need not concede the moral validity of this claim.

The more appealing grounds for priority lie in the inclusiveness of the society embraced by the state and the centrality of the state's purposes for human life; but these grounds also do not establish any clear priority for demands of the state. Reflection on the bases of moral duties to obey suggests one reason for skepticism. The most powerful sources of duty are reducible to duties to one's fellow citizens. Many duties are owed them directly, and even a promise to obey made to government officials mainly concerns what one owes other citizens rather than the officials who receive the promise. Suppose Richard believes that military nuclear weapons seriously threaten the lives of all his country's inhabitants, or that a particular war involves every citizen of the country in a great moral evil. If a violation of law will help to end one of these conditions, a duty to comply with the law would not necessarily win out over a duty to prevent major harm, or involvement in evil, that is ultimately addressed to the same group of fellow citizens.[8]

More fundamentally, any notion that a more inclusive relationship necessarily takes moral priority is misguided. Though modern emphasis on a powerful state limited by individual rights may give the notion some credence, the growth of supranational political entities certainly shows that inclusiveness itself is not the only relevant test. A citizen of a Common Market country is not likely to suppose that a duty to all citizens of that economic unit takes priority over a duty to citizens of his or her own country if the two come into irreconcilable conflict.[9]

If inclusiveness is not critical, perhaps the dependence of other relationships on the state is a basis for the priority of its claims. Within a single society, some institutions, such as local government and legally created corporations, are literally creatures of the state. The demands of the state's law may well take priority over any competing demands of these subsidiary organizations. But many relationships within a state are not subsidiary in this way. Strong family ties, for example, preceded complex political organizations. Even if modern maintenance of these relationships depends on the protections of an organized state, that does not mean the moral importance of the relationship is less than the moral importance of relations to the state. Especially if one thought the state could survive and accomplish its purposes pretty well on the basis of coercion, whereas families and other institutions depend more heavily on moral commitment, one might think one's moral duties in respect to the latter were as significant as one's moral duties toward the state.

Perhaps the most critical flaw in the idea of the priority of the state involves the variability of moral duties. In practical settings, the strength of moral requirements depends on how they are generated and their situational importance. An explicit promise to faculty colleagues might override a weak duty of fair play to fellow citizens, even though one's responsibilities toward the state should generally take precedence over responsibilities to one's faculty. A similar outcome may be reached when two duties derive from the same type of moral consideration—say, to preserve just institutions. A just government matters more than a just university; but if a disastrous university injustice could be averted by a relatively minor violation of law, such as a sit-in in the university president's office, that would have only the most marginal effect on the preservation of a just government, one might conclude the violation to be worth undertaking.

I do not want to overstate the basic theme of this section. Government is extremely important; and ineffective or unjust government can gravely thwart human potentialities. Much of what the government does sets a minimum floor for conduct that should rarely, if ever, be violated. One should take one's responsibilities toward one's government and fellow citizens with the utmost seriousness. Especially if a decent government is already unstable, one should be very hesitant to undertake serious acts of disobedience.[10] Usually the serious claims of law do carry substantial moral weight, but no easy formula exists for according the legitimate moral claims of the state priority over all other moral claims.

DEONTOLOGICAL STANDARDS AND CONSEQUENTIAL CALCULATIONS

The most frequent attempts to establish moral priorities involve an ordering between deontological standards and utilitarian considerations. At first glance, the issue itself may seem to be a relatively simple one about the relationship between pursuing overall welfare, or some other good, and performing a duty understood in nonconsequential terms. But examination of the nature of some deontological or non-utilitarian duties shows that what initially appears to be a single question about priorities is acutally three basic questions, with some variations.

Some deontological duties are themselves defined in a way that makes consequences relevant. In Chapter 8, I briefly discussed the aspect of Rawls's natural duty to support just institutions whose import is to "assist in the establishment of just arrangements when they do not exist," at least when we can do so at little cost.[11] Both the terms *assist* and *establishment* imply efficacious actions; I assumed that this duty to enhance the chances of justice in the future does not demand the performance of actions known to be useless toward that end.

Once we understand that a deontological duty may require the promotion of some future state of moral rightness, what I call a positive deontological duty, we can also understand the possibility that an act having that effect may violate another duty to avoid a present wrong.[12] The second duty may be cast in nonconsequential terms—"always obey the law"—or it may be cast to apply whenever certain negative consequences will occur—"obey the law if disobeying will undermine a just institution." I shall call such a duty a negative deontological duty, usually not pausing to distinguish between a wholly nonconsequential duty and one whose application or strength depends on the occurrence of some negative consequences.

If one is concerned with the possible priority of negative deontological duties, like the natural duty to obey, one must consider them in possible competition with positive deontological duties as well as with overall desirable consequences. The comparative priority of positive deontological duties and overall desirable consequences is yet another issue, one I shall touch on in passing. I should note that for purposes of this discussion of priorities, I treat a moral principle that includes distributive limits on maximizing good consequences as a positive deontological duty, a shift from my equation of it with utilitarian approaches, done for a different purpose in Chapter 6.[13]

I shall say relatively little about utilitarian approaches to these problems. A thoroughgoing act utilitarian, one who uses average or maximum welfare (or some other good) as the ultimate standard of behavior, would claim, of course, that any proper moral norms that are apparently deontological collapse into utilitarian concerns. Thus, neither avoiding injustice nor promoting justice would take priority over desirable consequences; indeed, desirable consequences would have priority over them if a genuine conflict was possible and justice was not relegated to the status of a subcategory of utility.

A self-conscious act utilitarian could accept standards of right and justice as "rules of thumb" for resolving difficult situations, but would violate these standards if persuaded that the total balance of consequences was in favor of doing so. If a moral rule about right or justice were itself understood to promote desirable consequences, a rule utilitarian might say that a violation would be morally wrong even if it promotes good consequences; but I need not add here to the treatment in Chapter 6 of that subject. More interesting questions arise if, as I have concluded, the application of a number of duties to obey the law is properly conceived as not depending on an overall balance of favorable consequences.

Once one grants the independent, nonconsequential, significance of these duties, it follows that they will sometimes override utilitarian considerations, that it will be sometimes right to perform those duties even though favorable overall consequences would result from their violation. Can one say more than this? Must conflicts between deontological standards and utilitarian considerations be resolved according to their respective strengths in various situations, or can more determinate guidance be offered?

One possibility is that true deontological standards, or at least true negative deontological standards, can never be overridden by considerations of utility or that they can be overridden only by overwhelmingly powerful utilitarian considerations. The appeal of an absolutist position about negative deontological standards is that one should not do what is immediately wrong to achieve good objectives in the future. This viewpoint accords negative duties priority not only over desirable consequences generally, but also over positive deontological duties. A morality based on such a principle places great emphasis on the distinction between negative duties to avoid wrong and positive duties to promote right and good and on the distinction between the quality of one's own act and predictable consequences of one's act that derive from the choices of others.[14] Negative duties rate higher than positive ones, and one's primary moral responsibility concerns the quality of one's own acts, not the likely reactions of others.

Whatever weight these distinctions should bear in moral evaluation generally, the notion that they will conveniently resolve conflicts over obedience to law is implausible.

Illustration 9-2:

Ruth is driving her car at 10:00 A.M., a time of ordinary traffic for which the thirty-mile-per-hour speed limit was developed. By exceeding the limit, she will very slightly increase risks beyond those judged generally acceptable. She has a strong reason to exceed the limit because (*a*) she is driving a stranger with a painful broken arm to the hospital; or (*b*) she is a councilwoman and the town council will shortly vote on whether to relax the present speed limit, and her presence is necessary to defeat this undesirable proposal; or (*c*) same as (*b*) except the undesirable proposal is to forbid resident aliens from teaching in the local public school. Neither the law setting the speed limit nor more general provisions[15] would be understood to allow speeding in any of these cases.

In this setting, Ruth would have a prima facie duty to obey the speed limit based on fair play or one or more of the theories of natural duty. The negative consequences of her observing the limit are substantial on each assumption—pain for someone or bad legislation—but by no means catastrophic. If the absolutist denies that a modest violation of the duty to observe the speed limit is morally justified, he adopts a position on obedience to law more rigid than that held by most citizens. He might contend that the limit on aliens teaching would be an injustice, but that position is harder to sustain about a speed limit that is too lenient.[16] To argue that shortening the length of someone's pain is a matter of deontological duty would be to erode any sharp distinction between overall bad consequences and positive deontological duties.

What the examples illustrate is that, as far as obedience to law is concerned, we are frequently constrained by negative deontological duties that have only moderate power.[17] When these duties conflict either with substantial positive deontological reasons or with straightforward welfare reasons, they will sometimes yield. Not only do the negative duties lack absolute priority, they can, as the three variations show and as people's actual views about morally acceptable speeding reflect, be outweighed by considerations that fall short of being overwhelming.

At least part of this conclusion is at odds with John Rawls's suggestion, first made in his original essay on fair play, that "the principles of justice are absolute with respect to utility."[18] He meant by this not only that utility cannot justify the creation of unjust institutions but also that "[O]ur obligation to obey the law, which is a special case of the principle of fair play, cannot be overridden by an appeal to utility, though it may be overridden by another duty of justice."[19] Although in A Theory of Justice Rawls casts the general duty to obey as a natural duty to support just institutions, his position with respect to the absolute priority of justice appears not to have altered.[20] Because Rawls's natural duty includes what I call positive deontological aspects, he does not say that compliance with just rules always overrides the promotion of future justice; but he is apparently committed to the proposition that welfare alone cannot warrant noncompliance.

Evaluating Rawls's position about obedience requires care, because neither its precise boundaries nor its grounds are entirely clear. A dominant theme of his social theory is that "an injustice is tolerable only when it is necessary to avoid an even greater injustice."[21] Promotion of overall welfare does not warrant treating people unjustly. As I will suggest shortly, the validity of this view is debatable; but even if it is correct, two other claims about the priority of justice do not necessarily follow from it. One concerns the relative status of positive future-regarding considerations of justice and other desirable consequences. Suppose I am faced with a choice whether to contribute money for political reform or for medical research; does my duty to support just institutions here override utilitarian considerations, if the medical research will contribute to welfare without affecting justice? Such a stark resolution seems implausible; my donation for research would not do an injustice and is made "at the expense of justice" only in the remotest sense. Since Rawls himself says that duties are not lexically prior to supererogatory acts of beneficence,[22] he probably does not suppose that I must here try to promote justice; certainly most people would not regard a choice to relieve the infirmities of the natural human condition in preference to improving justice as a moral mistake.

The second claim about the priority of justice is one that Rawls clearly does make, that obedience must prevail if it is in competition only with welfare considerations. The main point to be made here is that disobeying a law that does not protect individual rights is a special kind of injustice. Usually no other individual is made worse off; no one is subjected to an injustice in the ordinary sense. The only injustice involved is the actor's failure to conform with the duty to comply with just institutions. That this "injustice" is always enough to override favorable consequences is counterintuitive.

One aspect of the difficulties is evidenced by uncertainties about the practical import of Rawls's position. He speaks of a natural duty of mutual aid that, since it involves notions of reciprocity and is derived from the original position,[23] might be understood loosely as a duty of justice. In that event, Ruth's speeding to relieve the suffering of the stranger with the broken arm could be treated as satisfying a duty of justice. The duty of mutual aid, according to Rawls, comes into play when "one can [provide the help] without excessive risk or loss to oneself."[24] Imagine that by driving the stranger to the hospital, Ruth runs a serious risk of losing her job as a truck driver because of a trivial delay in a delivery. That risk might place her action outside the scope of duty into the category of supererogatory beneficence.[25] Surely that shift could not make her speeding *less* justified; if anything, her own need to get back on the job quickly would increase her justification. The line between disobedience that promotes justice or satisfies a positive duty and disobedience that only promotes good consequences cannot be the line between when disobedience is sometimes justified and when it never is.[26] Indeed, most people think that strong personal reasons also justify their breaking the law when they are confident no one else will be injured and the duty to obey seems relatively weak. Someone who has been unavoidably delayed and can get to a crucial job interview on time only by cutting across private property or speeding slightly will do so without believing he or she has committed a moral wrong.

The more important issues concerning Rawls's priority of justice lie closer to his main concern, circumstances in which the promotion of utility will involve injustice in a more direct and tangible sense. The underlying conflict in the *Hirabayashi*[27] and *Korematsu* cases[28] has often been thought to involve a conflict of this sort; I shall use a variation on it to consider, first, the dimensions of justifiable government action and, second, the related problem of obedience. Since the actual treatment early in World War II of American citizens of Japanese origin living on the West Coast smacked of virulent prejudice and extreme overreaction to any genuine danger, I need to formulate the conflict with assumed facts that eliminate these features.

Illustration 9-3:

In a West Coast city, ten percent of the population is of Japanese origin; the rest of the population is made up of whites and blacks. Early in a war involving Japan as an enemy, saboteurs from submarines have entered the city at night, blown up important military installations, and killed hundreds of soldiers. The task of the saboteurs is greatly eased by the presence of Japanese-Americans on the streets at night; authorities are not able by sight to distinguish the members of the two groups. No one doubts the loyalty of any Japanese-American and no prejudice exists against them. A curfew for Japanese-Americans would make a substantial difference in stopping the saboteurs; a curfew for the entire population would have the same, but no greater, beneficial effect. Neither the long-term survival of the United States nor its present political institutions is threatened by this war.[29] Authorities aware of all these facts must decide whether to impose a curfew, and, if so, whether to impose it on all citizens or only on those of Japanese origin.[30]

The curfew will substantially aid military efforts and save soldiers' lives, yet imposing a curfew on a minority group that has done nothing wrong seems unjust.[31] Though I shall not argue for the conclusion that a limited curfew is unjust, I am relying on the assumption that such restrictions on liberty are more just if imposed on wrongdoers or imposed on everyone. The curfew here could embrace the entire population, but then ninety percent of the people would be needlessly restricted in their nighttime movements. If the problem represents a genuine conflict between justice and utility, many people would believe the regrettable sacrifice in justice acceptable.[32]

How might a Rawlsian respond? He might say that a curfew that saves soldiers lives and furthers the war effort is not unjust, but that avenue seems to turn any pressing public need into a matter of justice; and those objectives could be served by a curfew on everyone. What if the narrow curfew is compared with a general one? The absence of need for ninety percent of the scope of the broader curfew would not render that curfew unjust,[33] since it would serve the practical purpose of making the burden fall more equally. If he makes the justice of a curfew for an innocent minority turn on the degree of public exigency and the absence of need for a broader curfew, the Rawlsian categorizes in a way that largely erodes the distinction between justice and utility, making us wonder how significant is any priority of justice over utility. Otherwise the Rawlsian must apparently conclude that the narrow curfew on Japanese-Americans is not a permissible moral option for the government. That conclusion conflicts with the general sense that no such easy ordering resolves dilemmas of this sort.

Related issues arise if George is deciding whether to disobey the narrow curfew, once it is adopted. George perceives a conflict between a general duty to obey and the injustice of the curfew and must decide which claim of justice takes priority. One would think that George should cast into the balance the usefulness of the curfew and whatever damage his violation would cause; but whether Rawls could accept the relevance of those considerations for George's duty is doubtful. If a valid claim of justice should never yield in a direct clash with utility, perhaps when two claims of justice conflict, utility cannot determine which should have priority. On the other hand, perhaps the strength of claims of justice and injustice may be affected by relevant utilitarian considerations.[34] If a Rawlsian adopts the latter analysis, he admits that utility can figure importantly, if only indirectly, in obedience to law.

Although I have certainly not disproved Rawls's claim about the absolute priority of justice over utility, I have shown that that notion is highly implausible if it means that *promoting* justice always takes preference over utility or that promoting welfare can never warrant the "weak injustice" involved in much law breaking. Rawls's more central concern that utility can never justify *causing injustice* is more debatable, but I have suggested that this position is also probably wrong and its implications for obedience to law are somewhat uncertain and likely misguided.

My own conclusion is that no simple principle exists for ordering justice and utility or for ordering negative deontological duties and morally worthwhile consequences. About the most that can confidently be said is that if a negative duty is present, consequential reasons to the contrary can override its power only if they are substantial *in relation to* the strength of the duty in that context, and that serious injustice should not be caused unless the utilitarian reasons for doing so are very strong. These formulations may be so vague as to provide little help, but they do realistically acknowledge that negative deontological standards themselves differ tremendously in their moral force, that they can be overridden by substantial considerations of consequence to the contrary, and that justice does not always win out over utility, when the two are genuinely distinct.

LAWS INFRINGING MORAL RIGHTS

The chapter thus far has concentrated on priorities concerning what one morally *ought* to do, though I have suggested that one possible significance of clashing moral claims might be to cancel what would otherwise be a duty to obey, leaving both obedience and disobedience within the range of the morally permissible. I now examine a particular possibility of that sort, that when a law violates a moral right, obedience to that law can never be a moral duty. Phrased differently, the claim is that if one is otherwise morally permitted to exercise a moral right, the improper intervention of the law cannot cancel the moral permissibility of that exercise.

The issue is suggested by Ronald Dworkin's proposal that when a law violates a moral right, the citizen has a moral right to disobey the law; in such circumstances he says, "it is silly to speak of a duty to obey the law as such."[35] Since what Dworkin himself means by a moral right in this context is the moral impermissibility of government interference with its exercise, it is not entirely clear, despite the language I have quoted, that his argument is really about the moral duty of the actor. However, a broader sense of a right to disobey might well imply that disobedience violates no moral duty. Apart from the justifiability of government enforcement, a rights-violating law raises at least three moral questions: can such a law change one's moral duties toward other individuals; can it alter what would be justifiable interference in one's life by other private individuals; and can it change one's moral duties toward the government or those it represents?

The first two questions can be answered fairly quickly on the basis of the example used in Chapter 8 of an unjust law barring interracial associations. I have suggested that the unjust law can affect what is a morally preferable act if one's attempts to associate will place others in serious danger. If the danger is great enough, one may speak of a duty not to bring harm to others. Thus, what is undoubtedly a rights-violating law can create conditions in which a full exercise of a moral right to associate would actually be a violation of one's moral duty to other persons.[36] Concerned friends and associates may not coerce one to do one's duty, but they may appropriately engage in activities such as blaming and avoidance when they think one is acting immorally. Such activities would be appropriate here to discourage someone from endangering others, even though the danger flows from a law that violates moral rights.

The more difficult question concerns the person's relationship with the government and with his fellow citizens as citizens. Can a duty to obey ever require compliance with a rights-violating law? When the violation of a right is as stark as in the law against interracial association, any duty an ordinary citizen owes to his government or fellow citizens is overridden; the forbidden association is not a moral wrong toward the government or the citizenry at large. This point can be roughly generalized to cover other violations of moral rights that deny a person's fundamental humanity.[37] One who is treated as subhuman or required to treat others as subhuman cannot have a moral duty to the state or its citizens to submit to such a constraint.

Not every violation of a moral right is of this dimension, however, and a milder example is needed to test the proposition that one never has a duty to obey a rights-violating rule.

Illustration 9-4.

All the professors at the Hughes Law School agree that to achieve more coherence in the curriculum, greater central supervision is needed of the subject matter in various courses. All recognize each professor's moral right to academic freedom and agree that reform should not infringe that right. An elected faculty committee produces recommendations for eliminating duplications, including a proposal that the privilege against self-incrimination, which is taught in a heavily attended criminal process course, no longer be taught in constitutional law. Only Professor Ristrante of the six constitutional law professors objects; she thinks that *Miranda* v. *Arizona* is central to understanding modern constitutional adjudication and that three prior sessions must be spent on coerced confessions and the privilege against self-incrimination if *Miranda* is to be understood. She dissents from the faculty's adoption of that proposal, dropping only a hint of worry about academic freedom. Over the summer she correctly decides that preclusion of matter she considers so vital for presentation of her own views does not constitute an impairment of her academic freedom. She deliberates about what she should do.

Would Ristrante act in a morally permissible way if she spent her usual four hours on the privilege and *Miranda*? Given the unanimous faculty belief in the need for central direction and the mutual sacrifices of autonomy, each faculty member may have a duty to observe restrictions placed on him or her, though some restrictions may go slightly beyond the hard-to-define borders of academic freedom. Anyone's refusal to abide by the faculty resolution may lead to other refusals by professors whose claims actually fall on the other side of the elusive line between academic freedom and legitimate control, the possible result being practical defeat of this needed reform and recrimination among colleagues. At the very least, Ristrante owes it to her colleagues not to disregard the resolution until she has presented her position about academic freedom in the fullest way possible. In short, the faculty's mistaken resolution does trigger a duty not to disobey, at least until the issue is fully aired, on the part of someone whose rights it violates.

In this illustration the grounds for obedience to rules are very strong, and the import of postponement or abandonment of this limited slice of academic freedom is not great. Given the multiple grounds for obeying the law of the state and their variant strength, and the ordinary citizen's relative incapacity to have his position closely attended to by legislators, showing that a particular breach of a rights-violating law would violate a moral duty to obey will be much harder. But the illustration does establish that no easy generalization about rights-violating laws will suffice; one needs to make a careful appraisal of the grounds of duty to obey and of whether they are canceled or overridden by the injustice of impairment of rights. Duties to obey will sometimes have enough power to override marginal and correctible impairments of moral rights, changing what would be morally permissible behavior in the absence of law into morally wrong behavior.

This inquiry, like the others in this chapter, has left us without any sharp, clear basis for assigning priority to conflicting moral claims that touch obedience to law. We must, regrettably, accept this evidence of the limited capacity of moral philosophy "to assign weights to . . . the normative requirements of life,"[38] and acknowledge that people facing decisions about obeying the law must do their uncertain best to take appropriate account of the relevant claims without plain rules of guidance. This general lesson is further confirmed in the next two chapters.

NOTES

1. I suggested in Chapter 3 that *obligation, duty, must,* and *required* are words that often connote a greater stringency than a simple "ought."

2. The idea that a person should not act against conscience, even when it is erroneous, goes back at least as far as medieval moralists. See Konvitz, Conscience and Civil Disobedience in Jewish, Christian, and Greek and Roman Thought, 29 Hastings L.J. 1619, 1635 (1978).

3. If Rachel is confident that the trespass would be morally wrong for her, she will probably find it easier to judge the trespass than the actors who engage in it. On some occasions, however, judging the actor may be easier than judging the act. We may think that a person deserves praise for a self-sacrificing act without being confident that the person did what was right.

4. See Mark 12:13–17; Matt. 22:15–22; Luke 20:20–26.

5. Rom. 13:1–7.

6. In the early church, of course, Christians refused to obey directives requiring acknowledgment of Roman gods and forbidding Christian services, but disobedience was limited to rules that directly concerned worship; and what disobedience there was did not involve active resistance of the state. See L. Buzzard and P. Campbell, Holy Disobedience 119–22, 168 (1984). This attitude of submission to the state, which surprisingly survived Roman persecutions, was given systematic defense in the writings of Augustine. See H. Deane, The Political and Social Ideas of St. Augustine 9 (1963).

7. See Buzzard and Campbell, note 6 supra at 155–71; Ball, Obligation: Not to the Law But to the Neighbor, 18 Ga. L. Rev. 922, 919–27 (1984).

8. It might be argued that the duty to prevent harm gives way to the nonconsequential duty not to disobey. I will discuss, and reject, that possibility later. In this chapter, I do not attempt any precise delineation of the best concepts to express the relations between conflicting moral reasons. Compare, e.g., Raz, Practical Reason and Norms (Hutchinson & Co., London, 1975); Nozick, Moral Complications and Moral Structures, 13 Nat. L. Forum 1 (1968). In part, the reason for this is clarity and simplicity of presentation; in part, the reason is skepticism that greater conceptual precision here does much to illuminate the substantive moral dilemmas. See Chapter 3, note 9.

9. Insofar as laws within a country that conflict with Common Market rules lose their validity, a citizen who decides to disobey such an (invalid) law is not faced with an irreconcilable conflict. When the conflict is irreconcilable, the fact that the Common Market has more limited purposes than individual

states may be relevant, but the difficulties of many African states in overcoming tribal loyalties suggests that broadness of purpose is not always the key.

10. As Peter Singer suggests, the more deeply ingrained the habit of obedience is, the easier it is to defend civil disobedience. Practical Ethics 194 (1979).

11. J. Rawls, A Theory of Justice 334 (1971).

12. Giving preferences in educational institutions to members of minority races is understood by some people in this way. See, generally, K. Greenawalt, Discrimination and Reverse Discrimination (1983).

13. In that chapter, a reason for obeying the law that turned exclusively on the promotion of good consequences counted as a utilitarian reason for obedience, even if promotion of good consequences contained a distributive limit. Because some notions of justice rely heavily on distributive limits, an important issue *here* is whether promoting consequences that respect or embody these limits has a favored status over good consequences generally.

14. See P. Foot, Virtues and Vices 25–27 (1978).

15. See Chapter 13 on the general justification defense. I am assuming the jurisdiction in question has a fairly restricted version of the defense.

16. I am assuming that a councilwoman does not have a duty to vote on every issue, and that occasional absence and tardiness do not violate her duties of office.

17. Compare Charles Freid, Right and Wrong (1978), who limits deontological standards to situations in which they operate with stringency, and supposes that when utilitarian considerations are overwhelming the matter is removed from ordinary moral discourse (id. at 9–13). By these devices, he manages to put his own position as an absolutist one.

18. Rawls, Legal Obligations and the Duty of Fair Play, S. Hook, ed., Law and Philosophy 3, 13 (1964).

19. Id.

20. J. Rawls, supra note 11 at 335–36. Joel Feinberg has an illuminating discussion of this topic in Rawls and Intuitionism, in N. Daniels, ed., Reading Rawls 108 (1975).

21. J. Rawls, supra note 11 at 4.

22. Id. at 339.

23. Id. at 114, 333–42.

24. Id. at 114.

25. See id. at 117.

26. See E. Nagel, Fair Play and Civil Disobedience, in S. Hook, ed., Law and Philosophy 72, 75 (1964), who uses an example of disobedience that will help avoid a restriction on medical research.

27. *Hirabayashi* v. *United States*, 320 U.S. 81 (1943).

28. *Korematsu* v. *United States*, 323 U.S. 214 (1944). In a discussion of Rawls's original paper on fair play, note 18 supra, Roland Pennock raised this problem. See Pennock, The Obligation to Obey and the Ends of the State, in S. Hook, ed., Law and Philosophy 77, 82 (1964).

29. I add this caveat only to eliminate the argument that successful prosecution of the war is necessary to preserve just institutions in the United States.

30. What I have outlined is part of the justification that was put forward for the measures during World War II. I focus on Japanese-Americans because countries traditionally have exercised substantial power over citizens of enemy countries during wartime, and I want to avoid the complicated questions about the justice of these powers.

31. Indeed, in a literal sense it is a violation of Rawls's principle of maximum equal liberties, though Rawls may not have meant to cover short-run expedients of this sort. I have unrealistically supposed that the sabotage efforts do not threaten civilians to avoid the argument that the unequal restriction on liberty will benefit the Japanese-American citizens themselves.

32. When the Supreme Court actually passed on the curfew for Japanese-Americans, it decided unanimously in its favor (*Hirabayashi* v. *United States*, 320 U.S. 81 [1943]), in sharp contrast to the three vigorous dissents to the exclusion of Japanese-Americans (*Korematsu* v. *United States*, 323 U.S. at 225, 233, 242 [dissenting opinions of Roberts, Murphy and Jackson, JJ.] [1944]).

33. Were uselessness treated as making the curfew unjust for all *but* Japanese-Americans, a negative consideration of utility would be transformed into an issue of justice.

34. One is inclined to say that the injustice of the narrow curfew is lessened if it supports vital interests.

35. R. Dworkin, Taking Rights Seriously 192–93 (1977). See also B. Zwiebach, Civility and Disobedience 147–48 (1975); Murray, The Problem of Mr. Rawls's Problem, in S. Hook, ed., Law and Philosophy 29, 31 (1964).

36. I am sliding over a tricky problem in the text. The example assumes that the person making the moral choice is white, and that the dangers of interracial association are much greater for blacks. Still if blacks *freely choose* to associate, can the white have a moral duty not to do so? I am inclined to think that the white would not have a moral duty to refrain from association. But an ordinary right to associate also includes a right to seek out and strongly encourage association. The white, especially if he or she occupies a powerful social position vis-à-vis the blacks involved, *is* under a duty not to press for associations that the blacks are hesitant to undertake.

37. See Murray, supra note 35; Richards, Conscience, Human Rights, and the Anarchist Challenge to the Obligation to Obey the Law, 18 Ga. L. Rev. 771–74 (1984).

38. P. Soper, A Theory of Law 60 (1984).

10

Nonviolent Disobedience: Reasons, Tactics, Justification

The last chapter explored some highly abstract questions about conflicts between reasons to obey and reasons to disobey. This chapter concentrates on narrower issues, the status of particular factors that have often been thought to be critical to whether disobedience of law is justified. I consider, in turn, the relevance of (1) claims that behavior is legally justified, (2) the exhaustion of political remedies, (3) the nature of objections to laws, policies, or practices, and the purposes behind violation, (4) the relation between the laws broken and the laws or policies protested against, (5) the interests affected by violations, and (6) the openness of behavior and acceptance of punishment. In this chapter I deal only with nonviolent disobedience, postponing the problem of violence until the next chapter. Here I treat situations in which the reasons for disobedience do not involve any fundamental challenge to the way the political order is constituted.

Placing the factors discussed here in the context of reasons to obey and disobey is complicated because of the variety of those reasons. Morally acceptable reasons for disobedience include overriding obligations to others, conscientious objection to performing required acts, belief that disobedience will promote justice or welfare, and, occasionally, strong personal motivations. Arrayed against these sorts of reasons are nonconsequential duties and consequential reasons in favor of obeying laws and whatever independent moral reasons support doing the acts the law requires. The factors I consider may occasionally affect the strength of a reason to disobey, but more typically their force concerns the reasons to obey. Their presence or absence may eliminate or mitigate a nonconsequential duty to obey or affect its application. The factors may also have consequential importance.

CLAIMS OF LEGAL RIGHT

People may disobey particular legal norms in the belief that their behavior is justified under a higher legal norm. Such situations can arise when an administrative or inferior legislative body exceeds authority granted by a superior legislature, but I shall focus on the familiar American context in which a law is thought to be invalid because it is unconstitutional.[1] The presence of a claim of legal right brings us to the definitional threshold of disobedience to law. If one's claim is upheld, one has not, in retrospect, disobeyed valid law; and if one believes one's claim will be upheld, one has not intentionally disobeyed valid law.[2] More important than the borders of what amounts to disobedience is the question of what effect a claim of legal right has on the moral reasons to comply with legal norms.

Among innumerable variations in circumstances I will consider three basic situations. In each, I assume that the actor's estimation of the likely success of his or her legal claim corresponds with the estimate an objective lawyer would make. I further assume that quick legislative review is unavailable, that a violation of the law is needed to get a judicial determination of validity,[3] and that the actor is willing to submit to the court's disposition.

In the first situation, Clay is reasonably sure his constitutional claim will be upheld. Any reasonable view of an individual's duties in a political order providing judicial review must include the appropriateness of testing the validity of laws that appear invalid.[4] No otherwise applicable deontological principle would require obedience when disobedience is the only avenue for testing validity. From a utilitarian perspective, a challenge to a probably invalid law serves the objective of eliminating improper legal norms; the existence of the legal claim will also affect perceptions of a violation, making it appear as something other than a challenge to the legal order. The question about obedience becomes somewhat more difficult if already pending cases adequately raise all legal issues, or if these can be raised without anyone's disobeying. Since one's own violation serves no testing objective, disobedience cannot be justified on that score. But, at least if the likelihood of invalidation is very high and disobedience will not be seriously unsettling, one should simply not be thought bound to comply with such "laws."[5]

In the second situation, Clay thinks that a significant doubt exists about the law's constitutionality but understands that a legal challenge is more likely than not to fail. Deontological standards and utilitarian considerations should be understood to permit disobedience, since serious but probably losing challenges are a healthy part of the legal order. Such challenges sometimes succeed, and even when they do not they may contribute to the development of constitutional law. When the likelihood of success is not great, however, the justification for disobedience may not extend beyond the cases necessary to raise the legal issues of invalidity.

In the third situation, Clay has a firm personal view about constitutionality that he knows will not succeed in court; he believes, say, that conscription violates the Thirteenth Amendment ban on involuntary servitude. If the courts will predictably dismiss his position as frivolous, his disobedience will not promote legal development; and given people's familiarity with wild ideas being dressed in the clothing of constitutional right, public perceptions of his violation of a draft law will be little influenced by his announcement of a constitutional justification.[6]

How nonconsequential duties are affected by Clay's view is more difficult. Clay might argue that his consent, duty of fair play, or natural duty extends only to laws he regards as valid. But that position would be too simple. A duty to obey the law should be understood in relation to a whole system of governance, including processes of interpretation, and one's own views about what *should* be declared legally invalid should not count for very much. Very few people even have reflective views about the content of constitutional standards; for them the constitutional claim will be little more than an elaboration of a moral or political conviction, one that does not gain greater force by being put in the language of legal validity.[7] Within a stable legal order and with respect to issues that courts adjudicate,[8] the special claim that one is really acting within the law changes the nature of obedience only when a real prospect exists that the norm that is disobeyed will be held invalid.

In the sections that follow, I will assume that no claim of legal invalidity is involved, that the actor is committing what he understands to be a violation of the positive law of his society.

PURSUIT OF LAWFUL ALTERNATIVES

A commonly stated condition of justifiable disobedience is that lawful alternatives for changing a law or policy have been pursued. The illustration involving the faculty resolution about the content of the constitutional law course shows the basic soundess of this position. Presenting one's views in a full and orderly fashion to those who have made or are to make a decision can be an important aspect of duties based on consent or fairness. Even if one is permitted finally to disobey, one at least owes it to one's fellow to try to avoid that impasse by persuading them to change their minds. From a utilitarian perspective, considerations of mutual respect and avoidance of unnecessary disruption counsel a similar course. Of course, in a large political unit, few individuals will have an opportunity to air their views fully; but individuals can wait until the positions they accept have been presented by someone about as well as they can be.

The principle that people should exhaust lawful political remedies before turning to disobedience requires some qualification. It, of course, does not apply when one has no objection to a law or policy, but simply believes he has an overriding obligation, say to a family member. Nor does it apply when the law requires an act that one cannot in conscience perform and one must perform the act before pursuit of lawful alternatives is possible. What the principle reaches are situations in which obedience is aimed at overturning a law, policy, or practice. Even then, pursuit of lawful alternatives may not be required if they are patently futile. When *some* efforts have been made to get ordinary political redress, people may sharply disagree over the adequacy of the efforts and whether they can yet be declared unsuccessful.[9] Though the basic principle itself is widely accepted, and properly so, the way it applies to particular circumstances will often be highly controversial.

THE NATURE OF OBJECTIONS TO LAWS, POLICIES, OR PRACTICES, AND THE PURPOSES BEHIND VIOLATIONS

People disobey the law with some frequency, believing that pursuit of their own personal objectives justifies rather trivial violations or that a competing obligation overrides the duty to obey. But the most serious and notable instances in which people who break the law think they are morally justified are ones in which they object to a law, policy, or practice. If the law compels an act that a person cannot conscientiously perform, say to join the military, an outsider cannot evaluate his justification for refusing to do the act short of assessing all the moral reasons that led him to think the act is absolutely forbidden. Not much of general application can be said about these clashes of conscience and law. Nor can much be said if the actor's position is that the harm done to other persons by a rule of law is so great that its circumvention is demanded by conscience—the position taken by those who aided fugitive slaves and, more recently, by many in the "Sanctuary" movement who have helped persons they consider victims of injustice to evade immigration restrictions.[10]

Some writers have thought that more definitive guidelines are possible when obedience is mainly aimed at changing a law or policy. Such disobedience is almost always a collective act.[11] Possible guidelines concern the reasons people disobey, the conditions in which they do so, and the tactics they employ. I concentrate in this section on the first of these factors, restricting myself to nonviolent responses to the law.

I ask particularly whether it is crucial to justification of nonviolent disobedience that it is directed at influencing the majority's sense of justice and is responsive to injustices of a substantial magnitude. Such limits have been offered either as part of the definition of civil disobedience or as conditions of justifiable civil disobedience. Although the possibility of otherwise justifiable disobedience may be left open,[12] the implicit assumption is that what does not qualify as justifiable civil disobedience will be harder to justify and may require qualitatively different justification.

Various authors have expressed the ideas that justified civil disobedience must appeal to the sense of justice of the majority[13] or must involve claims of genuine injustice,[14] or both; but since these notions receive systematic explication in John Rawls's well-known account, I will concentrate on that. According to Rawls, a person who engages in civil disobedience "invokes the commonly shared conception of justice that underlies the political order,"[15] declaring that principles of justice are not being respected[16] and aiming to make the majority reconsider the justice of its actions. Ordinarily, justified civil disobedience will be limited "to instances of substantial and clear injustice, and preferably to those which obstruct the path to removing other injustices."[17] Involving resistance to injustice within the limits of fidelity of law, civil disobedience will help inhibit and correct departures from justice and can contribute to stability in a well-ordered society.[18]

In excluding circumstances in which those who disobey seek mainly to bring the majority around by causing more inconvenience than the majority will tolerate, and also excluding appeals that are not directed at the majority or are not based on the majority's shared conception of justice, Rawls's concept of civil disobedience is a good bit narrower than many other formulations.[19] What I examine is whether disobedience that is either excluded by Rawls's definition or does not fit within his principles of justification is indeed much more difficult to justify than what he treats as justifiable civil disobedience.

Illustration 10-1:
Vegetarians who believe that the killing of nonhuman animals for food violates the animals' moral rights[20] consider whether to lie down in the midst of a stockyard as a protest against that practice. They think that publicizing their position by risking physical harm and suffering arrest may lead some people who already have qualms about the practice to beome vegetarians or quit jobs in the meat industry. They hope that others will begin to think more seriously about the problem and that over the long term a majority of society will come to accept their view and will outlaw killing animals for meat; but they recognize the latter development will take generations.

From the vegetarians' point of view, a grave moral wrong is being committed against defenseless beings who deserve protection. They seek to draw attention to this moral wrong in much the same way that other illegal demonstrations attempt to highlight wrongs. Even if human beings can have duties of justice to animals, the vegetarians do not appeal to the majority's shared conception of justice, which recognizes no rights of the sort they claim. No doubt, the vegetarians' hope to influence the views of their fellow citizens is based on a point of connection between their views and ordinary moral sympathies, which include respect for life and a limited concern for nonhuman animals. But when Rawls talks of "invoking a commonly shared conception," he requires a much stronger identity between the moral convictions of the majority and those disobeying than any the vegetarians can claim. Moreover, the vegetarians in this particular demonstration are mainly aiming at a passive minority that is already sympathetic to their position, so only in a very long-term sense are the demonstrators really addressing the majority at all. Yet if they are at all successful, the immediate result will be both *some reduction* in a practice they consider barbarous and an initial positive step toward wider reform.

If the aim of civil disobedience must be to keep the nearly just society true to its own present convictions, then the vegetarians cannot engage in justifiable civil disobedience. But what the illustration shows is that the reasons for open and peaceful disobedience are not limited to that purpose. The vegetarians do lack a justification derived from the existing political order that Rawlsian demonstrators will have,[21] but the two aims to transform a society's moral consciousness over time[22] and to reach a minority who themselves can quickly reduce the incidence of serious wrongs might also warrant peaceful disobedience. If the demonstrators submit to physical risk and to legal processes and possible punishment, their tactics are not likely to be so widely replicated as to threaten the society's stability. The claims of obedience are often weighty, and they are especially strong when the law represents the considered opinion of the majority; but these claims do not absolutely preclude every instance of disobedience that is intended to sensitize people to grave moral wrongs that are not yet widely recognized.[23]

Illustration 10-2:

A neighborhood is undergoing what has come to be known as "gentrification." Many buildings in which poor people live are being torn down to provide luxury housing, and in other buildings rents are being raised so fast that most present residents must leave. Poor residents and their sympathizers consider trespassory occupations of buildings doomed to destruction. They hope to persuade city officials that the laws and policies that permit such rapid change are unjust in conception; that, in any event, the strongly held feelings of injustice by those affected should not be overridden; and that attempts to override those feelings will cause inconvenience and embarrassment to the officials.

The potential demonstrators, unlike the vegetarians, have at least a plausible if debatable argument that failure to protect poor residents offends present conceptions of justice between rich and poor as they affect security of dwellings. The triple message the demonstrators wish to convey is common to most illegal political demonstrations. The first message is that, in its initial disposition, the majority or the government acted unjustly given the facts available to it. On this score, the demonstration is meant to illuminate the seriousness of the issue and encourage sober reconsideration. The second message introduces the intensity of the minority's feelings as a new element in calculations of justice. It says, "Even if you are still persuaded you were right in the first place, you should now change course when you realize the strength of our contrary feelings." Perhaps this notion is most familiar in the claim that a country should not fight a foreign war over an intense minority opposition. What Rawls says about appealing to the majority's sense of justice mainly refers to the basic merits of the issue, but the message that is grounded on the relevance of a minority's intense opposition is also an appeal to the majority's sense of justice and we should include it in what is a proper part of civil disobedience.[24]

The third message, that inconvenience and embarrassment will attend continuation of the present policy, is the most troubling and is not an appeal to a sense of justice at all. "Coercion" may be too strong a word, but the demonstrators in this respect seek to manipulate costs and benefits in a way that will persuade those in charge that the present course is too expensive. Rawls is certainly right that pressure of this sort involves subversion of ordinary processes of decision making in a way that appeals to justice do not. Because pressure is less reconcilable with adherence to ordinary processes, it does require stronger reasons to be justified. Both Gandhi and Marin Luther King, Jr., notable and reflective practitioners of civil disobedience, emphasized that the aim must be to transform opponents.[25] For them civil disobedience was not a sophisticated method of force but one of persuasion. But in their actions, both recognized that inconvenience for oppressors might be a necessary means to focus their attention on the issue of justice.[26] In reality, among instances of civil disobedience *pure* appeals to justice are rare; some element of pressure is usually present. The line between trying to persuade the majority that it is "unjust" to keep a committed minority in jail and trying to persuade the majority that jailing the minority will be inconvenient and unproductive is very thin indeed. Often those who disobey consciously seek to wear down as well as sensitize opponents; even when they do not, their tactics of disobedience are likely to exert pressure in fact.

Maintaining that success through such pressure is never a legitimate aim of civil disobedience may not be illogical; however, a more sensible position is that those who are willing to suffer to correct an injustice may sometimes convert that willingness into an aim to achieve a concession that the majority would not accord out of its own sense of justice.

Illustration 10-3:

Opponents of civilian nuclear power consider a trespassory demonstration at a site of a nuclear power plant to be built by a privately owned electric company. They hope both to persuade the company to abandon its plans and to alter public laws and policies that permit and favor such projects. Gerald believes that the public acceptance of such projects represents a clear injustice toward nearby residents and toward future generations. Wilma's view is somewhat different. She thinks that what has happened is an honest and understandable but terribly unfortunate misappraisal of the dangers of nuclear plants. She does not really blame anyone and thinks that the building of the plants would be warranted if the facts were as they are widely supposed. She has enormous respect for the minority of scientists who have estimated the dangers as very great and accepts their judgment.

One point of this illustration is to show how civil disobedience can be directed at decision makers other than public officials.[27] Often, as here and in many of the illegal protests on private university campuses during the late 1960s in the United States, demonstrators take aim at both private institutional and public targets. As long as it does not seriously threaten the legal order, disobedience to correct private injustice cannot be ruled out on principle, although, like the vegetarian demonstration, such disobedience lacks the particular political justification that may exist when public policy is the target and is claimed to violate prevailing principles of justice.

The main objective of this illustration is to use the difference between George's and Wilma's views to test Rawls's assertion that one must appeal to the majority's sense *of justice*, a claim that follows from his more general position, examined in the last chapter, that justice takes priority over utility. No doubt, Wilma is artificially drawn; those willing to put their bodies on the line usually find severe injustice someplace. But it is also true that many who consider illegal action draw no clear distinction between injustice and great harm. For Rawls, civil disobedience concerns only injustice, and a demonstration by Wilma and people of like view would be something other than civil disobedience. Rawls's approach would apparently require people considering disobedience to discount their fears about harms that do not derive from injustice. Yet if, as Wilma believes, what has happened is *only* a very bad policy decision[28] *and* disobedience is likely to produce a careful reappraisal and possible reversal, the disobedience might well be warranted.[29] The intensity of opposition demonstrated by self-sacrificing disobedience can serve to promote reexamination of crucial factual data as well as claims of justice.

Illustration 10-4:
Parents in a neighborhood where two children have been killed at a busy intersection that has no stop sign consider whether or not to publicize the need for such signs by blocking traffic for an hour. They have unsuccessfully sought for many months to get the town to install signs.

One may question whether the sloppiness and inertia that prevent stop signs from being placed where they are needed amounts to injustice, but they are common failings of all governments and perhaps all human endeavor. Certainly the failure to install signs is not a major injustice. Yet a contained illegal demonstration of the sort contemplated seems warranted to protect the lives of other children. A sensible approach to disobedience must calibrate the degree of injustice or likely harm to the magnitude of the disobedience. Much less is needed to justify minor localized disobedience than major illegal demonstrations.

The discussion in this section has addressed a number of factors: (1) appeal to the majority, (2) appeal to a sense of justice, (3) appeal to a present sense of wrong, and (4) appeal based on a substantial wrong. Each of these appeals may be important to measuring the magnitude of claims to obey and disobey, but none marks a critical dividing line between justifiable civil disobedience and other disobedience.

RELATIONSHIP BETWEEN THE REASON FOR PROTEST AND THE LAW BROKEN

Disobedience is easier to justify when a close connection exists between the injustice or wrong protested and the law being disobeyed. The force of the example of disobedience will be more contained and the interests that are compromised by disobedience will be less likely to warrant protection. But one cannot move from these matters of degree to the position of Justice Abe Fortas that "civil obedience . . . is never justified in our nation where the law being violated is not itself the focus or target of the protest."[30]

A preliminary difficulty with this sharp distinction is the elusiveness of its application. Would a "sit in" by parents at a house that a developer has refused to sell to them because they have small children be an improper violation of the general trespass law, to which the parents do not object, or a proper violation of the laws that allow developers to refuse sales on this ground? What of refusal to submit to the draft because one is opposed to an unjust war? Would that be a proper violation, because most draftees are sent to the unjust war, or an improper violation, because the draft itself is acceptable?

These perplexities of application mainly highlight the basic indefensibility of a sharp distinction of this kind. The moral legitimacy of the interests that will be undermined by obedience does not turn simply on the justice or injustice of the law that is violated. Even unjust laws may generate expectations whose disappointment is unfortunate, and some of those who benefit from a just law, say against trespass, may by immoral behavior largely forfeit their moral claim to the protection of that law. A demonstrator against apartheid trespassing on the property of a South African embassy might take such a view about the moral rights of the South African government.

If justifiable protests were limited in the way Fortas suggested, some laws and policies—for example, a highly unjust definition of treason or an egregious use of military force abroad—might be entirely immune from law-violating protest, as would be any injustice that results from a failure to enact laws to prevent great wrongs. A means of protest is more appropriate when it is reasonably related to the matter under protest;[31] a trespassory demonstration at the Pentagon is a better means of protesting an unjust war than setting a fire in a national forest. But the strict principle that the very law that is violated must be what is protested makes no sense.[32]

INTERESTS AFFECTED BY A VIOLATION

The power of claims to obey depends in part on the interests affected by a violation of law. In this connection, I discuss both the immediate impact on the interests of others and possible longer-term effects.

Violations of law can have radically different impacts on the interests of other citizens. Some involve no direct and perceivable interference with their interests. A law designed to protect those interests may not do so in the particular circumstances in which it is violated.[33] Other laws are not even designed to protect other people from harm to their interests. Some, such as those against drug use, are meant to protect the persons against whom they are directed; others, such as those requiring payment of taxes, concern shared burdens.[34]

Violations of law that affect people's interests do so in various ways. Some illegal acts cause inconvenience to others. A loudspeaker that exceeds permissible limits of noise disturbs people; a subway strike in a big city can disrupt travel for millions of commuters. In yet other situations, something that people own is taken, destroyed, or interfered with. The line between inconvenience and deprivation of rights[35] is not a clear one, and it depends largely on which interests the legal system recognizes as rights.[36] Some forms of illegality, such as illegal sit-ins, may involve aspects of both inconvenience and impairment of property or other rights. The most severe harm is physical injury to persons, a subject reserved for the next chapter on Violent Disobedience. On some occasions, harm to persons may be a greater or lesser risk of acts that would not be characterized as violent, such as an illegal strike in winter by fuel oil drivers, but I will disregard this complication.

One reason the nature of interference with the interests of others can affect justifications for obedience is that the independent moral reasons against behavior are stronger when more serious injuries are inflicted. Another reason is that some deontological standards favoring obedience have more force when schemes of social cooperation are designed to protect vital individual interests. There are consequential reasons as well. Human beings come to expect that certain of their interests will be protected by society. When this protection fails, the reaction is not only one of loss but also of frustration and insecurity, and the insecurity, at least, also extends to others who fear similar losses. For commuters and others, delays often translate into economic losses; but people suffer losses from inconvenience more readily than equally costly losses of property.[37] The deprivation of social expectations is felt more immediately and sharply when what is taken is something that one actually "owns." Beyond being unpleasant feelings, frustration and insecurity lead to withdrawal and retaliation, which are destructive. No doubt, as radical demonstrators during the 1960s often claimed,[38] on some occasions the person shaken by loss may reexamine complacent assumptions and recognize the injustice of the law or policy those who directly damaged him were protesting. But rejection of those who cause loss is much more typical, especially if the injury is a deprivation of rights.

Regarding many instances of obedience that cause harm to others, an important difference exists between expected harmful consequences and hoped-for beneficial ones. The former are virtually certain, the latter problematic. The greater the uncertainty that any good will be achieved, the greater that good would have to be to outweigh certain or highly probable harm.

I turn now to two longer-term effects that Rawls discusses. One of his conditions of justifiable civil obedience is that a group's violations of law will not lead to the kind of serious damage to the political order that may occur if too many groups, with various claims of injustice, disobey within a short time.[39] Within a nearly just society, such an overload should be avoided, although Rawls fails to suggest how hard it will be for any single group to decide whether its own choice to disobey will significantly worsen existing conditions.

The second longer-term effect Rawls addresses is provocation of the majority's harsh retaliation. If the danger is great, Rawls says a group may not be "wise" or "prudent" to disobey,[40] even though it has met the conditions for justifiable disobedience. Rawl's distinction between what is justifiable and what is prudent is another illustration of his priority of justice over utilitarian considerations. More specifically, he believes here that if victims of injustice are willing to risk further damage to their own interests triggered by their own otherwise justifiable response, the likelihood of further damage to them does not affect the justice of their own actions.

Unfortunately, this idea rests on an unrealistic picture of many large demonstrations against injustice. Typically, the protesters are a small slice of the victimized group plus sympathizers who are not victimized. The incidence of repression often falls on the entire minority that is the subject of the original injustice, including large numbers who have not violated the law and may have disapproved those tactics.[41] The caution of prudence is a heavy moral responsibility the demonstrators must bear with respect to the interests of all those they purport to represent.[42]

OPENNESS OF BEHAVIOR AND SUBMISSION TO PUNISHMENT

If obedience is to be justifiable within a generally just system, must those who disobey act openly and submit to punishment? I have already said enough to indicate that this cannot be an absolute rule about morally justified disobedience. Some applications of some laws are not reached by any obligation to obey, and many violations in these situations will not be open. Moreover, when an obligation to obey is outweighed by a more pressing moral duty to prevent severe injustice or harm to individuals, one's effectiveness may depend on secrecy. To take an extreme example, a person who *openly* tries to help a fugitive slave escape is likely to make escape impossible, and someone who surrenders to authorities after aiding a successful escape will compromise the chance of giving future assistance to others. Relieving people from the bonds of slavery justifies secretive violation of law, at least if it is nonviolent. Finding a noncontroversial example for more just societies is not as easy, but in the United States some concerned people now think that application of our immigration laws in certain instances is so unfair and inhumane that covert evasion is warranted.

The claims about openness and acceptance of punishment are mainly relevant to illegal protests.[43] The actual publicness of one's act may have some intrinsic significance, but its main importance is its linkage with submission to the operation of law. When people act openly, enforcement officials can arrest them and can also prosecute with clear evidence of their behavior. But two illustrations show that openness of the act itself is not critical. If people who sneak into a draft office and pour blood on the files come forward immediately and admit what they have done, the covertness of the illegal behavior at the moment it happened does not affect the quality of their whole course of action. And if easily identified illegal strikers use their economic power to ensure that no punishment is imposed, the unwillingness to submit to the law is not much affected by the openness of their actions.

A willingness to submit to punishment, which may combine two distinguishable elements, is often a critical ingredient of justified disobedience. One element is that the actor behaves so that authorities may impose punishment if they wish. The second element, not necessarily present with the first, is that the actor acknowledge the appropriateness of punishment if it is determined that the law has been violated. Raising possible legal defenses is not, of course, inconsistent with either element.

Acceptance of punishment often mitigates the force of a violation of a deontological duty. I have suggested that in some situations such acceptance may wholly satisfy the demands of a duty of fair play. Even when acceptance of punishment falls short of this, it can lessen unfairness by eliminating any unjust advantage the actor might derive. The ultimate commitment of one's fate to legal process means that under an obligation of consent or a duty to support just institutions, one's breach is also substantially lessened.

The actual effects of an illegal action are likely to be significantly different if the violators submit to punishment. In the first place, the frustration, resentment, and insecurity people feel when their interests are jeopardized are reduced if they realize that those who threaten them are willing to pay an even more costly price. Acceptance of punishment signifies the respect, even the love,[44] the protestor has for his opponents. Submission to punishment also demonstrates the depth of the actor's conviction, showing that his claim of substantial injustice is not just hypocritical rhetoric, rationalization of self-interest, or simple overstatement. Protestors wanting to convince others of the magnitude of their grievance are likely to be more persuasive if they submit to punishment.

Submission to punishment also serves as a helpful test of the actor's strength of conviction and contains the force of his example. When someone asks himself the hard question whether or not he is willing to be punished, he will be careful to consider his course of action and its value; thus, submission to punishment imposes some check on irresponsible judgment. It also sets an important limit on the message communicated to other persons considering disobedience, suggesting that they can think themselves justified in disobeying only if they believe a law or policy is so unjust that they are willing to suffer serious penalties to alter it.

The reasons so far suggested for willing submission are largely satisfied by a course of action that allows the authorities to impose punishment. An acknowledgment of its moral appropriateness goes even further, demonstrating a commitment to the fundamentals of the existing social order. Although the actor does not accept the judgment of society as expressed in the law about the proper course of behavior, he or she does ultimately accept that judgment in the form of punishment for behavior society considers wrongful. In so doing, the actor may express a certain humility about his moral judgment, but even if he does not, he reaffirms his sense of being a member of the community by admitting the appropriateness of enforcement efforts.[45] Such acknowledgments will reduce anger directed at protesters and minimize the chances of massive repression.

NOTES

1. Often a constitutional claim will be joined with a claim of moral right; here I am concerned only with the moral force of the claim that one's act is justifiable within the legal system itself.

2. People who raise test cases often have radically different motivations from those who engage in civil disobedience. See L. Buzzard and P. Campbell, Holy Disobedience 179 (1984), quoting an unpublished dissertation by Thomas Rekdal.

3. Generally, the validity of a criminal prohibition can be tested only by disobedience. Sometimes injunctions or declaratory judgments will afford a means to challenge legal norms without noncompliance.

4. The point is even more obvious if a statute is clearly and blatantly unconstitutional.

5. This conclusion would be strengthened if the probably invalid law inhibited an important personal liberty. Were the legal system to demand initial compliance with invalid laws, as the American system does demand compliance with improper injunctions, the conclusion would be altered.

6. The reactions of people who know him well might be significantly affected by his constitutional conviction.

7. I am not suggesting that the actor should disregard his moral conviction, only that his idiosyncratic view about the scope of the Constitution should carry little weight by itself.

8. If the actor's claim is that a law is unconstitutional and no relatively detached organ of government stands ready to interpret the Constitution with respect to that claim—say, because of the political question doctrine—the individual's interpretation may carry more moral significance, particularly if it enjoys some support by others.

9. The disagreement, of course, will not be merely or mainly factual. People will have different views on how great the efforts must be and how long they must continue without success before disobedience is warranted.

10. See Buzzard and Campbell, note 2 supra at 17, 148; Trial Opening in Arizona in Alien Sanctuary Case, New York Times, Oct. 21, 1985, Section A.

11. See M. Walzer, Obligations: Essays on Disobedience, War and Citizenship 4 (1970); Flynn, Collective Responsibility and Obedience to Law, 18 Ga. L. Rev. 845, 859 (1984).

12. See, e.g., J. Rawls, A Theory of Justice 363–68 (1971).

13. See, e.g., P. Singer, Practical Ethics 192 (1979), who speaks of civil disobedience as trying to get a genuine expression of majority rule.

14. See, e.g., Buzzard and Campbell, note 2 supra at 100. H. Bedau, ed., Civil Disobedience: Theory and Practice 23 (1969).

15. Rawls, note 12 supra at 365.

16. Id. at 364.

17. Id. at 372.

18. Id. at 382.

19. Compare Hugo Bedau's definition, in Bedau, note 14 supra at 218: "Anyone commits an act of civil disobedience if and only if he acts illegally, publicly, nonviolently, and conscientiously with the intent to frustrate [one of] the laws, policies, or decisions of his government."

20. Some may quarrel with the terminology of rights and justice for

entities that are not potential participants in the moral community. The crucial question is whether we can have moral duties toward such entities. Rawls assumes that we can (see Rawls, note 12 supra at 17, 512), although he apparently believes that the vocabulary of justice is inappropriate for those duties.

21. In Practical Ethics (supra note 13 at 182–95) Peter Singer discusses violations of law by Britain's Animal Liberation Front. He apparently supposes that the particular aims of the demonstrators, such as to stop the exploitation of factory farming, are consonant with the majority's moral sense.

22. See B. Zwiebach, Civility and Disobedience 154 (1975), who points out "the historical rule of disobedience in the development and articulation of new and valuable rights."

23. See P. Singer, note 13 supra at 192–95. Rawls himself, it should be noted, does not assert any absolute preclusion, and he does not develop how much harder it may be to justify nonviolent disobedience that does not quality as justified civil disobedience.

24. According to Rawls, "The intensity of desire or strength of conviction is irrelevant when questions of justice arise" (Rawls, note 12 supra at 361). One is hard put to understand how one could determine the justice of a policy that will lead to dislocation without knowing how strongly people dislike being dislocated; and their sense of resentment at being treated unjustly would also seem relevant. Compare Rawls, The Justification of Civil Disobedience, in H. Bedau, ed., note 14 supra at 240, 253, in which he indicates that the majority's sense of justice may be evidenced by an unwillingness to suppress the minority, but even there he seems to suppose that the sense of injustice does not depend on the minority's intensity.

25. M. K. Gandhi, Non-Violent Resistance (1961); M. L. King, Jr., Strength to Love 54 (1963).

26. See King's Letter from a Birmingham Jail (1963), reprinted in Bedau, note 14 supra at 72, 74–75.

27. See, generally, M. Walzer, note 11 supra at 25–43, who discusses illegal strikes mainly directed at changes in company policies.

28. One might argue that any stumbling decision by the government with very bad consequences is unjust to citizens but that extension of the concept of justice would turn any pressing utilitarian basis for public action into an issue of justice. For another interpretation of Rawls that sharply restricts instances of possibly justifiable civil disobedience, see J. Feinberg, Rawls and Intuitionism, in N. Daniels, Reading Rawls 108, 120–21 (1975).

29. What is said here also applies to conscientious avoidance of legal requirements. If one believes that following the law will be very harmful for people, one may be warranted in not following the law, although no issue of justice is involved.

30. A. Fortas, Concerning Dissent and Civil Disobedience 63 (1968).

31. See J. F. Childress, Civil Disobedience and Political Obligation 33 (1971); B. Zwiebach, note 22 supra at 181–84; and W. L. Taylor, Civil Disobedience: Observations on the Strategies of Protest, in H. Bedau, note 14 supra at 98, 104–5.

32. The thoughts in this section are developed at greater length in Greenawalt, A Contextual Approach to Disobedience, 70 Colum. L. Rev. 48, 67–69 (1970); also in J. R. Pennock and J. Chapman, eds., Nomos XII, Political and Legal Obligation 332 (1970).

33. I have in mind here examples such as the low speed limit that is really unnecessary at the time of day it is violated.

34. Of course, the citizenry, as beneficiaries of public expenditures, has an interest of a sort in each person paying his or her taxes, and each taxpayer may have an "interest" in fair sharing of the burden. I am referring here to more concrete interference with interests.

35. Obvious instances of deprivations of rights are interferences with property rights, but the sense of owning something might extend to other kinds of rights, such as contract rights. I do not pause over the subtlety of whether or not people generally attach a special psychological significance to property rights.

36. A sense of ownership does not always track legal ownership; a member of a family or a corporate employee, for example, may have such a sense about something he or she does not legally own.

37. This distinction may not apply when the only property that is injured is property held by the government or a large private institution.

38. Keeping other students away from class was considered a device for radicalizing them.

39. Rawls, note 12 supra at 373–75.

40. Id. at 376.

41. Rawls does recognize that possible injury to innocent third parties must be considered, but he does not seem aware of how typical the risk of such injury is.

42. See, generally, Peter Singer's account of escalating force in Northern Ireland. Democracy and Disobedience 139–45 (1973).

43. These matters are explored in a somewhat different way in Greenawalt, note 32 supra at 69–71. The discussion here proceeds on the assumption that the punishment to which one submits is one seriously intended by society. For the interesting suggestion that such was not the case when Socrates was sentenced to death, see Olsen, Socrates on Legal Obligation: Legitimation Theory and Civil Disobedience, 18 Ga. L. Rev. 828, 844–47 (1984).

44. See King, note 26 supra at 78.

45. See id.

11

Violent Disobedience

In this chapter I turn from peaceable to violent acts of disobedience. Violent acts are often, though by no means always, claimed to be justified because the whole political order requires change. Because the previous chapter deals with nonviolent acts that are not designed to accomplish such change and this chapter concerns violent acts, the use of nonviolent acts for revolutionary change is not explicitly discussed. I assume that any circumstances justifying violent acts of disobedience would also justify nonviolent ones, and that nonviolent acts are warranted sometimes when justifications for violent acts fall short.

Violent acts of law breaking, striking as they do at the most fundamental of human interests, are much harder to justify than peaceable acts of disobedience; and the idea that such acts can never be justified under a reasonably just political order has at least initial plausibility. This chapter explores the conditions under which violent illegal acts may be warranted. Any truly systematic effort of this sort would require an appraisal of violence as a technique of social change and a comparative evaluation of the harm it causes and the social harm it may alleviate. How violence compares with assorted social injustices and how the short- and long-term destructive potential of violence weighs against its ability to produce positive change are matters of deep controversy. Because the danger that one will end up simply rationalizing one's own predispositions is especially great with this subject, I have chosen initially to look at the law itself, at its treatment of violence, to try to discern moral principles for the appraisal of illegal violence. That endeavor is preceded by a brief discussion of the concept of violence, of why violence requires such powerful justification, and of the extent, to which the law's treatment of personal violence is relevant to the inquiry into moral evaluation.

The Concept of Violence

What I mean by acts of violence is acts of force against persons that cause death, substantial physical pain, or impairment of physical faculties or that restrain physical liberty for a significant period of time, and acts of force against property that destroy or gravely impair its physical integrity.[1] The term *violence* is itself often used to indicate condemnation, and perhaps the term implicitly conveys negative moral overtones, but I wish to avoid any implication that a violent act is necessarily wrong; rather, I assume that one can characterize an act as violent or not without settling the question of moral justification.[2] Partly because of the negative connotations of "violence," some wish to extend the term to cover psychological persecution or a social order that fails to afford opportunities to flourish. I restrict myself to the kinds of actions that the term undoubtedly covers and that typify the most troublesome questions about law breaking. Although an act that recklessly risks physical harm may be considered violent, I concentrate on the simpler cases in which an actor intends harm to persons or property or knows that that consequence will occur as a direct result of his act. I omit actions, such as winter strikes by drivers of fuel trucks, whose indirect effect may be to cause loss of life or grave harm; and I also omit actions whose risk lies in the violent response of others. Among actions that directly inflict harm, I do not discuss physical force to which the person on whom the force is used has consented or presumably would consent if conscious.[3]

The Harms of Violence

Death and physical injury are everywhere regarded as serious wrongs, impairing people's most fundamental interests. The most basic human right, perhaps, is to be free in one's person from unwarranted physical force. Illegal acts of violence generate intense resentment and insecurity among those who are injured and among those who fear they may be the next victims. Nothing is more destructive of a stable and peaceful social order than personal violence. Only the most compelling moral reasons can justify it.

Whether or not violence against property is especially harmful is more complicated.[4] Unless he holds out hope of recovery, an ordinary owner of tangible property is not likely to care very much whether his property has been destroyed or stolen; from his point of view, violence against property is therefore no worse than peaceable uncorrectible filching of property. When physical property is bombed or burned, however, a risk of injury to persons is often present; even when it is not present, people may fear that those who use such tactics against property today will use them against people tomorrow. Illegal use of bombs, at least, also symbolizes an extreme rejection of a social decision, even when property is their target. All this helps to explain why the bombing of abortion clinics is so disquieting, even when actors are careful not to jeopardize people. Because the main concern about violence is personal injury, I shall concentrate on violence that is directed at persons.

People sometimes threaten physical force without having to employ it. Private individuals getting their way by threatening violence is also unsettling to those affected, though generally somewhat less so than the actual infliction of violence. Because threats do not produce the same harm as actual violence, threats may be justified on occasion although the actual employment of violence would not be.[5] In what follows I will disregard this subtlety and talk simply about the use of physical force.[6]

Legal Rules and Moral Appraisals

Serious physical force directed at other persons or their property usually constitutes a crime and civil tort, but both branches of the law contain privileges justifying force that would otherwise be illegal. These privileges answer four major questions: (1) what kinds of rights and interests may people protect by the use of moderate or extreme physical force; (2) to what extent may one person use such force to protect another; (3) who may physical force be used against; (4) what limits, such as necessity, constrain the otherwise permissible use of force? No jurisdiction's law gives a clear answer to every issue that might be raised about the use of physical force, and some troublesome questions are answered differently in different jurisdictions; but the law does provide settled answers to a broad range of questions. The fabric of the law also provides hints about attitudes toward underlying moral premises, such as the places of moral rights and consequential evaluations.

As Oliver Wendell Holmes put it, "The law is the witness and deposit of our moral life."[7] The assumption of this chapter is that, at least in a liberal democracy, the law reflects social morality over a period of time and also provides a helpful starting point for thinking about a proper or ideal public morality for a society. One may, of course, conclude that the best public morality would diverge from present moral assumptions, but one cannot lightly disregard settled convictions about proper uses of force. Some areas of law, including in many societies the definition and protection of property rights, can be comfortably ascribed to class bias or the intense pressure of interested minorities; but people in all classes may be in the position of wanting to use force or being the victims of force. Perhaps members of "lower classes" commit more violence than the well-to-do, but these people are also more often its victims. With respect to violence against persons, no sharply competing class interests or perceptions are evident.[8]

Some aspects of law do render it an imperfect mirror of prevailing moral convictions about violence. The elite that makes and administers the law may put a higher priority on containing physical conflict than most people; and legal rules, whether developed by statute or judicial decision, are likely to exhibit a degree of sharpness, rationality, and generality that most people do not achieve in their everyday judgments. The crucial decision under the law concerns the legal consequence of behavior: is it to be allowed or made the subject of punishment or civil remedy? For this reason, when the law labels actions as acceptable, one cannot always tell whether the actions are really approved, are considered within a range of permissible moral options, or are regarded as wrong but excused. I shall concentrate on actions that the criminal law labels as justified,[9] but justification in this context may mean no more than morally permitted.

Even if the law tells us something about moral justifications for violent acts, the transposition of conclusions to illegal violence is troublesome, because unauthorized violence implicates duties to obey the law and produces distinctive consequences that flow from the breach of the legal order. Nonetheless, the thesis of this chapter is that the law itself illuminates the sorts of rights and interests people may appropriately protect and promote by using physical force against other persons.[10]

DEFENSE OF ONE'S RIGHTS AGAINST AGGRESSORS

Existing Legal Principles

The most obvious instances of lawful use of force are when a person acts to prevent someone else from attacking him or physically violating his property rights. A person may use deadly force against the threat of deadly force or to prevent a very serious crime. A person may not use more force than is necessary to defend his rights, and he may not use deadly force to prevent a minor injury, such as the simple theft of food from his store, even if deadly force is the only way to stop the fleeing wrongdoer.

Within these constraints, a victim of aggression need not engage in nice calculation of the benefits and burdens of using force. He may use nondeadly force to remove a trespasser, even though the harm he predictably will cause the trespasser may be greater than the harm the trespasser would otherwise cause him. Not only may a victim take the life of a single assailant if his own life is threatened, he may take the lives of any number of assailants if that is necessary to preserve his own life. Further, he may try to kill an assailant even though he might well survive if he refrained from taking action. Let us imagine the somewhat artificial case in which a victim realizes that if he does not respond to a single assailant, he will probably not die—the assailant is a bad shot and his chances of hitting the victim from the distance that separates the two is about twenty-five percent. The law, despite a lack of precision about the threshold probability of harm needed to trigger a justified response, does not demand that a person stand passively and accept a substantial chance of being killed when he can reduce or eliminate the risk by shooting at the assailant. Deadly force can also be used to prevent crimes such as rape and armed robbery that result in the death of victims only in a small percentage of cases. The permission to use such force may indicate both that taking life may sometimes be justified to protect interests of lesser magnitude than life and that any serious possibility of losing one's life at the hands of an aggressor may be enough to warrant the use of deadly force.

A victim need not retreat rather than use force, and he need not retreat from his home or place of work (or anywhere else in many jurisdictions) rather than use deadly force. He does not have to forgo his liberty to remain in a place where he has a right to be, even if the predictable consequence of his exercise of that liberty will be serious harm to an aggressor.

Innocent bystanders have a radically different status from aggressors. A victim may not use force against an aggressor if that force unduly risks harm to bystanders. A victim is supposed to accord the interests of bystanders as much weight as his own; he cannot intentionally kill an innocent bystander if that is the only way to save his life and he cannot place a bystander under greater risk than he stands under from an aggressor.

The law, as evidenced by the requirements that responsive force be necessary and not disproportionate to the original harm, does provide a degree of protection to the vital interests of aggressors; but the law also affords clear priority to the interests of innocent victims and bystanders. This priority may be explained by a utilitarian as discouraging improper use of force; but it more simply fits a deontological intuition that if someone's interests must be sacrificed, it should be the aggressor's.[11] This deontological perspective has two components, that people should not be required to sacrifice their most precious interests in the absence of wrongdoing and that aggressors forfeit their own rights to some degree by intentionally breaching the rights of others.

Illegal Force in Defense of Rights

Individuals sometimes believe that the law requires or permits infringement of their moral rights. If they are correct, may they morally use illegal physical force against government agents or private individuals who are invading their rights? One context in which this question can arise is when an actor falls just on the other side of the line of what the law permits. He may claim that the law has labeled as premature or excessive a use of force that is really warranted, and that his right to protect himself somehow outweighs whatever obligation he has to comply with the law.[12] I will disregard this context and focus on situations in which the law does not recognize, or self-consciously infringes, the underlying moral right whose protection is the basis for the use of force. I consider the extreme example of slavery and the plight of a person convicted of a crime of which he is innocent.

Slavery

Analysis of the moral right of a slave to use physical force to escape may seem unproductively anachronistic, but it helps to show that force, and even deadly force, may be warranted if violations of moral rights are extreme enough. The analysis also illustrates many of the difficulties of deciding when deadly force is warranted. If one could resolve what force a slave might justifiably use to escape, one could better assess claims of those suffering less gross and transparent injustices. Unfortunately, not all modern injustices are less severe than slavery; some modern governments have undertaken genocide, and a person marked for extinction on the basis of race, religion, ethnic origin, or class[13] faces a denial of moral right at least as extreme as that of the slave.

Illustration 11-1:

Sheila, who lives peaceably in the United States, is captured by alien invaders, who take her to another planet, where the dominant beings are humans who have attitudes about slavery that correspond with those held in earlier eras on earth. The point of Sheila's capture is that she and her offspring will be slaves. Under the planet's legal rule, no one may kill slaves, but masters may otherwise treat slaves as chattel property. Some masters are brutal; others, including Sheila's master, Manfred, exhibit a relatively humane concern for the welfare of their slaves. Slaves occasionally manage to escape and integrate themselves into the ordinary population.

At the moment the invaders try to capture Sheila, she may justifiably use force, and even kill the invaders, if that is necessary to avoid capture. Sheila's legal right to resist, by deadly force if required, reflects an antecedent moral right to protect her freedom. Assuming the invaders consciously violate the moral and legal norms of Sheila's society, she may consider them wrongful aggressors despite their own moral acceptance of slavery. Her moral right to use force against her captors survives her capture and removal to a ship in space where U.S. law no longer applies.

When Sheila finds herself in a society in which slavery is approved by law, and her status as a slave bears the stamp of legality, who counts as a wrongdoer is much less clear. There are people whose business is to maintain the system of slavery (slave dealers, private slave catchers, etc.) people whose lives involve implementing the laws regarding slavery but who have not selected a status uniquely involved with slavery (ordinary slave owners, ordinary law enforcement officials, judges, etc.), people who bear political responsibility for maintaining the slave system (legislators, important executive officials, etc.), and ordinary citizens whose lives are touched by slavery only indirectly. Who are the wrongdoers? Except for the tiny minority actively devoted to eliminating slavery, are all those who continue to live in a society in which this terrible evil is going on wrongdoers? Or is no one a wrongdoer, since no one can really be blamed for perpetuating slavery? The latter position reflects the important truth that one's personal degree of moral guilt depends heavily on one's awareness that what one is doing is wrong; if a social practice has longstanding acceptance, one receives a kind of reassurance that, from society's point of view, it is not objectionable. Even if one concludes, as a sensitive person might, that an institution like slavery is morally wrong, one may feel that little is to be gained by abstaining at a personal level from a widespread practice.

Sheila's case has an asymmetry that does not exist in ordinary self-defense cases; a clear moral right is being violated, but no particular person is now clearly to blame for the violation.

May Sheila use force against her master to escape? Certainly Manfred is not an innocent bystander; his actions continually infringe on Sheila's moral rights. Probably Sheila owes no respect at all to his interests that grow directly out of the institution of slavery, for example, his economic investment in her, and as to other interests, such as life and physical security, she certainly owes him no more than to treat his interests as equal to hers. Given the magnitude of Sheila's moral right to freedom, she would clearly be justified in using moderate physical force if that were necessary to escape.

Whether or not Sheila may use deadly force is a more troublesome question. The best argument on Manfred's behalf is that he is like an innocent aggressor in self-defense cases—someone who, without moral blame, jeopardizes Sheila's rights. Within the law, a victim is generally allowed the same response against an innocent aggressor, one who is insane or does not realize he is carrying a bomb, as a wrongful aggressor; but we should not too quickly conclude that the victim's moral rights are unaffected by the aggressor's blame. In self-defense cases, a victim must act quickly without much thought about the character of an assailant, and compact legal rules cannot develop every rare variation involving the known innocence of an aggressor. But a victim's knowledge that an aggressor is blameless would affect moral evaluation of the victim's failure to retreat or of his deadly response to a slight risk of injury. Escape usually occurs after deliberation, and Sheila has an opportunity to consider Manfred's moral status before she acts. Because he is fully aware of the facts that constitute Sheila's loss of rights, he is not as innocent as the true innocent aggressor, who is unaware that he threatens harm; but Manfred is less blameworthy than the typical wrongful aggressor. Exactly how much weight Sheila should give to Manfred's interests depends on how much her loss of rights dominates the moral evaluation.

One perspective is that she may do whatever is necessary to regain her precious right to freedom, including killing Manfred. An extreme version of this position would be that she may use deadly force rather than suffer any further loss of liberty: just as a victim of kidnapping may use deadly force to escape immediately even if he thinks he could escape later without using such force, Sheila would not have to delay to find a moment for less violent escape. The kidnapping analogy is somewhat misleading here, however, since kidnapping involves constant insecurity about the life of the victim and an unambiguous wrongdoer. Given the settled pattern of Sheila's loss of liberty and Manfred's decreased level of blame, the moral requirement that force be necessary should be understood to require that Sheila choose a moment when less force will be needed if such a moment promises an equal chance of success.

A different perspective sees Manfred and Sheila as caught up together in a grave social injustice, albeit one that makes Sheila suffer much more than Manfred. Because Manfred is not personally to blame for Sheila's condition, she should give weight to his legitimate interest. She certainly should choose a time for escape when expected force will be minimal, and perhaps she would be unjustified in killing Manfred if that were the only way to free herself.[14] The choice between this perspective and the one that emphasizes rights is difficult, and in context the correct choice may depend on whether or not Manfred has treated Sheila in a caring way.

When we consider others who might try to stop Sheila, questions about innocence and wrongdoing remain perplexing. If Sheila can use a level of force against Manfred, presumably she can use the same force against those specifically hired to bring her back. One might argue that as his agents, and perhaps as members of a less affluent social class, they are less to blame than he, but unlike him, they have chosen to engage themselves in the very business of catching slaves. The slave's position vis-à-vis Manfred's ordinary employees and other slaves who help hunt her down may be different. The employees have not chosen to hunt slaves, that is only a small part of their responsibilities; and the other slaves are essentially coerced by Manfred into hunting down their fellows. Although those groups do threaten Sheila's rights, they are innocent in a stronger sense than Manfred. Ordinary citizens who may try to restrain Sheila or report her have made a choice to prevent the escape that may distinguish them from those directed to participate in stopping her, but their fringe involvement in slavery may make them less responsible than Manfred.

How one should regard ordinary law enforcement officials is particularly difficult. They have a public duty to enforce the law, which happens to include slavery; this observation suggests a low level of personal responsibility. On the other hand, they have made a double choice: first, to take an enforcement position in which one important aspect of the law to be enforced is evil, and second, to participate directly in the enforcement enterprise, not only against those who break the law without any perceived moral claim but also against those who believe a moral justification underlies their behavior. As the visible representatives of the state that accepts slavery, the law enforcement official may in some sense assume the risk that he will be treated as a wrongdoer if the state is a wrongdoer, and perhaps the slave is thus justified in treating him as not innocent. Still, one should be hesitant to take this argument too far. If the enforcement official does not recognize, and perhaps cannot fairly be expected to recognize, that the particular act of enforcement is immoral, then whether he can somehow be taxed with the state's guilt because he happens to have chosen that line of work is doubtful.

Slavery pointedly combines extreme deprivation of personal rights with extreme deprivation of political rights. The law governing defense of rights strongly indicates that preservation of the bundle of rights that is lost when one becomes a slave is important enough to warrant even the taking of the life against a clearly identified oppressor. The illustration of slavery nicely shows how, even in this context, the system of legality and the problem of assessing responsibility can influence the dimensions of a moral right to use physical force.

Similar considerations apply to the more complex situations in which the claims of denial of moral rights are more uncertain and debatable and the deprivations plainly less severe.

Unjustified Punishment

Deprivations of moral rights perpetrated by the law need not depend on systematic injustice; they can result from the wrongful acts of isolated individuals or simple misfortune. In those settings, may illegal force be used justifiably against officials to prevent them from enforcing such a deprivation?

Illustration 11-2:
Susan, the sheriff, has framed Ralph for a murder she knows he did not commit. Ralph has been convicted and sentenced to death. He has unsuccessfully pursued all legal remedies. Shortly before the execution is to take place he has a chance to escape, but can do so only if he assaults, or kills Susan, who is his present custodian. Ralph has no legal right to escape at this point, since he is in Susan's lawful custody.

If Ralph's execution takes place, Susan will be a murderer, morally and legally. Ralph's moral right of self-defense extends to his using force against Susan; and he may even kill Susan if that is required to accomplish his escape. Unlike Sheila, Ralph does have normal duties to comply with law, and one might distinguish Susan as subverter of justice from Susan as lawful custodian, concluding that he cannot act violently against the latter. The distinction is artificial as it concerns Susan's well-being, and insofar as Ralph's violence does represent a kind of rejection of the state's authority, he cannot fairly be asked to give up his life when he knows the state's claims are grounded on plain error.[15]

Deadly force against Susan would be harder to justify if Ralph were merely escaping from imprisonment instead of from execution. An unjustified sentence of imprisonment may later be rescinded, and even if that prospect were dim, most imprisonment predictably comes to an end. However, if Ralph's sentence was very long, he might consider it like extended slavery.

In normal circumstances, the custodians, or those who seek to capture an escaped prisoner, will not be the same persons who bear responsibility for the wrong. Not only are they not blameworthy, they do not have the data that would allow them to identify the penalty as grossly unjust. Further, they are not merely innocent people who happen to pose a threat to the victim; they are persons performing necessary public duties; they owe an obligation to society to carry out the penalty that has been imposed. In one sense they are innocent aggressors rather than bystanders; their actions do pose a threat to Ralph's moral rights. But since they have acted with complete appropriateness, their interests probably deserve the consideration the law accords to the interests of bystanders. The magnitude of the wrong Ralph would otherwise suffer may be sufficient to justify moderate physical force to ensure his freedom, but deadly force against wholly innocent officials may be precluded even if Ralph's execution is the alternative.

When fortuitous error, such as sincere mistaken identification or substantial evidence of guilt that happens to be misleading (as in Dostoyevsky's *Brothers Karamazov*), produces a conviction of an innocent person, the analysis is essentially similar. Here no one—no private individual or state official—has injured the victim, but the innocent victim has nonetheless suffered a wrong. His obligations toward the state and toward innocent officials seems very much the same as if some single person, official or private, had intentionally framed him. As in that case, the government as a whole, and its custodial agents in particular, are carrying out a sentence that appears to be fully justified from their point of view but the victim himself knows to be unjustified.

Sometimes injustices result from the actions of high government officials (trials of leading party members during the Stalin era, for example) or from pervasive biases or preferences (e.g., in favor of whites against blacks) shared by virtually all government officials. These are intermediate cases between the legalized injustice of slavery and the isolated instance of injustice suffered by Ralph. As those who subvert the legal system of justice come closer to being the major representatives of the state or as the biases increase both in intensity and in the weight they are given, we come nearer to situations in which the government *qua* government is depriving one of rights.

Political Action to Protect Rights

Though the rights to life and liberty are ones that can be asserted directly against persons who threaten them, political action to alter the government or its laws often gives greater promise of achieving protection than direct assertion. Some other moral rights, such as a right to minimum welfare, that cannot be asserted directly because they require active participation by the government, can only be secured by political action. Political action to protect rights includes legal techniques such as speeches, nonforcible illegal techniques such as burning draft cards, moderate uses of force such as occupying buildings, major uses of force such as bombings, and full-scale warfare, as in armed revolutions. Our concern here is whether political action that includes physical force can be justified if nonviolent political action would be unsuccessful.

The law is of limited help in this inquiry. The law governing defense of rights deals with the direct assertion of rights. The law does not allow force to correct continuing injustices, say in an employer's treatment of its workers; but one cannot fairly infer from this bar the moral view that force is never justified to correct injustices the government perpetrates. Any modern society tries to structure private relations so that conflicts can be resolved without the use of force. The boss cannot bring physical force to bear against an employee, and the employee's use of force is deemed an improper response to whatever wrongs the boss has inflicted. With respect to private relations, the force of the state stands as a sort of neutral arbiter.[16] When the dispute is between the state and some of its members, no neutral arbiter exists. The state possesses a monopoly of relevant legal force. In such circumstances, aggrieved citizens may be morally justified in using force to combat or dislodge the force of the state that is denying their rights. The law may provide some vague guidance about sorts of rights for which such force may be appropriate, but one must turn mainly to history.

Rights that are so important their protection warrants direct force, even deadly force, against those who infringe them are the leading candidates for rights that warrant forcible political action. When basic rights are systematically suppressed, as with the institution of slavery, those who actually have power to alter prevailing law and practices are more responsible and blameworthy than those who merely take advantage of existing rules.[17] Political action may be more likely to succeed than direct assertions of rights, and success, if it comes, will rectify multiple violations. On the other hand, the initial brunt of forcible political action usually falls on lesser officials, mostly police officers and military personnel, and whether they can fairly be treated as wrongdoers is a troublesome question. Many forcible political acts are bound to harm innocent bystanders, and are more disturbing to a social order than direct assertions of rights.[18]

Although a moral justification to use force to assert one's rights directly does not necessarily imply a moral justification to use forcible political action, the kinds of rights for which one may use direct force are among those for which political force is sometimes warranted. The judgment of American culture on its own history is that certain political rights also qualify.

The initiators of the War for Independence relied heavily on claims that the government in power was denying their rights. The rhetoric of the time drew an analogy between the position of the colonists and that of slaves;[19] however, the claimed denials of rights were not nearly as extreme as others we have witnessed or can imagine.[20] Those who sought independence had not been marked for extermination, or enslaved, or arbitrarily imprisoned, or denied liberty of movement, or imposed on by an alien culture, or forbidden to worship as they chose, or foreclosed from expressing political opinions. Because the complaints that generated it, though conceived as part of a conspiracy to suppress liberty,[21] concerned inadequate political participation accompanied by harsh economic measures, the American Revolution must make one cautious in claiming that only the most extreme abuses justify armed insurrection.[22] To make the judgment that the Revolution was justified, as most Americans are inclined to do, one must acknowledge that gross (and widespread) denials of political participation and systematically harsh and unfair treatment can legitimatize forcible political action.

In terms of probable damage, armed military struggle is the ultimate degree of force for asserting political rights. A cause serious enough to justify military action is serious enough to justify lesser forms of force, such as forcible occupation of buildings or destruction of property. But how is one to judge a more selective use of deadly force, such as political assassination or terrorism directed at civilians, as an alternative? Many persons flinch at such tactics even when they deem military struggle defensible.

The comparative acceptance of armed struggle may be influenced by some factors whose relevance is dubious from a rational point of view. Because the army is viewed as an agent of the government for the purpose of fighting, killing soldiers may seem more appropriate than killing other persons associated with the government; but, especially when soldiers are draftees, the cogency of this attitude is questionable. There may also be a sense, perhaps shared by many participants, that open conflict is more honorable than stealthy murder. This view of the use of physical force probably has salutary effects on human relations generally, but it may also serve the interests of the powerful people who occupy positions of social authority, at the expense of the relatively inarticulate and powerless individuals who constitute the most vulnerable class in armed conflicts. Still, the sentiments of horror at political assassination and random terrorism are supported by their general destabilizing effect on social life,[23] the insecurity resulting when killing by stealth is approved, the greater likelihood that armed struggle will produce desirable changes, and the tendency for the comparative difficulty of mounting armed insurrection to serve as a check on the seriousness of an underlying cause.

Whatever the case when one is trying to assert a moral right against an individual who is directly violating that right, the grave consequences of armed struggle on innocent and guilty alike suggest that limits like those associated with the traditional just war doctrine are relevant.[24] Armed struggle should not be undertaken unless there is a reasonable prospect of success, unless the harm likely to be caused is not disproportionate to the good likely to be achieved, and unless other less violent alternatives would fail.

This last condition warrants brief comment. Whether violence is more likely to succeed than nonviolence will rarely be clear when one is judging overall political effects; and disagreements on that score will often underlie disputes over whether or not violence is justified.[25] On occasion those who support violence may even urge that it has independent virtues. Speaking of violence directed at colonial oppressors, Frantz Fanon stated:

> But it so happens that for the colonized people this violence, because it constitutes their only work, invests their characters with positive and creative qualities. The practice of violence binds them together as a whole. . . .
>   . . .
>   At the level of individuals, violence is a cleansing force. It frees the native from his inferiority complex and from his despair and inaction; it makes him fearless and restores his self respect.[26]

That a violent overthrowing of colonial rule is preferable to peaceful tactics, even if the latter are equally likely to win, is largely belied by Fanon's own account of mental disorders arising out of colonial war. And whatever its validity in the colonial context, the argument for violence is much less attractive when the oppressed must continue to live with the oppressors after their fight is won.[27] Generally, political violence has an immensely destructive effect on social relations, and its wounds take a long time to heal. Violence to change the law or government should be considered a step of last resort, even when protection of rights is at stake.

DEFENSE OF THE RIGHTS OF OTHERS AGAINST AGGRESSORS

Existing Legal Principles

When someone's rights are threatened, is an outsider justified in protecting those rights to the same degree as the victim? I shall assume that the rights, like those to life and liberty, are ones that the outsider is capable of protecting,[28] the outsider has available the same factual information as the victim, and the victim welcomes the outsider's aid. Movement within the law is now strongly in the direction of assimilating the rights of intervenors to the rights of victims; older restrictions, which limited intervention to family or friends or held strangers intervening strictly liable for mistaken appraisals of the facts, have now been largely abandoned. Defense of such restrictions has usually been cast in terms of the likely ignorance of strangers; but the older rules may also reflect some vague sense that intervenors are not always justified in doing what victims may do. If one tried to state a principle behind such a sense, it might be that a stranger has a greater moral duty to consider a balance of likely consequences than a person who is victimized by another's aggression.

Illegal Defense of the Rights of Others

Individuals defending the moral rights of others may believe they need to break the law. Of course, individuals who engage in political action to protect their own rights will also be trying to protect the rights of others suffering similar violations of right. But our focus here is on those who combat the denial of rights to a group that does not include themselves. A clear example would be white abolitionists who opposed slavery.

One might take the view that when the government systematically denies the rights of one group of citizens, it denies the rights of all. This proposition is based on the idea that people have a right to live in a just society and the lack of justice or evil inevitably poisons those who are not directly injured. Although some truth lies in this observation, it disregards the special and much more severe wrong that is done to the injured class. Thus, one is left with the problem whether persons not in that class have the same moral privilege to use force on behalf of members of the class as do the members of the class themselves.[29]

If intervenors generally have a greater moral responsibility to weigh consequences than do victims, that constraint would operate in these situations; but beyond that possibility, the intervenors' justification may be affected by ties that do not reach the victims. For the victim, moral reasons for obeying the law may be largely undercut by the violation of his rights. Slaves owe nothing to the government or to members of the society as such, though they may have universally applicable moral responsibilities to all humans that might bear on whether or not they should obey some laws. Abolitionists, on the other hand, have the rights and privileges of other citizens, including the possibility of participation in political processes. The injustice to another group may not relieve them of responsibilities they have as full citizens. Illegal aid, even forcible illegal aid, may be warranted if the injustice is severe enough, but the intervenor has a duty to weigh claims of obedience that are simply not present for many victims.

PUNISHMENT

Under the law, formal punishment of adults, involving serious physical force, is the exclusive province of the government. The law of justification thus provides no suggestion that private persons may appropriately punish other adults in this way.

This implicit judgment would clearly reach some situations in which private punishment may be contemplated. One of these is when a government operates with reasonable strength, honesty, and effectiveness, but some clearly guilty persons are not convicted, say because irrefutable evidence of their guilt is not usable at their trials. Some citizens may be tempted to take the law "into their own hands." Another kind of situation involves settings of close interpersonal relations that members believe should be carried on without state intervention. Brothers of a frequently beaten wife might believe themselves morally justified in beating up the husband in return, supposing that such action would be more productive than invoking public processes and not accepting the law's demarcation of public and private power for this situation. In each of these two sorts of situations, proponents of using private physical force might contend that the law's preclusion is stricter than prevailing, and correct, moral views and that its rigidity is to be explained in terms of misjudgment or administrative simplicity. But they could draw no support from the law itself.

The posture is different when the claim is that state machinery has failed so badly, because of weakness or corruption, that private individuals must undertake state functions of punishment. The criminal law as a whole does establish the importance of punishment as a social institution, and that premise may be used to argue that private infliction of punishment is morally warranted if the government fails in its task. During the colonial era, when no organized police force existed, the line between government and private citizens was much less distinct than it is now. Mobs, often led by respected public citizens, ventured outside the strict limits of legality with some frequency to enforce public ideas of justice, and on some occasions they did so with the acquiescence of local officials.[30] Those thinking and writing about political matters conceived a much more active role for the citizenry in this respect than any it would be accorded now.

Perhaps the weaker a government is, the more easily one can justify private illegal actions that perform functions that ordinarily belong to the government. A similar conclusion may apply when government officials are so corrupt they regularly decline to proceed against wrongdoers for wholly improper reasons.[31] Even in circumstances of weakness or pervasive corruption, however, private vigilantism is fraught with social dangers, creating risks of private feuds, a generally increased level of violence, and further breakdown of government authority. Very strong reasons in favor of action will be required to overcome its likely harm.

INDIRECT PROTECTION OF RIGHTS AND THE PROTECTION AND PROMOTION OF INTERESTS

Principles of Existing Law

On some occasions people trying to deflect a threat use physical force against persons who are not themselves the source of the threat. The threat may originate in the actions of another human being—A uses B as a shield in his attack on C, or A threatens to kill D unless C robs B. Or the threat may originate in natural causes—C, whose brakes have failed, can avoid going over a cliff with his two passengers only if he runs down pedestrian B. In each instance, C can prevent a harm by directing physical force at B.

The precise status of the law for such situations varies in different jurisdictions and is unclear in many. In most, a defense of necessity or general justification covers responses to natural threats; in some, responses to human threats are reached only by the defense of duress, but in modern American statutory formulations the defense of general justifications covers these as well. The defense of general justification, discussed in some detail in Chapter 13, provides that certain otherwise criminal injuries to persons or property are justified if they are required to avoid some more serious harm. One influential modern standard, that of the Model Penal Code, requires that the harm sought to be avoided "be greater" than that sought to be prevented by the law defining the offense.[32] The New York standard, also widely followed, demands that the need to avoid the harm "clearly outweigh" the desirability of avoiding the injury the statute seeks to prevent.[33] Among statutes, some sharp divergences exist, most notably over whether the defense should ever be available against charges of intentional homicide (many jurisdictions providing neither a justification nor a duress defense in such cases) and whether the harm to be avoided must constitute a grave harm or can include lesser evils. Uniform agreement apparently exists that if the threat to the actor's interests is grave, such as loss of life or severe physical harm, and the harm to the innocent person is less than grave, for example, taking of property or simple assault, the infliction of harm is justified. The law, thus, represents clear rejection of any notion that no intrusion on the rights of innocent persons is ever warranted. In these settings, the actor's claim of privilege does not depend on whether someone's vital interests are threatened by a willful rights-violating act of another or by a natural danger that does not jeopardize rights in any strict sense.[34]

The points at which legal rules diverge reflect some of the troubling points of moral disagreement within the society.[35] The Model Code and jurisdictions that follow it authorize an actor to use a straightforward consequentialist approach. The contrary position that the general justification defense is unavailable for intentional homicides corresponds, imperfectly, with the deontological view that intentionally taking the life of an innocent person is always wrong, however many lives may be lost as a consequence of one's failure to act. And the position that the defense cannot be invoked unless a grave interest is threatened roughly reflects another deontological view, that the rights of innocents may be invaded only when a substantial disproportion exists between the interest sacrificed and the interest protected.

Illegal Efforts to Protect Rights Indirectly and to Promote Vital Interests

When one thinks of personal uses of force, the line between direct protection of rights against offenders and force directed agianst innocent people is fairly sharp. The distinction largely breaks down when one thinks of political action to safeguard rights, though the officials or other persons at whom physical force is directed may be conceived as more or less to blame for rights violations. The previous discussion of forcible political action, including armed struggle, to defend one's own rights or the rights of others already embraces much of what can be said about action directed at innocent people. One major point is that if innocent people are likely to be injured, justified action requires a careful weighing of benefits against harm. The morality of serious injury to innocents is acutely important in this domain. If the *intentional* taking of innocent life is always wrong, random terrorism against innocent[36] civilians will never be morally justified. If innocent lives can be intentionally sacrificed in the pursuit of vital social objectives, then such tactics cannot be ruled out on absolute principle, though their extreme propensity to create insecurity and resentment may render their justification very difficult.

How far must justifications for forcible political action rest on assertions of right rather than claims about general welfare? The discussion is not easy, because the rhetoric of armed struggle has traditionally been a rhetoric of rights; and since those who use force against a government are inevitably accused of violating rights, they understandably wish to talk of protecting and promoting even more important rights.

Recognizing the immense complexity of trying to talk about what a government believes or intends, one might oversimplify some possible situations in the following way: (1) the government realizes that it is denying moral rights but is willing to do so in the interests of the powerful social class it represents; (2) the government intends the consequences that others characterize as a denial of rights but honestly disputes that characterization (e.g., the government supports slavery but regards slavery as benign); (3) the government follows a policy that it believes will have beneficial consequences but that others think will be destructive of vital interests such as life (e.g., the government thinks civilian nuclear power is safe; critics disagree); (4) the government recognizes the desirability of better satisfaction of vital interests but does not know how to contribute to that end (e.g., it understands the disastrous effects of sharp inflation but thinks it is impotent to stop inflation by any acceptable techniques).

In the first situation, the government is a wrongdoer in the most obvious sense. Whatever greater latitude to use force exists because a person or organization is intentionally violating rights is present here. In the second situation, the government may be less blameworthy, but it is intentionally doing what others consider a violation or rights. Action against the government can still be based on the claim that it is violating rights. When one reaches the third and fourth situations, the claim of rights violation is much more dubious. Opponents of civilian nuclear power may think millions of lives will be lost because of the government's misguided policies, but the ordinary notions of rights and violation imply something more than the unfortunate consequence of mistaken policy judgment, and they also imply something more than the actual helplessness or ineptitude revealed by the fourth situation. Cases, of course, will never be as simple as the situations suggested. Opponents of government policies will be able to point to indifference, corruption, inappropriate priorities, and other matters as bases for blaming officials even when no intention exists to violate rights.

Just as the general justification defense permits forcible action to protect important interests in the absence of a violation of rights, government actions that do not violate rights may be harmful enough to warrant illegal force, if that is required to alter things. This conclusion receives some historical support from the 1776 Virginia Bill of Rights, which talks of government being instituted for "the common benefit, protection, and security" and claims on behalf of a majority a right to abolish any government that "shall be found inadequate or contrary to these purposes."[37] Whether or not gross ineptitude alone is a subject of moral blame may be debatable; if it is not, a principle that innocent lives cannot be taken would constrain possible uses of force against government officials whose only failure was extreme ineffectiveness. For countries without techniques for orderly change of officials, at least moderate illegal force may sometimes be warranted to alter rulers whose main fault is incompetence. In liberal democracies, on the other hand, gross ineptitude that cannot be remedied by ordinary political processes is highly unlikely.

The discussion in this chapter has shown that in some circumstances the use of serious physical force is morally justified. In relatively common situations the law approves the use of such force, moral judgment largely coinciding with legal permission. In more unusual circumstances illegal physical force may be employed in a morally justifiable manner, although justification for serious physical force that is illegal will rarely be available in a liberal democratic society that recognizes its members as equal and functions with reasonable effectiveness.

I have concentrated on whether violence is morally permissible according to proper standards of public morality. Dedication to some absolute principle of nonviolence, such as that adopted by pacifists and by Gandhi[38] and King, exacts a higher standard than public morality can reasonably demand. On the other hand, given the self-sacrifice and constructive witness of nonviolent disobedience, one could rarely, if ever, say that a person had a moral *duty* to choose violent law breaking in preference to nonviolent acts designed to combat injustice.

NOTES

1. A more precise categorization is achieved by Ronald B. Miller, Violence, Force and Coercion, in J. Schaffer, ed., Violence 15–27 (1971). For other illuminating treatments of the concept of violence, see Holmes, Violence and Nonviolence, in id. at 110–12, and P. Macky, Violence: Right or Wrong (1973).

2. The two notions of "great physical force" and "unlawful force" derive from the Latin roots *violentus* and *violare*.

3. I thus exclude not only ordinary surgery but also instances of consent to homicide and to sadistic acts.

4. In discussing activities of the Animal Liberation Front, Peter Singer, Practical Ethics 182 (1979), sharply distinguishes property damage from personal violence.

5. In the law, for example, special restrictions on the justifiable use of deadly force do not apply to threats to use deadly force. A critical question about nuclear weapons policy is whether national threats to use weapons are warranted even if actual use of the weapons in the circumstances would not be.

6. In some circumstances the justifiability of actual use (judged by what is a reasonable act based on the facts then available) may depend on a threat's having first been made. An unsuccessful threat against an aggressor may demonstrate the necessity of using actual force and may help to establish that the aggressor is really dangerous.

7. Holmes, The Path of the Law, 10 Harv. L. Rev. 457, 459 (1897).

8. Even with respect to property rights, those who regard themselves as oppressed and want a redistribution of property are not likely to favor radically different principles about the use of force against justly held property. Property rights differ a great deal between Communist and capitalist societies, but the use of force against legally held property is similarly treated.

9. See, generally, Greenawalt, The Perplexing Borders of Justification and Excuse, 84 Colum. L. Rev. 1897 (1984). I omit citations for most of the relevant principles of criminal law. See, generally, Model Penal Code and Commentaries §§ 3.01–3.12 (1985); W. LaFave and A. Scott, Handbook on Criminal Law 381–407 (1972); Kadish, Respect for Life and Regard for Rights in the Criminal Law, 64 Calif. L. Rev. 871 (1976); Greenawalt, Violence— Legal Justification and Moral Appraisal, 32 Emory L.J. 437 (1983).

10. The presuppositions on which the analysis rests are more fully developed in id.

11. How far the law of justification can be explained in wholly deontological or wholly consequential terms is discussed briefly in id., at 453–56. A mixed account, an account of rights and duties qualified by consequential considerations, provides the most straightforward defense of existing principles.

12. Of course, in many cases of ordinary self-defensive force, an original victim may respond without precise knowledge of what the law provides and without careful thought; his moral claim will therefore be that a person with such knowledge and time to consider would judge his action to be appropriate.

13. I assume in including "class" that no simple correlation exists between one's class and one's perpetuation of grave injustices in the past.

14. I omit in the text the exact conditions under which Sheila uses force, but these could make a difference. If Sheila starts to escape and Manfred takes actions that threaten Sheila's life, she could, morally, use deadly force in self-defense. The difficult examples are when Manfred uses nondeadly force to prevent the escape and Sheila can gain her liberty only by using deadly force and when Sheila uses deadly force before her escape to prevent subsequent recapture. Ordinarily one can use deadly force only responsively, because one cannot know that someone else will try to stop the exercise of a moral right. But if Manfred always uses force to recapture slaves, Sheila can be confident that he will do so in her case. The intuitive sense that even here reactive use of deadly force is easier to justify than initial use may rest partly on necessity. If one can plan an escape that will not involve deadly force, its necessary use because of an unplanned occurrence differs significantly from making such force a part of one's plan.

15. That conclusion lies in tension with Socrates' view in the Crito that he was morally required to submit to unjust punishment. However, the tribunal convicting Socrates had relatively full evidence and, in effect, interpreted the "laws" against impiety and corruption of youth in a mistaken and undesirable way. The flaws in the process by which Socrates was convicted were not as stark as those affecting Ralph.

16. However, in some societies an employer's economic power may be so great or the government's support of the prevailing social class so strong that physical force on behalf of the disinherited may appear a necessary and morally justified means for righting some "private" wrongs. Michael Walzer makes such a suggestion about some union employment of force. M. Walzer, Civil Disobedience and Corporate Authority, in Obligations: Essays on Disobedience, War and Citizenship 38–43 (1970). Even if one does not object to the role of the state or believe that a private organization has excessive power, he may believe that on certain occasions physical force is warranted to achieve a change in the policy of the private organization.

17. This judgment would require qualification for political actors who are

trying to change the rules or do not attempt to do so only because general opinion overwhelmingly supports slavery.

18. Perhaps like slaves, people suffering the most extreme deprivations of right need not take this last consideration into account.

19. See B. Bailyn, The Ideological Origins of the American Revolution 118, 232–46 (1967).

20. Comparing the colonists' situation with the plight of actual slaves, the slavery the colonists complained of, as Samuel Hopkins put it in 1776, "is lighter than a feather compared to their heavy doom, and may be called liberty and happiness when contrasted with the most abject slavery and inutterable wretchedness to which they are subjected." Id. at 244.

21. Id. at 94–159.

22. The claims on behalf of the Confederacy were no more powerful, though they were joined with an argument that secession was a legal right under the Constitution.

23. See, e.g., P. Singer, note 4 supra at 198–200; M. Walzer, note 16 supra at 66–67.

24. See, generally, Wells, Is "Just" Violence Like "Just" War?, 1 Soc. Theory Prac. 26 (1970).

25. Compare, e.g., Gandhi's hope that peaceful suffering might transform the situation of the Jews in Nazi Germany with the more pessimistic appraisals of Martin Buber and J. L. Magnes in Two Letters to Gandhi, The Bond, Jerusalem, April 1939.

26. F. Fanon, The Wretched of the Earth 93, 94 (E. Farrington trans., 1968).

27. See Walzer, note 16 supra at 66–67.

28. By contrast, if constant humiliation by A has deprived B of self-respect, B may have to make claims on his own to restore his self-respect. See Richards, Rights, Resistance, and the Demands of Self-Respect, 32 Emory L.J. 405, 420–21 (1983).

29. There are more complex intermediate cases in which the intervenor's original assistance is peaceful—he hides runaway slaves—and his need to use force arises only when he is threatened for giving peaceful assistance, when others intrude on his property to discover if he is doing so, or when others attempt to capture persons who have relied on his assistance. In the first two instances, one might view the intervenor's use of force as opposing a denial of his own rights, including his right to offer nonforcible assistance to those whose moral rights are denied. In the last case, the intervenor may have a responsibility to use force based on his undertaking toward the slaves relying on his help.

30. See, generally, J. Reid, In a Defiant Stance (1977); Maier, Popular Uprisings and Civil Authority in Eighteenth-Century America, 27 Wm. & Mary Q. (n.s.) 3 (1970).

31. If the corruption is subject to correction by the political process, that

alternative is preferable to meting out private punishment to those who have profited from the corruption.

32. Model Penal Code § 3.02(1)(a) (Official Draft, 1985).

33. N.Y. Penal Law § 35.05 (McKinney, 1975).

34. I assume that if a mountaineer freezes to death because of a snowstorm, no deprivation of rights occurs.

35. The variant implications are explored in greater detail in Chapter 13.

36. Some terrorists may take the view that virtually everyone in the target population really is to blame for the social injustice against which they fight.

37. Virginia Bill of Rights, § 3.

38. Gandhi, note 25 supra at 42, indicates clearly that Jews should respond to Hitler with nonviolent resistance even if their massacre would be the result.

IV

INSTITUTIONS OF
AMELIORATION

12

Responses Within the Law to Moral Claims to Disobey

In previous chapters, we have considered reasons why people may believe they are morally justified in disobeying the law. This last part of the book concerns the legal system, how formally or through the exercise of power by legal officials it may respond to choices to disobey made on moral grounds. Succeeding chapters analyze particular techniques of accommodation. This chapter clarifies certain central issues, indicating why claims of moral justification can matter for the law and how the law can respond to them.

The Relevance of Moral Claims to Disobey

Why should moral claims to do what is otherwise illegal matter at all for the law? If society has judged behavior to be wrongful and the actor has engaged in that behavior, should he not receive the same treatment as others who engage in the behavior? I will address this question mainly in terms of criminal punishment, commenting briefly at the end of the section on civil liability.

The basic reason a moral claim may matter is that the actor who sincerely asserts such a claim is not like other violators. The difference is clearest when officials can rightly say that the actor is correct in his or her moral claim. Whatever may be true when exisiting social standards diverge from proper standards of public morality,[1] an actor's claim will be "correct" if it follows both the moral evaluations of most of the community and proper standards. The actor's claim may be that what he did was morally permissible, even given the law against it, or that legal interference violates his moral rights.

Could society ever agree with such a claim, or does the law always represent "the moral judgment of the majority and its sense of justice"?[2] Even if we put aside the many highly technical legal rules that embody no obvious moral judgments,[3] we cannot say that the law invariably reflects a community's moral judgments. Because of the intensity of a minority's sentiments or its disproportionate political influence, legislatures may adopt laws that are at odds with the moral judgments of the majority. More commonly, legislators fail to repeal laws embodying traditional moral views (e.g., against homosexual acts) even when those views cease to be embraced by most citizens. Most important, the majority's approval of a law does not mean that it disapproves every violation. People may suppose both that the acts required by the law are generally desirable and that the law's existence provides further strong moral reasons for performing the acts, and still agree with an actor that pressing conflicting considerations justify disobedience. All will agree that a good speed limit should be broken when it is necessary to save a life, and many people will believe that disobedience of a good law as a protest is sometimes justified. Few people regard intentional interference with traffic as generally acceptable, but many would approve blocking of traffic to protest a dangerous failure to install a traffic light or a president's hasty decision to use tactical nuclear weapons. On some occasions, actors will rightly regard disobedience as morally justified and the majority will agree.

When these conditions are met, many of the ordinary reasons for punishment simply do not apply. Morally justified acts tend on balance, not to be harmful to the legitimate interests of the members of society;[4] and society should not try to discourage those acts by means of incapacitation, general and individual deterrence, and norm reinforcement.[5] When moral delinquency is absent, and understood to be absent, retribution, reform of character, and vengeance are also inappropriate.

Is fairness to those who have not violated the law a more substantial argument in favor of punishing morally justified law breakers? Such an argument has little force when a disobedient act involves no special personal gain for the actor.[6] But even when an actor benefits by a justified illegal act, it will usually be hard to call this benefit unfair. The law breaker's likely acquisition of fortuitous advantages denied to others may affect the initial justifiability of his act, in ways that fair play, natural duty, and utilitarian reasons for obedience reflect. But if these reasons for obedience are outweighed and the illegal act is morally preferable, or at least permitted, whatever residual unfairness is involved will not be a matter of blame for the actor.[7] Apart from preventing actual unfairness, punishment might be defended as preventing perceived unfairness. Some who conclude that an act was warranted may still harbor resentment that they did not profit in a similar way; and others who remain unpersuaded about justification may have more fully developed ideas about the actor's unjust gain. Punishment might at least serve the purpose of reassuring those with such perceptions.

Perhaps the strongest arguments for punishment of violators who might be justified rest on the difficulty of identifying accurately which acts of disobedience are really justified and on the inappropriateness of officials making such judgments. Any principle that officials may excuse justified illegal acts will result in some failures to punish unjustified acts, for which the purposes of punishment would be more fully served. Even when officials make correct judgments about which acts to excuse, citizens may draw mistaken inferences, and restraints of deterrence and norm acceptance may be weakened for unjustified acts that resemble the justified ones. For these and other reasons, the appropriateness of government officials setting themselves up to determine when illegal acts are morally justified is subject to doubt. This problem is explored in the next section and in subsequent chapters. Once we see that the more straightforward bases for punishment do not apply to morally justified illegal acts, however, we should be receptive to the basic idea of amelioration within the law.

The analysis of responses to correct claims of moral right is somewhat different. If the actor's behavior is itself morally justified, the law's violation of a moral right against the intervention of society is simply an additional reason why punishment may not be appropriate. The interesting problem concerns an assertion of a moral right (say, to engage in adult sexual relations) on behalf of behavior that is not morally justified (by deceitfully professing affection, the actor has engaged in sexual relations solely to improve his business position).

What exactly does it mean that despite the immorality of his particular sexual acts, the actor really does have a moral right to engage in them? One sense would be that society's interference by punishment is morally unjustified; in this sense, the conclusion that a moral right exists would inexorably imply that punishment is inappropriate. A second, more modest sense is that the actor's original moral right to engage in the behavior was violated by the law that prohibits such behavior.

Based on this second sense, whether or not the original moral right yields a moral right to be free of punishment is a genuine moral question. Ronald Dworkin has suggested that an original moral right does have this consequence, that when the government violates a moral right, it "does a further wrong to enforce that law."[8] This is a powerful claim about the force of moral rights. I have suggested in Chapter 9 that an individual's possession of an original moral right does not inexorably imply that he has no moral duty to obey a rights-violating prohibition. In that context, I drew on an illustration involving a faculty restriction on a member's teaching criminal procedure cases in constitutional law, a restriction that violates academic freedom.[9] The same illustration shows why the rights-invading character of the original restriction does not necessarily obviate the appropriateness of punishment.

Although enforcement of the restriction, of course, continues the original wrong, the desirability of applying rules when disagreement exists over whether they violate rights and the need to back up duties of fairness with sanctions might make enforcement of a misconceived restriction, even of a rights-violating one, preferable to nonenforcement. Because in the faculty resolution example, the government as legislator is indistinguishable from the government as enforcer, we can pass over critical problems about appropriate roles of variant government officials that loom large in subsequent chapters. One might view the faculty, as a body, as having entered a kind of implied contract with its members to enforce the rules as they exist and to have a duty of fairness to that effect toward other faculty members who comply despite the belief that their own moral rights may be infringed. If the reasons for faculty *enforcement* are partly deontological, determining the appropriateness of enforcement requires measuring the moral right (and the correlative duty not to infringe it) against the duty to enforce; two deontological standards are in competition. Even if the reasons for enforcement are exclusively utilitarian, the existence of the rule against teaching certain cases could make a difference. The utilitarian reasons in favor of enforcement, when *added* to the utilitarian reasons for the original restriction, might be strong enough to override the right to teach what one thinks best.

This possibility may be affected by the underlying bases for moral rights. One might conceive of moral rights against government interference in certain domains as resting heavily on distrust of government judgments, an ultimately utilitarian grounding of the sort presented in J. S. Mill's On Liberty.[10] Utilitarian reasons that support a heavy presumption against government interference with designated moral rights might or might not support a practice of nonenforcement when the government has mistakenly, but in good faith, transgressed moral rights. The best balance between deontological principle and utilitarian calculation with respect to restrictive legislation is not necessarily the best balance for questions of enforcement of laws that may possibly violate rights.

In summary, we can see that legislation that violates moral rights people have against the government can not only affect what is morally right for an actor to do and the appropriateness of private interference, points covered in Chapter 9, it can also affect whether the government's further interference by enforcement is warranted.

I have thus far assumed that the actor's claim of moral justification or moral right is correct and is accepted by a majority of society. When society rightly disagrees with his claim, the arguments in favor of punishment are much stronger. The actor has engaged in harmful, unwarranted behavior, and society wishes to prevent him and others from committing similar acts. Still, not all the ordinary reasons for punishment apply. Unless his moral sentiments are themselves abhorrent, the actor who behaves out of conviction deserves condemnation less than the criminal who acts in the pursuit of private gain or from undisciplined passion. Moreover, he typically will not be a suitable candidate for reform. The strength of conviction and willingness to sacrifice that are required to act against self-interest in doing what one believes to be morally correct are rightly considered admirable traits, not usually to be visited with harsh penalties. When such penalties are inflicted, they are likely to produce alienation and bitterness in the conscientious actors who bear them. Thus, even when the majority of society is firmly convinced that the actor's assessment of relevant moral claims is mistaken, it may have substantial reasons to avoid punishment or reduce its severity.

In the first part of this study, civil wrongs were treated as violations of law. The substantive civil law may be contoured to treat as privileged acts that would otherwise be wrongful but are supported by powerful moral claims. When an act does not fall within any such privilege, a private citizen suffering a civil injury should properly consider the actor's moral claims before proceeding against him. Civil juries and judges might to some extent temper their treatment of cases because of such moral claims; but in a civil case the legal rights of the person harmed are involved as well as the general interests of the state. Lenient treatment for the actor means ungenerous treatment for the person suffering the breach of civil duty. When the moral claim to breach concerns the comparative relation of the two parties (e.g., the plaintiff's cruelty has led the defendant to strike him), a finding of nonliability or reduced damages may work no genuine unfairness; but if plaintiff's position is more fortuitous, the unfairness to him of leniency is a serious concern.

Modes of Response Within the Law

Discretionary Nonenforcement

The most obvious way in which the legal system can provide for amelioration is by authorizing officials to disregard violations altogether or temper treatment of violators according to the wrongfulness of their actions. One reason for doubt about the law's conferring discretion on officials to disregard violations is the value of uniform application of legal prohibitions. Substantial reasons, however, support some discretion. Given the choices about allocation of resources that enforcement agencies must make, judgments may need to be made about less serious violations and less blameworthy violators.[11] Were administrative officials left free to decide in each case what behavior was criminal, their discretion would offend the principle of justice that people should have ample warning their behavior is criminal; but this basic principle is not violated if all executive officials do is to decline to proceed against someone who has committed a crime. In any particular system of criminal law, many offenders will not be proceeded against because they are not discovered. To extend this class to include others who are known, or strongly suspected, by executive officials to be offenders violates principles of liberal government only if the discretion involved confers arbitrary power or is at odds with a principle of equality.[12]

A conceivable principle of equality is that all discovered offenders should be given equal treatment in relation to the criminal process. But if there are substantial reasons why application of the criminal process is inappropriate for some offenders, these offenders may be unequal in relevant ways to those who should be proceeded against. Whether or not the principle of equal treatment of equals is offended will depend on the criteria for distinction and consistency of administrative behavior. If, under conditions of perfect consistency in application, the reasons for differentiation concern relevant characteristics of individual offenders, such as the seriousness of the crime or degree of participation, then similar offenders are not being given unequal treatment; but if the reasons concern such matters as temporary case overload or a need for a highly publicized single prosecution, ideals of individual justice and equality are sacrificed.[13] When criteria are not evenly applied, discretion will, of course, conflict with the principle of equality.

The geniune concern about equality largely merges with the concern about arbitrary power. When decisions are made by individual law enforcement agents, the dangers of inconsistency of treatment are very great, although guidelines from higher-ups can reduce the problem somewhat. That executive officials may use their discretion to proceed against particular persons for inappropriate reasons (personal dislike, political disagreement, etc.) is a special danger, a potentiality for abuse that reaches beyond the general evils of inequality of application. Administrative discretion not to proceed against some who break the law does involve dangers of arbitrariness and unequal treatment of similar offenders, but weighty reasons for such discretion may counsel attempts to contain it rather than do without it.

Police and prosecutors are possible agencies of discretion to disregard violations, and, when judges are permitted to dismiss charges independent of proof of guilt,[14] they have a similar authority. Executive pardons (or legislative amnesties) issued before any criminal process is invoked constitute another method of exercising discretion to disregard violations of law. Later chapters examine these techniques.

Discretionary Leniency

Whether or not they have discretion to disregard violations, officials may be given discretion to vary the nature and severity of treatment given those who have violated the law. Examples of such discretion are prosecutorial authority to reduce charges below the level of an actual offense and to bargain over the precise amount of punishment, judicial authority to determine the original severity of a sentence,[15] or even to divert the offender to some noncriminal disposition, parole board discretion to determine the time of initial release and to decide on the possible consequences of parole violation, and legislative pardon or executive pardon or reduction of sentence for those who have already begun to serve their sentences.

The reasons for this sort of discretion are essentially the same as the reasons for excusing some offenders altogether. Although less sharply posed when only variant treatment is involved, the concerns about inequality and possible abuse are also similar, and these largely underlie the strong recent movement for greater equality in sentencing.[16]

Unauthorized Nonenforcement and Leniency

Authorized disregard for violations and authorized distinctions in treatment of violators are two straightforward means by which the legal system provides for variations in response to law violation; a third means by which the legal system may respond to moral claims to disobey the law is through unauthorized acts of officials that result in exoneration or difference in penalty. My inclusion of these exercises of power requires some explanation, since acts that the law does not authorize might be regarded simply as outside the legal system and beyond our concern.

One reason for inclusion is that whether officials are authorized to disregard offenses or accord more lenient treatment, their power to achieve those results may be made possible by their legal authority. Twelve independent citizens do not have the ability to acquit a defendant; twelve jurors plainly do have that power even if their act is unauthorized. In their dependence on legal authority, unauthorized acts of officials differ from the acts of private citizens who help others to avoid punishment. In conferring authority, the legal system makes possible a range of responses that it does not explicitly, or even implicitly, authorize.

A second reason for considering unauthorized acts is that the line between unauthorized acts and authorized acts is sometimes not very clear. Whether jurors have legal authority to acquit defendants whom they know to be legally guilty, whether judges can legally disregard mandatory sentences in very appealing cases, whether police can decline to proceed against people they see violating the law—these are difficult and sharply debated questions. Full treatment of these subjects, and indeed full understanding of the significance of deciding whether or not a practice is legally authorized, requires consideration of the possibility of unauthorized practices that benefit some offenders.

The third reason for concern with unauthorized official acts is broad interest in the responses of officials to claims of moral justification for disobeying the law. To review the entire range of their choice, one must consider acts that exceed the boundaries of legality as well as those that fall within them. The breadth of this inquiry further illuminates the nature and moral force of official duties.

We have seen in Chapter 5 that officials, by taking oaths or voluntarily undertaking known responsibilities, are bound by a promissory obligation to perform duties attaching to their offices. Because their power and prestige make regular officials obvious beneficiaries of the political process and they are among its most active participants, officials have duties of fairness, both a duty of fair play and a natural duty of justice, to other citizens to perform their responsibilities. Because order and security depend heavily on reliable performances of official duties, utilitarian reasons also strongly support fulfillment of official roles.

Despite these powerful reasons for performing official duties, situations can arise in which the moral inequity of doing so makes declining enforcement the morally proper choice. Some may believe that the only moral alternatives for an official are to perform or resign; but this view neglects, or gives inadequate attention to, two sorts of situations. One concerns practices that are so evil the official should not forfeit his power to prevent terrible things from happening by resigning. One thinks, for example, of judges in Nazi Germany who were distressed by rules depriving Jews of property and liberty and who knew that their resignation would result in appointments of Nazi sympathizers. The second situation concerns a single isolated evil. An official may not think a matter grave enough to warrant resignation when performance of his other duties is acceptable and desirable; but he may believe that carrying out his official duty on this occasion will have serious adverse effects that could be avoided by nonperformance. One thinks, for example, of the plight of the junior officers trying Billy Budd in Herman Melville's story.[17] Straightforward application of the Rules of War required them to find Budd guilty of a crime with a mandatory death sentence, but they understood that Budd was morally innocent in striking his own false accuser, Claggert. If they viewed the case as a truly exceptional one calling for an exceptional response, legally unjustified leniency would have seemed a more proper response than resignation, even if resignation had been an option.[18] Resignation will often be the best course for officials required to perform morally unacceptable responsibilities, but sometimes officials should continue in office and decline to perform particular duties.

One way of reaching this conclusion would be to deny that agreements to perform functions of office, or duties of fairness, really cover performing one's designated responsibilities on every occasion. I have suggested that an oath of a naturalized citizen can be reasonably understood not as a promise to obey every law on every occasion but to be a law-abiding citizen in general. Can it be argued that what officials really promise is to do their official duty most of the time, rather than always?

Perhaps one should not assume that an official is promising to follow each detailed specification of duty whenever it is relevant. To take a trivial example, an official has a duty to refrain from using his or her position for private gain. Because the federal government makes personal use of government supplies criminal, a member of the executive branch who takes pencils home for his family is committing a crime and violating the duty not to seek private gain. Yet, it seems a strain of the law to say that each government officer has promised not to perform acts of this kind.

Nevertheless, whatever may be true of trivial breaches of duty, the argument that the promise of performance is comprehensive for matters of importance is much stronger for officials than for private citizens. The scope of the promise is already limited to official functions, rather than all aspects of one's life touched by legal demands. And an official referred to his oath after a clear and substantial breach of official duty would be unlikely to respond, "Well, I didn't mean I would always perform my duty."

Similar questions arise if one conceives of officials as having a duty of fair play and a natural duty to perform their responsibilities. If a possible violation of official duty is meant to benefit, or at least is thought unlikely to hurt, joint participants in the political order, perhaps the official would not be acting unfairly toward them or violating a duty to promote their welfare; but it might be argued that the duties of fair play preclude the official's making an independent judgment about whether or not a violation of legally prescribed duty will benefit the citizenry.

If one assumes that a promise or other moral duty covers all substantial official duties, that does not settle how to define the duties of office. An official is not simply free to pursue the ends of his office in any way he thinks best; established procedures and other subsidiary constraints bear on what he may do. But is every breach of a subsidiary restraint necessarily a breach of duty if the reason for the breach is to serve the overall goals of the office? Insofar as such breaches are not failures to perform official duties, the notion of performance of duty is made more flexible and instances of clear violations are lessened. These troublesome questions about what constitutes official duty cannot be answered in the abstract; one needs a closer look at particular official responsibilities of the sort offered in subsequent chapters.

Legal Justification of the Original Action

A final respect in which the legal system may respond to moral claims to violate the law is by making the behavior involved a nonviolation. My inclusion of this technique also requires some explanation, one that will reveal the rather thin line between what is discussed in the next two chapters and what is not.

Many legal rules carve out exceptions for acts that would be illegal if they did not contain some special feature that makes treating them as offenses inappropriate. Often, people who exhibit this special feature would think they had a powerful moral reason for disobeying the law if it did not excuse their conduct. An obvious example is the use of force in self-defense, treated in Chapter 11. In delimiting areas of privilege, justification, and excuse, a large part of what the law does is to accommodate competing moral claims, generally conferring legal permissibility on behavior that is assumed to be morally justifiable. Views about moral justification and moral rights also influence the areas in which legislatures choose to enact basic proscriptions. A strong argument against legal prohibition of consenting sexual acts among adults, for example, is that many in the population now believe people have a moral right to express their sexuality in any manner that does not directly injure others. Repeal of an existing law on this subject might be viewed, in part, as a response to moral claims to disobey that law.

Because this is not a broad study of all the ways in which moral claims appropriately underlie legislative action and affect the scope of the substantive law, I need to identify narrower senses in which the substantive law can respond directly to moral claims to disobey. The most obvious of these concerns generally illegal behavior that is excused for people with a special moral claim to engage in it. Exemptions for conscientious objectors fit most clearly into this category; an exception to a general prohibition is carved out for those who cannot in conscience comply with the general rule. Another narrow sense in which the legal system responds to moral claims is with open-ended standards that permit those applying the law to take such claims into account when they determine whether or not the law has been violated. Although no legal standards call for a direct and complete moral evaluation of behavior, moral evaluation is a substantial aspect of many open-ended standards found in the common law, in statutes, and in written constitutions. Legal terms such as negligence, reasonable, and reckless call for some moral appraisal, but the range is usually constricted by the comparative narrowness of the issue and by prior legal determinations about appropriate behavior. I will concentrate on standards that are more completely open-ended and call for something closer to an overall moral evaluation.

Stages of the Process

Another way of classifying possible legal responses to moral claims to disobey is in terms of when the responses occur. A substantive standard that permits otherwise illegal behavior operates at the earliest point, altering the legal quality of a person's acts. If the standard is open-ended and its application is not plain, effective exoneration may have to await a determination by a prosecutorial official. If applicability is seriously disputed, only a court or jury may finally determine that the actor has not really broken the law.

Effective disregard of law violation may occur at different stages and have different degrees of finality. A police or prosecutorial decision not to proceed occurs early; in vast numbers of instances, a single decision ends the matter, but formally an offender remains subject to prosecution until the statute of limitations has run. Dismissal of charges by the judge, jury acquittal, or a judge's decision against imposing a sentence operate later, but, given principles of double jeopardy, they do typically bar any subsequent action. Although these actions relieve the offender of any formal penalty, the very exposure to the criminal process will usually be perceived as unfortunate in itself.[19] Full pardons or amnesty given before prosecution is launched operate after the act but before these other techniques of exonerating the actor; unlike an individual prosecutor's determination not to proceed, these actions do preclude a later decision to prosecute.

Differentiations in terms of treatment typically operate after a determination of guilt, either when a judge initially imposes sentence or by some subsequent decision of a parole board or other body. A commutation of sentence or a pardon given during the sentence also reduces the severity of punishment. Sometimes effective decisions to give more lenient treatment do precede findings of guilt. The prosecutor may reduce the level of charges in return for an agreement to plead guilty or (less often) for other reasons; in some jurisdictions the prosecutor or the judge may divert a case to some noncriminal proceeding, under which the offender is assured of escaping criminal punishment but may be subjected to other consequences he would prefer to avoid.

Situations in which officials violate their duties in letting offenders "get off" or in moderating their penalties can obviously occur at all stages of the process, right up to the term of confinement that follows sentence.

Subsequent chapters address the following questions about agencies of possible amelioration: Does the law authorize officials to excuse or treat more leniently those whose commission of otherwise illegal acts is based on some moral claim, or are such decisions outside the law? How far does the law supply criteria by which such decisions can be made? What position about possible leniency and what criteria of decision should be accepted by officials working within the American legal tradition? What alterations in existing law or institutional understandings could help achieve more appropriate responses to conflicts between mandatory laws and the perceived claims of morality? The importance and difficulty of each of these inquiries varies greatly among the different agencies of amelioration, and as we will see, many of the basic questions hardly yield simple "yes" or "no" answers. Facing these questions nonetheless helps us to develop considered opinions about the crucial issues.

By concentrating on each possibility of amelioration in turn, I may underemphasize the extent to which each is related to the others in a whole system. Intelligent reflection about the present scope of one kind of official responsibility and about directions of desirable change must rest on an appreciation of how one role meshes with other roles in enforcing the law.

NOTES

1. I explain in Chapter 3 what I mean by proper standards of public morality.

2. Rostow, The Rightful Limits of Freedom in a Liberal Democratic State: Of Civil Disobedience, in E. Rostow, ed., Is Law Dead? 46 (1971).

3. Many of these might be said to *implement* fundamental moral judgments of the community. For example, a technical rule about the quality of ceiling sprinklers in hotels might implement a moral judgment that hotel guests should be protected from the dangers of fires.

4. This thought involves some oversimplification. If the act is justified because the actor has a special moral obligation (say to a sister), people may approve the act (hiding her from the police) while believing that the act is harmful to society in general. In these cases reasons do exist for discouraging people from doing what is morally justified. More generally, if justified acts include all morally permitted acts, people may think some morally permitted acts will predictably produce consequences that, overall, are harmful.

5. For a brief survey of purposes of punishment, see Greenawalt, Punishment, in Encyclopedia of Crime and Justice, Vol. IV, p. 1336 (1983), 74 J. Crim. Law Criminol. 343 (1983).

6. A possible benefit to the whole population, such as a reduction in the risk of nuclear war, would not be a special personal gain. A. D. Woozley draws a distinction between "pure" law breakers, who act exclusively from conviction, and "impure" law breakers, who have something to gain by breaking the law. Law and Obedience 35–36 (1979). According to Woozley, the only bases for excusing impure law breakers are ones of convenience. As impure law breakers, Woozley mainly has in mind those who will enjoy acts of disobedience or derive immediate material profit from them; but blacks certainly stood to gain in the long run from civil rights protests, as did whites who believed that integration would produce relations between whites and blacks that were better for whites as well as for blacks. To classify as "pure" only protesting whites and blacks who did not expect (or hope) that illegal protests would enrich their lives would be odd; certainly a distinction *thus* drawn could not be critical in determining how the legal system should respond to violations.

7. Sometimes morally justified illegal acts may produce comparative benefits and harm that are in some sense fortuitous. Suppose that Leon is extremely law-abiding and refuses to obtain and use a medicine that has not yet received official approval. Nancy, convinced that an indefensibly inefficient and corrupt system of drug approval has worked in this instance, decides that the likely benefits of the medicine justify her obtaining it illegally. Her life is saved because she uses the medicine, and Leon dies because he did not. Even if Nancy's behavior was morally as good as Leon's, her benefit is out of proportion to desert and we feel Leon is a kind of victim of unfairness. But here the distribution of benefits is unfair in the sense that life is unfair in its unequal conferral of looks, health, intelligence, and other attributes; this sort of unfairness is not the kind that would warrant punishing Nancy.

8. Dworkin, Taking Rights Seriously 192–93 (1977).

9. Illustration 9-4.

10. Whether or not Mill presents a persuasive case on utilitarian grounds for unqualified principles of noninterference is debatable.

11. One can certainly conceive of a system in which ample resources were available to proceed against all violators against whom adequate evidence could be gathered; but the criminal justice system in the United States does not fall into this category.

12. Another possible worry is that discretion conflicts with executive responsibility to the legislature, but that worry is either circular or rests on complex assumptions about what various government bodies should decide. If the legislature has meant to confer such discretion, then its exercise is not an executive usurpation; thus, the concern about legislative supremacy may be another way to claim that the legislature has meant to bar such discretion. Arguments about the inappropriateness of such discretion that are independent of what a particular legislature desires require some reason beyond simple legislative supremacy to show why executive discretion is improper.

13. Comment on this differentiation between reasons that relate to particular offenders and those that do not is offered in Greenawalt, How Empty Is the Idea of Equality, 83 Colum. L. Rev. 1167, 1173–74 (1983).

14. See, e.g., Model Penal Code § 2.12 (1985).

15. A judge's power to impose a completely suspended sentence, which is not operative unless another violation is committed, or to impose no sentence at all, falls very close to authority to disregard a violation.

16. Model Penal Code, Introduction to Articles 6 and 7, Part I, Vol. 3 (1985).

17. H. Melville, Billy Budd (1948).

18. Officers on ships in wartime are not, of course, free to resign. For a statement by an American judge on why he refused to apply the law regarding abortion and also refused to assign the case to another judge, see L. Buzzard and P. Campbell, Holy Disobedience 3–5 (1984).

19. However, some conscientious law violators welcome the publicity for their point of view that prosecution involves.

13

General Justification—Necessity

The law, as Aristotle observed,[1] cannot speak "universally" and "correctly" for some matters, because rules laying down precise standards may yield inappropriate results for extraordinary cases. Many specific exceptions to rules, such as the right to use otherwise illegal force in self-defense, are, of course, based on accommodation of competing claims. Though some of these exceptions contain such general evaluative terms as *reasonable* or *necessary*, in other respects they are relatively precise; therefore, those applying the law need not make a sweeping judgment as to whether or not the actor's behavior was morally justified. The inability of these specific exceptions to capture every case in which application of the main rule would be inappropriate generates the question of whether a more sweepingly open-ended exception should authorize a broad assessment of an actor's claim that his or her transgression of the rule was justified. The question arises mainly in relation to crimes and torts based on intentional acts;[2] I will concentrate on criminal liability for such acts.

THE APPROPRIATENESS OF A STATUTORY DEFENSE

In the criminal law, the defense of general justification, or necessity, has operated as an open-ended exception to liability. In addition to troubling problems about the formulation of the defense, there are serious questions as to whether the defense should exist at all, whether, if it should exist, it should receive statutory elaboration, and whether it should be applied by judge or jury.

The argument against having the defense does not rest on the belief that conviction is appropriate for all circumstances covered by the criminal law. Donald breaks the speed limit to get someone urgently in need of care to a hospital; Harriett, who has become lost in a storm during a remote hiking expedition, breaks into an unoccupied cabin for shelter and food. No one really supposes that Donald and Harriett deserve treatment like criminals.[3] Rather, the argument is that these matters can be trusted to the good sense of prosecutors and judges;[4] that when criminal conviction is obviously inappropriate prosecutors will not go forward and, if prosecution is brought, judges will either find some way to dismiss charges or to impose negligible sentences.

That very few cases actually raise the defense does show that most appealing claims of justification are handled in some informal way; yet, despite its limited practical significance, the defense fills important offices. It serves most plainly as a safeguard against prosecutorial abuse. Even when prosecutorial policy is enlightened, actors who are genuinely justified should have legal confirmation that they have acted appropriately,[5] rather than having to conceive themselves as depending on a prosecutor's grace. Moreover, when claimed justifying facts are in doubt, or the crime is very serious, or the balance of relevant values is controversial, formal adjudication may be preferable to prosecutorial judgment of whether or not a possibly justified actor should be punished.

Should the defense be codified in statutory form or left to judicial development? This essay is not the place to discuss the general virtues of criminal codification, which concern clarity, systematization, and the need to tell people in advance what behavior is criminal. In the United States, that basic crimes should be defined in statutes is now settled as a matter of penal policy and constitutional principle. Whether or not justifications should also be codified is perhaps not quite so clear, but the great majority of states revising their penal laws over the past two decades have incorporated statutory formulations of self-defense and other common justifications.

Even if the wisdom of codification, and of codification of justifications, is granted, one can doubt that statutory definition of the general justification defense is warranted.[6] The worry is that the situations in which actors should be relieved of liability are so complicated and various that any attempt at compact verbal definition will prove much too crude; the recommendation is that this subject be left for judicial elaboration in the rare cases when the issue is critical. Starting from the assumption that statutory formulations of justifications are generally desirable, we should be hesitant to abandon that aim for this justification unless the problems of statutory drafting prove intractable. Part of the burden in the remainder of this chapter is to illuminate what some of those problems are and how they may be addressed. The discussion seeks to show that statutory formulation is feasible enough to make it worthwhile.

THE BASIC NATURE OF THE DEFENSE

Justification Rather than Excuse

The origins and the present status of the defense of necessity are shrouded in uncertainty and confusion.[7] The fundamental difficulty involves the line between justification and excuse[8] and goes all the way back to ancient discussions whether one person can push another off a plank that is capable of supporting only one of them. Is trying to preserve one's life in this way something that is morally desirable, indifferent, or within the range of permissible acts? Or is the point that the person is not to blame for pushing his fellow off because of the extreme emotional strain created by a life-threatening situation? In the first appraisal, the actor was, in some sense, justified, in the second, only excused. Because exigent natural circumstances often affect both the wrongness of an act and the actor's capacity for rational choice, the threads of justification and excuse are not easy to separate even when one is confident that no punishment is called for. The same conceptual difficulty arises when the source of danger is a human threat, and the threatened person performs the otherwise illegal act that is demanded. Duress is typically labeled an excuse, but yielding to a threat is sometimes the morally preferable response, as when a person is told and believes that five innocent children will be killed unless he steals a diamond.

Analytical clarity is served by legal recognition that both exigent natural circumstances and human threats can justify some otherwise illegal acts, that is, can at least put those acts within the permissible range of responses. Most modern formulations of the general justification defense do achieve this objective by language broad enough to include choices of evils generated by threats. Analytical clarity and fair penal policy would also be served by recognition that natural circumstances, as well as human threats, can sometimes undermine one's rational capacities so much that actions that are not justified can be excused.[9] Modern American law is anomalous in allowing such an excuse for responses to threats but not for responses to natural extremity.[10]

My focus here is on necessity only as it relates to genuine justification. For that purpose we can imagine that the actor faced with a difficult choice is fully rational and has time to deliberate. To say that he is justified is to say that his deliberate rational choice to commit an otherwise illegal action is within the range of legally acceptable responses to his situation. To what extent actors who fall short of such a justification should nevertheless be excused is a critical question for any criminal law, but that question is beyond the scope of this effort.

The crucial aspect of justification is whether what the actor does is warranted. That statement might seem obvious and unilluminating were it not for recent suggestions that the central feature of justified action is that others may aid the actor and may not try to stop him.[11] Typically, it is true that when action is warranted others are permitted to assist it and forbidden to interfere with it; but the rights of third parties in respect to an act do not themselves determine its justifiability. A prisoner's escape to avoid a grave threat to his life may be justified even if the guard's attempt to stop him is also justified. In this chapter's discussion, I concentrate on the actor who claims that his act is justified, not on how others affected may respond to his acts.

A Supplement to Legislative Judgment

One critical question about a general justification defense is its appropriate relationship to legislative determinations about criminal liability. Should the defense be conceived exclusively as a supplement to legislative choice, dealing with extraordinary situations in a manner legislators probably would approve, or should the defense be understood also to impose a higher level of review of legislative determinations? In a notable 1917 case, the judge spoke a law of necessity resting on "natural rights" that "cannot be taken away by statute."[12] This language suggests the idea that a defendant can put the question of justification to a judge or jury regardless of how clearly the legislature has forbidden his behavior.

Any benefits reaped from a defense that overleaps the confinement of legislative judgment would be likely to be outweighed by the harmful impact of the defense on the system of criminal justice. Judges are less representative than legislators and already have the authority to declare legislative decisions unconstitutional; giving judges further authority to cancel the legislature's decisions about punishable behavior would not make sense. The notion of jury review of legislative choice, a voice of the community passing on what its representatives have done, is much more comprehensible. As to that possibility, confident judgment is more difficult, particularly if the judgment reaches beyond a particular system and point of time. Nonetheless, whatever authority juries should have to acquit guilty persons,[13] jurors within the modern American system of law should not be told that if they think the defendant's acts were justified, they should conclude that the defendant has not really violated the law. Such a practice would thrust an unpredictable wild card into jury determinations and would open trials up to congeries of evidence and argument about the moral merits of assailants and victims and other moral claims. The diminished sense of legislative authority that might result could prove an encouragement to irresponsible legislative action; legislators might adopt criminal measures in the expectation that juries would negate their application. Were there a deep fear of legislative abuse in defining crimes and no other effective checking mechanism, these difficulties might be worth embracing. But judicial review under our written constitution allows a more structured form of review that reaches most gross abuses legislatures may perpetrate.

The principle of justification should be viewed, therefore, not as an encouragement to some other body to second-guess judgments made by the legislature, but rather to provide opportunities for supplementary, particularistic judgments that are beyond legislative capacity.

THE SUBSTANTIVE REACH OF THE DEFENSE

One can most easily consider issues about the formulation of the general justification defense with reference to a particular codified version; I have chosen Section 3.02 of the Model Penal Code, which has exercised a substantial influence on recent state codes.[14] It provides the following:

(1) Conduct that the actor believes to be necessary to avoid a harm or evil to himself or to another is justifiable, provided that:

(a) the harm or evil sought to be avoided by such conduct is greater than that sought to be prevented by the law defining the offense charged; and

(b) neither the Code nor other law defining the offense provides exceptions or defenses dealing with the specific situation involved; and

(c) a legislative purpose to exclude the justification claimed does not otherwise plainly appear.[15]

Subsections (1)(b) and (1)(c) reflect the appropriate view that the defense should be viewed as a supplement to legislative determinations. If the legislature has carefully worked out the situations in which deadly force may be used in self-defense, a defendant who fails to qualify is not free, according to Subsection (1)(b), to contend that his shooting of someone in self-defense was nevertheless warranted under the broader standard of general justification. A legislature's plain intent to exclude a justification controls, under Subsection (1)(c).

Which Acts Are Justified—A Consequentialist Approach to the Weighing of Evils

In the introductory language of Subsection (1), the Model Code follows earlier law in requiring that the conduct be believed necessary[16] to avoid an evil; what would otherwise be a violation of law is not warranted if the actor supposes only that it is one way among others for avoiding the evil. The section thus represents the appropriate judgment that breaches of law should be a last resort for avoiding harm.[17]

Section 3.02 does not include a requirement found in many formulations that the evil to be avoided must be imminent. The point of demanding imminence is to ensure that breach of a legal standard is really a necessary last resort; but one should be able to violate the law now in the rare instances when it is genuinely necessary to avoid a future harm. If Vicki, sharing a two-week vacation with Fred at a remote mountain cabin, learns that Fred plans to kill her in six days, she may take Fred's car *now* if that promises to be the only way to escape safely. Although the evil is not imminent, taking the car is a necessary last resort for Vicki and should be privileged.

Subsection (1)(a) contains the theoretically most important and controversial standard of the provision; it establishes a thoroughgoing consequentialist approach to the question of justification, implicitly excluding alternatives that have been followed in some common law decisions and statutory formulations.

An actor is justified if the evil sought to be avoided is greater than the evil sought to be prevented by the law he has violated. Although the language chosen is imprecise on the point, the notion of "greater" is to be understood as referring to evils and risks in particular circumstances, not to some wooden reading of all the interests a statutory rule is meant to safeguard. The point can be illustrated with Donald's breaking of the speed limit to get his passenger medical care. One aim of speed limits is to save lives. The harm of loss of the life of Donald's passenger is not greater than the harm of loss of life of someone hit by a speeding automobile; thus, one harm sought to be prevented by the statute is as great as the harm Donald meant to avoid. Donald is, nevertheless, justified. The reason is that the risk of his causing death by speeding on this one occasion is very slight; the chance that his speeding will save his passenger is much greater.[18] When these probabilities are taken into account, the harm avoided is greater than the harm sought to be prevented.

The determination of which harm is greater is left to the judge or jury applying the law. Whereas the actor's belief that action is needed to avoid an evil is determinative,[19] the actor's personal conviction that the evil avoided is more serious than the evil prevented does not control. Suppose an actor is threatened that his house will be burned unless he beats an acquaintance severely. He decides that having his house burned would be worse than his acquaintance suffering a beating, and he yields to the threat. Under the justification defense, the jury or judge would weigh these comparative evils. This disposition is obviously sound because the law should be treated as justifying only behavior that society generally considers justified; the actor's idiosyncratic evaluations are not sufficient. Further, a jury may be able to assess someone's appraisal of the facts reasonably well, but outsiders will be hard put to determine the sincerity of an actor's claim about how he compares evils.

Section 3.02 contains no express restrictions in terms of evils avoided and crimes committed. In contrast to some other formulations, it does not require that the harm avoided be very serious,[20] taking the view that acts amounting to minor crimes—say ordinary trespass—might be warranted to avoid something less than a serious evil. More controversially, the section also fails to limit the defense by excluding some crimes from its ambit. Its allowance of the defense even for murder is related to its consequential character, to which I now turn.

The relevant comparison under the Model Penal Code is between the harm avoided and the harm the law was designed to prevent. The emphasis on harm in the section bears a strongly consequentialist cast. Conceivably, one might argue that the inherent wrongness of an actor's conduct counts in the balance of harms, so that the intentional killing of an innocent person might be viewed as a greater harm than the loss of two innocent lives that would occur if the victim were not killed. However, it takes a considerable strain of the apparent import of the code language to make deontological factors count. I shall treat the provision as undilutedly consequentialist.

So understood, Section 3.02 calls for an evaluation that might differ from the inquiry as to whether the actor, given his belief about necessity to avoid an evil, was morally justified in acting as he did. The standard does not leave room to say that although the conduct predictably caused more evil than it avoided, it was nevertheless justified because of some special responsibility the actor had to the person who would have been harmed had the actor obeyed the criminal law. A defendant who helps a close friend avoid arrest or saves the lives of his own family by sacrificing a greater number of lives of innocent strangers is not justified under this provision. From the law's point of view, avoidance of arrest remains an evil, not a good; and the loss of five innocent lives is a greater evil than the loss of three innocent lives. One underlying principle of the criminal law is to encourage people to respect the fundamental interests of strangers, and the creation of ad hoc exceptions justifying special protection of friends and family members would be ill-advised.[21]

The language of Section 3.02 also forecloses any argument that someone is justified simply because he or she is exercising a moral right. By making behavior criminal, the legislature has implicitly rejected most claims of moral right that are independent of evils avoided. In passing laws against marijuana use or consensual homosexual acts, for example, the legislature has decided that individuals do not have a general moral right to engage in such behavior. On occasion, however, an actor might claim he is exercising a moral right the legislature did not mean to reject. For example, a person who believed that marijuana was helpful as treatment for his glaucoma[22] might assert a narrow moral right to preserve his health as he thought best. Given government licensing of medical drugs, which renders unavailable many drugs that some people think would help them, the argument that the legislature has not meant to reject the asserted right is a hard one; and similar difficulties will plague many arguments that special claims of right are consistent with general prohibition. In any event, whatever the ability of judges and juries to decide that favorable consequences will result from breaches of legal rules, they are not, in the absence of constitutional guarantees, as well equipped to decide claims about moral rights to be free of government interference. A general justification sensibly excludes such claims.

A much more important and controversial feature of the consequentialist approach of Section 3.02 is its nonrecognition of absolute moral prohibitions and the force of deontological norms. Many people agree with the traditional Roman Catholic position that intentionally taking innocent human life is never morally justified;[23] they will object that the law should not treat such actions as within the realm of possible justification. Others believe that extremely weighty considerations of consequence might warrant such actions but that the inherent quality of acts also matters. On this view what is an inherently wrongful act should not be committed to achieve a moderately favorable balance of consequences. No doubt, notions like these partly underlie disagreement over whether or not homicide should be covered by a general justification defense.

Assessment of the inclusion of homicide demands careful understanding of what divides an "absolute" or more moderate deontological position from the consequentialist one embodied in the Model Penal Code. The most common version of the absolute position admits that acts that predictably cause the loss of innocent life may be morally justified under the principle of "double effect." This principle permits death as a virtually certain but unintended consequence but precludes the purposeful killing of innocents as a "necessary evil" to accomplish a greater good.[24] When a mountaineer cuts the rope that attaches him to a companion who has fallen over a precipice and whom it is impossible to save, or when an engineer diverts a flood to save a town, knowing that the inhabitants of a farm will be inundated, loss of life is an unwanted and unintended, although almost inevitable, consequence. The principle of "double effect" does not allow purposeful killing to achieve a desirable objective; under it, townspeople may not kill their mayor (who is in hiding) under the credible threat by a foreign invader that everyone in the town will otherwise be destroyed, nor may a surgeon kill a healthy person to acquire body parts whose transplant will save the lives of five others. Where the Model Code diverges from the principle of double effect is in giving the townspeople, as well as the mountaineer and the engineer, a potential legal justification.

Understanding what divides an absolute view from the consequentialist one shows why excluding the defense for all instances of homicide, or murder, is not an appropriate solution.

A person commits murder if he acts in a way that is virtually certain to cause the death of another, even if he hopes that death will not occur. In the absence of a justification, both the mountaineer[25] and the engineer would be murderers. Thus, nonapplication of the defense to murder would leave unjustified people who would be innocent even under absolute approaches. Such a step could be defended as a kind of symbol of the sanctity of life or as a concession to the difficulties of administering the defense in a way that is fair, and perceived to be so, in cases of death; but excluding the defense for murder or homicide is definitely not a precise way to represent the typical "absolute" moral position. More obviously, it is not a precise way to represent any moderate deontological position that permits intentional killing if the alternative would be catastrophic.

An accurate representation of the absolute position would be to bar a general justification for homicides that are "intentional" in the narrow sense excluded by the principle of double effect.[26] If other intentional acts were regarded as always wrong regardless of consequences, language could be drafted to exclude those as well.

A measure short of using such specific language as a limit on the reach of the justification provision would be to draft language to leave flexibility for those applying the law to reject a claim of justification if they thought fundamental moral standards had been transgressed.[27] The main advantage of this approach is that, without having to define the precise boundaries of accepted moral standards,[28] legislators could authorize disallowance of the defense when defendants, such as the surgeon killing a healthy person to get body parts, who might seem to be reached by Section 3.01, have clearly transgressed accepted moral standards without a sufficiently overwhelming reason. A second possible advantage would be to permit the jury, as representatives of community sentiment, to make these delicate moral judgments.[29] Leaving the matter open in this way would introduce the disturbing possibility of discrepancies depending on the moral views of those applying the law on particular occasions; however, this course does sidestep the tricky problems of achieving comprehensive legislative resolution of deep disagreements over morally acceptable conduct and of formulating that resolution in clear definitions of the cases to be excluded from the defense.

In a society in which no consensus exists about an alternative moral principle, one need not embrace the consequentialist approach as the correct moral principle to defend the idea that at least some acts that are wrong under absolute standards but have the foreseeable consequence of effecting a net avoidance of relevant evils should be considered justified as far as the law is concerned. In practical terms, this position does not represent adoption of the consequentialist approach in favor of more deontological standards, because the actor who adheres to deontological standards will not have engaged in punishable behavior. What the justification defense does, in effect, is place the actor who aims at a net saving of lives on a parity with the actor who refuses to breach ordinary moral standards. That is the appropriate posture for the law when society is divided over the morally preferable choice.

Yet the problem remains of acts that may come within the terms of Section 3.01 that virtually no one regards as acceptable. An independent requirement that the act "justly respect the interests of everyone involved" would meet this problem in an appropriate way, as well as deal with the fairness difficulty discussed later.

If the general consequentialist flavor of Section 3.02 is accepted, questions may still be raised as to whether the balance between harms is appropriately struck. The harm avoided must be *greater* than the harm the statute tries to prevent. One possibility is that the standard is too harsh from a defendant's point of view. Certainly a person should not be able to cause a criminal harm to avoid a harm that is smaller than the one he causes; but perhaps he should succeed if the two harms are equal. Ancient suggestions that one can push someone else off a plank that can hold only a single person may lend plausibility to this position, but the grounds for its rejection are clear. As far as harms other than death are concerned, even imagining likely instances of equal harms is difficult. In any event, for lesser harms, intuition hardly supports justification in such settings. If natural events or a threat put one person under a danger, say loss of $10,000 in property, we do not suppose that shifting precisely the same loss onto some other innocent person is warranted. The same conclusion applies to cases of death if the life of the actor or his loved one is not at stake. A person is not likely to suppose he should shift the burden of impending death, caused by a natural catastrophe or threat, from one stranger to another. The appeal of the plank example lies in basic instincts of self-preservation, and, if the actor who pushes his fellow off the plank should be exonerated, the grounds should be excuse rather than justification.

A more serious practical issue about the standard of Section 3.02 is whether or not it is too lenient toward the defendant. Many states have chosen to follow New York, which alows the defense only if "the desirability and urgency of avoiding such injury *clearly outweigh* the desirability of avoiding the injury sought to be prevented . . ." (emphasis added).[30] Although the difference between the two standards will not matter in most cases, one might defend New York's approach as a sort of imprecise way of giving effect to general deontological sentiments or as representing a discrete principle that one should not violate criminal standards or shift expected harms unless the balance of gain is substantial.

Requiring that one harm clearly outweigh the other is patently not a sensible method of hanging onto any absolute standards of wrong. And since "clearly outweigh" is not the same as "substantally outweigh"—one harm might only slightly outweigh another but do so clearly—the language is not well chosen to demand a substantial imbalance between the comparative harms. In any event, at least if he does not impair the rights of innocents, a person who achieves a net diminution of harm should usually be free of criminal liability even if the harm avoided is not substantially greater than the harm involved in the violation.

The strongest argument for the language of the New York provision undoubtedly concerns administration of the defense. The standard attempts to constrain success when those applying the law may be overly sympathetic toward the defendant or deeply uncertain about the balance of harms. Which standard will work more appropriately in cases in which a genuine dispute exists over the balance of harms is arguable, the extreme rarity of the defense giving little basis for confident judgment.

Any formulation of a general justification defense, whether statutory or developed in judicial opinions, is bound to be highly open-ended. Are such formulations objectionable for failing to provide fair warning and permitting uneven administration? If the defense is rarely relied on in advance, few actors will be put in a worse position because it exists. The fair warning concern has much less force for rules that confer immunity that would otherwise not exist than for basic definitions of criminal behavior. Because many practical questions about necessity and relative values will prove relatively simple,[31] issues of general justification are not quite as uncertain as the open-ended phraseology might suggest; and a degree of necessary vagueness is tolerable when a subject does not lend itself to more precise definition. Insofar as uneven administration remains a worry, abolishing the defense on that ground would be largely self-defeating, because unevenness would remain in the exercise of prosecutorial discretion, jury nullification, and sentencing determinations.

The Question of Fairness

One difficulty with the Model Code's single-mindedly consequentialist cast is that it makes no reference to the fairness of the decision of who will suffer, a problem evident in the two famous lifeboat cases, *Regina* v. *Dudley and Stephens*[32] and *United States* v. *Holmes*.[33] In the former case, a weak cabin boy was killed and eaten; in the latter, sailors threw passengers overboard. To what extent one can reasonably expect those in dire straits to act in morally sensitive ways may be debatable,[34] but some methods of choice of who will be sacrificed must be beyond the pale, from the perspective of justification.[35] Although fairness of selection might be viewed as an aspect of whether the law-violating act was believed necessary, the problem is not strictly one of necessity. When one of five persons must be thrown overboard, the casting out of a person who was fairly chosen (say, by lot) is no more "necessary" than the casting out of someone unfairly chosen (say, by race or income level). A requirement of fair selection could be left to interpretation and implementation, but a better resolution would be to demand in the statute that the actor's conduct "justly (or fairly) respect the interests of everyone involved" or that it not involve an unfair infliction of harm. As I have previously indicated, at least the former language would also be capable of authorizing exclusion of the defense when other deontological standards have been breached without sufficiently strong reasons.

Administrability and Levels of Evaluation

Section 3.02 is framed to put the overriding emphasis on the particular event in which the actor was involved: on that occasion did his conduct predictably do more good than harm? But if one is evaluating the desirability of the defense for certain classes of cases, another relevant question is whether the net effect of allowing the defense will be desirable. Both because of possible misjudgments by those applying the defense and because of influences on the behavior of future actors, it is conceivable that allowing the defense will be undesirable for some sorts of individual circumstances in which the actor's behavior was warranted. This more general level of evaluation introduces troublesome questions about the competence and detachment of those applying the standard, the appropriate bases for judging individuals, the import of the Model Penal Code and other existing formulations, and the effects of legal standards of this sort on people's behavior. I shall try to illuminate these questions with reference to prison escapes, protests, official illegality, and mob action against minorities.

Prison Escapes

Were the defense of general justification to encourage actors to violate the law without sufficient assessment of whether their actions were really necessary to avoid greater evils, that would be a serious drawback. For private actors and in most circumstances this worry is implausible because such a rarely used defense is not likely to affect how someone reacts to an unexpected emergency situation;[36] but the concern is serious with respect to prisoners contemplating escape.

When one prisoner is threatened with a serious assault by another and authorities provide inadequate protection, escape may be a necessary lesser evil to prevent the assault. But if prisoners who escape are subsequently returned to the same institutions, the level of freedom from assault will not rise much if the defense is recognized. Because the closed community of fellow prisoners learns of such rulings, allowing the defense may well encourage more escapes, and the burden upon those applying the defense of assessing the adequacy of in-prison protection and the existence and credibility of purported threats of assault would be formidable. One might reasonably conclude that although the evil of escape is less than the evil of assault, and escape is sometimes necessary to avoid assault, the defense of general justification nevertheless should not be admitted for such situations. Some courts, including the Supreme Court, have worked around this problem by requiring that escapees turn themselves in at the earliest safe opportunity if they want successfully to claim the justification,[37] a requirement that makes some administrative sense but does not display great sensitivity to the prisoner's fear that conditions in prison will not have improved.

The following is the more generalized question for which the escape problem poses a possible illustration: what should the legal system do if, despite some actors being justified on the facts of their isolated situations, recognizing the defense for classes of those situations would be undesirable? The easiest answer is that the law should not recognize defenses that are undesirable from the broader point of view, and if classes of situations for which the general justification defense is undesirable can be discretely identified, they should be excluded from its ambit.

A possible rejoinder is that sacrificing the individual who has achieved a net diminution of harm is unfair. This fairness claim must be sharpened. One concern might be that the actor has not been given adequate notice that his act will be treated as criminal. I want now to put the concern about notice unfairness aside and assume the actor is told in advance that the contemplated conduct will be regarded as legally unjustified. If the actor is considering aiding some strangers at the expense of others or protecting a greater property interest of his own at the expense of a lesser property interest of others, there is no substantive unfairness in the law's telling him that, in light of overall policies of legal administration, he will not be permitted to choose the lesser evil on this particular occasion. The concern about substantive fairness is more appealing if one's life or bodily integrity is at stake. It does seem more harsh to say that a prisoner must suffer grave injury or be penalized because permitting a defense to a charge of escape would have bad effects for the overall system. This particular problem is nevertheless probably capable of being handled to an adequate degree by prosecutorial discretion, sentencing determinations, and perhaps the duress defense (an excuse).[38] Although the acceptability of this approach is debatable because of its undeniable element of harshness, I will assume that the defense may appropriately be denied for all cases within a class for which recognition of the defense would be undesirable.

Should a provision like the Model Penal Code's be understood as implicitly including such an exception to the defense? The harm avoided must be "greater than that sought to be prevented by the law defining the offense charged." A possible construction is that the harm sought to be prevented includes all the difficulties of administration that would arise if the general justification defense were recognized. On that construction, the judge or jury applying the law could survey the "big picture" before deciding whether or not to hold a particular defendant justified. There are two problems with this construction. The first is that it requires a great strain of the language, which seems to refer to the harm of a single escape rather than the harm of administering an exception from liability for justified escapes generally. The second problem involves fairness to the defendant. Certainly the language gives him no warning that he may be denied the defense if it will encourage others to escape and be too hard to administer. Admittedly, few, if any, defendants will look at the statute in advance, but it remains troublesome to deny a justification on grounds that a defendant cannot have been expected to take into account and that are not evident from the statute. The fair notice problem might be met by a court's accepting the defense in the first case but announcing that, in subsequent cases,[39] defendants will not succeed because the defense would be too difficult to administer. Such a paradoxical development of the law, however, would hardly be a happy solution.

A better resolution of this problem would be to state explicitly in the statute that the general justification defense would not be afforded when its recognition would tend to undermine principles of justice. It would be preferable, of course, to have more specific language, but exclusion of particular crimes is probably not called for. A defense could comfortably be recognized for escape, for example, if the jail is on fire.[40] The more generalized condition of application would focus attention on the long-term effects of recognizing the defense and allow a sensitive assessment of problems of administrability; it would also provide defendants at least a vague warning that a more complicated inquiry is involved than the facts of their particular cases.

Protests

When actors violate one law, for example, a traffic regulation, to protest another law or a government policy, should they be able to claim a general justification? Courts have not been receptive to such claims,[41] and it is easy to see why; determining whether the harm of one law or policy is so great that citizens are justified in causing the harm another law is aimed at preventing hardly seems an appropriate task for judges or juries.

The language of present provisions poses difficulty for justification claims by protesters, but it does not appear to exclude them. The New York requirement that the evil avoided "clearly outweigh" the evil sought to be prevented may be a more effective barrier than the balancing standard of Section 3.02, since it will be difficult to establish that one is clearly greater than the other with such incommensurable harms. The demand that the conduct be believed necessary to avoid the evil also poses some obstacle, but a protester against an unpopular war, for example, might be able to persuade others that illegal acts were required to halt the war, or at least that he believed such acts were required. Even the imminence requirement of many formulations would not be an absolute bar. Illegal acts of protest are usually addressed at what the actors consider to be a continuing evil, and the further continuation of an evil may be regarded as an imminent harm.

The heart of the difficulty with allowing the defense for cases of protest is that it conflicts with a conception of the defense as particularizing general legislative aims. Certainly the legislature would not authorize illegal protests against its own enactments, nor would it be likely to approve such tactics against controversial executive policies, most of which the legislature has the capability to alter.[42] Illegal protests should be precluded from the defense on the theory that permitting a justification for such cases is not consonant with the legislature's general purposes. Section 3.02 does bar the defense when a legislative purpose to exclude it "plainly appear[s]".[43] Since legislators have neither thought about this problem nor adopted a specific provision that excludes illegal protests, the language of the Model Penal Code does not effectively bar the defense for these cases. The standard should be worded more broadly to exclude the justification when acceptance would conflict with "ascertainable legislative purposes."[44]

Official Illegality

One of the greatest dangers with the defense of general justification is that it will be used by officials to support illegal actions. A notable example is the 1917 Bisbee Deportation case, in which a sheriff organized a huge posse that kidnapped more than one thousand striking IWW members and sympathizers and transported them out of the state, an action claimed to be necessary to protect the lives and property of local residents.[45] A more recent illustration is the defense of John Erlichman, one of President Nixon's two most important advisers, who directed that the office of Daniel Ellsberg's psychiatrist be broken into so that Ellsberg's files could be examined. His claim was not cast as a general justification, but Erlichman did argue that the act was legal because it was necessary for national security.[46] Blatantly illegal actions by officials may, in times of local or national crisis, be defended as necessary to prevent grave harm, and the officials who raise such defenses will not usually be as tarnished as were the members of the Nixon administration by the time they got to trial. In such cases, public sympathies concerning well-known official defendants and their victims may count for more than the particular acts; when the victims are criminals or proponents of unpopular political positions, officials may be especially likely to succeed.

The Model Code partly addresses this problem about public officials by barring the general justification when other justifications are relevant, but the apparent result is somewhat paradoxical. Official duty is a separate justification,[47] so when the official is acting as an official but oversteps the limits of his authority, he must do without the choice-of-evils argument. What is considered a proper exercise of official duty, however, will often depend on the exigencies of a situation. If the official's action is plainly illegal, and if, despite his relying on his position within the government when performing the action he lays no claim to official authority in the usual sense, then he may be free to claim choice of the lesser evil as would a private individual. In the Bisbee Deportation case, the court instructed the jury that because the sheriff lacked official authority to organize the posse, he had acted as an individual and member of the community and was subject to the principles governing private actors.[48]

The defense should be barred altogether for officials who act under the color of authority[49] in any sense. An official authority justification can be sufficiently flexible to cover almost all defensible acts by officials, and an official who cannot succeed under it or a more specific justification should be excluded from a justification defense. An exclusion of this sort could be easily added to statutory language, or the defense could be phrased as one for private individuals.

Private Action Against Feared Minorities

A more intractable difficulty is private mob action against unpopular minorities, which may be based on prejudice and exaggerated fears. The acquittal in the Bisbee Deportation case suggests that claims that drastic measures are needed to curb uncertain dangers may sometimes be viewed sympathetically. Are there any principles that might be employed to preclude the defense in such situations?

One possibility is not to allow the defense whenever a prompt plea to officials could have provided relief from feared dangers if officials had responded effectively. But such a principle would leave some persons who accurately perceive that officials cannot or will not protect them against serious threatened harms without the justification. A narrower principle would bar the defense when private citizens take upon themselves the responsibilities of government officers after the government has had time to act. Such a rule would still be too broad, eliminating the defense not only when a private mob overreacts to some supposed danger, but also when private persons respond with minimum force to a real danger that officials refuse to recognize, are too frightened to meet, or are unable to contain. Moreover, in situations when prompt and effective official action not taken could have stymied the person making a threat, it would be anomalous to allow people to respond to the threat by harming the interests of an innocent person but not to do something public officials should do, such as temporarily confing the person making the threat. In short, no sensible principle emerges that would prevent misuse of the defense on behalf of those who take action against unpopular groups without also preventing its use by persons whose claim of justification should be sustained.

THE APPROPRIATE AGENCY OF EVALUATION AND THE PERSPECTIVES IT EMPLOYS

Which aspects of the general justification defense should be assigned to the judge and which to the jury are delicate questions. No doubt, the judge should decide whether a more specific defense applies, whether the legislature has otherwise meant to bar a defense of general justification, and whether recognition of the defense in situations of a particular sort would harm the administration of justice. And jurors should decide whether a defendant believed in the necessity of his or her action to avoid an evil.[50] The troublesome question concerns the choice of evils: who should decide if the evil avoided was sufficiently great to warrant the act forbidden by the statute?

The Model Penal Code does not resolve this question, and sound arguments can be made on each side. In part, the issue turns on how expansive a defense is desired. New York and the states following it have explicitly committed the determination to the judge, the assumption being that judges will be more constrained than juries. Judicial decision about the balance of evils also admits of greater consistency and, over a long period, the building up of relevant precedents.

Some older formulations of the necessity defense assume that its application is up to the jury, and this approach has been defended more recently on the ground that a body "representative of the community should be allowed to decide the issue of relative values."[51] A subsidiary reason for assignment to the jury involves cases in which defendants claim to have avoided various potential evils—say, damage to the lives and property of many people, as in the Bisbee Deportation case. A judge responsible for the balance of evils may be hard put to indicate precisely what combinations of potential evils the jury would have to find for the justification claim to succeed, though the judge might repair to some general formula such as "Find for defendants if the physical welfare of many people was threatened."

The agency to which evaluation of the choice of evils is committed is interestingly related to the possible criteria of evaluation. Mortimer and Sanford Kadish speak of the evaluation as whether "on balance it is better in terms of the ultimate ends of the criminal law for a person to violate a given rule than obey it."[52] One might plausibly argue that a judge weighing conflicting evils should be guided mainly by the law's weighting of relevant interests, drawing subtly, and perhaps even unconsciously, from related legal standards. In this view, the principle of general justification is a reference away from a narrow and explicit rule—the violated criminal statute—to the whole body of the law. If the judge finds that he must go outside the law in making his comparison between the evils, he is presumably to be guided mainly by community standards, insofar as these are identifiably different from his own. Jurors are not trained to make evaluations by reference to peripherally relevant legal norms; in difficult cases, they will compare evils as representatives of community sentiment, each juror relying initially on his own judgment and then perhaps bending to some extent if he finds that his judgment is out of line with those of his fellow jurors. Any notion that the law itself supplies the materials for evaluation of the choice of evils is closely linked to the assumption that the judge will make the evaluation.

Although the idea of the balance being struck by community representatives is an appealing one, the dangers of inordinate sympathy for some undeserving defendants and the interests of regularity and reference to other legal materials make judicial determination of the balance of evils preferable.

CONCLUSION

The overall theme of this canvass of the boundaries of a general justification defense and the agencies of its application is that a broad statutory formulation is feasible and desirable. Although the consequentialist and context-centered flavor of modern versions of the defense should be qualified, the general outlines of the defense are appropriate. The resolution of the various problems I have noted might be left to the courts over time, but I have argued that most of these problems can best be handled by modest additions to statutory language.[53]

NOTES

1. Aristotle, Ethica Nicomachea, Book X, Part 9 (W. Ross trans., 1925).

2. Conduct is not characterized as reckless or negligent if the risks taken were justified. Thus, for crimes or torts depending on reckless or negligent action, claims of justification affect whether or not the basic elements of liability are present, not whether an otherwise wrongful act is treated as appropriate. Separate justifications could be offered for some breaches of strict liability standards.

3. How Harriett should be regarded for civil liability is less clear. Although she should not be viewed as a wrongdoer, there is a powerful argument that she, rather than the owner of the cabin, should bear the costs of saving herself. See *Vincent* v. *Lake Erie Transportation Co.*, 109 Minn. 456, 124 N.W. 221 (1910); Second Restatement of Torts, § 263.

4. See G. B. Law Comm'n, Criminal Law: Report on Defences of General Application 19–32 (1977), reprinted in 9 Law Comm'n Reports 25–38 (1980). Because tort suits depend on the wishes of an injured party, this argument against recognizing a defense would not apply to civil liability.

5. I refer here not only to formal determinations but also to the belief of unprosecuted actors that they have not committed a crime.

6. National Commission on Reform of Federal Criminal Laws, Final Report § 601 Comment (1971).

7. See, generally, D. Cohen, Necessity as a Justification: A Comparative Critique (paper presented to 1984 Freiburg Conference on German–Anglo-American Criminal Law Theory).

8. I explore this general subject in greater depth in Greenawalt, The Perplexing Borders of Justification and Excuse, 84 Colum. L. Rev. 1897 (1984); and in Greenawalt, Distinguishing Justifications from Excuses in Ethics and Law, forthcoming in J. Law Soc. Prob. (1986).

9. In the German Penal Code of 1975, § 35 has this import, complementing § 34, which deals with justification.

10. See Model Penal Code, §§ 2.09 (duress), 3.02 (general justification) (1985).

11. See, e.g., G. Fletcher, Rethinking Criminal Law 760–61, 830, 850 (1978); Fletcher, Should Intolerable Prison Conditions Generate a Justification or an Excuse for Escape? 26 UCLA L. Rev. 1355, 1357–58 (1979);

Robinson, Criminal Law Defenses: A Systematic Analysis, 82 Colum. L. Rev. 199, 274–75 (1982). The ill wisdom and internal difficulties of a view that the existence of a justification *depends* on others being allowed to assist and not being allowed to interfere are canvassed in Greenawalt, The Perplexing Borders of Justification and Excuse, note 8 supra at 1918–27. That essay also indicates why it is incorrect to suppose that justifications are always objective and general and that excuses are always subjective and individual. Id. at 1915–18.

12. See Comment, The Law of Necessity as Applied in the Bisbee Deportation Case, 3 Ariz. L. Rev. 264, 267 (1961) (containing a report of the judge's instructions). The facts of the case are discussed later.

13. This authority is considered in Chapter 15.

14. See Model Penal Code, § 3.02(1) and Comment (1985).

15. I have omitted Subsection (2), which deals with situations in which an actor is reckless or negligent in bringing about the situation requiring the choice of evils or in his appraisal of the necessity for his conduct. Its treatment of these situations, which I do not discuss, differs from that in many other formulations.

16. The section focuses on the actor's beliefs rather than what actually turns out to be necessary. If the actor's beliefs are reasonable, he should be regarded as justified in acting on them. See Greenawalt, The Perplexing Borders of Justification and Excuse, note 8 supra at 1907–11. The theory of the Model Code, § 3.02(2), is that beliefs that are reckless or negligent should yield liability for crimes of recklessness or negligence only.

17. "Necessity" does not always require a high probability that the evil will occur if the act is not performed. Speeding might be warranted even if one realized that the chances it will help an injured person are only around 20%.

18. The same conclusion would apply even if the harm avoided did not include loss of life at all. Donald would be justified in creating the very slight increase of risk of death that one instance of speeding involves to save his passenger's limb or to shorten his suffering of excruciating pain.

19. There is a subtle qualification here. The term *necessary* includes a factual assessment of the probability that certain action will avert a certain harm, but it also includes a judgment as to whether or not action should be taken on that probability. Plainly the defendant's factual assessment controls, but it is doubtful if his assessment of what amounts to a justifying probability controls. For example, suppose Donald said, "I knew the chances my passengers would benefit from my speeding were very slight but I still thought it necessary to go ahead." A jury, taking a view that the exigency required by the statute was stronger than that Donald perceived, might decide that Donald's beliefs did not amount to belief in the necessity of speeding despite Donald's assumption to the contrary.

20. In Wisconsin, for example, the defense can be raised only when the evil to be avoided is public disaster, death, or great bodily harm. Wis. Stat. Ann. tit. 45, § 939.47.

21. Giving preference to the vital interests of one's family and close friends when one is subject to a threat or to an exigency created by natural forces may properly be excused, as the duress defense contemplates for common responses to threats.

22. See Medical Necessity as a Defense to Criminal Liability: *United States* v. *Randall*, 46 Geo. Wash. L. Rev. 273 (1978).

23. A strong defense of that position in terms of a theory of moral rights is provided in J. Murphy, Retribution, Justice and Therapy 3–25 (1979). See, generally, P. Foot, Virtues and Vices 19–31 (1981); Thomson, The Trolley Problem, 94 Yale L. J. 1395 (1985). I discuss this problem at greater length in Greenawalt, Natural Law and Political Choice: The General Justification Defense; Criteria for Political Action; and the Duty to Obey the Law, forthcoming in Cath. U. L. Rev. (1986).

24. See, e.g., J. Finnis, Fundamentals of Ethics 80–133 (1983); J. L. Mackie, Ethics 160–68 (1977). Supposing that it is not better that one innocent person be killed than that the whole people perish, Finnis generalizes that one should not choose directly against any basic human good. Finnis at 100, 106.

25. A quibble might be raised about whether the mountaineer's act caused death if it merely hastened death by a minute or two; but standard doctrine is that the person who kills someone already on his deathbed is guilty of murder.

26. Under the Model Penal Code, one must have a "conscious object" to cause a result in order to act purposefully with respect to it. §2.02(2)(a)(i).

27. One passage in the original commentary to the Model Penal Code suggested such an approach under the Code's standard (Model Penal Code § 3.02, Comment 4, Tent. Draft No. 8 [1958]). The passage, however, was in severe tension with other passages indicating that lives are to count equally and that a net saving of lives is justified within the compass of Section 3.02. See id. § 3.02, Comment 3.

28. The treatment of subtle variations by Judith Jarvis Thomson is particularly helpful in indicating the complexity of the moral evaluations involved. Thomson, note 23 supra.

29. However, this possibility would be related to the general allocation of administration of the defense, discussed below.

30. N. Y. Penal Law (McKinney 1975) § 35.05.

31. Cases in which facts are undisputed and the balance of harms definitely favors the defendant, however, are not likely to get to court.

32. 14 Q. B. D. 273 (1884).

33. 26 F. Cas. 360 (C. C. E. D. Pa. 1842).

34. There is always the possibility of *excusing* those who use unfair techniques of selection because of overwhelming emotional pressures.

35. Requiring fair selection might be viewed as a limited deontological element of an otherwise consequentialist standard. However, a consequentialist would note that fair methods of selection have better long-term consequences than unfair ones. (Whether or not one was a consequentialist might have some bearing on what one considers fair methods of selection.) The main

difficulty is not that a consequentialist standard is incapable of incorporating a principle of fairness, but that a standard that emphasizes the harm avoided and the harm designed to be prevented by the statute does not refer to that factor.

36. A narrow related concern is that people will more freely threaten others if the persons threatened yield more often because justifications are available to relieve them of liability. Whether or not possible escape from liability affects many people subject to threats is dubious; in any event, as long as the duress defense exists, elimination of the general justification defense in this context would hardly matter.

37. *United States* v. *Bailey*, 444 U.S. 394 (1979); *People* v. *Lovercamp*, 43 Cal. App.3d 823, 118 Cap. Rptr. 110 (Dist. Ct. App. 1974). Compare *State* v. *Green*, 470 S.W.2d 565 (Mo.) (rejecting defense), cert. denied, 405 U.S. 1073 (1971), with *People* v. *Harmon*, 53 Mich. App. 482, 220 N.W.2d 212 (1974) (acknowledging defense), aff'd, 394 Mich. 625, 232 N.W.2d 187 (1975).

38. I say "perhaps the duress defense" because similar objections might be raised to allowing its use in this context.

39. All those cases arising from escapes that preceded the decision of the first case might be treated like it.

40. This sentence assumes that even an attempt to leave conditions of confinement temporarily counts as an escape.

41. Arnolds and Garland, The Defense of Necessity in Criminal Law: The Right to Choose the Lesser Evil, 65 J. Crim. Law Criminol. 289 (1974).

42. Matters are somewhat more complicated if one introduces the dual levels of a federal system, but the basic point is not much affected.

43. The defense is also barred when the legislature provides exceptions or defenses dealing with the specific situation.

44. No doubt, the restrictive "plainly appears" language of the Model Penal Code was chosen to prevent improper reliance on dim legislative purpose by judges unsympathetic to the defense. My suggestion reflects the view that some broadening of the language will not unduly increase this risk.

45. See Comment, note 12 supra.

46. 376 F. Supp. 29 (D.D.C. 1974). His claims were that the president had authority to order a break-in required by national security and that, in any event, he acted in the belief that the president had such authority. A very slight shift of the first claim could turn it into one based on general justification.

47. Section 3.03.

48. See Comment, note 12 supra at 272.

49. Analogy to principles governing "color of law" and "state action" in civil rights cases might profitably be employed here. See, generally, Lewis, The Meaning of State Action, 60 Colum. L. Rev. 1083 (1960); Comment, The Civil Rights Act and Mr. Monroe, 49 Calif. L. Rev. 145 (1961); Note, State Action and the Burger Court, 60 Va. L. Rev. 840 (1974).

50. See note 20 for an elaboration of what a judgment about necessity involves. I assume that the jury will determine evaluative aspects of necessity

as well as factual ones, though one might argue theoretically that the evaluative questions are not really distinct from choice of evils issues and should be assigned to the court if it determines the balance of evils.

51. Arnolds and Garland, note 41 supra at 296.

52. M. Kadish and S. Kadish, Discretion to Disobey 120 (1973).

53. I doubt that these problems are serious enough, given the rarity of the defense, to warrant separate amendment; but in a jurisdiction that is codifying or recodifying justification defenses, I would recommend use of the suggested additions.

14

Conscientious Objection and Constitutional Interpretation

The main problem for this chapter is whether, and when, society should excuse people from obligations because they strongly feel that performing them would be morally wrong. The general justification defense envisions a kind of formal approval of defendant's claim of moral justification; the question here is whether or not people should ever be relieved of legal obligations when their primary moral claims are not endorsed by society.

Possible exemptions from military service, the subject that comes immediately to mind when one thinks of conscientious objection, illustrate the issue. A typical pacifist believes that countries should not wage military conflicts and that individuals should not participate in them. Neither any national government nor the majority of any country's citizenry presently endorses those propositions in the absolutist manner in which the pacifist accepts them. At this level, therefore, his moral claims are not accepted. Yet many countries, including the United States, have decided not to compel military service of pacifists. If that decision is sound, does it yield principles for extension to other concerns?

In this chapter, I attempt a generalized approach to the problem of conscientious objection, analyzing both the grounds for exemptions and the sensible range of their coverage. I concentrate primarily on legislative choice, not on how those applying the law should fulfill their duties. My major practical conclusion is to reject the premise that the typical way of affording relief to conscientious objectors should be the specification and administration of relatively precise criteria of exemption. Rather, when possible, self-selection should be employed as a preferable alternative.

In the United States some exemptions based on conscience have been held to be constitutionally required. In the last part of the chapter I offer some brief comments on the complex topic of constitutional interpretation. These comments apply to debatable claims about constitutional rights to conscience, but they also concern other claims that moral rights warrant constitutional protection.

CONSCIENTIOUS OBJECTION AND OTHER MORAL CLAIMS AGAINST PERFORMANCE

The common assumption, drawn perhaps from the history of exemptions from military service, is that if an exemption is to be given, it should be limited to conscientious objectors. Subsequently I will suggest that whenever possible, an alternative approach should be employed that does not require government officers to place people in categories; however, I do assume that when programs are based on criteria for exemption, and when the treatment given those exempted would be preferred by many people to performance of the basic obligation, the category of those exempted should be limited to conscientious objectors. This category is considerably narrower than the class of all those who think performance of a legal obligation would be morally wrong.

Henry Thoreau, near the end of his essay "Resistance to Civil Government," talked of a truly "enlightened State, in which the State comes to recognize the individual as a higher and independent power, from which all its own power and authority are derived, and treats him accordingly."[1] The gist of this passage is elusive, but Thoreau may have supposed that the ideal state would not demand of persons actions they thought were morally wrong. The term *conscientious objection* sets up hurdles regarding intensity of conviction and willingness to suffer alternative harms that exclude many who think doing an act would be wrong.

A conscientious objector is not someone who thinks he or she is committing only a minor moral wrong. Although a conscientious objector need not feel certain of the moral rightness of his view, he must believe that performing the required act would probably involve him in grave moral wrong. Gravity can be measured to some extent by what the objector thinks he should be willing to suffer rather than commit the act. A person could be a conscientious objector despite his actual submission to threats of alternative harm, as long as he believed strongly that such submission was wrong and felt great remorse over his own weakness. But if a person thought some moderate harm would actually make submission morally justifiable, he would not be a conscientious objector. If the issue were military service, a genuine objector would hold his own death preferable to killing enemy soldiers. For less momentous acts, such as jury service, the label "conscientious objector" might be conceded to persons who thought submission morally preferable to death; but a minimum standard for conscientious objection is belief that one should submit to penalties that society (or any decent society) has deemed appropriate rather than perform the obligation. In other words, a true conscientious objector must think it would be morally preferable not to perform a required act even if no exemption were afforded for conscientious objectors and enforcement against him were certain.

A defense given to all those who thought performance of an act morally wrong would be much broader.

Illustration 14-1:
Michael takes the following position: "I think it is morally better for me to devote myself to saving young lives as a social worker than to be a soldier. I give due weight to the government's view that I should be a soldier, but I still believe the morally better course of action is not to submit to military service. Yet, if my only alternative is going to jail, then military service would be morally preferable."

Michael is not a conscientious objector, but he might qualify under a standard that exempted all those who thought military service morally wrong under the circumstances.

Should a young person be exempted from compulsory military service because he thinks that a moral obligation to his family outweighs the country's need or that he can serve his country better by continuing as a social worker? The answer is clearly "no."[2] The moral judgment that the standard would require of individuals would be extremely difficult, forcing them to decide just how much weight to give to the social judgment reflected in the law and the actual military needs of the country. Their honest judgment of what is morally best would often be so heavily tinctured by self-interest that compulsory military service with such an exemption would not be very different from a volunteer army. If the social judgment embodied in compulsory military service is an appropriate one, as will undoubtedly be thought by those who adopt the judgment, it should count for something more.[3] Society properly requires people to do things other than what they regard as morally best when a corporate determination has been made that their contribution is needed for the general safety and welfare; and the law properly aims to influence the moral judgments of citizens, both by affecting their calculation of relevant consequences and by encouraging moral perspectives that favor the required act.

Any exemption based on moral conviction faces difficulties of administration greater than those presented by a general justification defense. Although part of a claim of justification concerns what the actor was trying to do—he was driving fast *because* he had an injured person in the back seat—the claim requires strong support in the objective circumstances. An exemption based on "moral conviction," at least one tailored to individual as opposed to group perspectives, depends exclusively on the moral sense of the person involved, something more difficult for outsiders to assess. Deciding if someone is really a conscientious objector can be very hard; deciding if someone, on balance, thinks an act morally preferable would be harder still.

Moral claims falling short of conscientious exemption may well be relevant for other strategies of exoneration or mitigation, discussed in the next chapter; however, I will assume in what follows that an exemption to legal obligations based on stated criteria will be limited to conscientious objectors and that the task of applying the criteria will include determining not only what convictions someone has but also whether these amount to a conscientious objection.[4]

CONSCIENTIOUS OBJECTORS AND THE PURPOSES OF PUNISHMENT

Even though society deems the position of the conscientious objector to be mistaken, many of the purposes of punishment that apply to ordinary offenders do not, as Chapter 12 has already suggested, apply to him at all or do not apply with the same force.

Incapacitation and Reform

The usefulness of isolating a conscientious objector from society will depend on his crime. If his moral convictions lead to continued violations of the rights of others—say he steals because of a moral conviction that private property is an outrage—then putting him behind bars serves a purpose; if he refuses to perform a single sort of positive act, such as submitting to military service, his presence among his fellow citizens itself poses no danger, and separating him from society is not needed.

Whatever the realistic possibilities of criminal punishment reforming the character of offenders in a positive way, that controversial aim of punishment has little relevance for conscientious objectors. Jail is not an appropriate means for encouraging thoughtful reevaluations of firm moral convictions.

Moral Blameworthiness and Vengeance

Ordinarily, serious criminal penalties should be imposed only on people whose acts occasion substantial moral blame. Rather than seeking to advance his own interests or giving vent to his own impulses in disregard of the legitimate claims of others, the conscientious objector responds to a perceived moral duty, usually believing that his refusal to comply will better serve his fellows than would the behavior that the state requires. At least if his underlying beliefs strike sympathetic chords in nonadherents,[5] a conscientious objector will seem morally blameless or much less to blame than those who break the law out of self-interest.

The satisfaction of justified anger may be one legitimate, if subsidiary, purpose of punishment. One who understands the bases for a conscientious objector's refusal to obey a law will not be likely to regard anger as an appropriate response. Perhaps others, less understanding, will feel anger; but the satisfaction of *unjustified* anger should rarely be an aim of criminal penalties.

Deterrence and Education

A dominant purpose of punishment is to deter illegal acts, both by creating immediate fear in those tempted to perform the acts and by helping people develop self-control over time. The firmly committed and courageous conscientious objector is not likely to be deterred by the law's penalties. Some conscientious objectors, however, are susceptible. Not all are actually willing to go to jail. Deterrence of those who lack the will to act on their convictions exacts a terrible price. Their feeling that they have yielded to compulsion and violated their most deeply held beliefs and principles may involve profound resentment and loss of self-respect. Further, if the acts they are forced to perform do, like military service and jury duty, require active cooperation over a period of time, they are not likely to be the best candidates for the jobs involved.

Serious criminal penalties not only frighten, they educate people about behavior the community deems to be acceptable. Although existing conscientious objectors are not easily deterred, young people growing up in a society that does not exempt objectors, that does not accord the recognition to autonomy that an exemption reflects, may be influenced against adopting a position that has been placed outside the range of the socially tolerable. Although many other factors matter, a systematic refusal to exempt will reduce the number of people who find themselves opposed in conscience to performing particular legal duties.

Fairness, Perceived Fairness, and Administrability

The fairness of exempting conscientious objectors is a somewhat more complex issue and warrants fuller discussion. If onerous burdens must be borne on behalf of society, a sharing of the burden that is equal in some sense will be most fair, barring some countervailing reason.[6] What exactly will constitute a roughly equal sharing or its closest feasible approximation will often be a subject of intense debate, but we can conceive universal military service as based on a principle of equal sharing realized in terms of equal contributions of time. Should equal sharing among those capable of rendering service not be possible, a lottery imposing an equal risk would be a second-best fair distribution.

If someone is incapable of performing the task that would constitute his share, fairness does not demand a pointless effort to make him perform. The allocation of burdens will be fairer, however, if he is imposed on in some other way than if he is simply relieved altogether. A system is fairer if persons physically unable to engage in combat are given desk jobs than if they are excused altogether from service.

This general conclusion about fairness applies to conscientious objectors. Their morally grounded unwillingness to contribute may be viewed as making them incapable in a special sense, or at least as making the burden much more onerous for them than for others. Among friends engaged in a common endeavor, say a camping expedition, a person will not be forced to engage in a task he abhors, say killing animals for meat; but other burdens will be allocated in a manner designed to equalize sharing overall. Excusing conscientious objectors is not unfair to those who carry the burden the objectors refuse, but excusing the objectors altogether is less fair than requiring them to bear some roughly equal alternative burden. This principle underlies the rule that those who object only to combatant military service must perform noncombatant duty and the rule that those who object to all military duty must perform alternative civilian service. Because time in jail is a fate most people deem more unpalatable than military service, criminal punishment may itself be viewed as one method of equalizing burdens. But a method that conveys harsh condemnation, wastes social resources, and involves maximum interference with personal liberty is much worse than permitting objectors to make a positive contribution that is alternative to the task they reject.

Those who decide on systems for allocating burdens must worry about perceived as well as actual fairness. When citizens must bear onerous burdens, it is important that they sense no unfair share is being imposed on them. Perhaps some people who submit to the risks and rigors of military service, themselves lacking any options, may not believe any noncriminal alternative task is equally onerous. Their belief that anyone exempted is "getting off too easy" is not by itself a sufficient reason for punishing conscientious objectors as criminals; but the presence of such perceived unfairness is socially undesirable.

Concerns about fairness and perceived fairness are magnified in any system requiring determinations whether particular persons are conscientious objectors. As long as some of those who do not qualify for an exemption have a powerful incentive to seek it, instances of successful fraud will occur,[7] as will instances of mistaken denial to claimants who really do qualify. Faulty determinations reduce the overall fairness of any system of exemptions; and when those compelled to perform the primary task believe that faulty determinations are common, the system will be perceived as unfair in practice, however fair it may appear in theory.

This survey of the purposes of punishment and their relevance for conscientious objectors has indicated that certain bases for punishment do apply to conscientious objectors but that good reasons exist for excusing them for some otherwise common obligations. When objectors are excused from shared burdens, fairness is enhanced by imposing on them some roughly equal burden.

TYPES OF LEGAL REQUIREMENTS AND POSSIBLE EXEMPTIONS FOR CONSCIENTIOUS OBJECTORS

General considerations about punishment obviously do not establish whether or not an exemption is warranted from any particular legal requirement. Some types of laws lend themselves much more comfortably to that possibility than do others, and an exercise in rough classification can illuminate important differences. Conscientious objectors may be unwilling to comply with four different sorts of standards: (1) rules that directly protect others from harm; (2) rules that impose shared burdens, such as taxes or military service; (3) rules that protect actors from doing harm to themselves; and (4) rules that establish conditions for receiving benefits or acquiring licenses or privileges.

Rules Directly Protecting Others from Harm

Reflection on laws protecting life, liberty, and property quickly reveals why no universal principle of exemption for conscientious objectors would be appropriate. We may face some initial difficulty understanding what conscientious objection even means in this context. Almost no one thinks he is bound in conscience constantly to violate particular legal rights of other people, but a person may feel bound in conscience to violate such rights on particular occasions. For example, a person might think God has ordered him to kill a heretic or that family honor demands personal vengeance. Societies cannot afford to excuse persons who inflict injuries out of conviction. Civil law properly does not take account of idiosyncratic moral perceptions when it imposes the cost of injuries on the person who intentionally causes them; the criminal law properly declines to sacrifice maximum possible deterrence and educational effect by exempting classes of person who violate the rights of others.

If this point seems obvious with respect to violations of personal rights, it may seem less so when violations of the "rights" of the government and large private organizations are involved. Conceivably, people who trespass on public or corporate property could be excused if they are acting out of conscience. Yet deciding whether or not persons with some point to make feel bound in conscience to make it at a single place and time will usually be very difficult. Further, if it is assumed that trespassers may be forcibly removed from property, exempting objectors from criminal punishment would create an anomaly. As soon as they were released, having established the basis for their exemption, they could return to the property to recommence their trespass.[8] Though more might be said about this problem, I will assume that even for such violations no exception based on conscience is appropriate.[9]

Another possible exception to the principle that no exemptions should be given from rules that protect others directly from harm concerns violations of duties of care by actors who seek the welfare of those to whom the duties are owed. Parents may refuse to procure medical treatment for their child because they believe such treatment is less efficacious than spiritual healing or will jeopardize the child's immortal soul. Even if one grants that the state should ensure appropriate medical treatment for children when it can, the appropriateness of imposing criminal liability on parents who fail to fulfill their duty of care does not follow. Perhaps the propensity of some people to accept bizarre ideas about what is good for them and their loved ones is so great that the law must, for educative purposes, insist on uniform minimal standards of appropriate physical treatment. On the other hand, parents have such an intense concern for the physical welfare of their children that an exemption for those with strong convictions against medical treatment may promote little imitation.

Rules Imposing Shared Burdens

Because refusals to comply do not directly violate the rights of others and because alternative tasks are usually possible, laws imposing shared burdens are better candidates for exemptions than laws forbidding infliction of harm. When some people conscientiously refuse to perform burdens, such as taxes, jury duty, or military service, their share must be borne by others or the total amount of benefits will be slightly reduced. Increased shares of burdens or reduced benefits may be spread among all participants or borne by particular individuals, who, for example, may be called to serve only because conscientious objectors have declined to serve. Even in the latter instance, the individual called will have no right to be free of the burden; and ordinarily he will not identify himself as one who has replaced a conscientious objector. In any event, as long as conscientious objectors would refuse to perform whether or not they are exempt, a perfectly administered exemption itself does not affect the burdens others will have to bear. Because a belief that one should never perform an act may be established more easily than a belief that one must perform a certain act on a particular occasion, identifying conscientious objectors will generally be simpler when the government requires acts than when it prohibits acts.

If the law imposes a duty not to infringe on the rights of others, no alternative restraint or action can offset a violation; but performance of alternative acts is a way for conscientious objectors to bear burdens equal to those carried by persons who comply with rules imposing shared responsibilities. Finally, a persons's claim against being enlisted by society to do what he finds abhorrent may simply be more powerful than his claim to perform some act he thinks is right but society deems wrongful.[10]

Paternalistic Laws

Some laws, such as those forbidding the use of drugs, are designed mainly to protect the persons whose acts are forbidden; since violation of these laws affects other persons only indirectly, generous acknowledgment of conscientious objection may seem apt. But this conclusion about paternalistic laws would be too hasty. Most paternalistic legislation would not be adopted unless substantial numbers of people wanted to perform the forbidden acts. Those who wish to perform the acts typically will regard them as not dangerous or harmful[11] and often will feel the government has no business forbidding them. If everybody who believed he or she has a moral right to engage in the acts were given an exemption, prohibitive legislation would have little point. Strong beliefs about rights to perform self-regarding acts are indeed a very good reason for legislatures to forgo paternalistic measures. But once the judgment is made that legislation is valuable enough to override this consideration, no broad exemption will appear warranted. Whether some narrow exemption can be justified and formulated in an administrable manner depends on the particular subject involved.

Rules Establishing Conditions for Benefits and Privileges

Conditions on benefits, such as workers' compensation, and privileges, such as driving, do not pose the same direct conflict between law and conscience as do the three kinds of rules just discussed. Willingness to work on Saturday may be a prerequisite for receiving public money, but one who objects to working on Saturday has the option of simply giving up the benefits. From this perspective, the need for an exemption for conscientious objectors appears less strong. On the other hand, some benefits and privileges are very important to people, and granting them to objectors harms no one.[12] Unless the condition that the objector will not perform is generally regarded as onerous, attempted fraud will be minimal; and the objector's failure to satisfy a condition will not ordinarily leave any burden to be borne by someone else.

For these reasons, the state interest in denying an exemption will usually be less than for other sorts of rules.

THE RELEVANCE OF RELIGION IN
FORMULATING EXEMPTIONS

I have thus far proceeded on the assumption that the class of persons to whom an exemption is to be granted should be cast in terms of conscientious objectors. What possible role does "religion" have to play in defining the eligible class? If every conscientious claim is automatically regarded as "religious" in some broad sense,[13] the question loses importance, but religion in a narrower sense does not include all conscientious claims. Whether or not religion in the narrower sense matters is an important question.

A modern liberal state, composed of people with widely diverse religious beliefs, should not have as a purpose the promotion of any particular religion or the promotion of religion in general over nonreligion. Such a state should not make the judgment that a belief is better or more accurate simply because it has some religious underpinning. Thus, the connection of a belief to religion does not in and of itself confer any special claim to be accommodated.[14] However, other possible reasons remain for making religious belief or practice a criterion for exemption.

Conceivably, only religious persons would be thought likely to have a particular kind of conscientious objection—say to receiving a vaccination—and an exemption might be restricted to them on this ground. Or nonreligious objectors might be barred from an exemption on the basis that those with religious scruples have, in some psychological sense, stronger reasons not to perform than they do. Even if it were assumed that some nonreligious persons had objections as powerful as those of religious believers, they might be excluded to minimize problems of accurate administration and perceived unfairness. Finally, were an exemption cast in other than religious terms, religious ties

might still be used as evidence of sincerity and as a means of construing the views of inarticulate claimants. The weight of these various
considerations is assessed in context in the ensuing discussion.

APPLICATION TO SPECIFIC PROBLEMS

I now address some particular problems concerning conscientious
objection and suggest their appropriate resolution in light of the
general principles thus far suggested.

Military Service

The problem of exemptions from compulsory military service has
dominated discussion of conscientious objection. The demand that
people stand ready to kill others and to sacrifice their own lives is the
most severe demand a society can place on its citizens; the first part of
that demand, the readiness to kill others, is in some tension with the
Christian religious tradition that has underlain American culture.
That is not to say that most Christians at any time in the country's
history have believed killing in war is morally wrong, only that the
perfectionist ethics of the Gospels, including, for example, the invocation to "turn the other cheek," and the pacifist inclinations of the early
Church pose a serious question about whether such killing can be
justified. Throughout our history some sects have been pacifist, and
their pacifist views have been thought worthy of some accommodation.

If compulsory military service is ever reintroduced, a self-selecting
alternative to military duty should be adopted. I will defend and
amplify this position, but first I will examine how an exemption
should be cast if the traditional approach, which requires proof of
eligibility, is followed. This discussion has significance partly because
such an approach may be used again for draftees,[15] as it is now for
persons presently within the military who develop conscientious opposition to service, and partly because some exemptions in other areas
must necessarily demand proof of eligibility. Another important reason for the exercise is to demonstrate how troublesome drawing
eligibility lines with respect to military service can be.

I shall assume that an exemption is properly tailored to the scope of
the objection, that one who objects only to combatant military service
should be given noncombatant military service, and that only those

who object to all military service should be wholly exempt. I address two major questions: whether an exemption should be grounded in religious belief and whether it should be restricted essentially to pacifists.[16]

Religious Belief and Eligibility

A religious criterion for eligibility could be cast in terms of personal belief or membership in a pacifist sect. Although eligibility for an exemption from combatant military service was limited in the United States as recently as World War I to members of pacifist sects, few would now suggest reversion to that position. Some traditionally pacifist sects, notably the Society of Friends, have such a wide diversity of beliefs that someone's membership in the sect is hardly an assurance of his pacifism; and many who adhere to other religious groups or to none are also pacifists. Limiting an exemption to those affiliated with pacifist denominations would make administration simpler, but it would unjustly exclude others with virtually identical convictions and would inappropriately encourage people to join particular religious groups.[17]

Whether or not an exemption should be limited to religious believers is a more difficult question. The Supreme Court, in two landmark cases,[18] has construed a statutory exemption originally aimed at religious believers who accept a Supreme Being to include all those who are truly conscientious. Constitutional objections to the lines Congress intended may well have underlaid these exercises in construction, but nonetheless it formally remains open to Congress to try again to narrow the category of exempted objectors, and some Justices would undoubtedly accept the fruits of such an effort.[19] My interest here is not in constitutionality but in whether such an effort would be appropriate for a legislature free to make it.

We can pass rather quickly over two possible arguments for limiting an exemption to claimants whose belief is religious in a sense narrower than one covering all conscientious objections. The first is that such a limit would enhance public acceptability. Though some citizens may resent the ability of nonreligious objectors to avoid military service, their attitude is a doubtful basis for public policy; since the country exempted nonreligious objectors during the latter years of the Vietnam War, the broader exemption is clearly tolerable, and a slight increase in acceptability is an inadequate reason to confine it.

The second argument is that administering the exemption for nonreligious objectors is too difficult. Measurements of administrative ease are hard to come by, and whether or not difficulties in this area are too great is a delicate matter of judgment. I will simply register my own opinion, based on review of a substantial number of draft cases,[20] that determinations of sincerity are somewhat more troublesome when persons lack religious belief and affiliation.[21] Nonetheless, some administrative difficulty is not a weighty basis for narrowing the exemption, particularly if, as I believe, most people are not willing to lie about their deepest convictions.

A third, more interesting argument for confining the exemption is that religious objectors are special, that they face a more painful choice than other objectors. I will consider arguments that belief in "extratemporal consequences" or a transcendent source of moral truth make the claim of a religious person more powerful than that of a nonbeliever.

Jesse Choper has urged that conflicts between legal demands and conscience have a particular cruelty for the religious believer because of the extratemporal consequences he thinks will ensue if he violates his conscience.[22] Acknowledging the impossibility of empirical proof, Dean Choper writes that "intuition and experience affirm that the degree of internal trauma on earth for those who have put their souls in jeopardy for eternity can be expected to be markedly greater than for those who have only violated a moral scruple."[23]

Although just such belief in harmful extratemporal consequences may make it easier for an objector to suffer jail if he sticks to his conscience, given his assurance that his present sacrifice will eventually be redeemed for his own benefit, Choper is probably right in supposing that what matters most for a possible exemption is not how much a class of persons will suffer if they violate a law but how much they will suffer if they comply with the law and violate their consciences.

The major problem with a distinction based on extratemporal consequences is that it loses force as soon as one considers the diverse views taken by adherents of this country's traditional religions. Those who fear that a choice may lead to eternal damnation will find that choice particularly painful. But for many practicing Christians and Jews the connection between grave moral wrongs and possible extratemporal consequences is much less direct or is highly uncertain. Many persons believe that most or all sins are within God's loving forgiveness and that a contrite heart can wash them of potential extratemporal consequences. Many persons suppose that sins will be visited by definite negative consequences in this life or a next existence, such as purgatory, but that a penitent person may avoid damnation. Others who believe in extratemporal consequences may not think they relate to particular sins. A strict Calvinist, for example, believes that election to heaven is determined on some basis beyond human comprehension.[24] Some persons simply do not believe in divine eternal punishment, or any divine punishment, while they retain belief in divine love and an afterlife. Others confess uncertainty about exactly what will happen after death, while expressing faith in the continuing power of God's love. Many religious persons are deeply unsure about the precise relationship of sins in this life to the nature of existence in an afterlife.

This summary survey exposes serious objections to using a standard of extratemporal consequences. Many persons who accept a connection between potential harmful extratemporal consequences and particular sins do not think these consequences are inevitable or eternal. Whether such persons suffer more torment from violating conscience than those who think they have done a terrible wrong in the only life they have to live is far from clear. For persons who doubt any strong link between extratemporal consequences and particular sins exists, the likelihood of special suffering is even weaker. The rationale for focusing on extratemporal consequences would largely evaporate if all who believed in the possibility of an afterlife were to qualify for an exemption. If a tighter connection between moral wrongs and extratemporal consequences were demanded, administrative bodies and courts would be put in the impossible position of sorting out the immense variety of beliefs that are found in traditional religious denominations and of trying to settle just how close the believed connection would have to be before an exemption should be granted.

An alternative approach would be to repeat Congress's earlier attempt to exempt only those whose pacifism is connected to belief in a transcendent being.[25] The theory would be that persons who think they violate the norms of a higher power will feel more severely disturbed than those who think they breach moral principles without such transcendent significance. As with the broader version of an extratemporal consequence standard, the basic problem with such a limit is that belief in a transcendent being probably does not correlate sharply with intensity of feeling that one should not violate one's convictions. The firm conviction against killing in war is one that can arise outside of belief in a transcendent being, and many pacifists who do not believe in a transcendent being have convictions as intense as those who do.

The most plausible form of the argument for limiting the exemption is that *most* nonreligious people sincerely opposed to participation in war have less intense feelings against participation than *most* pacifists who are religious; since a substantial percentage of nonreligious pacifists, when forced, would choose military service before jail without feeling terrible remorse, the inability to identify these persons in advance requires withholding the exemption from all nonreligious pacifists. The factual predicates of this argument are much too uncertain a basis for public policy, but even if they are granted, the resulting punishment of many nonreligious objectors who do have intense feelings against military service and will go to jail rather than submit would not be warranted.

If an exemption continues to be given to pacifist conscientious objectors, no religious restriction should be adopted.

Selective Objection and Eligibility

Another dilemma, sharply exposed by the Vietnam War, is whether an exemption should include nonpacifists who object to participation in a particular war. In 1971, the Supreme Court, in accord with the plain intent of Congress, construed the statute to exclude "selective objectors" and also declared that Congress could permissibly distinguish them from persons who object to participation in all wars.[26]

The most familiar basis for refusal to fight in a particular war is belief that the country's involvement does not meet the criteria of a just war, a concept developed in the post-Constantine Church from Greek and Roman roots, elaborated in subsequent Christian eras, and now subscribed to in one form or another by most of the major Christian denominations. According to traditional just war doctrine, a war must, among other things, be for a just cause, and be waged by means that are just and proportionate to the good likely to be achieved. Objection to particular wars can also be based on international law analogs governing the reasons for fighting and the military means employed. More rarely, selective objectors may regard as crucial the dominant race or religion of an enemy country or their own previous associations with that country.

Some selective objectors undoubtedly have as intense convictions against participating in a war as do most pacifists, and the basic harm in coercing their conscience is as great, so a strong argument exists for extending an exemption to them. On the other hand, selective objectors much more closely than pacifists resemble persons who have ordinary political objections to particular wars; they are more difficult for others to identify; the grounds for their objections are subject to change over time; and their objection to fighting in a particular war is much less closely tied to objection to performing military service away from that war than objection to all wars is tied to objection to all military service. Although these reasons against an exemption for selective objectors are substantial, the grounds for extension of an exemption to them are more powerful.[27]

Self-Selection: A Far Better Alternative

The preceding comments about who might be exempted reveal how imperfect each possible formulation of the eligible class is. Yet our society can handle conscientious objections to military service in a manner that effectively circumvents all the difficulties that accompany even the best test of eligibility. If a draft is reinstituted, Congress should establish an alternative civilian service that anyone could choose.[28] Since the draft's aim is to get soldiers, the conditions of civilian service should be set so that the great majority of people will prefer military service, but the conditions should be no more onerous than are needed for this objective. Civilian service could carry substantially less pay and subsidary benefits or be for a longer period of time, or both. If a lottery were used for military service, young men (and perhaps young women[29]) might choose between a certainty of two years of civilian service and a chance of two years of military service. For a more nearly universal draft, the choice might be between two years of military service and two and a half or three years of civilian service. Someone already serving in the military (or previously chosen by lot) could transfer to civilian service by accepting a period of work substantially longer than his remaining military duty.

This approach exhibits powerful advantages over any version of a traditional exemption. It eliminates worry about how to draw the lines of exemption and the nagging sense that any lines incorporate elements of unfairness. It eliminates the incredible practical problems of accurately identifying sincere conscientious objectors. Beyond its great expense, potential for delay, and intrusiveness concerning personal convictions, the administration of a limited exemption inevitably excuses some who are not really eligible and refuses to excuse others who are eligible; it inevitably breeds resentment among those wrongly denied exemptions and those who serve believing that the system of exemptions is unfair. No one in the military could feel unfairly treated by the choice of others to do civilian work, as long as he or she could have made the same choice.

Conceivable objections to such a plan prove to be insubstantial. Concern might be raised that too many people would opt for civilian service. If the country were not engaged in a war or were fighting in a fairly popular one, a relatively small percentage would opt for a civilian service with conditions substantially less favorable than those of military service. In any event, the United States since World War II has never needed anywhere near all those of conscriptable age in the military; the increasing technological sophistication of modern warfare should ensure a continuation of this pattern (which the conscription of women would further accentuate). Ample personnel for the military would remain even if substantial numbers chose civilian service.[30] No doubt adjustments in institutions would be needed to accommodate a great number of persons in civilian service, but there is plenty of useful work they could perform. The value of that work should be sufficient to cover the modest salaries of the workers and administrative costs.

A different sort of objection, that the less favorable terms of civilian service are unfair to genuine objectors, is also misconceived. Roughly equal burdens are justified to achieve fairness between those who accept military service and those whose conscience forbids them from doing so. Since risk of death and prolonged separation from loved ones characterize much military service, some adjustment in ordinary terms (pay, benefits, period of duty) for civilian service is needed to strike a fair balance. And moderate additional unfavorableness in civilian service, needed to lead most persons to prefer military duty (or a chance of military duty), is required to make the system work and to avoid the serious injustice of jailing whole classes of objectors or of making uncertain judgments about eligibility for an exemption that may be fraudulently claimed.

Draft Registration

Resolving the proper treatment for those whose conscience forbids even registration for conscription is more difficult, but room exists for more accommodation than has yet been afforded. Congress traditionally has not granted any exemption for persons who refuse to register, and a good many pacifists unwilling to cooperate with the draft system even to this degree have gone to jail. The country's present registration requirement[31] also lacks any exemption based on conscience.

For some people, the potential conflict between conscience and a registration requirement may be avoidable. In a system permitting anyone to choose civilian service as an alternative to military duty, persons should be permitted to register directly for civilian service. Though some persons would consider any such registration as unacceptable cooperation with military conscription, others who would not register for a draft might register for civilian service.

A more general device for avoiding the conflict between conscience and draft registration would be to accomplish a person's registration without his cooperation. Schools, employers, and unemployment offices, for example, could report all persons who reached the age of eighteen. Although such a system might manage to register virtually all young people, as a general substitute for self-reporting it would carry significant costs. Military service involves a momentous relationship between the individual and his government; the natural and simplest way of determining who is eligible is for individuals to report to the government. That method, which symbolizes an individual's willingness to undertake shared burdens of citizenship, should not be altered because some people are conscientiously opposed to registering. Although jury lists are compiled without individual cooperation, with no controversy, such a procedure for military conscription may even derogate from the autonomous choice of those who refuse to have themselves registered. A system should permit indirect reporting for individuals who find that more acceptable than registering themselves; but indirection should not circumvent an individual's own unwillingness to have himself registered by any means.

For those situations in which the conflict between conscience and registration requirements cannot be avoided, appropriate resolution depends on the context of nonregistration. Presently, registration exists without conscription. The existence of persons who are conscientiously opposed to registering is one powerful reason for abandoning a program whose benefit to the country is extremely conjectural. If that step is not taken, proof that one cannot in conscience register should be made a defense to a criminal charge of nonregistration. The person who has refused to register would have to persuade the prosecutor or the jury not only that he could not in conscience submit to military service but that registration alone would conflict with his deepest convictions.[32] This defense would create no unfairness to those who do register, since simple registration imposes no serious burden on them.

A person who refuses to register when registration is linked to an actual draft should not have a similar defense, since he has taken an important step to avoid or decline a very serious obligation placed on others. However, if he can establish, at some time before sentence, that his grounds for refusal were conscientious and he also expresses his willingness to perform civilian service, any criminal penalty should be suspended while he performs civilian service, and the penalty should be erased upon his satisfactory completion of that service. The objector unwilling to perform civilian service should be imprisoned; this outcome is tragic for those whose total noncooperation is required by conscience, but fairness to those who serve at great cost requires that no one be able by personal choice, however motivated, to escape all obligation to serve.

Taxes

The payment of taxes is a basic but onerous responsibility of citizens; a complete escape from liability cannot properly be granted to those with strong moral objections to contributing, but governments could do more than they have to work out alternatives that meet public needs and satisfy claims of conscience. Since most people strenuously dislike paying taxes and many believe that their own taxes are unfairly high, any scheme to lift the burden from the shoulders of conscientious objectors would create a tremendous temptation to fraud and would subtly influence many people toward an honest conviction that they could not, in conscience, pay. Administrative difficulties would be immense, and high levels of unfairness and perceived unfairness would be generated. For these reasons conscientious exemption from tax liabilities has never seemed a serious option. Moreover, with respect to taxes, the state need not worry, as it must in regard to pacifist soldiers, that successful coercion will produce ineffective performance; money collected under protest buys as much as money cheerfully given.

Yet some people are appalled that contributions coerced from them are used for evil purposes. They may feel that their payment of taxes unacceptably involves them in military efforts or in publicly funded abortions they consider murder; or they may believe that the very practice of coerced payments to the government is morally abhorrent. Such views may lead persons to believe they should not pay taxes at all, should not pay the percentage of assessed liability that goes to the purpose they consider evil, or should not pay any money to be used for that purpose.[33]

Without granting any formal exemption, the government can make some accommodation to those whose refusal to pay taxes is obviously conscientious. It can proceed to collect the amount owed without the objector's full cooperation, garnishing pay checks or a bank account, while reserving criminal prosecution for persons who dishonestly attempt to evade taxes. Although occasional prosecutions have been mounted in the United States against prominent people who conscientiously refuse to pay taxes, one has the sense that persons who openly declare their liabilities and balk at payment are less likely to be the subject of criminal proceedings than those whose declarations are false.[34]

For major taxes, such as the income tax and property tax,[35] governments could make a formal and more serious effort to meet the claims of conscientious objectors, and they could do so without engaging in the worrisome task of determining eligibility. If people wished not to have their own taxes go for some abhorrent purpose, the government could direct their particular payments elsewhere, charging in return a substantial fee, one high enough to cover administrative expenses for this bookkeeping operation and to discourage most people from exercising this option. If people refused to pay all or a share of their taxes, they could be permitted as an alternative to direct their money to private causes, such as hospitals and other charities. The cost of this privilege would be a significant addition to the sum owed, say 10%. Since few people would willingly undertake this added expense, not many would take advantage of such a program unless they had strong moral convictions about taxpaying.

Because paying taxes against conscience may not portend the moral horror that the pacifist feels about the possibility of killing, the case for formal accommodation with respect to taxes is less pressing than that regarding military service, but the intense indignity some people feel about the use of their taxes is sufficient to justify such a program. Proposals offered thus far have been cast in terms of particular uses of tax money, namely, military expenditures.[36] That limitation is a mistake—at least it is a mistake if the aim is really to accommodate conscience rather than label military endeavors suspect. A program permitting optional choices about the direction of payments for one's tax liabilities should stand neutral among government uses of money, representing a general concession to strong moral convictions instead of acknowledging the moral dubiousness of particular kinds of expenditures.

Jury Duty

The few people conscientiously opposed to jury duty should be excused.[37] Though imposing some alternative donation of time on them would be fair, the administrative effort is almost certainly not worthwhile. False claims of conscientious opposition to jury service will be rare, and persons called for jury service will not feel the system of selection is unfair because an insignificant number of conscientious objectors is excused or because an exemption for them provides an infrequently used opportunity for fraud.[38]

Drug Use—Paternalism

We have thus far looked at requirements that impose shared burdens. I now turn to paternalistic legislation, taking laws against drug use as representative. Of course, one cannot apply the conclusions reached here to other paternalistic laws without careful analysis of similarities and differences; but thinking about possible exemptions from drug laws does suggest problems whose scope is much broader.

When the state forbids use of a substance such as marijuana, should any class of potential users be afforded an exemption? We may have some initial difficulty conceiving who a conscientious objector would be in this case. No one is likely to believe that he is under an absolute duty to ingest a particular substance; after all, the substance might be unavailable. Someone might think he must use a substance if it is physically possible to do so; but that seems a strange position, barring some special religious significance to use. Defying a threat of death to perform a religious ceremony is comprehensible, but we cannot imagine someone would believe, despite a threat of death, that he has a moral duty to ingest a substance in a nonreligious setting.

Many people do think the government has no business barring use of marijuana and some of these think they have a moral right to use, but these opinions may be held by persons who never or rarely use marijuana or regard its use as no more satisfying or uplifting than a great many other activities. Perhaps a more promising class for an exemption would be persons who believe that marijuana use produces deep insights about ultimate truths; but just what sorts of insights would be reached, and how unique would marijuana use have to be regarded as a source of truth for a claimant to be exempted?

As long as the focus remains on individual reasons for personal use, the difficulties of categorization appear insurmountable, even in theory. When one asks how any such exemption would be administered, one realizes that attempted application of some amorphous standard to individual cases[39] would work serious injustice and would quickly undermine the efficacy of the general prohibition.[40] This latter result may not disturb those critical of the law's existence, but it will hardly commend itself to legislators persuaded that a broad prohibition is desirable.

Any feasible exemption would need to be cast in terms of specialized use. One such use is medical. For this use, objective requisites would suffice; a person whose physical condition qualified him would not also need to have a particular moral view about the necessity of use. Another specialized use is in the context of religious services. An exemption that reaches persons who use drugs in corporate religious services but does not cover either nonreligious group use or individual religious use can be defended. One argument for distinguishing religious from nonreligious use is that a person who thinks he needs a drug to maintain a connection with a transcendent being, or to understand ultimate reality, makes a claim to use that is of a different dimension from the claim of a person who seeks pleasure, personal adjustment, or even generally enhanced perception. Accompanying the basic claim that access to higher reality is simply a more compelling interest is a related point about the inappropriateness of government determination, even by indirection, of how people seek such reality. Of course, the state should generally be hesitant to cut people off from what they perceive to be sources of happiness and fulfillment, and occasionally it must prohibit extremely self-destructive acts that participants believe bear a close connection to higher reality. Still, the point remains that among paternalistic exercises the state should be particularly wary of limiting the search for a higher reality and the maintenance of perceived connections with that reality.

A second argument for excluding nonreligious use from an exemption concerns administrability, and this argument also supports the distinction between corporate religious use and individual religious use. Were it granted that some nonreligious persons had reasons for use as compelling as those engaged in religious use, separating use for pleasure from use for deep insight or some other compelling purpose would still be too difficult. An administrable exemption could not go beyond religious use. Further, given the impossibility of assessing individual claims that purely personal religious pursuit leads to marijuana use, exempted religious use must be corporate or at least closely tied to corporate religious practices.[41]

If the general desire to use a drug is widespread, and serious enforcement efforts support a legislative prohibition, claims based on corporate religious practices will have to be reviewed with some stringency, so that groups of drug users will not succeed by creating bogus religions to cover their use.[42] Once the genuineness of the religion and an individual user's bona fide membership in the religious community were established, no further inquiry into his particular convictions about the use of marijuana would be called for.

Conditions on Benefits—Saturday Employment and Refusals to Perform Abortions

Many acts that are not absolutely required may have to be performed if a person is to receive particular benefits. Since the person may forgo the benefits involved, these conditions do not pose an absolute conflict between duty and conscience; but the benefits are often important enough that their loss puts considerable strain on complying with conscience. If the benefits are provided by the government, the issue regarding accommodation concerns possible concessions to conscience by the government itself.[43] I will concentrate on this aspect, not discussing the more complex question of when the government should compel private persons and organizations to make accommodations in the conferral of benefits they control.[44]

The conceivable conflicts of condition and conscience are almost infinite. I first consider refusal to work on Saturday as representative of the tension between a claim of conscience and ordinary conditions of employment; then I turn to refusals to perform abortions, which might be a ground for withholding monetary support that would otherwise be provided or even for denying a medical license. What emerge as central to the question of possible accommodations are the dangers of unfairness or independant harm to others and the incentives to fraud.

Members of some Sabbatarian denominations believe that they should not work on Saturday, which God has ordained as a day of rest. The issue in a notable Supreme Court case, *Sherbert* v. *Verner*,[45] was whether a state that conditioned eligibility for unemployment compensation on availability for Saturday work could withhold that compensation from someone whose religious convictions forbade work on that day. Whether or not one endorses the Supreme Court's conclusion that the state's action was unconstitutional, the legislative question is relatively straightforward. Most people would strongly prefer working permanently to receiving unemployment benefits that may last only a temporary period,[46] so they have little incentive to feign an unwillingness to work on Saturday. Granting unemployment benefits to people like Mrs. Sherbert involves no hardship or unfairness to other individuals; and the slight drain on the public treasury is a small price to pay for the accommodation.

Whether unemployment benefits should be afforded people who refuse Saturday work for reasons of principle that do not amount to a conscientious opposition to such work is more troublesome. No one is likely to have a nonreligious belief that work on a particular day is absolutely wrong; but a person might have strong moral grounds, based, say, on family responsibilities, against working on Saturday. Also, Saturday employment may render attendance at religious services difficult or impossible for members of sects that worship on that day but do not regard work on that day as wrongful. Given the propensity of most people to want to work, the extension of benefits may be warranted. As far as members of Sabbatarian groups are concerned, trying to distinguish individuals or sects who believe Saturday work is wrong in principle from those who merely think Saturday worship is very important might prove complicated.

A still more difficult question is whether as employer the government should exempt from Saturday work persons who would otherwise work on that day but cannot do so out of conviction. Typically, freedom from Saturday work will be based on seniority; an exemption would give a preference to those who qualify over more senior nonqualifying employees.[47] In any event, if some persons are exempted, others will bear a heavier share of Saturday work, so a question of fairness is posed. Ideally, the "benefit" of freedom from Saturday work might be balanced by some corresponding detriment (lower wages, longer hours); but such precise refinements in working conditions may not be feasible. When a choice must be made between accommodation, with its accompanying unfairness, or placing a heavy burden on those whose conscience forbids Saturday work, my own judgment is that the interest in accommodation predominates; but the exemption in this setting should be limited to those who combine membership in a Sabbatarian group with a strong conviction against Saturday work.

The belief of a large number of doctors that abortion is tantamount to murder presents at least a potential conflict between conscience and benefit or privilege.[48] If a medical license were conditioned on a willingness to perform accepted medical techniques including abortions, a person unwilling to perform abortions might lose his license or fail to get one. Alternatively, a hospital whose owners were committed to that view might be deprived of funds otherwise available. I shall not try to work out resolutions for the variety of contexts in which such a conflict might arise. As a general principle, doctors should be free to decline to engage in treatment to which they are conscientiously opposed, as long as patients can get the treatment elsewhere and are aware of its availability. No inquiry into stated objections to abortions need be undertaken, since neither doctors nor hospitals have any apparent reason to make false claims that they find abortion morally unacceptable. The setting of conditions for medical licenses and grants of funds for medical facilities should accommodate conscientious conviction up to the point that it seriously compromises the capacity of patients to take advantage of accepted medical practice.

Conclusions About Legislative Choice

This brief survey of various contexts in which issues of conscientious objection may arise gives a fair indication of the complexity of the questions. It suggests that liberal societies should make greater efforts to accommodate conscience than have yet been achieved. It also suggests the general desirability of using self-selection between alternatives, rather than administration of eligibility requirements, when that course is feasible. In some areas, judgments about eligibility are unavoidable. What exactly the appropriate standards of eligibility are depends strongly on the nature of the activity from which the exemption is sought and the possibilities of fraud and other unfairness.

CONSCIENTIOUS OBJECTION, CONSTITUTIONAL RIGHTS, AND JUDICIAL INTERPRETATION

Moral and Constitutional Rights to Act or Refrain from Acting

Although the Supreme Court has indicated that the exemption from military service is a matter of legislative grace, certain exemptions from obligations or conditions have been bestowed upon conscientious objectors as constitutional rights. The Supreme Court has strongly hinted that an objector has a constitutional right to be free of jury service[49] and has held that a person with a religious conviction against Saturday employment cannot be declared ineligible for unemployment compensation because of an unwillingness to work on that day.[50] These cases exemplify instances in which what may be regarded as moral rights are given constitutional protection. In cases of this sort the constitutional right depends on the actual moral convictions of the actor or of some group with which he is associated. Though some constitutional rights of this sort have been based on a broad right of conscience derived from the free speech clause,[51] most have been grounded on the free exercise clause. When the asserted right is one that lends itself to possible fraud, the courts have usually required some connection to the corporate activities of a discrete religious group.[52]

Although the constitutional status of claimed moral rights to engage in or refrain from particular actions free of government restraint arises in only a limited domain,[53] the domain is by no means exhausted by claims of conscience. Often, claims about free expression, free exercise of religion, and so-called substantive privacy (e.g., abortion, sexual liberty) do not depend on the particular motives of actors.

Many such rights do not depend at all on an individual's beliefs and attitudes. Under present law, a woman who has been advised by a doctor has a constitutional right to have an abortion through the sixth month of pregnancy. Her own personal reasons for having an abortion and her convictions about abortion do not matter. She shares a right of action that applies to all pregnant women. Similarly, if the government attempts to confiscate a supposedly obscene book one is attempting to bring into the country, the quality of the book rather than one's attitudes about it are what matters.[54]

Some other constitutional rights depend on the beliefs and intentions of the actor. One aspect of the constitutional test of punishable advocacy of crime is whether or not the speaker's words are directed toward encouraging commission of the crime.[55] In theory at least, of two speakers uttering exactly the same words in like settings, one could be punishable because of his intent to encourage the criminal act while the other would be protected because he lacked that intent. Whether one who libeled a public figure is constitutionally protected depends on whether or not he was aware of the possible falsity of what he wrote.

In this section of the chapter, the main question I address is whether, when a court assesses a statute or common-law doctrine against a defendant's claim of constitutional right, its evaluation should depend partly on the nature and strength of the defendant's moral claim. That broad question arises in difficult cases involving claims of conscience, as well as in other situations when moral rights are asserted to have constitutional status. The question is the subject of an extensive literature,[56] and my primary effort here is to clarify its dimensions for those not already familiar with that literature. Although stating my own views, I do not attempt any systematic defense of them here. Nor do I attempt any critical assessment of existing constitutional decisions,[57] a task too far removed from the subjects of this book.

Constraints on Constitutional Interpretation

Like ordinary legislation, constitutional provisions protecting rights reflect the moral judgments of those who adopted them, in this case complex judgments that certain activities should be put beyond the range of control by the political branches of the government.[58] In constitutions, as in statutes, language may embody a compromise of competing moral claims, though nothing in our federal Constitution resembles the relatively precise accommodation of the criminal law rules governing use of force in self-defense. The fact that the Constitution itself represents moral evaluations does not, of course, establish that moral evaluation is also the task of those who must decide if statutes and their applications fall afoul of constitutional restraints.

Widespread agreement exists on the appropriateness of some other techniques of interpretation. The point is clearest for actions that the language of the Constitution, the intent of the Framers, and the decisions of earlier courts place squarely within the area of constitutional protection. For these actions, a modern court will rarely need to engage in any debatable moral evaluation. Usually it will apply the plain law, perhaps after determining that no overwhelming argument has been made contrary to the indications of these powerful sources.[59] Even for harder cases, judicial interpretation is not simple moral evaluation; the implications of the textual language, the Framers' intent, and the precedents count for something if they point in one direction or another. The questions, rather, are whether moral evaluation should count at all, and if so, what kinds of moral evaluation are proper.

The questions as they are usually put, and as I shall address them, concern an appropriate conception of the judicial role. I am thus putting aside the possibility that in particular cases judges should transcend the duties of their positions to achieve a morally just result. Whatever room may exist for judges to place moral results over the confines of their legal duties, that room is decidedly slight when they issue public interpretations of constitutional rights. Given their general scope, legally unwarranted interpretations are not justified by reaching desirable results in a single case.[60] Lower courts intentionally misinterpreting the law are likely to be frustrated by reversal; and higher courts must worry about erosion of support for the judiciary if they are perceived to be using their final power of decision in a lawless way.[61] Only in rare instances could judges defensibly exceed the legal limits of their interpretive roles.

Courts and Moral Evaluations

The central question is whether or not, in hard cases involving claims of constitutional rights to perform or avoid actions, courts should inquire if the claimants have a moral right to perform or avoid the acts, either direct deontological rights against government interference or more complex sorts of rights, based in part on which subjects can be trusted to shifting majorities. Answering the central question is complicated by the different ways in which it may be understood. Most constitutional provisions are cast at a high level of generality, and they must be applied to social conditions, such as radio and television and extensive public welfare, not envisioned by the Framers. Unless a modern court should limit its constitutional holdings to actual practices the Framers meant to forbid—a stultifying approach to interpretation that few endorse—courts must somehow apply the broad constitutional provisions to changing circumstances. One possibility is to ascertain what moral and social principles led the Framers to adopt the open-ended language that they did and to try to apply those priniciples faithfully to the different circumstances. Such an endeavor would involve a kind of applied moral analysis, but one whose basic premises were, in theory, drawn from an authoritative legal source. Of course, in practice, no judge is wholly capable of ascertaining and applying the moral perspectives of the Framers without relying to some degree on his or her own categories of moral appraisal and substantive judgments, but the effort at least would be to draw one's perspective of evaluation from the Framers. A second interpretive exercise is reasoning by analogy from clearly proscribed practices to practices whose status is in doubt. One asks, for example, whether electric shock is like the tortures that the Framers regarded as cruel and unusual. Inquiry by analogy need not involve moral evaluation, but if the central features of the Framers' evaluations of cruel punishment themselves involved moral judgments, inquiry by analogy might be hard to distinguish from a direct moral inquiry, one that starts with the premises that a particular punishment is immoral and asks if another punishment that resembles it in certain respects is also immoral. Although many observers doubt that attempts to apply the Framers' perspectives and to reason by analogy from clearly proscribed practices can allow a judge to escape present moral evaluations, judicial employment of these strategies is relatively uncontroversial.

The question that engenders serious disagreement is whether or not modern courts should make fresh moral evaluations. One argument in their favor is that they contribute to making the Constitution a document that can have relevance for succeeding generations. A contrary argument is that courts, usually not democratically selected and not politically responsible to the electorate, have no business altering the basic limits of the Constitution.

The import of the Framers' intent and constitutional language is itself a point of contention. One view is that the Framers invited constitutional developments in response to changing moral evaluations and that the open language of the Constitution authorizes these. Plainly the Framers did adopt broad language, and the sensitive among them realized that the Constitution might be understood to forbid particular practices they had not conceived. But any approval by them of future moral evaluations that differed from their own is more dubious.

Believing that the constitutional document needs to be accorded an evolutionary interpretation and that a suitably complex theory of liberal democracy can accord such power to judges, especially given the political checks that exist on their authority, I conclude that fresh moral evaluations are appropriate. Perhaps, as some have suggested, courts have a special role to play when constitutional claims involve inadequate participation in the political process and unfair representations;[62] but their authority to develop constitutional law on the basis of moral appraisals is not restricted to those cases.

What kind of fresh evaluation should judges be making? Do some parts of the Constitution call on judges to elucidate the correct moral understanding of the basic concepts; or should judges remain voices of the community, guided by the community's moral sense insofar as it can be discerned. Neither of these possibilities receives clear endorsement from the constitutional language, and each is overly simplistic.

The competing positions require synthesis in two important ways. A judge cannot be expected to disregard his or her strongly held moral convictions in cases of geniune doubt. A sensible approach to the role of judges concedes them some latitude to rely on their views of what is morally right in marginal cases. But such an approach also accords significant independent weight to community sentiment. Precisely what community sentiment counts can, of course, itself be a troublesome question. If one is interpreting a countermajoritarian guarantee, one cannot simply ask whether the community presently recognizes a right to engage in the behavior the legislature has prohibited. One must ask whether or not community practices over time and the rights that people assert on their own behalf imply that the prohibited behavior should be protected.

The second aspect of synthesis looks at different aspects of moral judgment. In some cases, the problem is essentially to derive by rational means conclusions about a particular problem from broadly accepted and deeply held moral premises. If the community has yet to reach the conclusions that its moral premises clearly imply, then the judge should perform the exercise of derivation as rationality dictates, not as the illogical or confused community sentiments would have it.[63] When the issue is what starting premise to adopt, however, and the premise is not easily susceptible to rational judgment one way or the other, the weight of the community's judgment should be more substantial.

How much weight should fresh moral evaluations carry? Some constitutional standards such as the cruel and unusual punishment clause themselves give more prominence to these evaluations than do others such as the jury trial guarantee. Moreover, when the legal arguments in a narrower sense are themselves inconclusive or tend to cancel each other out, then the moral evaluation will be more important. Even when the issue involves a claim of moral right and the legal materials are inconclusive, we should not suppose that the court's evaluation will necessarily be a straightforward one about moral rights in any direct sense. A judge might, for example, conclude that in a liberal democracy, individuals have no moral right to engage in revolutionary speech but still treat such speech as a constitutional right because doing so will encourage a stable polity and social progress. Thus, even when courts properly engage in fresh evaluations, those may include much more than weighing of claims of moral right in any narrow sense.

This summary of some complex issues about constitutional claims of conscience and other claims of constitutional right produces the following general conclusion. In deciding such constitutional questions, courts may properly engage in evaluations of claims of moral right, relying both on community sentiments to some degree and on their own attempt to resolve moral dilemmas. The weight of such evaluations depends very much on the precise legal issue.

NOTES

1. H. Thoreau, Resistance to Civil Government, in E. Peabody, ed., Aesthetic Papers 189, 211 (1849).

2. The same conclusion applies in relation to those who think that any military conscription constitutes a denial of individual rights.

3. Someone who thought instead that military conscription is indefensible might well wish to water down its force as far as possible.

4. The category of conscientious objectors largely conforms with the category of those who have a strong moral conviction that a required act is morally wrong and that the government should not require it; but I should mention some clarifications or qualifications. First, some objectors in conscience form their convictions on the basis of what they take as God's revealed word, and these convictions, such as those against taking blood transfusions, need not be related to moral obligations toward others. By the criteria suggested in Chapter 2, these would not be "moral" convictions. Second, some people may think their special status makes their participation in war wrong without holding a view that participating in war is wrong for everyone. Third, some people may not necessarily suppose it is wrong for the government to order them to perform a certain act, though they do think it would be wrong for them to comply.

5. Some sorts of moral beliefs, e.g., in favor of killing members of a particular race or religion, are so unacceptable that blame is not withheld from those who act on these beliefs.

6. This sentence skirts the complicated question of whether or not norms cast in terms of equality are meaningful. My own views on that subject are developed in Greenawalt, How Empty is the Idea of Equality? 83 Colum. L. Rev. 1167 (1983).

7. Typically, someone must decide if an applicant is sincere and if his sincere belief amounts to a conscientious objection. I do not pause here over possible surrogates for these inquiries, such as whether a claimant belongs to a sect most of whose members have sincere beliefs that qualify.

8. This anomaly could be avoided by acknowledging that the state could remove and detain people in these circumstances whom it could not lawfully punish.

9. I am not addressing the related issue of whether some actions that would otherwise be trespassory should be permitted (by statute or constitutional interpretation) because they are a form of political expression. Such permis-

sions would not turn on whether politically expressive acts were grounded in conscience.

10. See Harlan Fiske Stone, The Conscientious Objector, 21 Colum. Univ. Q. 253, 268 (1919); Michael Walzer, Obligations: Essays on Disobedience, War, and Citizenship 135–36 (1970). Although they do not enlist private persons in the performance of official tasks in the manner of jury duty and military service, duties of care toward children do require parents to perform certain acts.

11. In some instances, an element of increased danger—say in driving a motorcycle without a helmet—will be recognized but the benefits of the act, an increased feeling of freedom, will be thought to outweigh the danger.

12. Of course, the grant of benefits often represents an overall drain on public resources. If the objection is to establishing one's competence to perform a licensed act (say by taking a driving test), the grant of a license to an objector might create a danger to others.

13. See the plurality opinion in *Welsh* v. *United States*, 398 U.S. 333 (1970). On the general problem of defining religion for legal purposes, see Greenawalt, The Constitutional Concept of Religion, 72 Calif. L. Rev. 753 (1984).

14. A written constitution might, of course, give religious claims some special status; at least in some respects, the Constitution of the United States does so.

15. The rules regarding conscientious objection to military service, 50 U.S.C. App. 456(j) (1977), are incorporated into the Military Selective Service Act, ch. 625, 62 Stat. 604 (1948) (codified as amended at 50 U.S.C. app. 451 73 (1977). Presidential authority to induct men into active military service expired in 1973, 50 U.S.C. app. 471(a) (1977), but may be renewed by an act of Congress.

16. In the United States, the exemption has included persons who believe they should never fight in a war even if they think it is all right for others to fight. Such persons are not strictly pacifists. What exactly makes a person a pacifist or opposed to participating in any war is itself a troublesome issue when either concept is applied to a person who thinks some historical wars may have been justified but believes that, given modern weaponry, no war or no war fought by this country can now be justified.

17. On the basis of the Supreme Court's decisions under the religion clauses, such a limitation would almost certainly be unconstitutional.

18. *United States* v. *Seeger*, 380 U.S. 163 (1965); *Welsh* v. *United States*, 398 U.S. 333 (1970). In *Welsh*, only four of eight justices found the claimant eligible under the statute; Justice Harlan thought him excluded by the statute but considered that exclusion to be unconstitutional. 398 U.S. at 344.

19. See the dissenting opinion of J. White, in *Welsh* v. *United States*, 398 U.S. at 367. Indeed, the overruling of *Welsh* is a possibility, in which event continuance of the old statutory standard would limit the exemption to persons religious in a sense narrower than that adopted by the plurality

opinion in that case. After *Seeger*, Congress had amended the Selective Service Act to drop the requirement of belief in a Supreme Being. Pub. L. No. 90–40 § 1 (5), 81 Stat. 100–2, 104 (1967) (codified as amended at 50 U.S.C. app. 456(j) [1977]).

20. Reviewing such cases was part of my job as deputy solicitor general in 1971–1972.

21. Very likely, in this respect, religious affiliation is the most important element. Even if draft boards and others had more *trouble* determining the sincerity of nonreligious objectors, that does not establish that sincerity was really more difficult to determine. Conceivably, some persons who are insincere fool administrators by feigning religious belief and establishing religious affiliation.

22. Choper, Defining "Religion" in the First Amendment, 1982 U. Ill. L. Rev. 579.

23. Id. at 598. Choper's comments are directed to how religion should be defined for constitutional purposes, but the basic argument he puts forward is also relevant for legislative choice. My reasons for rejecting Choper's position as the basis for a constitutional definition of religion are elaborated in Greenawalt, note 13 supra, at 802–06 (1984).

24. A frequent strand of this position has, however, been that a good life is *evidence* of election. A Calvinist who took this view might find commission of a grave wrong particularly painful because it constitutes evidence of his nonelection.

25. In 1948, Congress restricted the exemption to those who believed in a "Supreme Being." Section 6(j) of the Military Selective Service Act of 1948, c. 625, 62 Stat. 613. The effect of the restriction was largely gutted by *United States* v. *Seeger*, 380 U.S. 163 (1965), and the restriction was removed from the act two years later. See supra note 19.

26. *Gillette* v. *United States*, 401 U.S. 437, 454–56 (1970).

27. The arguments on both sides are developed at greater length in Greenawalt, All or Nothing At All: The Defeat of Selective Conscientious Objection, 1971 Supreme Court Rev. 31, 47–66. Were an exemption to be granted to selective objectors, it need go no further than the scope of the objection: a person who in conscience could serve outside the theater of the war to which he objects should not be excused altogether from military service (except on possible grounds of administrative convenience).

An exemption for selective objectors might conceivably be limited to those whose convictions are rooted in some traditional religious belief. The aims would be to enhance accurate identification and temper resentment in those who serve in unpopular wars from which persons not so different from themselves are being exempted. However, such a limitation would raise many of the objections already discussed in connection with pacifists. Further, since many religious persons adduce essentially the same reasons for concluding that a war is immoral as do many nonreligious persons, tricky questions about the required connection between one's religious beliefs and one's opposition to a particular war would be raised. Finally, if nonreligious pacifists were exempted, restricting eligible selective objectors to religious believers would be both odd and confusing.

28. Similarly, anyone should be able to choose noncombatant service in the military over combatant service by accepting somewhat less favorable conditions of work.

29. Although I do not develop the point in this essay, what I say about fairness points to the injustice of limiting conscription to males.

30. Another conceivable concern might be class differentiations between those who chose military service and those who chose alternative service. Very likely, a high percentage of those choosing alternative service would come from the middle and upper classes. Still, most young persons from those classes would choose military service; and the resulting composition of the military would be much less skewed toward poorer people than the volunteer army is.

31. 50 U.S.C. app. § 453 (1977).

32. In phrasing the sentence in text in this way, I do not mean to indicate that the so called "burden of persuasion" as to this issue would necessarily be on the defendant, though such a shift in the ordinary burden of persuasion for criminal cases might be justified on the grounds that the government will be hard put to disprove conscientious motivation once a defendant has made any claim to it.

33. The arguments in favor of granting some exemptions are developed in Comment, The World Peace Tax Fund Act: Conscientious Objection for Taxpayers, 74 Nw. U. L. Rev. 76 (1979). Though it has been suggested that nonpayment of taxes is a particularly revolutionary form of civil disobedience (see H. Bedau, ed., Civil Disobedience 22 [1969]), refusal to pay taxes is not especially dangerous or radical in principle. See B. Zwiebach, Civility and Disobedience 188–90 (1975).

34. Of course, prosecutions of tax violators in all classes is so highly selective, one cannot be confident that the percentage of conscientious refusers prosecuted is actually less than the percentage of evaders prosecuted.

35. I do not think accommodation is feasible for sales and similar taxes.

36. See Comment, note 33 supra.

37. See *In re Jenison*, 267 Minn. 136, 120 N.W. 2d 515 (1963), on remand from 375 U.S. 14 (1963); *United States* v. *Hillyard*, 52 F. Supp. 612 (E.D. Wash. 1943). Both cases upheld a constitutional claim to refuse to serve.

38. A sense of unfairness is much more likely to arise because of broader categories of excuses from jury service or because of feelings that one's time is being wantonly wasted.

39. The claim for an exemption might be made in the form of an application for a license to use or as a defense to criminal prosecution.

40. In passing on constitutional claims to use drugs, courts have been sensitive to the problems that exceptions would undermine the effectiveness of prohibitions. See, e.g., *Leary* v. *United States*, 383 F.2d 851, 859–62 (5th Cir.

1967), reversed on other grounds, 395 U.S. 6 (1969); *United States* v. *Middleton*, 690 F. 2d 820 (11th Cir. 1982).

41. Cases granting constitutional exemptions from prohibitions have involved corporate religious practice. *People* v. *Woody*, 61 Cal. 2d 716, 394 P.2d 813, 40 Cal. Rptr. 69 (1964); *In re Grady*, 61 Cal.2d 887, 394 P.2d 728 (1964), 39 Cal. Rptr. 912 (1964); *State* v. *Whittingham*, 14 Ariz. App. 27, 504 P.2d 950 (1973), cert. denied, 417 U.S. 946 (1974). Use might be individual but closely tied to corporate practice if a tenet of a religious group were that individual use on some occasions was required or recommended.

42. Enforcement of marijuana laws is now so relaxed in most jurisdictions that people would probably not take the trouble to create bogus religions to exempt their use of that drug.

43. In a federal system, of course, one question is whether or not the federal government should mandate concessions by state governments.

44. An example of such legislation is the Title VII requirement that employers make reasonable accommodation to the religious requirements of employees, involved in *T.W.A.* v. *Hardison*, 432 U.S. 63 (1977). See also *Estate of Thornton* v. *Caldor, Inc.*, 105 S. Ct. 2914 (1985).

45. 374 U.S. 398 (1963).

46. Regular unemployment benefits usually run from thirteen to twenty-six weeks. See, e.g., N.C. Gen. Stat. § 96–12(d) (1981). During the recessions of the 1970s and 1980s, recipients who have exhausted their eligibility for regular state unemployment benefits have been able to receive extended benefits for additional periods under supplementary federal funding. But these additional benefits have been contingent on ad hoc congressional appropriations and the existence of a relatively high unemployment rate, computed on the basis of the employment rate among employees covered by unemployment insurance programs in the first place. See, e.g., N.C. Gen. Stat. B 96–12(e) (1981)

47. I am assuming the needs of the government as employer are not thwarted by a person's unavailability for Saturday work.

48. As far as I am aware, no such conflict has yet arisen. The Ninth Circuit has ruled, in accordance with existing legislation, that the failure of a Catholic hospital to perform sterilizations is not grounds for denial of federal funding. *Chrisman* v. *Sisters of St. Joseph of Peace*, 506 F.2d 308 (9th Cir. 1974).

49. *In re Jenison*, 375 U.S. 14 (1963), reversed on remand, 267 Minn. 136, 120 N.W. 2d 515 (1963).

50. *Sherbert* v. *Verner*, 374 U.S. 398 (1963).

51. See *West Virginia State Board of Education* v. *Barnette*; 319 U.S. 624 (1943); *Wooley* v. *Maynard*, 430 U.S. 705 (1977).

52. *Wisconsin* v. *Yoder*, 406 U.S. 205 (1972); *People* v. *Woody*, 61 Cal.2d 716, 394 P.2d 813, 40 Cal. Rptr. 69 (1964).

53. Much of the Constitution allocates the powers of government and has little to do with moral claims in any ordinary sense. Other provisions, like the Fourth Amendment's ban on unreasonable searches and the Eighth Amend-

ment's ban on cruel and unusual punishment have moral analogs and confer rights on private persons; but the rights are to be free of particular invasions rather than to perform actions. The right to have fair notice of prohibited behavior indirectly gives a right to engage in action not presently forbidden, but involves no primary right to perform or avoid particular sorts of actions. Various rights of equality also do not create such primary rights but demand forms of evenhandedness.

The question of exactly which constitutional rights fit into the category of protected activities is somewhat arguable. The rule against state impairment of the obligation of contracts certainly protects the activity of enforcing a contract already made and likely gives some protection to the whole enterprise of contract making. Similarly, rules limiting government interference with property can be viewed as protecting the activities of acquisition, use, and disposal.

54. I put aside people, such as social science researchers, that may have some special privilege to import obscene books.

55. See, generally, Greenawalt, Speech and Crime, 1980 Amer. Bar Found. R. J. 647.

56. See, e.g., R. Berger, Government by Judiciary (1977); J. Ely, Democracy and Distrust (1980); M. Perry, The Constitution, The Courts, and Human Rights (1982); D. Richards, The Moral Criticism of Law (1977); Bork, Neutral Priniciples and Some First Amendment Problems, 47 Ind. L.J. 1 (1971); Dworkin, The Forum of Prinicple, 56 N.Y.U. L. Rev. 469 (1981); Grey, Do We Have an Unwritten Constitution, 27 Stan. L. Rev. 703 (1975); Greenawalt, The Enduring Significance of Neutral Principles, 78 Colum. L. Rev. 982 (1978).

57. Such assessments are attempted in my articles cited in notes 27 and 55 and, to a more limited extent, in the article cited in note 13.

58. As originally adopted, the Bill of Rights in the U.S. Constitution mainly limited federal government; but most states had similar constitutional provisions, and the major federal restrictions are now considered applicable against the states.

59. This exercise may involve the modest moral evaluation included in the decision that existing protection is not itself morally abhorrent.

60. This point has less force if the judges are able to write an opinion that is so narrow it has no clear implications for other cases.

61. These remarks presuppose that the institutions of law do impose constraints even on courts that are not subject to higher review. They also presuppose the more difficult judgment that these constraints are better viewed as legal ones than as role constraints of a more general kind that might apply to choices within a legally permitted range.

62. Ely, supra note 56.

63. Admittedly the matter is more complicated because the failure to draw a certain conclusion may sometimes cast doubt on whether or not members of the community really subscribe to the broader premise to which they give lip service.

15

Techniques of Amelioration in the Criminal Process: Nonprosecution, Nullification, Sentencing, and Pardon

The last two chapters have indicated how the law itself may exonerate some people who would violate particular legal rules out of moral conviction. Most people who violate such rules, however, do not have any legal defense. If their cases went to trial, the facts were accurately found, and the law was correctly applied, they would be found guilty. This chapter suggests how legal officials may ameliorate the force of the law for these cases.

NONPROSECUTION

This first section deals with the power of certain officials to decline to move cases forward. Among cases in which guilt is clear but no conviction is ever obtained, the vast majority are ones in which prosecutors or police have decided against going forward.

Prosecutorial Decisions Not to Proceed

Decisions by prosecutors not to press charges are not formally conclusive—later criminal proceedings may still be brought—but, for practical purposes, such decisions are usually final. Prosecuting agencies do not process all cases in which there is probable cause of someone's guilt or even all cases in which conviction would be highly likely.[1]

Prosecutors in common-law countries[2], including the United States, have legal authority not to proceed against all offenders. Statutes typically do not demand that they prosecute every case, and the courts have consistently refused to direct that prosecutors take action against possible offenders some citizens want prosecuted.[3] In contrast with the case in England, where prosecution by private citizens remains permissible, U.S. jurisdictions give public officials exclusive power to bring criminal actions; and the exercise of prosecutorial discretion in favor of leniency effectively precludes invocation of the criminal process and imposition of criminal penalties.

For many minor crimes, no heavy presumption exists in favor of prosecution; for these, one may speak of prosecutors as possessing an implicit delegated discretion to decide whether to go forward. A presumption may exist in favor or enforcement for more serious offenses, but even for them a failure to proceed cannot be described as a violation of any legal duty.

Moral Claims and Reasons Not to Prosecute

Prosecutors have many reasons for declining to proceed against offenders for the crimes they have actually committed: a prosecutor may think evidence insufficient for a conviction, he may trade immunity for testimony against other offenders, or he may reduce charges in return for a guilty plea. Because our interest is in situations in which actors have some moral claim to disobey the law, our concern here is limited to failures to prosecute (or to prosecute for crimes as serious as those actually committed) based, at least in part, on judgments about the gravity of offenses or the character of actors.

Faced with a vast array of criminal statutes and given limited resources by the legislature, prosecutors are unable to proceed against every petty offense, but their discretion goes well beyond using legislative categorizations to assign priority to cases. A legislature's classifications must necessarily be crude, and within any class of offense, some acts will be less serious than others. The taking of a single hotel towel is petty larceny, for example, but ordinarily it hardly warrants prosecution. Quite apart from resource problems, some misbehavior is so trivial that the formal condemnation of a criminal conviction is inappropriate, and prosecutors may assume that legislators would take the same view.

Behavior can be, on balance, less serious than ordinary instances of the offense for reasons other than the triviality of the harm. Leniency may be warranted because an actor is a less serious offender than most of those who commit crimes of similar gravity; his participation may be marginal (e.g., lending an automobile); he may be a passive, unenthusiastic follower of a more dominant personality; or his mental condition may render him less blameworthy than the ordinary offender. In other circumstances of more interest for us, a fully responsible actor may possess motivations and beliefs about the legality and morality of his conduct that suggest his wrongdoing is less than that of most offenders. In this sense, driving seventy miles per hour is a less serious wrong, or not a wrong at all, if the aim is to get an injured passenger to the hospital.

A prosecutor properly decides not to proceed when he thinks that an act served the overall good of avoiding evils and would qualify as permitted under the general justification defense;[4] but he may also decline to go forward when he thinks the actor had substantial reasons for what he did but not reasons that provide a full justification. Because of the reasons favoring the act, it would fall among "less serious" instances of the offense.

Illustration 15-1:

In two cases of simple, unprovoked assault, the victims have suffered bruises but not serious wounds or broken limbs. In the first, Adrian tried to intimidate a victim for personal advantage; in the second, Bruce attacked the victim because he had intercourse with Bruce's fifteen-year-old sister. Although Bruce understands that the victim's having had intercourse with a minor is not a legal justification for an assault, he considers it ample moral justification.

The prosecutor may reasonably decide not to prosecute Bruce though he prosecutes Adrian, because of the social sense that moderate physical force in retaliation for crimes committed against family members is less wrongful than most assaults.

Something akin to the conscientious objector principle may also be operative; the actor's moral perspectives may count even if they are unorthodox. Suppose that Bruce's victim has had consensual intercourse with Bruce's twenty-five-year-old sister, and Bruce believes that the chasteness of single women should be enforced by male relatives. If the marriage of his only sister sharply reduces the danger of future attacks by Bruce and general deterrence is not a concern,[5] a prosecutor might decline to proceed on the ground that Bruce's motives and moral beliefs, though gravely at odds with those of most of society, render him less blameworthy and less dangerous than other offenders.

As the analysis thus far implies, beliefs about moral rights or moral duties may be relevant to leniency. When an actor's genuine belief that he had a moral right to do what he did does not indicate that future illegal acts are likely,[6] or reflect a general insensitivity to the interests of others, then the belief is one reason for a prosecutor not to go forward. Also relevant will be the actor's perspective about the legality of his acts. If the actor reasonably thinks that what he did was legal, or reasonably thinks its legality was geniunely uncertain, his blame and likely propensity to commit future illegal acts may be less than those of most offenders.[7] Although prosecutorial leniency may be inappropriate when the actor has selfishly done something undeniably antisocial in the mistaken hope that it will prove not to be legally proscribed, a prosecutor does have reason not to proceed against an actor who is firmly convinced that what he did is legal or who has a morally grounded reason, such as establishing the limits of a law he thinks is unjust, for performing an act he thinks may or may not be within his legal rights.[8]

An account of reasons for prosecutorial leniency would be incomplete if it did not recognize that some of the same factors favoring nonprosecution also constitute reasons for going forward. Because prosecution is a major means of establishing the statutory and constitutional limits of criminal law, prosecution of some of those who may have acted on the borderlines of legality is needed to clarify the law.[9] Further, the deliberate and open quality of much law violation engaged in by protestors not only demonstrates their moral convictions but also represents a settled defiance of the authority of law and indicates the likelihood of future violations. Persons in authority may quietly let minor breaches of rules pass, but when the violations are announced in advance and take place in their presence, their failure to act may undercut claims that the rules, and the persons who administer them, deserve respect. One thinks, for example, of parental disciplinary rules, athletic training rules, and employer regulations concerning work that are breached after prior announcement in front of the authority who set the rules. It is not easy to let such violations slide. In the realm of public affairs, open breaches of law are attended by much greater publicity than most surreptitious violations, and legal authorities must concern themselves with the possibility that law-abiding citizens will feel distressed, insecure, and perhaps put upon if no action is taken, although in some instances of mass demonstrations, dispersement or arrests may appear to be a sufficient response even if prosecution does not follow. Another reason to proceed is closely related to the last. Not all kinds of conscientious law violation presage future breaches, but many acts of open defiance, such as trespass on nuclear facilities, strongly suggest that similar acts may be forthcoming, since the actor's public aims are rarely achieved by one instance of law violation. Discouragement of further violations is an important reason for prosecution and punishment.

I have thus far argued that the overall harmfulness of behavior and an actor's sincere belief in moral justification, factors crucial for standards of general justification and conscientious objection, are also important ingredients in the exercise of prosecutorial discretion; that claims of moral right and opinions about legality that receive little recognition in the substantive law may properly influence decisions by prosecutors; and that some aspects of acts supporting lenience also support prosecution.

Perspectives for Judgments

More subtle questions arise over the vantage point prosecutors should take in assessing the critieria just discussed to decide whether or not to go forward. Should the prosecutor view himself or herself as a deputy of the legislature, an interpreter of the law, an organ of community sentiment, or an independent agent working to rationalize the law and make its application more just? The answer is that he should be a mixture of all these and that simpler versions of his responsibilities are inadequate.

When we talk about a prosecutor's duty in this context, we are not, in the main, concerned with his legal duty, since the law leaves him free to perform in a variety of ways. Properly conceived, however, his role may still require reference to values contained in the law.

Most narrowly, the prosecutor might be guided by the legislature's views reflected in applicable criminal statutes. For example, the prosecutor would treat ordinary instances of consenting acts between homosexuals as seriously as intentional assault if these crimes have been classified as equally serious in the penal code. Given the irrationality that has characterized grading in American jurisdictions, and the failure to repeal, or reduce the severity of, many crimes when community mores have shifted radically, the idea that prosecutors should not look beyond the grade fixed by the legislature cannot be seriously urged.

A somewhat more plausible view is that the prosecutor should be guided by how the legislature would presently act. This approach, however, also has defects. How to decide what a majority of persons would do about questions they have not faced would be difficult, and in any event, the prosecutor should not regard himself as a transmitter of irrationalities that present legislators might accept but have not yet written into law. There is more to executive judgment than trying to mirror the elusive sentiments of the legislature. Room exists for creative attempts at rational administration, even when the present majority of the legislature might not accept all the elements of that administration if they had the time and energy to focus on them as carefully as the executive.

The "whole law" would no doubt properly be one source of such a rational administration. Thus, the prosecutor might decide that, given constitutional values of liberty, the law of torts, and the interests that statutes protect in other contexts, the "law as a whole" does not regard consenting homosexual acts as being as grave as assault, even if the two are classified as equal in the jurisdiction's criminal code. Even this perspective, however, should not be regarded as completely constraining. If a substantial shift has taken place in community morality about sexual relations among consenting adults, prosecutorial policy may properly be responsive to that shift, though the shift is not yet fully reflected in the various branches of the law.

A prosecutor also rightly makes some judgments about needs of criminal law enforcement that are neither implicit in the law nor yet generally accepted by the community. Within a limited range, he may be guided by what he believes to be right principles of enforcement. Not only is the prosecutor less constrained by legal standards than judges who apply the law, he is also politically more responsible, subject to dismissal or being voted out of office. Moreover, like most administrative officials, prosecutors will generally do a better job, and better people will be attracted to the job of prosecutor, if they conceive of their role as involving some scope for individual judgment about desirable policy rather than as transmitting with as accurately as possible the uncertain sentiments of the legislature or the community.

Although the prosecutor's role leaves some scope for individual judgment, the prosecutor does not have the same range of authority as the legislature to decide what measures comport with justice and social welfare. This point can be illustrated by referring to a position that might be taken to imply he does have such authority for at least one situation—when legislation violates the moral rights of citizens. I have already discussed Ronald Dworkin's view that, if the government adopts a law that violates a moral right, it "does a further wrong to enforce that law."[10] I have suggested some reasons why enforcement of a rights-violating rule might be the right thing for the government to do; but here I want to assume that the government, taken as a whole, should not enforce a particular rights-violating law.

This conclusion is crucially incomplete as a guide to action—indeed, has little practical significance—until the problem of allocation of roles, including that of the prosecutor, is addressed. At a minimum, the notion of "further wrong" suggests that the legislature, if it comes to see the error of its ways and repeals its prohibition, should exempt from punishment previous violators not yet prosecuted; this is, in fact, the usual prinicple of interpretation when criminal prohibitions are repealed. The legislature should also free all violators then being punished, which is not the usual practice. Because legislatures rarely reach focused judgments that they have previously violated rights, the implications of a principle of "further wrong" will not often be carried out in the setting of legislative repeal.

Once we depart the relatively solid ground of legislative reconsideration, the idea that government enforcement is an additional wrong is much less clear in its practical import. If the claim is that each executive official should decide whether or not a statute violates moral rights, and that each should refuse to carry out his enforcement functions whenever he makes that judgment, then the claim is wrong. Although I focus here on the prosecutor, the point has wider application.

Illustration 15-2:
The state legislature has recently deliberated about the problem of abortion. Conforming to Supreme Court interpretations of constitutional requirements, it has recognized the right of women to have abortions with the consent of their doctors through the sixth month of pregnancy, but it has decisively taken the view that in the absense of strong health reasons, termination of a viable fetus is a very serious wrong, punishable by up to twenty years in jail. A woman who enters the hospital at the beginning of her labor tells her doctor she has decided she does not want the baby and asks the doctor to abort the fetus in a

manner that will cause its death. The doctor does so, and outraged members of the hospital staff present evidence of this crime to the prosecutor. The prosecutor is firmly convinced that the fetus has no moral rights until actual birth, that no moral wrong was done in this case, and that following the law would deny women their moral rights.[11] The prosecutor also recognizes, however, that his is a decidedly minority sentiment, at odds not only with the views of the vast majority of the population but also with the recently considered and strongly expressed views of the legislature.

In these circumstances, the prosecutor's political duty is to prosecute. However broad the appropriate range for individual judgment, he is, first and foremost, a representative of society at large and of the legislature, which is society's formal voice.

Fallible as they are, legislatures and courts are more appropriate organs to assess claims of moral right than prosecutors. Quite apart from comparative ability to evaluate claims of moral right, legislatures in our system have the political authority to violate moral rights if they do not violate the Constitution. The prosecutor's oath of office implies an obligation to accept the underlying distribution of political power and basic judgments of superior legal authorities, so a political duty that goes beyond consequentialist calculation is involved when he refuses to enforce a law against violations the legislature regards as grave.

Institutional Development of Standards for Cases

Only radical alterations in our system of criminal justice could eliminate prosecutorial discretion; and serious proposals for reform have concentrated on limiting and channeling that discretion.[12] Policy about the kinds of cases I have discussed, as well as other bases for prosecutorial lenience, is best set by higher authorities in the prosecutor's office, not by individual staff members. The higher authorities carry the political responsibility that makes reliance on their individual judgments appropriate, and without central direction, consistency is impossible. Given the complex ways in which claims of moral justification, moral right, and conscience can bear on decisions whether or not to prosecute, however, one cannot reasonably expect highly specific standards that will easily dispose of particular cases.

Affording potential defendants some formal right to argue that they should not be prosecuted would probably be inappropriate. The standards of decision and relevant facts would often be too intractable, and such a procedure would involve a quasi-limitation on the apparent coverage of the substantive law that would undermine some of the law's symbolic offices.

The wisdom of publicizing whatever open-ended standards prosecutors are able to evolve is also doubtful, mainly because publication would also seem to cut back on the reach of the law. Notifying the public in a general way of the obvious fact that the wrongfulness of behavior and the character of the actor may count would do no harm; but publicizing the flexible criteria used to make judgments about prosecution within classes of cases is probably not a good idea. When a definite decision has been made against any prosecution of some clear category of cases,[13] such as private use of marijuana, that information might be made available. Widespread knowledge of such a decision may appear to restrict the substantive law; but concerned people are likely to realize anyway that enforcement is not occurring.

Police Discretion Not to Enforce

When a police officer sees someone violate the law, or has substantial evidence of a violation, he or she may make an arrest.[14] In many circumstances if the officer on the scene does not make an arrest, the chances of any future enforcement are nil, though the officer's inaction has no formal significance for the suspect.

Police discretion is somewhat more controversial than prosecutorial discretion.[15] Many states have "full enforcement" laws that require an arrest for any offense committed in an officer's presence; and if these laws are read literally, many police decisions not to arrest would themselves be illegal. Police forces are not capable of full enforcement, however, and legislators are aware of this. Yet they maintain laws (e.g., in many jurisdictions, against all private use of marijuana and jaywalking) that are blatantly unenforced, and they decline to authorize resources with which full enforcement could be approximated. Perhaps because prosecutors *can* prosecute without initiatives by the police and because private persons can appeal directly to prosecutors, court cases on police discretion are less dispositive than those on prosecutorial authority, but no one would expect the courts to enforce a duty of full enforcement. Thus, despite statutes that seem to indicate the contrary, the police may be viewed as having legal authority not to arrest some violators. The statutes should nonetheless be taken as reflecting uneasiness with conferring too broad a discretion on the police. Police are not hired to decide what crimes are more serious than others, and they must usually act on the spur of the moment; their warrant to sift among the moral claims of various violators is much weaker than that of prosecutors.

At a minimum, police officers are permitted to engage in selective nonenforcement for social order reasons, not spending their time and energy on trivial violations that would divert them from more important responsibilities,[16] and they should have some scope in weighing the importance of obvious aspects of the particular factual context, including moral claims the actor explicitly or implicitly makes. If it is granted that police should arrest for some assaults but not others, it will make a difference if Al, who has punched Bill, says without contradiction, "Bill just beat up my younger brother." Even when resource allocation is not at issue, denying the police any flexibility would be harsh. They should, for example, be able to let go with a warning traffic violators who have a credible and appealing story that falls short of a general justification defense. The police should nevertheless not take upon themselves the responsibility of resolving debatable and troublesome moral questions that might affect prosecution; those should be left to the prosecutors.[17]

If police policy is to be set about crimes for which arrests will not be made, that policy should be made, insofar as possible, in the higher levels of police departments.

Pardon and Amnesty Issued Prior to Prosecution

The executive may issue pardons to individual offenders, as Gerald Ford did for Richard Nixon, or to classes of offenders, such as draft law violators, before any prosecutorial steps are taken or prior to trial. These actions represent determinations not to proceed that are final. Decisions about who will receive pardon or amnesty are essentially unlimited by law, constrained only by possible allocations of authority between executive and legislature and by a bar against using impermissible criteria, such as religion or race, to define the group benefited. Often, pardon or amnesty is granted because those benefiting are regarded as less dangerous or culpable than the legislatively determined severity of their offenses might indicate, and the same considerations that bear on prosecutorial decisions to be lenient are relevant here.

The major difference is that those deciding on amnesty and pardon owe less deference to any original legislative decision about the magnitude of a crime. This point is most obvious when the legislature grants amnesty. Values of continuity may caution some respect for existing law and the continued operation of presently imposed punishments, but if the present legislature determines that an original legislative judgment was misconceived or that grounds of protest warranted illegal action, no political loyalty to a superior prevents it from acting on that judgment by forgiving the offenders. Politically responsible legislators are also much better suited to decide that earlier political decisions, such as to fight in Vietnam, were actually misconceived or are now generally understood to have been misconceived, than are judges or prosecutors. Moreover, legislators may appropriately give more weight to contemporary political factors, such as the subsidence of resentment toward draft violators or the need to heal bitter divisions that termination of the conflict may have brought.

Similar conclusions apply to executive pardon, though with somewhat diminished force. Prosecutorial discretion is, within our system, a necessary consequence of the authority to execute the laws, but the pardoning power has separate historical grounding and independent specification in federal and state constitutions. In the exercise of that power, the executive has greater latitude than a prosecutor to deviate from legislative judgment and to take account of relevant political factors. I say "greater latitude," because I think a degree of deference is still owed to the decisions of the coordinate branch. Thus, even a president or governor would need very powerful reasons simply to pardon everyone who committed a crime that he thought should not be on the books.

Grand Jury Refusals to Indict

In jurisdictions retaining the grand jury, the first formal stage of some criminal cases is an indictment by that body. In other cases, indictment follows arrest and a preliminary judicial determination of likely guilt. If no grand jury is willing to indict, prosecution may not go forward. The refusal of one grand jury to indict is not finally dispositive, but typically prosecutors are not allowed to put the same case before another grand jury unless they have new evidence or a persuasive argument that the first body was biased.

The formal function of the grand jury is to consider evidence put forward by the prosecution and determine whether it sufficiently establishes the likelihood of guilt to warrant a trial. The grand jury, however, has the power to refuse to return an indictment despite substantial evidence of guilt. Many observers think that is precisely what happened in the case of Bernhard Goetz, who shot four menacing teenagers on a New York subway.[18] Although it is conceivable that a majority of the original grand jury refused to indict Goetz for homicide because they believed all he did fell within the scope of the self-defense justification, his own statements to police gave an account not easily squared with that defense. Some grand jurors may simply have approved Goetz's acts as ones of justified retaliation and refused to vote for an indictment for that reason.

The grand jury resembles the petit jury for trials in that its members are not informed about any dispensing function. Votes by grand jurors that effectively "nullify" the law are theoretically similar to nullifying votes by trial jurors. These are discussed at some length in the next section, so I will not pause here to explore the boundaries of the grand jury's legal authority or how its dispensing power should be exercised.

Proceedings Based on Violations of Civil Norms

As I have been at pains to point out in this book, talk about law observance cannot sensibly be limited to compliance with criminal statutes. People may have moral reasons for breaching contracts or committing torts, or for violating civil duties imposed by statute. When the source of a civil action is an injured private party, the decision whether to proceed rests in private hands, and that decision is one of the more important that ordinary citizens can make about involvement in the legal system. With respect to some sorts of breaches, at least, a person contemplating suit or deciding on what settlement to accept might properly be influenced by the moral claims of the person who has violated his or her legal rights.

Other decisions about proceeding to enforce civil obligations are made by government officials. The range of their discretion whether to go forward or not would generally approximate that of the prosecutor with respect to criminal statutes.

NONCONVICTION AND "NULLIFICATION" OF THE SUBSTANTIVE LAW

Once the stage of trial is reached, plain discretion not to apply the law plays a much less significant part in the system of criminal justice. Prosecutors generally retain the authority to abandon charges; if they do so during trial, the double jeopardy guarantee bars subsequent prosecution. But prosecutors who have decided a case is worth trying are not likely, absent some failure to establish evidence, to change their minds in midstream. In a few American jurisdictions, judges have explicit authority to dismiss de minimis infractions, though defendants are technically guilty.[19] Most jurisdictions do not confer such authority on judges, however, and its use in those jurisdictions that do is fairly rare.

For the most part, then, trial proceeds as if what is at stake is discovery of the facts and application of the law to them, not the decision whether to exercise some discretion to dispense. Jurors and judges, however, have the power to "nullify" the substantive law; that is, they can make a determination that someone has not violated the law when in fact he has and they know he has.

Jury Nullification

The jury's power to nullify is the most obvious. In civil cases, a jury can decide against the party that has presented the most persuasive evidence; unless the evidence in favor of the losing party is extremely strong, the jury's decision will survive an appeal. Its power in criminal cases is more absolute; if it acquits, the constitutional rule against double jeopardy precludes further proceedings against the defendant. I will concentrate here on the role of the jury in criminal cases. Much of what is said also applies to civil cases, though, of course, the claim of the opposing party to have his lawful expectations satisfied is a powerful argument against subverting the rules of civil liability to his disadvantage.

Lay jurors in common-law countries can nullify the criminal law by acquitting a defendant they believe is guilty of the crime charged. They can also nullify the written law in a more moderate fashion, by returning a verdict for a lesser offense when they believe the defendant is guilty of the more serious offense with which he has been charged. One juror alone (or a minority of jurors in jurisdictions that allow conviction with less than unanimity) can, if sufficiently strong-willed and persistent, block application of the law to an offender by refusing to vote for conviction.

The Legal Authority of Juries

Whether or not jurors have legal authority to engage in such refusals to apply the law is a complex question. Their dispensing power has been a fundamental element of the administration of the criminal law since the medieval period, and indeed, because of the capital sentence for most homicides and thefts, was once a more integral aspect of the law's administration than it is now.[20] In the sixteenth and seventeenth centuries, jurors were occasionally fined and imprisoned for refusals to convict;[21] now when they acquit, not only is their verdict unreviewable, they are immune from any punishment for failing to fulfill their temporary official duty. Nevertheless, jurors are instructed to apply the law as the judge gives it to them, and they take an oath that they will do so; and despite three narrowly interpreted state constitutional standards that grant jurors authority to determine the law,[22] the earlier dispute over whether jurors are the ultimate finders of law as well as fact has now been decisively resolved: jurors must take the law according to the judge's instructions. Defendant's counsel can neither argue that the jury should disregard those instructions nor present evidence in favor of the proposition that the defendant should be acquitted despite violating the law.

How is the legal duty of jurors to be understood? One view is that the power of acquittal establishes a right of acquittal. As Chancellor James Kent put it, "The law must . . . have intended, in granting this power to a jury, to grant them a lawful and rightful power, or it would have provided a remedy against the undue exercise of it."[23] Without more, however, this position is too simple. The law may confer unreviewable power for a variety of reasons. Judges of highest courts, for example, have essentially unreviewable authority to determine the law, because in a practical system of government such power must be placed somewhere. Yet certainly some interpretations of law could be so egregious, so far beyond permissible bounds, that we should say the judges who made them violated their legal duty and acted outside their authority. In cases in which substantial evidence is produced against the defendant, jurors have, as George Christie has pointed out, effective power to convict on less than the reasonable doubt standard.[24] That is to say, if the jurors consciously determine that the evidence does not meet that requisite, but the defendant is probably guilty and is certainly a dangerous character who should be locked up, they can convict, and no other organ of government will be able to go behind their verdict and undo their finding of guilt. We should, nevertheless, hesitate to say that the jurors have legal authority to convict on less than beyond a reasonable doubt. Power does not necessarily demonstrate right.

The contrary position—that the jury's legal duty is always simply to apply the law as the judge instructs it—also presents some difficulties, because the undoubted power to acquit rests on something more than the impracticality of review. One of the historic arguments for jury trial is that a community check against enforcement of arbitrary laws and unduly harsh penalties is desirable; and jury refusals to convict publishers charged with seditious libel and petty thieves facing mandatory death penalties are celebrated as civilizing the administration of justice. Before the American Revolution, John Adams conceived the jury as introducing a democratic element into the executive function by which "the subject is guarded in the execution of the laws."[25] When the Supreme Court held that the Fourteenth Amendment required states to afford jury trials in criminal cases, the possibility of jury nullification was considered one of the characteristics making jury trial fundamental to our system of justice.[26] Since judges may direct judgment for either party in a civil case or acquittal in a criminal case, a judge's inability to direct a finding of guilt in a criminal trial rests not on impracticality, but on special solicitude for the criminal defendant—a sense that he should not be convicted without a supportive judgment by members of the community. Even such an apparently innocuous technique as requiring the jury to make particular findings of fact as well as returning a general verdict has been said to undercut its "historic function . . . of tempering rules of law by common sense."[27] Thus, the jury's power on occasion to nullify the law is viewed as a positive feature of its operation, one that is self-consciously protected by ancillary doctrines.

Finding each of the two simple competing views to be unsatisfactory, Mortimer and Sanford Kadish, in their insightful book *Discretion to Disobey*,[28] conclude that juries are under a legal obligation to follow instructions and have a legal right to disobey the instructions if the reasons for doing so are strong enough. Jurors are exemplars of officials who occupy "recourse roles" and who are permitted to depart from the prescribed means for exercising their roles when they believe the ends for which their roles are created will not be served if they fail to digress. The obligation to follow the prescribed means is like a promissory obligation in ordinary life—one that must be given considerable weight but can be overridden by very strong contrary reasons.

This account of the juror's responsibility under our system may make us somewhat uncomfortable, because we are used to thinking that the law forbids, requires, or permits actions. But the Kadish view reflects sophistication about subtle variations in the messages that may be conveyed to actors in a social enterprise.

One need only reflect on parental injunctions to small children to grasp the point. When my three boys have wanted to do things I regarded as part of the birthright of every youth but in later life saw as fraught with potential danger, such as walking on high walls, shooting metal clips with slingshots, throwing sticks and small rocks at the enemy of the moment, hitting brothers in assorted parts of the anatomy, and climbing out of windows, I have discovered that, whether I am presented with a fait accompli or involve myself before the event, my responses are modulated according to my feelings of danger and acceptability. For the actions I regard as the worst, I may say something like "This is absolutely forbidden. You should never do that. If you do it again, you will be seriously punished." On other occasions I say things like "That's a bad idea. You really shouldn't do that," or "That is really stupid. You know you can hurt someone (yourself) that way," or "I am very disappointed in you for doing X" (hitting a brother in a part of the body not absolutely forbidden), or "You really shouldn't do that, but if you must, be very careful." The last comment comes close to a grudging permission, but what I am struggling somehow to do in many instances is to avoid conveying a genuine permission, something that may connote approval or acceptance, and yet to steer clear of absolute prohibition. I should not want to make too much of this analogy, especially since what underlies my variations is a wish not to dilute the prohibitions of the worst acts or overburden the boys with absolute "no's" and a hope that their own sense of responsibility will develop—reasons quite different from those that underlie the uncertain signals the legal system conveys about jury responsibilities. But if a small amount of self-study reveals such variations in parental attempts to guide children, we should hardly be surprised that something as complicated as a legal system may not offer straightforward directions about the performance of some important responsibilities.

If the Kadishes are right that the legal authority of jurors cannot be described in simple terms, it does not follow that their own theoretical account is the most satisfactory. The thrust of their suggestions has a rather paradoxical air—that the obligation to apply the law faithfully continues in force even in those situations when nullification is warranted by the powerful reasons in its favor. As Kurt Baier has pointed out,[29] the conflict between possible nullification and applying the law is not just an ordinary conflict of obligations one cannot practically fulfill at the same time.[30] Nullification is logically incompatible with applying the law; if nullification is required by the ends of justice, one cannot conceivably fulfill that end of one's role and the obligation to apply the law. Without challenging the Kadish account of what jurors may do, Baier tries to dispel the element of paradox by suggesting that jurors should be thought to be under an obligation to follow instructions unless compliance would seriously frustrate some of the ends of their role.[31] In that event, they would cease to be under the obligation to apply the law faithfully.

I do not believe that Baier's revision is philosophically more compelling than the original account of the Kadishes. Having suggested that the obligations of promise and fair play may run into conflicts with more compelling duties of justice, I have assumed that obligations may be outweighed rather than cease, even when performance of the obligation is not logically compatible with satisfying the duty of justice. Imagine that A previously helped B to capture B's escaped slave; B has promised to do the same for A if the need arises. B, who has by now freed all his own slaves, sees A's escaped slave on his property. His obligations of promise and fair play toward A compete with his natural duties toward the slave. Performance of one duty is logically incompatible wth performance of the other. I should say the promissory or fair play obligation is outweighed by the natural duty rather than nonexistent. Similarly, a jury's obligation to apply the law could be outweighed by its duty to do what is morally just in an individual case.

In any event, whatever the strength of Baier's position as an account of how outsiders should view the jury's responsibilities, it fails to capture the perplexities facing jurors themselves, who are not instructed about any authority to disregard instructions. Because no one tells them under what conditions they may nullify the law, they are likely to feel themselves being pulled in two different directions, with the uneasy feeling that whatever they do will be wrong from some point of view. The Kadish paradox is much more faithful to their disquieting dilemma than is Baier's simpler resolution.

Criteria for Nullification

Because judges do not instruct juries about their power to nullify the law, the dearth of writing on how conscientious jurors should exercise that power is not surprising; but I want to consider what standard might be applied by a thoughtful juror who is considering acquittal, even though he recognizes that application of the judge's instructions to the facts would yield a guilty verdict. Few now believe that lay jurors should supplant the judge's instructions with their own interpretations of the law, and such authority would be hard to defend. The authority that is implicitly conceded to jurors is rather that they may disregard the law when its application would be highly unjust. As the Kadishes put it, the jurors must place a "significant surcharge" on denial of their obligation to apply the law. A juror should not acquit unless he is firmly convinced that a gross injustice would be done by conviction. He must believe more than that the actor's motives were good or that the law is a bad one. He must think that the actor was performing an act that was clearly justified or was exercising an undeniable moral right. Ordinarily, he would have to think either that the law on which the prosecution is based is itself highly unjust or that the particular circumstances of the case are so far outside what the legislature had in mind that the law's application in this case would be unconscionable. In rare cases, for example, when jurors are strongly persuaded that protesters had an overwhelming powerful reason to break a law, acquittal may be warranted even though jurors do not consider the law itself unjust or the situation to be outside the legislature's intentions.

Perhaps the jury needs less strong reasons when the form of nullification is to reduce the crime involved (say from murder to manslaughter) without justification in the law and facts. Because the defendant will still be convicted and receive a sentence, the jury's defiance of the law in this situation is not quite so great.

One final distinction needs to be drawn. Some cases will present a genuine issue of guilt on the basis of the evidence, and an outsider may not be able to tell whether the jury honestly disbelieved the prosecutor's version of the facts or believed it but nevertheless determined not to convict. Indeed, the jurors voting for acquittal may represent both positions, and the jurors wishing to nullify may deceive the other jurors about the grounds for their votes. In such cases, nullification may be surreptitious; no one will be sure it has taken place.[32] Such violations of the ordinary premises of the system still require strong justification, but since the practical damage will be less if others are not aware of what has occurred, such manipulation may occasionally be warranted even if an open and clear nullification would not be.

The law itself supplies the guiding criteria for jury nullification only to a limited degree. In some cases, jurors may reach behind the letter of the broken law to its ascertainable spirit, perceiving that the individual violator was simply not a person that the legislature really wanted to penalize. In other instances, jurors may be aware that a particular prohibition is out of line with other, more important provisions of the law. For the most part, however, a juror must call on his own, individual sense of justice to decide if a legally warranted conviction would be so intolerable that he should not vote for it. Thus, if jury nullification is an instance in which agents "undertake actions outside the role's prescribed means to achieve the role's ends,"[33] the "ends" are general ones of justice and fairness. The jurors themselves will fill in the content of those ends, not from any special conception of the criminal law as it then exists, but from a less focused appreciation of when condemnation and punishment is acceptable.

Possible Reform

Practical interest in the status of jury nullification increased greatly with the trials of those who refused military service in Vietnam or protested the war there. Change in the present understanding of jury role could take place in either direction. Jury nullification could be more clearly labeled an illegitimate exercise of power, perhaps stripped of some of the support it now enjoys from tangential rules of law, no longer forming the basis of any constitutional doctrines about right to jury trial or providing a subject of admiration for thoughtful commentators. Conversely, jury nullification could be formally recognized, with juries instructed about their power and, perhaps, with lawyers presenting evidence and argument about the appropriateness of deciding against the law in particular cases.

There can be no doubt that jury nullification played a critical humanizing role during stages of English history when the substantive criminal law and its penalties were extremely harsh.[34] The lay jury has also served as an important safeguard against outright oppression. One can certainly conceive of systems of criminal justice that can do without lay jurors and their nullifying powers; but these systems would lack a significant check on official abuse. In any event, the tradition of such power is too deeply rooted in our law to be abandoned.

For the law implicitly to recognize and approve a power it does not admit to those who must exercise it is anomalous. Jurors lacking instructions about authority to nullify can hardly be expected to have reasonably compatible notions of when the duty to apply the law is outweighed by other considerations; on that score defendants are at the mercy of the private notions of members of their particular juries.

Formidable objections to a shift exist, however. If jury nullification could be effectively discouraged, jury power to prevent injustice would be diminished. If jury nullification were formally approved, the proper authority of the written law might be undermined. As all recognize, juries may nullify for bad reasons as well as good, and no one has yet thought of a formula that would produce nullification only in deserving cases. The sensible assumption is that if juries were instructed about their power to nullify, this would increase the instances of nullification; some of these would be just refusals to apply the law, others victories for prejudice or overly generous sympathy.

George Christie has made the further observation that such instructions would tend to have the undesirable effect of relieving the moral responsibility that jurors feel for nullification and increasing their sense of moral responsibility for convictions, because jurors could no longer view themselves as simple agents of the law sworn to do as it directs.[35] If defense attorneys could present evidence and argument in favor of nullification, the dangers of appeal to prejudice would be greatly enhanced, and trials of many political protesters would be turned into unconstrained debates over controversial political issues.

Some language should be discoverable that would alert all jurors to the existence of the nullification power but would indicate in the strongest terms that it should be reserved for only the most exceptional cases. Jurors might be told the following, for example: "Your basic responsibility is to apply the law as given in the judge's instructions. You do have the legal authority to acquit a defendant who is guilty under the law, but that should be done only in an extreme case of a terrible injustice." The gains in openness and consistency should outweigh any harm from a slight increase in instances of nullification. Because a crucial value of the law is its capacity to focus and narrow issues, however, to make cases turn on something other than the political and social sympathies of juries, no evidence or argument on the possibility of nullification should be permitted.

Judge Nullification

Judges in criminal cases also have some power to nullify the substantive law. In jury trials, they can direct jurors to acquit when evidence clearly supports a finding of guilt; when a trial is before the bench, a judge can acquit though persuaded of legal guilt. Such determinations are unreviewable, and the possibility of any disciplinary action for isolated instances of nullification is remote.

Judicial power to nullify the substantive law has never been suggested as a desirable feature of trial before judges, and the nonreviewability of their decisions to acquit may be thought to derive more from implications of the defendant's right against double jeopardy than from any sense that the judge is an appropriate agent to second guess the legislature about what behavior should be criminal. Judges are permanent officers of the law sworn to uphold the law, not representatives of community sentiment. In a system with jurors and judges, judges are much less appropriate candidates than jurors to assess the moral acceptability of applications of the law.[36] Perhaps in serious cases,[37] judges have no authority like that of the jury to engage in justified departures from the rules of the substantive law. If judges do have any authority to nullify the criminal law, it is much more limited than the parallel authority of juries.

Nevertheless, it is conceivable that some convictions would be so abhorrent that judicial defiance of the law would be defensible, and this conclusion may be true even if such action is considered to be outside the law in every sense. Given the judge's greater understanding of the law, its values may more fully inform his or her evaluation of possible justifications for nullification than will be true for jurors. Both because of the nature of the office and because they usually find a way of mitigating the rigors of the law through their sentencing power, judges will need much more powerful reasons than juries to engage in outright nullification.

Judges also have the power, in their roles as fact-finders, in their supervision of jurors, and even in their construal of the law, to achieve nullification of the civil law. Except when they resolve factual disputes, what trial court judges do is subject to appeal, but the reality often is that a case is not worth appealing and the powers of trial judges are frequently much greater than a formal analysis of their relation to appellate courts indicates. Nullification of the civil law means denial of legal rights to a litigant who is claiming them; but especially in areas of law in which the power of litigants is unequal, such as landlord–tenant, judges may sometimes be disposed to mitigate the rigor of applicable legal standards.

SENTENCING AND OTHER DETERMINATIONS ABOUT TREATMENT

Apart from decisions about prosecution and guilt or innocence, officials make a variety of determinations about how offenders will be treated. One way in which conflicts between the law and an offender's moral convictions can be ameliorated is by affording comparatively lenient treatment. This section explores these possibilities briefly; its enumeration of the different kinds of officials who determine treatment shows forcefully how important the particular roles officials play are.

Judicial Sentences

Statutes in most jurisdictions confer great discretion on judges to decide how severe sentences will be; as long as he sentences within the specified range, the judge does not exceed his legal authority.[38] Judges and prosecutors making influential recommendations about sentence properly respond to the reasons for lenient treatment of violators who have plausible claims of moral justification or moral right or were moved by conscience. If these reasons are not strong enough to warrant nonprosecution, they may still dictate a lighter sentence than is given to other offenders. When the law contains general standards for guiding the judge's decision about severity, those standards typically are broad enough to encompass the sorts of considerations discussed in previous sections, including matters such as the character and likely future dangerousness of the offender and the gravity of his crime.[39] Indeed, one of the strongest arguments for discretionary sentencing is that it permits mitigation of penalty for actors whose moral culpability is less than that of the average offender. The general statutory standards designed to guide judicial discretion, of course, provide no precise direction about the weighting of particular factors; judges, like prosecutors, must rely on a broad sense of appropriateness to make particular judgments, one that includes but is not limited to the practices of other judges and the intimations of legal materials that go beyond the specific substantive crime and sentencing provisions.

Within essentially discretionary sentencing structures, legislators may establish substantial mandatory minimum sentences for specific offenses or for habitual offenders; and the recently popular "just deserts" approach to sentencing followed by a number of states leaves judges little latitude even in ordinary cases.[40] Although undercharging by prosecutors often saves judges from a nasty dilemma, judges are sometimes presented with cases in which they strongly believe the minimum sentence would be unduly harsh, and with some frequency they decline to impose the sentence called for by the statute. Given the legislative decision to impose mandatory minimum sentences for designated classes of offenders, these judicial acts cannot be considered exercises of delegated power; but if it is generally understood and accepted that judges will smooth the rougher edges of required sentences, the occasional refusal to impose these sentences may be viewed as authorized in the sense in which jury nullification is authorized. For a judge to decline to impose a specified sanction, his reasons should be very powerful. To some extent, the law as a whole may help guide him, as when the specific statute applicable to the case is uncharacteristically harsh or rigid in comparison with other provisions relating to similar matters; but in other circumstances, the judge will have to rely on some wider evaluation of the proper aims of criminal law.

Parole Determinations

Parole boards traditionally have had very extensive discretion in determining when to release offenders from prison. Statutory criteria have been cast in broad terms that permit evaluation of the actor's character and the harm to society of the crimes he might commit if he violates the law after release. For our purposes, discretionary parole board decisions about release are not different in principle from sentencing decisions, though postsentence behavior and the general character of the actor will usually loom larger than reevaluations of the underlying criminal act.

Considerations about the gravity of conduct and character may also help determine other matters. The rigor and the content of the conditions under which an offender will be released will be determined partly by judgments about the offender and the danger he poses; the board's assessment of the reasons behind the underlying criminal act may be relevant for this purpose. Similar evaluations are called for when conditions of parole have been violated, and parole authorities must make a discretionary decision whether or not to revoke parole.

Pardon and Amnesty

When pardon or amnesty is granted after conviction, its main significance is to affect the sentence imposed as well as the collateral consequences of criminal conviction. As already indicated in connection with pretrial pardons, executive and legislative judgments about excusing offenders will be influenced by the character of the offenders and the gravity of their crimes. When such determinations are made, less deference needs to be given to prior legislative policy than should be afforded by prosecutors, judges, and parole authorities. The extended debate over amnesties to those who violated military law or conscription requirements during the Vietnam War illustrates how claims of moral rightness and conscience can figure in decisions whether or not a pardon or amnesty should be granted.[41]

Pretrial Confinement

One important decision about treatment that precedes conviction is a magistrate's determination of whether to confine a charged offender, set bail, or release him on his own recognizance. Even if the ostensible orthodoxy is correct that the only proper purpose in setting bail is to ensure that the person charged will not escape trial, evaluation of the nature of the crime will be relevant to the likelihood that someone may try to escape. Of course, the offender's sense of moral rectitude is not always a guarantee against flight; one need only think of revolutionary activists who are part of a larger organization for whom flight may actually be more likely than for ordinary offenders. Often, however, the offender's powerful belief that he has acted rightly will coexist with a willingness, even a desire, that his claim be aired in the public forum of a trial.

An offender's moral claims will also play a more subtle part. Once the magistrate has a sense of the likelihood of flight under various conditions—imprisonment, high bail, low bail, release without bail—the seriousness of the crime will count in calculating the acceptable degree of risk. Possible moral justifications will tell here. If Alan has killed for pay and Beth has given poison to a terminally ill relative who asked to be killed, both are guilty of murder, but a certain risk that the offender will go untried might appear tolerable for Beth but not for Alan.

In practice, magistrates making bail decisions also may consider the danger that an offender poses to the community during the pretrial period, at least when very serious crimes are involved. Whether or not that consideration is in some sense legally authorized is itself a troubling question, but in any event, moral claims in favor of disobedience would matter for such determinations, shedding light on the likelihood that the released offender would commit further crimes.

Administration of Punishment and Conditions of Confinement

Prison wardens and some other officials have as their primary responsibility the administration of confinement or other aspects of punishment, the basic nature of which has been determined by another authority. A warden makes limited judgments about security needs and promising programs for particular offenders; except as he credits good time, determinations about the length of imprisonment are not his business.

Reflection on the warden's responsibilities bring home most sharply the point about role allocation. Although his estimations about the character of the offender may properly influence his decisions about the precise conditions of confinement, surely his job does not include responsibility for making judgments that a section of the substantive criminal law or a conviction violates moral rights. If the warden releases a prisoner or designedly permits escape because he thinks moral rights have been violated, he does so wholly outside the law. Only the most compelling reasons of morality could justify such a course. Although other legal norms might help the warden identify gross injustice, that he would conceive of his choice to permit escape as being guided mainly by the law as a whole is very improbable. Rather, only a profound dissatisfaction with major features of the law would be likely to produce a belief in reasons strong enough to warrant the extreme departure from his ordinary role that a personal determination to release would involve.

CONCLUSION

In the last part of this book, we have reviewed various agencies of amelioration between the demands of the law and the perceived demands of morality. Instead of no further room existing to accommodate the moral claims citizens acknowledge once the basic legal rules have been established, these claims can affect the disposition of offenders in a variety of ways. Far from being over, the dialogue between citizens and legal officials over what constitutes acceptable behavior has simply entered a new stage. Some of the ways in which the impact of the law can be moderated are plainly within the law, others involve official defiance of law, and still others enjoy a twilight status, receiving no explicit authorization but some degree of acceptance from the legal system.

Questions about an actor's full or partial justification or his claim of moral right can arise at various stages and be dealt with by different persons exercising authority—legislators, police or prosecutors, juries, sentencing judges, and pardoning authorities. The exact mix of responsibilities in the United States in the late twentieth century is the product of history, and we can certainly imagine other systems of criminal justice working reasonably well with significantly different role allocations. But the present combination of legislative attention to special situations, the jury's check on the justice of conviction, and official discretion to tailor prosecution and punishment to individual circumstances do yield a significant degree of sensitivity to plausible moral claims in favor of disobedience. Each of the institutions must be viewed as a part of a complicated process, and proposed reform of any one institution must be assessed in terms of the likely functioning of the others.

Many decisions in favor of amelioration require delicate judgments about complex considerations. To some extent, the guides to these judgments may be found within the law as a whole, but often the decision-maker must reach outside the law and make an independent determination of the legitimate purposes of the criminal law and of the proper bases for social interference with individual action. One is tempted to generalize from these examples that, in carrying out social roles, officials draw partly from the conception of the role as publicly understood, partly from their individual judgments about the special responsibilities of the role, and partly from a sense of broader social values and purposes to which a particular role contributes.

It would be surprising if judges making legal decisions are wholly different in this respect from other officials. When they make determinations of substantive law, they are undoubtedly more fully constrained by existing legal materials than the officials who make the decisions I have examined; nevertheless, some room remains for references outside the law. Understanding of judicial responsibilities to decide legal issues, the subject of extensive jurisprudential discussion, can be enhanced by a comparison with the responsibilities of other officials acting under the law. Apart from their own intrinsic importance, the matters discussed here help focus that comparison.

The roles of officials enforcing the law can also be profitably compared with the roles of ordinary persons as subjects of the law. The moral reasons for departing from the path of law observance are similar, but officials require much more powerful justifications before they are warranted in deviating, both because their voluntarily accepting an office and swearing to perform its duties creates a strong bond of obligation and because the consequential reasons for official compliance with law are usually of greater magnitude than those applicable to ordinary citizens.

NOTES

1. See, generally, K. Davis, Discretionary Justice 162–214 (1969); M. Kadish and S. Kadish, Discretion to Disobey 73–85 (1973).

2. The tradition in civil law countries assigns much less role to the prosecutor in this respect. See, e.g., Jescheck, The Discretionary Powers of the Prosecuting Attorney in West Germany, 18 Am. Jour. Comp. Law 508 (1970); Herrmann, The Rule of Compulsory Prosecution and the Scope of Prosecutorial Discretion in Germany, 41 U. Chi. L. Rev. 468 (1974); Langbein, Controlling Prosecutorial Discretion in Germany, 41 U. Chi. L. Rev. 439 (1974).

3. See *Inmates* v. *Rockefeller*, 477 F.2d 375, 379 (1973).

4. There is an argument that in cases of homicide, a prosecutor should not make this determination, that only an authoritative community judgment should exonerate.

5. General deterrence might well be important if Bruce belongs to a closely knit religious sect whose members share his view.

6. Often, of course, a claim of moral right *will* suggest the actor's willingness to violate the law again in similar circumstances.

7. Though a strong argument can be made that actors should not be treated as criminals unless they are aware, or actually should be aware, that their behavior is criminal, I assume here that the substantive law rightly does not make belief in legality a defense, expect in limited circumstances. Demanding that juries decide whether defendants honestly held such beliefs would be troublesome, as would judicial determinations of whether those beliefs are reasonable; and encouraging behavior at the very edges of legality is usually not desirable.

8. Ronald Dworkin suggests that the argument for nonprosecution applies when the actor reasonably believes the law, understood as a correct view of the relevant legal materials, is in his favor even if he is quite certain the courts will decide against him (e.g., the actor thinks that compulsory military service is involuntary servitude forbidden by the Thirteenth Amendment, though the Supreme Court has consistently rejected that position and no one predicts a contrary result in the foreseeable future). Dworkin, Taking Rights Seriously 214–15 (1977). Dworkin then goes on to say that those with analogous moral beliefs to the hypothetical actor's should be treated similarly, because they should not be penalized for lacking the legal sophistication to transform their moral perspectives into the relevant legal conclusions (id.). This rather legalistic approach to the problem is very nearly backwards. There are good reasons to refrain from prosecution of those with strong moral beliefs in support of their acts, and these also apply to persons whose private view of the law (as it should be interpreted) supports their position; but to ascribe deep significance to such views about the law—often formed in enthusiastic response to positions advocated for public consumption by lawyer-activists who represent a miniscule proportion of the profession—would be mistaken.

9. A system of law may be more humane and sensitive to claims of right if it allows challenges by means other than criminal violations.

10. Dworkin, Taking Rights Seriously at 192, discussed in Chapters 9 and 12.

11. The problem is somewhat complicated by the relationship between doctor and pregnant woman, since prosecution might be limited to the doctor. The woman's moral right to an abortion includes a moral right to assistance of a competent person to perform the abortion. One may think of the doctor as having a derivative moral right to provide the assistance. In any event, punishment of the doctor will make it very difficult for other women to get similar assistance, so their rights will be effectively frustrated by a successful prosecution of the doctor.

12. See, generally, K. Davis, Discretionary Justice 189–214 (1969).

13. I realize that the line between classes of cases and criteria within these classes is not a sharp one.

14. For some petty violations, such as traffic offenses, an officer's summons may initiate criminal proceedings.

15. See Heffernan, The Police and Their Rules of Office, in W. Heffernan and T. Stroup, eds., Police Ethics: Hard Choices in Law Enforcement 3 (1984).

16. Heffernan talks about an arrest of someone for smoking marijuana in a deserted public place as involving two or three hours of an officer's time to book the suspect and possibly an equal amount of time for a court appearance. Id.

17. Id. at 15–20.

18. See, e.g., Newsweek, March 25, 1985, p. 58.

19. See Model Penal Code § 2.12 and Comment (1985).

20. See, generally, T. A. Green, Verdict According to Conscience (1985).

21. Id. at 209.

22. Ga. Const. Art. 1, 32–201; Ind. Const. Art. 1, § 19; Mo. Const. Art XV, § 19.

23. See M. Kadish and S. Kadish, Discretion to Disobey 51 (1973).

24. Christie, Lawful Departures from Legal Rules: "Jury Nullification" and Legitimated Disobedience, 62 Calif. L. Rev. 1289 (1974).

25. See J. Adams, Works III, 481, quoted and discussed in B. Bailyn, The Ideological Origins of the American Revolution 74 (1967).

26. *Duncan* v. *Louisiana*, 391 U. S. 145, 153 (1968).

27. *United States* v. *Spock*, 416 F.2d 165, 181 (1st Cir. 1969).

28. See note 23, supra.

29. See Baier, Book Review, 124 U. Pa. L. Rev. 561, 576 (1975). M. B. E. Smith has criticized the Kadishes' assumption that one can speak of legal obligations independently of moral obligations. Smith, Concerning Lawful Illegality, 83 Yale L. J. 1534 (1974).

30. If A has promised to pay B his only $2000, he cannot both fulfill the promise and pay $2000 for C's badly needed operation, but no logical compatibility exists between the two actions.

31. Id. at 581.

32. The initial grand jury disposition of the Bernhard Goetz case illustrates the possible uncertainty. Outsiders cannot be sure whether grand jurors refused to indict for homicide because they genuinely believed Goetz had a good claim of self-defense or because they just did not want to see him convicted given the circumstances surrounding his shooting of four youths.

33. Kadish and Kadish, supra note 23 at 31.

34. See Green, note 20 supra.

35. Christie, note 24 supra at 1304.

36. An assessment based on established constitutional or legislative criteria is much more appropriate for a judge. Both the application of the necessity defense and the interpretation of constitutional standards can involve judges in such assessments.

37. With respect to some petty offenses, such as traffic violations, it may be thought that judges have an implicit authority to decline to hold technically guilty offenders criminally liable.

38. If, however, he gives the lightest sentence only to whites and consistently sentences otherwise similar blacks more severely, he violates the equal protection clause. U. S. Constitution, Amendment XIV, § 1.

39. See Model Penal Code, § 7.01 (1985).

40. See Model Penal Code, Introduction to Articles 6 and 7 (1985). The critique of the "just deserts" approach in the Introduction, for which I was substantially responsible as chief reporter for the revision of the commentaries, substantially, though not completely, corresponds with my own views about the comparative merits of "just deserts" and constrained discretion as philosophies of sentencing.

41. See Greenawalt, Vietnam Amnesty—Problems of Justice and Line-Drawing, 11 Ga. L. Rev. 1 (1976), for my own thoughts about appropriate guidelines in that context.

Index

377